A JOURNEY
OF FAITH
and
COMMUNITY

Praise for *A Journey of Faith and Community*

"All churches think of updating their history when a significant anniversary approaches, but few have had the tremendous impact on its community and the nation as has Augusta's First Baptist Church. Often remembered as the birthplace of the Southern Baptist Convention, the 200-year history of the congregation is a reflection of American religious thought from both a micro and macro perspective. Bruce Gourley has written an engaging and well documented bicentennial history that should be on the shelves of every student of history from both a local, national and religious perspective."

—*Erick Montgomery, Executive Director, Historic Augusta, Inc.*

"With two hundred years as an organized body of worshipers, the First Baptist Church of Augusta, Georgia enjoys a rich history of faith and service. As host of the founding meeting of the Southern Baptist Convention and one of the earliest participants in the Cooperative Baptist Fellowship, the church can complicate simple notions of southern Baptist history and identity. Bruce Gourley has done a marvelous job recovering the church's story and telling it in regional, national, denominational, and Christian context."

—*Dr. Charles Israel, Associate Professor of History and Associate Dean for Academic Affairs, Auburn University*

"There has always been more to church life than Sunday morning preaching at First Baptist Church, Augusta, Georgia. Bruce T. Gourley's *A Journey of Faith and Community* tells the fascinating story of this historic church in considerable detail. Read and see!"

—*Dr. Keith Harper, Senior Professor of Baptist Studies, Southeastern Baptist Theological Seminary*

"While it is true that every church has its story, it is also true that some stories are better than others; and within that category some of the better stories are better told than others. Bruce Gourley's *A Journey of Faith and Community* is wonderful combination of an insightful scholar telling the story of an important church. Readers will gain a deep appreciation of the interplay between congregation and culture as they encounter the rich history of The First Baptist Church, Augusta, Georgia."

—*Dr. Anthony Chute, Professor of Church History and Associate Dean, School of Christian Ministries, California Baptist University, Riverside, CA*

A JOURNEY OF FAITH
—— *and* ——
COMMUNITY

The Story of the
First Baptist Church
—— *of* ——
Augusta, Georgia

BRUCE T. GOURLEY

Mercer University Press
and
Baptist History & Heritage Society

MUP/ H937

ISBN   978-0-88146-613-3
Cataloging-in-Publication Data is available from the Library of Congress

Dedication

Dot Fowler Thompson
Jack W. Thompson

This book was made possible by a generous bequest from the estates of Jack and Dot Thompson. The Thompsons were dedicated church members who taught the kindergarten Sunday School class for more than forty years. Jack was ordained as a deacon in 1990. Their love of God was made evident in their service at First Baptist Church Augusta.

Illustration by Gloria Jennings

Contents

Acknowledgments

This book is possible because of the contributions of many people. Unfortunately, there is not enough room to list all by name.

Not the least of contributions are the many faith legacies of now-deceased pastors and lay leaders of First Baptist Church Augusta, including those who thought it important to preserve early church records for future generations.

The work of early church historian Isabella Jordan was especially valuable, including her 100th anniversary volume and her preservation from memory of a twenty-year period of congregational history of which the documentation was lost in an early twentieth-century fire.

Just as valuable were the contributions of Anna Olive Jones Bannister in expanding the church's historical documentation, keeping the congregation's heritage alive in the minds of members, penning the 150th anniversary history of the church, and answering my many questions in a lively and delightful interview.

Frank and Nanci McPhail on many occasions welcomed me as family when I visited Augusta for research and interviews over the course of three years. Stimulating conversations, laughter, wonderful home-cooked meals, and excursions around Augusta and beyond were among the highlights of my time spent in Augusta in their beautiful home. My gratitude to the McPhails is immense, and I hope they will yet visit the Gourley family in Montana so that I might give them a personal tour of Big Sky Country and Yellowstone National Park.

Janet and David Hudson, a remarkable couple and among the best advocates of Baptist principles and beliefs that I have known, provided invaluable support for the book project. As anniversary committee chair, Janet spent many years planning for and envisioning not only the writing and publication of a 200th anniversary history volume, but also the oversight of a churchwide, yearlong celebration of the congregation's bicentennial. She provided valuable feedback, guidance, and encouragement during the book project. David, too, offered encouragement and helped move the project along at key junctures.

Rodger Murchison, retired associate pastor, offered much-needed assistance, encouragement, and guidance in navigating the local logistics of the book project. He also demonstrated great patience as well as reliable and timely feedback when requested, as did other anniversary committee members.

Jackie Blanchard, from her local history expertise, led the way with the help of Bobby and Jane Anderson in selecting church photographs and images to match the text.

From behind the scenes Dede Maddox, ministry assistant to pastors, and Lavinia Polatty, financial director, helped keep the project on track. From behind the video camera David Rose facilitated many oral interviews of current and former staff and lay leaders, of whom all the interviewees offered valuable insights.

Finally, I wish to express special appreciation for Erick Montgomery, longtime executive director of Historic Augusta, Inc. Historic Augusta is dedicated to the preservation of historic sites and structures in Augusta and the Central Savannah River Area, and Erick is a foremost authority on local history. The author of two books, *An Augusta Scrapbook* (2000) and *Thomas Woodrow Wilson: Family Ties and Southern Connections* (2006), Erick generously lent his time and assistance in reviewing chapter drafts and gently setting me straight where I, as an outsider, erred in matters of local history. To the extent that this volume effectively incorporates the story of First Baptist with that of Augusta, Erick deserves much credit.

A JOURNEY
OF FAITH
and
COMMUNITY

First Baptist Church
Eighth and Greene Streets, Augusta, Georgia
Dedicated on May 6, 1821

First Baptist Church
Eighth and Greene Streets, Augusta, Georgia
September 9, 1902

Interior of First Baptist Church
Eighth and Greene Streets, Augusta, Georgia
Dedicated on December 1, 1903

First Baptist Church Walton Way Campus
Architectural rendering

First Baptist Church Sanctuary, Walton Way
Photo by Bruce Gourley

Daniel Building

Mission Activities Center

Fellowship Hall

Storey Chapel

Memorial Garden

William Theophilus Brantly
First Pastor, 1820–1826

William Theophilus Brantly, Jr.
1840–1848

Lansing B. Burrows
1883–1899

Sparks Melton
1900–1909

R. Paul Caudill
1937–1944

Albert Warren Huyck
1944–1953

Robert Jackson Robinson
1953–1974

George L. Balentine
1975–1982

Charles B. Bugg
1982–1989

Timothy L. Owings
1990–2003

Clark Gregory DeLoach
2005–2015

Laying of Cornerstone, 1902

Centennial Celebration of the Southern Baptist Convention and Victory in Europe Day. Dr. Louie D. Newton (preaching): Dr. A Warren Huyck to his right and Mrs. Kate T. Corbett and Mr. Marion S. Symms to his left

Lucy Wright Parker, Missionary Emeritus of our church
November 18, 1894–February 18, 1987
Missionary nurse to China and South Korea: 1928-1964

Martha Tanner
Missionary to Nigeria, appointed November 8, 1946

Anna Olive Bannister and Margaret M. Parker
First Women Deacons, Ordination on January 11, 1981

Joan C. Puryear
First Woman Moderator, 2011

Installation of Historic Marker, Georgia Historical Commission 1956
(l to r)Fred Schuvie, Brotherhood Vice President,
H. M. Tarpley, Brotherhood President, and Dr. R. J. Robinson, Minister

Sesquicentennial Celebration, 1817–1967
Bell Auditorium

Scenes from Dedication Sunday in the Activities Building
October 19, 1975

Dr. R. J. Robinson, Minister (left) and
Sesquicentennial Celebration Keynote Speaker, Billy Graham

Television broadcasts initiated on Easter Sunday, 1955
Wilbur T. Herrington (left) and Dr. R. J. Robinson

Dr. George L. Balentine
Dedication of Buildings, October 19, 1975

Worshipping in the Activities Building

Sanctuary Ground Breaking, December 2, 1979
Walton Way and Jackson Road
Dr. George L. Balentine, Pastor

Prayer before entering the Sanctuary for the first time led by Thomas
Walter Blanchard, Chairman of the Board of Deacons, March 3, 1983

First service in the Sanctuary
Dr. Charles B. Bugg, March 20, 1983
Attendance: 2,210

Stained Glass Windows
Gospel side

Installation of Schantz Pipe Organ
Dedicated on February 7, 1981

Installation of the steeple
November 14, 1982

Resolution to T. Richard Daniel for 15 years serving as Chairman of the
Building Committee, February 19, 1984: (l to r): Robert C. Norman, T. Richard
Daniel, Margaret Daniel, Thomas W. Blanchard, and Dr. Charles Bugg

175th Anniversary, March 22, 1992: Celebration of Heritage and Hope
From left to right: Dr. & Mrs. George L. Balentine, (1975–1982),
Dr. & Mrs. Timothy L. Owings (1990–2003), Mrs. A. Warren Huyck,
Dr. & Mrs. Robert Jackson Robinson, (1953–1974),
Dr. & Mrs. R. Paul Caudill (1937–1944)

The Dedication of the Sanctuary Addition and Covered Walkways

First Baptist Church
Augusta, Georgia

October 1, 2000

OFFICE, CLASSROOM & MUSIC SUITE ADDITION
FIRST BAPTIST CHURCH, AUGUSTA, GEORGIA

THE
WOODHURST
PARTNERSHIP

Dedication of the Sanctuary Addition and Covered Walkways
October 1, 2000

Chung Yong, first Chinese convert, 1885

Chinese Sunday School organized 1885

Chinese Sunday School , 1945
P. K. Jue, Director

Construction of Storey Chapel

Installation of windows in Storey Chapel

Dedication of Storey Chapel
June 12, 2011

June 12, 2011
Portrait of Barbara Nan Longley Storey, 1931–2002
Wife of Mallie Bert Storey

Wall of Faith Mosaic, June 12, 2011
Sanctuary, Chapel and Fellowship Hall

Dave Welter, Chairman and Creative Artist constructing Wall of Faith

Dave Welter standing in front of the Wall of Faith

Dedication of Fellowship Hall and Storey Chapel, June 12, 2011:
(l to r) Wade Blount, Joan Puryear, Milton Martin, and Gregory DeLoach

Dedicatory Luncheon in Fellowship Hall
June 12, 2011

First Communion in Storey Chapel
June 12, 2011
Clark Gregory DeLoach

Honduras Mission Trip

Bridge Ministry under Calhoun Expressway at 15th Street,
the ministry began in 2007 and FBC joined in 2011

"English As a Second Language"

Benevolence Ministry

1

An Elusive, Radical Freedom

Heretics. Seditionists. Anarchists.

Many respectable Christians of the seventeenth century openly detested early Baptists.

Why? Because imprisoned human minds ensured proper belief and social order, the status quo of religious conformity protected by church-state alliance. By demanding freedom of conscience for all, religious liberty for everyone, and church-state separation, Baptists threatened to destroy traditional Christian civilization.

Colonial civil and religious leaders prioritized the suppression of religious dissent. Yet despite unleashing some 150 years of often violent persecution upon Baptists, the determined minority sect bravely persisted, finally triumphing in the securing of religious liberty for all and church-state separation enacted in the 1791 First Amendment to the United States Constitution.

Over the next 200-plus years, however, many Baptists in America gradually forgot or willingly abandoned their faith's historical freedom commitments. Today, far too few Baptist pulpits of the twenty-first century testify to the freedoms central to traditional Baptist faith and heritage. But among the faithful is the First Baptist Church of Augusta, Georgia, a vibrant congregation worshiping in a magnificent sanctuary in which Baptists' freedom heritage is enshrined in architecture and etched in beautiful stained glass.

Baptists' freedom heritage has often been preached from the church's pulpit. One such occasion, a 2007 sermon series by Dr. Gregory DeLoach (pastor from 2005-2015), explored Baptist identity in five parts:

1. Soul Freedom
2. Personal Identity and the Priesthood of All Believers
3. Religious Freedom and Liberty
4. Freedom and the Authority of Scripture
5. Church Freedom and Our Autonomy
6. Believer's Baptism and the Mark of Christ.[1]

As DeLoach indicated, the Baptist story is grounded in the liberating freedom of Christ.

Baptist Origins

Among the magnificent stained glass windows in the First Baptist sanctuary, panes portray an ancient story of new hope for the world. The biblical New Testament portrays Jesus Christ, the Son of God, bursting the bonds of tribalism and offering freedom to all, including the lowliest of persons. Executed on a cross by powerful men unable to envision a God of such radical freedom, the scriptures tell of a risen Christ who instructed those who believed in him to take the message of freedom throughout the world, a freedom enabling human salvation.[2]

Yet in the centuries following Christ an institutionalized, hierarchical, and self-serving Roman Catholic Church structure often allied with emperors and kings in sacrificing Christ's freedom on the altar of creeds and dogma. Many who dared reach for liberty were put to death. Accruing riches and earthly glory, the Church failed to serve the needs of the people. Salvation, tightly controlled and regulated, became a commodity available only for the right price—whether of mind, ritual, or money. Throughout Europe despair welled in the shadows of towering religious edifices.[3]

Long-simmering discontent finally spilled over in the Protestant Reformation of the sixteenth century, breaking the Church's monopoly over salvation. Freedom, so long suppressed, peeked cautiously through the cracks. Even so, early Protestant denominations clutched tightly to their own doctrinal formulations, fearful of allowing freedom to get out of hand. Persecution of dissenters continued, death remaining the lot of those who dared openly stray too far from official dogma.[4]

Despite suppression and persecution, small glimpses of freedom brought about by the Reformation empowered greater boldness on the part of the people. Even the Church of England, the most powerful of the early Protestant expressions, could not constrain calls for ever greater reform. By early seventeenth-century England a growing reformist movement divided along two broad fronts: "Puritans" remained loyal to the Church of England but demanded changes from within, while "Separatists" abandoned the Church from convictions that true faith required total separation. While grudgingly allowing room for Puritans, the Church viciously persecuted Separatists.[5]

Within this heated religious vortex arose a new breed of dissenters that would, in time, bear the name Baptist. The earliest such congregation emerged from Separatism in 1609 in the safety of liberal-minded Amsterdam, Holland. Leading the group were two well-educated, former English Separatists who had fled their native England to avoid severe punishment for their religious beliefs: John Smyth, a minister, and Thomas Helwys, a layman.

This little band of Baptist believers staked out their religious claims unabashedly. Casting aside creeds and sacraments, they held aloft the New Testament as their sole written authority and Christ as their spiritual king. Coerced faith they rejected as illegitimate, voluntary faith alone as authentic. The New Testament Jesus, after all, never forced anyone to believe in him. Adult believers only were to be baptized, following repentance of sins and confession of faith in Christ. Infant baptism, standard practice in all of official Christendom, was without biblical basis. (By 1640 Baptists also rejected the traditional baptismal practice of sprinkling, or affusion, embracing instead immersion as the proper, and biblical, mode of baptism.) Religious hierarchy had no place in the true church. Rather, the New Testament church modeled democratic, congregational autonomy as the proper model of church governance.

Voluntary faith as taught by Jesus required freedom of conscience and religious liberty for all. The only way to achieve these universal freedoms was by abolishing religious hierarchy and separating church from state, thus rendering unto Caesar's what was Caesar's, and to God what was God's (Mark 12:13-17).

Undaunted by a centuries-long tradition of dogmatic religion enforced by the state, Smyth and Helwys took the offensive. Not content to seek freedom for themselves only, they also advocated for freedom on behalf of all persons, including those with whom they vigorously disagreed in matters theological.

At the same time, however, the two Baptist leaders struggled with their own disputations.

About a year following the emergence of what historians recognize as the first Baptist church in 1609, the small congregation of perhaps three dozen members split into two factions. Helwys assumed leadership of the original congregation while Smyth led away a disgruntled faction. Their parting centered on the question of the legitimacy of the original congregation. Plainly, Smyth and Helwys' establishment of their little band of believers independently of any other Christian entity represented a historical anomaly. Helwys remained comfortable with this unusual methodology, pointing to scriptural legitimacy for the church's founding. Smyth and his followers expressed their doubts by seeking acceptance in a nearby Mennonite fellowship, a more established group of dissenters. Unfortunately, Smyth died in 1612. Three years later the Mennonites accepted his little group of followers into their congregation.[6]

To Helwys, therefore, fell the leadership of the Baptists. In 1611, the same year that King James' *Authorized Version* Bible debuted in an attempt to tamp down on religious dissenters, Helwys wrote a confession (or statement) of faith. Therein he voiced Arminian theology (the belief that Christ died for all persons) and declared that kings, like their subjects, must spiritually submit to God. In addition, Helwys insisted, citizens owed fealty to rulers only if their administrations were "lawful," that is, confined to temporal matters. When kings sought rule over spiritual matters, the people could rightly resist.[7]

In short, these earliest of Baptists staked out a position of freedom on both the inclusive nature of the gospel message and individual religious conscience. Opposing establishment Christianity and kingly authority, they positioned themselves in heretical territory, placing their lives in daily danger.

Convinced of the truth of their unorthodox convictions, Helwys and his congregation of some dozen individuals threw caution to the wind in moving back to England in 1612 in order to speak out for religious liberty for all and against religious conformity.

Having returned to London, Helwys immediately published a book titled *A Short Declaration of the Mystery of Iniquity*. Within this volume the Baptist leader condemned the dogma of traditional Christian religion—the Roman Catholic Church, Church of England, Puritans, and Separatists—only to turn around and argue that they, as well as his little group of Baptists, should have full and equal religious liberty. And not only should all Christians, orthodox or not, have complete religious liberty, but also Muslims, Jews, pagans, and all others.

Rebuking King James, Helwys declared "that our lord the King hath no more power over their [adherents of establishment religion] consciences than over ours, and that is none at all; for our lord the King is but an earthly King...mens religion to God is betwixt God and themselves...Let them be heretikes, Turcks, Jewes or whatsoever, it apperteynes not to the earthly power to punish them in the least measure."[8]

While Helwys' declaration seems humdrum by contemporary standards, it was an explosive and treasonous claim in the early seventeenth century. In a Western world long under the grip of theocracies, the state-enforced mandatory faith and freedom of conscience did not exist.

Yet not only did Helwys boldly and publicly advocate treason in his book, but he also sent a copy to King James with a personal note: "The king is a mortall man & not God," Helwys declared, and "therefore hath no power over ye [the] immortal Soules of his subjects, to make laws and ordinances for them, and to set Spiritual Lords over them."[9]

Remarkably, in a pre-Enlightenment world Helwys established the basic trio of principles of the historic Baptist faith that would one day revolutionize the world: freedom of conscience, religious liberty for all, and church-state separation. For treason James had Helwys arrested in 1613 and thrown into the notorious Newgate prison, the Alcatraz of that day. There the courageous Baptist died about 1616, a martyr for his dissenting faith.[10]

To the king's dismay, however, Baptists in England did not wilt away. In the face of mounting persecution, the little sect hunkered down in determination, gathering for worship in the back alleys of London and in out-of-the-way small towns.

Early Baptists in America

Following Helwys' death, small groups of dissenters migrated to the New World, beginning with the Separatist Pilgrims of 1620 among the passengers of the *Mayflower*. Puritan migrants came next, their numbers and influence quickly absorbing the Pilgrims. The Puritans viewed themselves as children of God providentially called to carve out a New Israel in the wilderness of the New World. In their new home they established theocratic settlements and colonies based on Old Testament law, eventually becoming known as Congregationalists. While rejoicing in their own religious freedom, they denied religious liberty to others. Of the others, Baptists were among the worst of infidels.[11]

To English lawyer and Separatist Roger Williams fell the distinction of introducing the Baptist faith into the New World. Arriving at Boston in 1631, the well-connected but troubled Williams found himself conflicted almost from the beginning. His dissenter convictions, growing ever more radical, deepened in the face of the colonial theocracies he encountered in New England. By the winter of 1635 his religious beliefs had become so unacceptable that Massachusetts Christian authorities ordered his banishment.

Barely escaping deportation to England, Williams fled into the wilderness in the midst of winter. Sleeping in hollow logs and nearly starving, he eventually stumbled upon a tribe of Indians, the Narragansett, whom he had earlier befriended. Sheltered by the natives through the harsh winter months, in the spring the refugee Williams purchased land from the tribe and established Providence Plantations, later known as Rhode Island, a democratic colony and the first government to guarantee religious liberty for all citizens. Williams' freedom and democratic convictions reflected those of Baptists, the faith to which he soon converted, thereupon in 1638 founding the first Baptist church in America, the First Baptist Church of Providence. Although soon abandoning the Baptist faith congregationally, Williams remained committed to Baptist convictions for the rest of his life.[12]

While Williams made history as both the founder of Rhode Island and of America's first Baptist church, another English immigrant, medical doctor and Baptist pastor John Clarke, deserves foremost credit for securing the continuity of the Baptist faith in the New World.

Clarke, like many other newly-arrived Baptists of the late 1630s, made his home in Rhode Island in order to escape Puritan persecution. Venturing into other colonies risked beatings, whippings, imprisonment, the stocks, or even death. Like many Baptists, Clarke suffered imprisonment. In addition to prison, some Baptists experienced public lashings in the Massachusetts Bay Colony for publicly speaking of their faith.

Meanwhile, the English Civil War and overthrow of the monarchy in the 1640s and 1650s created disarray in the New World. Theocratic colonies appealed to England for the dissolution and absorption of the Rhode Island colony. Fighting to save the lone haven of freedom in the New World, Clarke returned to England. Writing of persecutions in New England and penning a new colonial charter for Rhode Island, he spent years petitioning for the charter's approval in the midst of political intrigue and turmoil.

Finally obtaining a new royal charter enshrining the original's guarantee of religious liberty for all, Clarke secured Rhode Island's freedom. Words from the 1663 charter are yet enshrined on the facade of the state courthouse in Providence: "that a most flourishing civil state may stand and best be maintained, and that among our English subjects, with a full liberty in religious concernments."[13]

With Rhode Island an exception (later alongside the middle colony of Pennsylvania), Baptists in colonial America faced ongoing persecution from Christian theocratic governments. While the Congregationalist Church (Puritans) mandated religion in most Northern colonies, the Anglican Church (Church of England) did so in most Southern colonies. Baptist offenses against the Christian colonies included refusal to baptize their infants, pay taxes in support of the state churches, or obtain government licenses to preach.

Theologically, Baptists' beliefs ranged across a wide spectrum, anchored by each person's personal faith in Christ as savior, direct access to God through Christ (the "priesthood of all believers"[14]), and individual interpretation of scripture. In each congregation members democratically established theological boundaries, chose their ministers, and developed ecclesial practices. Some groups of Baptists issued confessional statements outlining their community's generally-accepted beliefs. Acceptance of any statement of faith remained voluntary. If a person came to disagree with his or her community's particulars, he or she remained free to seek a more like-minded Baptist community elsewhere. Upon such religious diversity Christian colonial leaders often frowned.

As late as the 1760s and 1770s in Anglican Virginia, many Baptists were beaten, whipped, jailed, and even waterboarded for refusing to conform to the religious laws of the colony. Government authorities took away the unbaptized children of some Baptist families, giving them to proper Christian families, and sometimes confiscated Baptist homes and lands. State thugs frequently disrupted Baptist worship services, variously pelting ministers with fruit and other objects, urinating on preachers, and dragging pastors off to jail. Meeting houses were destroyed, and some Baptists stoned. As many as one half of all Baptist ministers in Virginia during the decades of the 1760s and 1770s served jail time by order of Anglican colonial officials. Despite such abhorrent persecutions at the hands of Christian officials, Baptists in Virginia demanded that the colony dismantle the state church.[15]

While revolutionary era Baptists suffered in Anglican Virginia, their counterparts in Congregationalist Massachusetts endured similar persecutions. As the political revolution for freedom from Britain gained traction, Baptists in Massachusetts and Virginia alike spoke out forcefully for religious liberty for all. Among leading Baptist voices of the 1770s was Rev. Isaac Backus of Massachusetts. A former Congregationalist, Backus converted to the Baptist faith during the First Great Awakening, a religious revival that embraced voluntary faith and drove many establishment Christians into the Baptist camp.

Thereafter demanding church-state separation, Backus in 1773 published a book titled *An Appeal to the Public for Religious Liberty, Against the Oppressions of the Present Day*. Of the theocratic Massachusetts colonial government, Backus declared, "Now who can hear Christ declare that his kingdom is, not of this world, and yet believe that this blending of church and state together can be pleasing to him?"[16] He also wrote other treatises advocating church-state separation and in 1788 voted for the U.S. Constitution as a member of Massachusetts' ratifying convention, expressing approval of the Constitution's refusal to restrict public government service to Christians only.[17]

Meanwhile, Baptists in 1770s Virginia also petitioned colonial officials for religious liberty for all and church-state separation, demanding religious freedom as a condition for taking up arms to fight for political freedom from Britain. Needing the dissenters' help in defeating Britain—Baptists by then being a sizeable number in the state, with some Presbyterians standing alongside Baptists in demanding religious liberty—the Anglican government reluctantly promised to enact religious liberty in the colony following the war.[18]

After the British surrendered at Yorktown in October 1781, however, Virginia's Anglican officials ignored their promise to Baptists and other dissenters. In 1784, hoping to appease dissenters, Virginia's House of Delegates passed a resolution calling for a General Assessment tax on citizens for the funding of Christian churches at large.

Baptists did not find the treachery amusing. State support of religion in any capacity remained unacceptable. Baptists led the way in swamping the legislature with hundreds of petitions, the statements in some instances bearing thousands of signatures opposing the new religious taxation proposal. Thomas Jefferson and James Madison sided with the dissenters, and the bill died the following year.

The immediate threat swatted aside, Virginia Baptists remained determined as ever to permanently secure religious liberty for all and church-state separation. Famed Virginia Baptist evangelist and religious liberty champion John Leland allied with Jefferson and Madison to press the matter. Whereas Baptists fought for religious freedom from a biblical perspective, Jefferson, a Deist, fought from a philosophical perspective. Their alliance represented the partnership of faith and Enlightenment. Baptists, having championed religious freedom before the Enlightenment, now had a powerful ally in one of the foremost champions of the Age of Reason. With the fervent support of Baptists, Jefferson drafted the Virginia Statute for Establishing Religious Freedom, of which the state's General Assembly adopted on January 16, 1786.[19]

At long last, religious liberty for all and church-state separation had been established in Virginia.

Now Baptists South and North turned their attention to securing the same for the new nation. Exerting great pressure upon congressional representatives, their efforts in concert with Madison came to fruition in the enactment of national religious liberty for all and church-state separation in the First Amendment to the U.S. Constitution in 1791.

"Congress shall make no law respecting an establishment of religion, or prohibiting the free exercise thereof," the opening sentence of the First Amendment proclaimed. After nearly two centuries of enduring persecution and shedding blood, of alternatively hiding from Christian government authorities and openly defying theocratic laws, and of demanding equal freedom for all persons, Baptists had won the prolonged contest over the very nature of religious faith. In the new United States, religion now stood as a voluntary matter between the individual and his or her god, gods, or no gods. Having played a pivotal role in the establishment of the world's first secular national government, Baptists returned to their houses of worship praising God and rejoicing that imprisonment, beatings, and other state-supported religious persecutions were now a thing of the past.

Europeans marveled over America's separation of church and state. Some applauded the new concept. Others thought it would not last.

America's Congregationalists and Anglicans, formerly the state churches in the colonies, neither enthused nor marveled. How would their churches survive without government-mandated church membership, government-paid ministers, and government-funded meeting houses of worship? How could God bless America now that Baptists and other dissenters—nonconformist Christians, Jews, Muslims, and even pagans—were free to follow their consciences? How could the new nation possibly survive when its founding documents were based on Enlightenment principles rather than biblical law, and government legislators were no longer required to be Christians?

These questions and others confronted the Anglican authorities of the former colony, and now state, of Georgia. Dissenters such as Baptists yet had no meeting houses in the state's largest towns. With neither king nor Christian courts in place to deter such religious rabble, town leaders faced new realities.

Outsiders still, Baptists nonetheless faced a much brighter future.

2

Early Baptist Efforts in Augusta

Few stories worth the telling are absent tension, struggles, and eventual triumph. The narrative of Baptists in America from their beginnings in 1638 to the enactment of the First Amendment to the United States Constitution in 1791 is a remarkable account of how a minority and persecuted people of faith changed the world. Threaded within this larger narrative and the decades following is the story of the emergence of the First Baptist Church of Augusta, Georgia.

Although neither the first nor largest church established in the state, the long, circuitous birthing of the Augusta congregation is a dramatic journey replete with mystery and intrigue, danger and daring, challenges and contradictions. It is a story as much about the colonial province and early state of Georgia as it is about theology, faith, and religious edifices.

The story begins in a prison, a place only too well known for generations of religious dissenters such as Baptists.

The Establishment of a New Colony

A successful military officer and politician, General James Oglethorpe of England felt troubled in the year 1729. A close friend who had fallen into debt had been thrown into jail, where he subsequently caught smallpox and died.

Angry at a London prison system riddled with corruption and abuses, Oglethorpe used his influence to launch an ambitious campaign of reform. Quickly bringing about much needed changes in the city's prisons, within three years Oglethorpe became one of Britain's leading humanitarians. Still unsatisfied, he turned his attention to the struggles of the impoverished masses. A century earlier the New World had provided hope for Britain's poor citizens. Now, Oglethorpe and his friends petitioned for the establishment of a new colony for poor British citizens, five decades after the establishment of the last colony, Pennsylvania.

In 1732 King George II granted a charter for the new colony of Georgia, appointing Oglethorpe as a governing trustee. Some 114 men, women, and children boarded the *Anne* and sailed down the Thames River in November, arriving at Port Royal, South Carolina in January 1733. Continuing southward and aided by African slaves from South Carolina, they cleared land at the mouth of a major river, the Savannah. Perhaps coined after a derivative of Shawnee, a nearby Native American people, the name soon identified Georgia's first town. A royal charter defined the province as between the Savannah and Altamaha rivers and westward to the Mississippi.[20]

Central to the new colony, the Savannah River enhanced fur trade with Native Americans, Georgia's initial major industry. Some 100 miles upriver, shoals—created by geological uplift—prohibited commercial navigation. Below the shoals Augusta emerged in 1736, named after the new bride of Frederick Louis, Prince of Wales. Although South Carolina fur traders from across the river viewed Augusta with suspicion, Oglethorpe considered the town critical to Georgia's economy. The surrounding fertile land offered enticing agricultural opportunities.

The initial construction of the town was completed by 1739. Four streets deep and three streets wide with a plaza, Augusta looked somewhat similar to Savannah, including a military outpost, Fort Augusta. Located within the town proper, the fort offered protection should Indians display hostility. Into the 1740s Oglethorpe directed the colony, prohibiting the importation of slaves (to little effect) and fighting off aggressive Spanish forces operating out of St. Augustine. Oglethorpe's effective military leadership permanently drove the Spanish out of Georgia in 1742, elevating him to the status of national hero in England.

Augusta, meanwhile, soon reflected prosperous and established Charles Town more than Savannah. Sensing financial opportunity, planters from the South Carolina city purchased land near Augusta and imported slaves. Free white laborers soon complained of the lack of work.

Returning to London and marrying, Oglethorpe gradually withdrew from the affairs of Georgia. As his leadership waned, the remaining colonial trustees formally loosened laws against rum, slavery, and large land holdings. In 1751 the trustees gave up their charter, surrendering colonial rule to the British government. Carolina planters soon expanded further into Georgia, importing thousands of slaves to work large, coastal rice plantations. Far wealthier than Georgia's original settlers, within twenty years some sixty or so leading planters effectively controlled the economy, society, and culture of coastal and intercoastal Georgia, their domain reaching many miles inland, including up the Savannah River.

As wealthy elite planters commanded the economic and social life of Savannah and Augusta, by the mid-1750s frontier areas along the tributaries of the Savannah River experienced a new wave of immigration in the form of poor, uneducated whites. Tensions with Native Americans inevitably followed, but colonial leaders proved adept at negotiating peaceful resolutions. A treaty signed in Augusta in 1763 opened additional new lands for white settlement, generating another wave of settlers in the form of middle-class, educated, slave-owning Virginia families who provided a leavening influence up and down the Savannah.[21]

Tribulations and Triumph: Baptists in Early Georgia

As the fruits of the land drove the early economic engine of the Georgia colony, the Anglican (Church of England) faith infused legal precepts and determined cultural norms. The first worship services in the colony took place in Savannah in 1733, within months of the founding of the town. Christ Church, Georgia's first church, was built adjacent to Johnson square. John Wesley, Anglican minister and founder of Methodism (initially a movement within the Church of England), briefly served Christ Church, establishing the first Sunday School and publishing the first English hymnbook for use in the American colonies. Upriver, Augusta's first church building, constructed in 1750 adjacent to the fort, became known as St. Paul's Church.[22]

While Georgia's original charter granted limited free exercise of religion to all except Catholics, in 1758 colonial officials formally established Anglicanism as the state church. Governors thereafter were charged with ensuring the proper worship of God in accordance with the Church of England. Religious freedoms of dissenters were curtailed, although Georgia's frontier status effectively negated ecclesial enforcement.[23]

On the Appalachian and Southern frontiers of 1750s and 1760s colonial America the Baptist faith often prospered. A branch of Baptists known as Separate Baptists, a rural, common-folk people emphasizing individual salvation, practical theology, and emotional worship, benefited greatly from the religious Great Awakening of the 1730s and 1740s that originated in New England and then spread southward along the expanding frontier.[24]

Success, however, proved elusive for the handful of Baptists who initially migrated to the Georgia backcountry. Indians roamed the forests, Anglicans ruled the towns, and the hardships of eking out a living on hardscrabble remote farms consumed time and energies. Few opportunities existed for Baptists to organize themselves in any formal manner. The first known Baptist congregation in the colony, the Tuckaseeking Seventh-Day Baptist Church established in Effingham County near Savannah in 1759, failed to take root, disbanding about 1763.

Eight years passed after the demise of the Tuckaseeking congregation, a period void of formal Baptist activity in Georgia. During this time the persecution of Baptist preachers in Anglican Virginia escalated, leading many Baptists of the colony to seek friendlier climes. Some eventually settled in Georgia, including a charismatic husband-wife preaching team.

A native of Connecticut, Daniel Marshall formerly served as a deacon in the state Congregational Church. Like many other New England Congregationalists during the Great Awakening, Marshall, disillusioned with coerced religion, left the state church and converted to the Baptist faith. Daniel married Martha Stearns, sister of a Baptist evangelist, in 1747. Their first child, Abraham, arrived the following year. Moving to Virginia in the 1750s, the couple pastored Baptist churches, Martha quickly gaining a reputation as an inspiring orator. Migrating further southward, they established eighteen churches in North and then South Carolina.

In the late 1760s, while living near the South Carolina and Georgia border about fifteen miles north of Augusta at Horse Creek, South Carolina, and pastoring at Stephens Creek, Daniel periodically crossed the Savannah River to preach in Georgia. In the words of Samuel Boykin, a nineteenth-century chronicler of Georgia Baptist history, Marshall "made frequent evangelistic tours into Georgia, preaching with remarkable zeal and fervor in houses and groves." He preached in Georgia at a Quaker settlement and a small outpost known as Kiokee.[25]

Georgia officials, however, were "violently opposed to the Baptists."[26] Not one to shy from confrontation, Daniel sometimes preached dangerously close to the city of Augusta. Local authorities became aware of Marshall's presence, and Constable Samuel Cartledge determined to suppress Baptist activity. About 1770 the inevitable happened. Possibly at Appling, about seven miles from Augusta, "While upon his knees offering the opening prayer he [Marshall] was suddenly interrupted by a heavy hand being laid upon his shoulder with the exclamation, 'You are my prisoner.' Rising from the posture of devotion, the venerable man of God, with benignant face and snow-white hair, stood front to front with a stern officer of the law."[27]

Brought before the magistrate and church officials, Daniel stood trial. Coming to his defense, Martha quoted scripture extensively and advocated religious liberty for all. Impressed by Martha, the magistrate waived prison time and instead sternly warned Daniel to cease preaching in the colony, to which Marshall refused. Nonetheless, Daniel was soon released.[28]

The first attempt to establish a Baptist presence in the vicinity of Augusta seemed a failure. Yet the Marshalls' insistence upon religious liberty for all and defiance in the face of persecution by Christian authorities made an impression upon their opponents. Constable Cartledge soon converted to the Baptist faith. In addition, one or two other Anglicans in Augusta possibly extended friendly overtures to Daniel in the next few years.[29]

With the seeds of a Baptist fellowship planted near Augusta, the Marshalls determined to advance the Baptist faith in Georgia. On January 1, 1771 the Marshall family moved across the Savannah River and settled on Kiokee Creek in present-day Columbia County, Georgia, about twenty miles from Augusta. There the couple resided for the remainder of their lives.[30]

Daniel quickly busied himself preaching among the inhabitants of the surrounding countryside, in 1771 or 1772 establishing the Kiokee Baptist Church, the first permanent Baptist congregation in the Georgia colony. Apparently a number of members of the Stephens Creek Baptist Church in South Carolina moved across the river to be a part of the congregation. Church members remained vigilant, but parish authorities did not disturb the fledgling congregation. [31]

The American Revolution paralleled the founding and earliest years of the Kiokee church. British warships sailed into Savannah in 1776, leading the Provincial Congress to move to Augusta. In January 1779 the British occupied Augusta, forcing patriots across the river into South Carolina before the invaders were driven back in the Battle of Kettle Creek. Georgia's constitutional government, established in Augusta in the fall of 1779, preceded a return of the British in 1780. Augusta reverted to permanent American control in June 1781, four months before Cornwallis' surrender at Yorktown, Virginia signaled the end of major fighting in the war. The British abandoned Savannah in July 1782, and the Paris Peace Treaty of May 1783 concluded the War for Independence. An aged Daniel Marshall alone among the colony's Baptist ministers remained in Georgia throughout the war. Daniel's son Abraham served as a soldier and chaplain in the Continental Army.[32]

Following the war Augusta prospered as Indians retreated further westward. Selected as the post-war capital of Georgia in 1786, Augusta hosted the colony's ratification of the U.S. Constitution in 1788. A new state constitution followed. Judge George Walton emerged as a man with no equal in the city, a former member of the Provincial Congress, delegate to the Continental Congress in Philadelphia, signer of the Declaration of Independence, trustee of Augusta, governor of Georgia, and later U.S. senator.[33]

Kiokee, however, remained the state's hub of Baptist activity. There Daniel Marshall presided over the formation of the Georgia Baptist Association in 1784. Weeks later he passed away, his legacy as Georgia's first great Baptist leader secure.[34] Abraham succeeded to the Kiokee pulpit. Georgia Baptists' new statesman, the younger Marshall was soon put to the test.

Baptists in America, allied with Thomas Jefferson and James Madison, had not yet secured religious liberty for all and church-state separation. From Massachusetts to Virginia to Georgia and many points in between, legislators determined to preserve church-state unions. Abraham Marshall took up the fight in Georgia, where only Protestants were allowed to serve in state offices and legislators in 1785 passed a bill for "the establishment and support of the public duties of religion" through taxation.

Alarmed, the Georgia Baptist Association turned to Marshall and two other ministers to craft a response to Georgia's lawmakers. An autumn 1785 presentation of "The Baptist Remonstrance to the General Assembly" before legislators convened in Savannah voiced the concerns of the state's Baptists. Echoing Baptists elsewhere in America, they declared that government had no business establishing religious laws, whether Christian or otherwise.

Georgia Baptists insisted that the "Act for the regular establishment and support of religion" was "injurious to both" and that "civil and religious government ought not to be blended together." Thus, "religious societies, or churches, are not, as many conceive, to be formed by the Legislature...religion does not need such carnal weapons as acts of assembly and civil sanctions, nor can they be applied to it without destroying it." And "statesmen derive no authority from God or men, to judge heresy and establish systems of religious opinion or modes of religious worship."[35]

Marshall's written eloquence, however, did not then convince Georgia's legislators to abandon the continued "blending of church and state." Voting in favor of taxation to support Christian churches, Georgia's lawmakers ensured the continued anger of Baptists, although some other Christian denominations were not at all displeased. Elected to the 1789 Georgia Constitutional Convention, Marshall continued pressuring the state. Still, Georgia, like some other states, initially ignored the national separation of church and state in the 1791 First Amendment to the U.S. Constitution. Not until 1798 did the state finally prohibit religious taxes and make religion a voluntary affair. In 1804 a jubilant Marshall noted that "Civil and religious liberty have spread with astonishing rapidity."[36]

When not advocating for religious liberty for all and church-state separation, Abraham Marshall preached with great power. Contemporary accounts indicate that few rivaled Marshall's oratory skills. More than compensating for a lack of formal education, the imposing Marshall's voice was "bugle-like," of "great power, melody, and flexibility" and "with the most graceful facility." According to a friend, when preaching Marshall would "portray the glories of Heaven with such matchless force and beauty, that his hearers could scarcely remain upon their seats; and then he would depict the miseries of the lost in such terrible, burning language, as almost to make the hair stand erect upon your head."[37]

The most prominent Baptist in Georgia of his day, Marshall also became one of the more notable Baptists in all of America. A six-month preaching tour north to his home state of Connecticut in 1786 evidenced Marshall's popularity. Covering some 3,000 miles on horseback through eleven states he preached approximately 200 sermons, baptized hundreds, and preached to some 50,000 persons total, including crowds as large as 3,500.[38]

Fresh from his evangelistic tour, Marshall in 1787 led the Kiokee Baptist Church in a year of great growth, baptizing some 100 persons. The church, meeting once a month as customary of the era, fluctuated between 200 and 300 members in the years following, even as the average size of Baptist churches in Georgia in 1801 stood at a mere 63. The church constructed a brick meeting house in 1808. Utilized regularly for about a century, the building yet stands and is used on special occasions to this day.[39]

The Challenges of Augusta

In addition to pastoring the Kiokee church and conducting revival services as far north as New England, Marshall for almost two decades served as moderator of the Georgia Baptist Association. During this time Augusta, a regional hub of commerce, became a source of contention. On many Sundays some church families were absent from the Kiokee church, having gone to the market in Augusta for the weekend. Marshall brought his complaints against city-infatuated members to the annual gathering of the Georgia Baptist Association in 1810, eliciting agreement that routine absences from Sunday services constituted a serious spiritual offense.[40]

A successful preacher and associational leader, Marshall led Georgia Baptists in a time of great growth. At least fourteen men answered a call to preach the gospel due to Marshall's ministry. Although lacking formal education, Marshall advocated strongly for educated ministers, serving as a trustee on several college boards, including that of Franklin College (later the University of Georgia) from 1802 to 1811. During this time he led Georgia Baptists in an effort to establish a Baptist institution of higher education, resulting in the formation of Mount Enon College in 1806. In a remarkable incident revealing the great progress of Baptists in the state as well as ongoing prejudices against them, the Georgia legislature refused to charter the institution, citing concerns that since Baptists were now the largest denomination in the state, the presence of a Baptist college would provide an unfair advantage over other denominations. Legislators need not to have been alarmed, as many Baptist pastors in the state remained suspicious of education, ensuring the failure of Mount Enon.[41]

Alongside preaching, associational leadership, and educational advocacy, Marshall enthusiastically supported mission work. Only in the 1790s had Baptists begun to embrace missionary activity. The historical influence of Calvinistic theology in much of Baptist life resulted in the belief that God, without human help, would save those who were predestined for salvation. Andrew Fuller and William Carey, English Baptists, are credited with helping some Baptists move beyond this stumbling block and embrace mission work in foreign lands. Marshall became one of many Baptists in America who embraced the missions movement, apparently having read of the work of William Carey and others in faraway India. Closer to home, the Kiokee pastor advocated missionary work among Indians.[42]

Even before the modern missions movement led by Fuller and Carey, however, Marshall excelled at starting new churches, itself a type of mission activity. He may have founded more churches in Georgia than any other one person, although the records are inconclusive.[43]

The Kiokee pastor counted among his most notable church-planting accomplishments the founding of the First African Baptist Church in Savannah, Georgia, in 1788. With roots in black Baptist worship on a nearby plantation, the Savannah congregation emerged as the first formally organized black church in Georgia. When enslaved Baptists in Savannah encountered resistance in establishing a church, they turned to Marshall, who traveled by horseback some 165 miles to the port city. There he baptized forty-five persons of color, formed them into a church, and baptized their first pastor, Andrew Bryan. Five years afterward, in 1793, Marshall constituted a second black Baptist church, the Springfield African Church, Augusta's first black Baptist church and claiming roots earlier than the Savannah African Baptist Church. For furthering the work of black Baptists, Marshall became known as a "friend of the black people."[44]

Despite Abraham's tireless church-starting efforts, Augusta remained on the periphery of white Baptist life. Earlier in 1774 Daniel Marshall had founded Red's Creek Baptist Church (now Abilene Baptist Church, the third oldest surviving Baptist church in Georgia) some six miles west of the city. In 1777 a group of Baptists, including some members of the Red's Creek congregation, obtained a deed of land 100 feet square near the center of Augusta. Whether services were ever held or a meeting house constructed on the property is unclear, but by 1787 attempts to establish a Baptist church in Augusta were abandoned and the deed sold.[45]

Meanwhile, the trustees of the Academy of Richmond County were appointed by 1783, charged with establishing an academy and rebuilding St. Paul's Church, destroyed during the Revolutionary War. Funding came from the sale of unclaimed and loyalists' confiscated lands within the city. Academy classes began about 1785 in a large house on Bay Street, where St. Paul's congregation also met until the 1789 opening of the new sanctuary. In addition to the Episcopalian (Anglican) congregation, other religious groups sometimes worshiped in St. Paul's. A permanent building for the academy opened in 1802 on the 500 block of Telfair Street. Seven years later the trustees hired the school's first full-time rector (headmaster): young William Brantly, a graduate of the University of South Carolina and a Baptist.[46]

Few Baptists called Augusta home at the time of Brantly's arrival. Naturally wishing to worship with persons of like faith, the academy's rector obtained permission to hold Baptist services on campus. For at least two years a few Baptists in Augusta met in some capacity, the frequency unknown, at the Richmond Academy under Brantly's leadership. On December 2, 1809, the trustees of the academy expressed their confidence in the president by voting to set aside "a lot of ground between Telfair and Walker streets, not exceeding half a square, for the purpose of building a Baptist Church thereon." The title to the land was to be transferred to the appropriate Baptist body. Unfortunately, nothing else came of the matter. The details of this failure to act are seemingly lost to time, but once again Baptists of the city let slip an opportunity to build a church in Augusta. Perhaps the group's small numbers, lack of financial resources, and paucity of connections among the city's elites collectively contributed to the inaction. Upon Brantly's departure in 1811 to pastor the First Baptist Church of Beaufort, South Carolina, what became of the group is unknown.[47]

So while the Kiokee church and other congregations thrived, Augusta remained a spiritual wilderness for Baptists. Methodists (1801), Catholics (1807), and Presbyterians (1804/1812) had established churches in the city. How much longer would Baptists have to wait?

The Emergence of a Baptist Congregation in Augusta

What was it about Augusta that hindered a viable white Baptist presence in the city? Perhaps socioeconomic factors stood at the fore-front. Baptists of the late eighteenth and early nineteenth centuries in rural areas of the American South largely lived in poverty and lacked formal educational training, while Episcopalians, the dominant church-men of the South's cities, were often financially well-off, culturally sophisticated, and highly educated. Historically suspicious of salaried pastors (often paid by government-levied taxes), Baptists of the South typically did not pay their ministers. Recently-achieved church-state separation, however, changed the minds of some. In 1808 the Georgia Baptist Association debated the merits of pastoral salaries, a conversation that spurred financial compensation for pastors and contributed to the establishment of Baptist educational institutions designed to produce professionally-trained ministers.[48]

In addition, Baptist worship services in the rural South usually con-sisted of emotional preaching and spontaneity, while other Protestant services evidenced order and formality. The folksy religion of rural Bap-tists likely did not translate well in the city of Augusta. Nonetheless, a

21

new period of national religious revival, the Second Great Awakening, bestowed experiential faith with greater respectability.[49]

While figuring into the equation only indirectly, a third factor pertaining to Baptists' late establishment in Augusta involved missions. Historically uninvolved in missionary activity other than church starting, some Baptists in the South following the turn of the century gradually embraced the concept. Many, in turn, formed organizations designed to carry out missionary work more efficiently and cooperatively. In 1814 the General Missionary Convention of the Baptist Denomination in the United States of America for Foreign Missions (or Triennial Convention; the organization met every three years) was formed in Philadelphia, the first national Baptist denomination in the United States. Supported by significant numbers of Baptists North and South, the organization enhanced the Baptist witness in America.[50]

A pronounced focus on prayer attended the missionary movement, with prayer "societies" increasingly preceding the establishment of local congregations. Within this context a new organization emerged in Augusta on March 25, 1817. "The Baptist Praying Society of Augusta," while not yet a fully-functioning church body, proved to be the beginning of a church long hoped for by the city's scattered Baptists. According to church records, eighteen persons attended the historic gathering. Sensing the importance of the moment, in democratic fashion they drafted a statement of their intent and signed their names as charter members of the Society:

> We, the Baptist Brethren of Augusta, Georgia, being in a destitute state, without preaching, church union, or communion, and at the same time believing it is our duty, privilege, and high calling to be more united; believing also that it is inconsistent with the principles of true and vital religion, and hoping it will not be offensive to the particular churches to which any of us belong or have belonged, have thought proper to enter into the following covenant, viz.:
>
> We agree to join in a society to be known and styled 'The Baptist Praying Society of Augusta'; to meet in evening prayer meetings as often as convenient; to use our individual influence among our preaching brethren to get Sabbath preaching among us.

Further, we agree to watch over each other in faithfulness, in love, and in all things taking the Word of God for the man of our counsel.

We hope to conduct all matters amongst us in decency and order as required by the Gospel. We agree to appoint a clerk to keep a fair record of all matters that they may be thought worthy of notice; also to appoint a moderator to preside over our society's meetings, and to preserve order amongst us.

As the desire of all is the furtherance of the Gospel of Jesus Christ, we agree that when it may be thought by sister churches around about us that we are in a fit state for constitution, to become constituted, or so soon as it can be done on Christian and Gospel principles.

Done in society, this 25th day of March, 1817, and signed by the following persons:

Members of the Praying Society
Jesse D. Green, Martha Greenwood, James Hunter Randolph, Woodson Ligon, Polly Ligon, Patsy Ligon, Elizabeth Williams, Henry Mealing, Joseph Phillips, Betsy Goss, Mary Ann Mimms, Edward Martin, Sarah Collier, Hannah Jelks, John Garner, Sarah Garner, Caleb Morgan, Lydia Wallace[51]

Layman Jesse D. Green spearheaded the effort, signaling his prominence. Henry Mealing lived immediately across the river adjacent to downtown Augusta in Edgefield District, South Carolina, and owned a meat market. Joseph Phillips (or Philips) resided in Burke County, Georgia. The Garner family lived in Orangeburg County, South Carolina. Women comprised ten of the eighteen signatories. Charter trustees included Mealing, Randolph, and Ligon, alongside Abraham Marshall and John McKinne (or McKenne), a local businessman who vouched for the upstart Baptists. Though not a member, the venerable Marshall more than any other was responsible for the church's birthing.[52]

Two months afterward, on May 24 and 25, the Praying Society met in the Richmond County courthouse and constituted as a church. A proud Marshall assisted in the ceremony. As often customary in Baptist congregations, the men and women gathered referred to one another as "Brother" or "Sister." Brother Matheny preached from Matthew 16:18: "And I say unto thee, that thou art Peter, and upon this rock I will build my church." In a called conference (business meeting) following the sermon, Brother Davis moderated, receiving and reading the "letters" (statements of faith) of the Praying Society members who applied for church membership. During the weekend's events, Brothers J. D. Green and Woodson Ligon received ordination as the congregation's first deacons.[53]

Steady growth followed, with six persons joining the congregation by August.[54] As in other Baptist congregations of the South, church membership came with both privilege and responsibility. Against a backdrop of uneven municipal legal codes and judicial systems on the expanding frontier, churches frequently served as arbiters of morality and judges of personal disputes, their decisions carrying ramifications within civic life.

Remaining in the good graces of one's congregation, however, required personal diligence appropriate to congregational socioeconomic status as filtered through scripture. Most Baptist churches of the South, yet to attain the upper echelons of society, valued personal piety rather than social standing as a measure of religiosity. Sins of the flesh, avarice, and entertainments—all easily accessible to persons of wealth and position—were especially egregious to Baptists who, by avoidance of such personal weaknesses, could demonstrate religious superiority.[55]

Reflecting the democratic nature of local congregations, reception into membership required a majority vote of members, as did expulsion from a church body. As long as one avoided sin, or when guilty expressed repentance and asked for forgiveness, one would remain in good standing with the congregation. Sin paired with defiance, however, often resulted in expulsion. Elizabeth Williams, a founding member of the Praying Society, became the first to formally fall out of favor with some members. She may have been a bit of a rebel all along.

Church records between May and August of 1817 are unusually terse, offering no hint of troubles concerning Williams. Church minutes of the era often chronicle extended efforts, usually months and sometimes more than a year, to reconcile with members accused of sinning. No such written record exists in the case of Williams, although most likely the congregation did seek reconciliation. Church minutes of August 23 make it plain that any such efforts failed. The congregation's judgment is communicated in brief and veiled, yet pointed, wording:

"Sister Williams being guilty of intemperness and of keeping bad company was expelled this day."[56] Thus dismissed from fellowship, the details of Williams' offenses remained off the books, her story of unrepentant sin left to the whispers and rumors circulating about town.

In a much more pleasant development the church requested admittance to the Georgia Baptist Association in October. The same month Abraham Marshall, John McKinne, James H. Randolph, Woodson Ligon, and Jesse D. Green were named as "The Trustees of the Baptist Society in the city of Augusta and county of Richmond," charged with holding real estate, building a meeting house, and securing a pastor for the congregation.

Also in October 1817 the church petitioned the Georgia legislature for donation of land "back of the Presbyterian or of the Catholic Church for the purpose of building thereon a place of worship." The request, at odds with Baptists' commitment to church-state separation yet pragmatic, apparently went nowhere. On December 19 the state passed an act "to incorporate the Baptist Church in the city of Augusta and county of Richmond," and to authorize the trustees of the Academy of Richmond County "to convey a lot of land in the city of Augusta to said Baptist Society." The potential lots, however, proved unsuitable, and the search continued.[57]

3

A Church Birthed, A Community Transformed

In 1820 Adam Hodgson, a visitor from England, found himself surrounded by the "pomp and circumstance" of commercial activity along Augusta's riverfront Broad Street. He described "carts coming in from the country with cotton, and crowding the streets, or other avenues, of this rural town; tradesmen and agents bustling about in different directions; wharves loaded with bales; and steamboats darkening the air with their black exhalations."[58]

Among the most commercial two miles in the American South, Broad Street defined Augusta. Here the Federal Road and the Savannah River intersected. Stage coach lines linked the city to Savannah, Milledgeville, Columbia, and Charleston. Some 100 shop owners hawked their wares along the main street of a frontier town with big ambitions.[59]

At the center of enterprise stood a small number of wealthy planters who lived in the city part-time, yet generated enormous riches from their outlying cotton plantations worked by large numbers of slaves. From there the cotton economy rippled downscale. Middle class white men typically worked as lawyers, merchants, and shopkeepers. White craftsmen, mechanics, and laborers represented the lower class, which also included free black men (and some slaves) in the occupations of carpenter, barber, blacksmith, boat hand, and other service-related jobs. Many slaves worked as manual laborers in warehouses and along the wharves. White women, meanwhile, usually filled the role of homemaker. In addition to raising children and cooking, they tended garden plots and raised chickens, hogs, and the occasional milk cow. Some worked in the shops along Broad Street. Many middle and lower class white families operated small businesses (workshops, stores, private schools, and boarding houses) from their homes, structures often no more than 20 x 40 feet in size. Some 42 percent of Augusta households owned slaves.[60]

Isabella S. Jordan, in her centennial account of the history of the congregation that eventually became known as First Baptist Church, described the recreational and social life of middle-to-upper class Augusta at the time of the church's formation: "Horse-racing, card-playing and drinking were the gentlemanly pastimes of the men, while balls, visiting and the latest fashions from Paris occupied the thoughts of the women."[61] A surviving diary from the era reveals the attire of the young female journalist when attending the races: a purple skirt, scarlet-colored velvet jacket with matching slippers and turban, the latter replete with ostrich feathers.[62]

With good transportation infrastructure, a growing population, and a booming economy, Augusta in 1820 offered vast opportunities for enterprising individuals.

A Congregation Without a Home

In the twenty-first century, slavery is often referred to in shorthand as "America's original sin." North and South shared in this sin alike, although the practice faded away in the North in the early nineteenth century. Unlike in many other cities and towns of the South of this time, white Baptists of Augusta could not be found among the ranks of large slaveholders, or planters. At least six founding members of the white Baptist church, however, owned slaves.[63]

Nonetheless, the Baptist menfolk shared a commonality with elites: an appreciation of alcoholic spirits. While typically frowning upon drunkenness, few Christians of the era embraced tee-totaling. Baptist congregations, like others, used fermented wine for communion services. Church families often grew the grapes and produced the communion wine.[64]

Samuel Cartledge, the constable who had earlier arrested Daniel Marshall for preaching near Augusta only to be converted by the testimony of Daniel and his wife Martha, later recounted a story about Abraham, the younger Marshall. The occasion is the home of a friend in which Marshall and Rev. Hope Hull, an early Methodist leader in Georgia, were dining.

When dinner was announced, as the universal custom was then, they were invited to the sideboard where stood a decanter, and by it a glass, to take the usual drink before dinner. Marshall, being the older man, stepped up, poured out his dram and drank it down without ceremony; Hull reproved him, saying, "Brother Marshall, we should thank God for his good creatures, and ask his blessing upon them before we partake." Marshall received the rebuke in silence. Then up stepped Hull, and poured into the glass his dram, and closing his eyes and raising his hand, said a long grace over it. While Hull was saying his grace, Marshall raised Hull's glass to his lips and emptied it down his own throat. When Hull opened his eyes and reached to take it, behold it was empty, and Marshall said, "Brother Hull, the Scriptures command us to watch as well as to pray."[65]

A man of both good taste and ready humor, in addition to evangelistic renown and political acumen, Abraham Marshall's presence and influence among the early Baptists of Augusta knew no parallel. The legacy and legend of "Father Marshall," secure by the time of the founding of Augusta's first white Baptist church, for some converged in the prowess for publicity he displayed during the early days of the congregation.

A cherished story handed down orally from generation to generation of Augusta church members captures the creativity and panache of Marshall's efforts to attract Augusta's residents to the Baptist faith. Isabella Jordan recalled her "aged aunt," who was converted under the preaching of Marshall. "Ay, Child!" she would say, "the whole town would go out to see Father Marshall when he came riding down the street on his old white horse, his saddle-bags full of testaments and tracts, which he freely distributed, at the same time inviting the people to come and hear the gospel preached at the courthouse. I, with a merry group of young people, went there to scoff, but, my child, after hearing Father Marshall, I stayed to pray."[66]

Whether or not Abraham Marshall really caught the attention of the "whole town," he nonetheless steered the fledgling congregation of Baptists from the years 1817 to 1819. With prospects of land unrealized in 1817, Pastor Marshall on February 18, 1818 led the congregation in taking up a collection, totaling $32.50, for a church building fund.[67]

Months passed with no further movement toward obtaining land or a meeting house. The deacons explored another land possibility that led to yet another dead end. Nonetheless, the church carried on. Jesse Green was selected to represent the church at the October 1818 meeting of the Georgia Baptist Association, taking with him $40 to contribute to missions work. In November the church's membership increased by five, including Joshua Key, who would prove to be a key lay leader in the years to come.[68]

Meanwhile, Abraham Marshall's health rapidly declined, his appearances in Augusta growing less frequent in the fall months. He tried but failed to persuade his friend Jesse Mercer to assume the Augusta pastorate. The winter months, however, brought encouraging news. On February 28, 1819 church members discussed the prospects of acquiring land deeded by a deceased city resident and designated for the building of a church. In addition, members were informed that "it appears that a lot of land was granted to this church by the Legislature."[69]

With a lot of land seemingly at hand, the church decided it was time to begin raising money for a building. An ad placed in the April 5, 1819 edition of the *Augusta Chronicle* summarized both the disadvantages and the hopes of the yet struggling congregation:

> The Trustees of the Baptist Church in the city of Augusta, desirous of erecting a house in honor of Almighty God, and encouraged in their desire by the liberal patronage which a generous community has extended towards the erection of churches in favor of other denominations, make this humble appeal to an enlightened public. They have obtained an estimate of the probable expense of such a building as that which they contemplate, and perceive that the amount considerably exceeds what they can procure by voluntary donations. They therefore propose that those who are disposed to extend a friendly countenance to this desire shall have the right of obtaining for a given consideration a limited number of pews to be held as permanent interest by each subscriber, who on entering his name shall explicitly state his design to take a pew. And those who shall furnish any donations toward the contemplated building shall be considered as having a privilege in the distribution of such pews as shall not be disposed of by original subscription.[70]

A common Baptist practice of the era, pew rents provided congregational income, those near the front of the church costing more than seats in the rear.

Unfortunately, the hopes of the congregation yet again proved premature. The land prospects did not materialize, nor did enough money to construct a building. Identical newspaper notices taken out by church trustees in July and August thanked community members who "beyond expectation subscribed for Pews" in the church. The apparent generosity of some notwithstanding, the statement noted "the extreme scarcity of money" in declaring the church's decision to postpone "until January next" the "commencement of the building." At that time, the notice continued, "it is fondly hoped the times will be such as to justify calls being made on those who have subscribed, and induce others to do likewise."[71]

Augusta's Baptists were not the first of their faith to watch in dismay as plans of land and a building unexpectedly fell through. Perhaps someone among the little group knew the story of how the same fate had befallen America's first Baptist church, the First Baptist Church of Providence, Rhode Island, in the early 1770s as members strove to find a suitable place to build a new meeting house.[72] Yet for America's original Baptist church, success followed failure, and so it would be with the fledgling Baptist church in Augusta.

A Rapid Ascension

Whispers of hope wafted into town during the spring months of 1819. The Richmond Academy, seeking a new rector, courted someone with whom the institute was quite familiar: Rev. William Brantly, who eight years earlier had left the Academy to pastor the First Baptist Church of Beaufort, South Carolina. In response, on May 22, 1819, almost two years to the day of the formal constitution of the Augusta congregation, "Father Marshall" returned to the city in order to moderate the church's most important conference (business meeting) to date. Years earlier Brantly had been baptized by Marshall and lent a much-appreciated helping hand to the city's Baptists. Nineteenth-century Baptist historian Samuel Boykin described Brantly as "a courtly, courteous, highly cultivated and thoroughly educated minister and scholar," while another observer called him "one of the most eloquent preachers of the day." In addition to his oratory fame, Brantly had also made a name

30

for himself as a writer for the national *American Baptist Magazine*, "known to readers of that journal as a nervous and powerful writer." Excited about the prospects of his return and seizing the moment, the congregation voted "to call to the pastoral care of the church the Rev. William T. Brantly."[73]

Meanwhile, congregational transitions and growth marked the summer months. Jesse Green in June was granted a letter of dismissal, a document certifying him as a member in good standing and typically required for a person to join another Baptist church. Upon Green's departure, Joshua Key stepped into the role of church clerk. In August the church appointed messengers to the upcoming October meeting of the Georgia Baptist Association, to be held at Kiokee Baptist Church. The church also "Resolved that each member pay into the treasury 25c monthly for the purpose of buying candles, wine, etc."[74]

Yet apart from internal church matters, trouble brewed in Augusta, hinted at in church records. "Brethren were appointed to visit Springfield Church to advise them in the settlement of some cases of discipline," church records of July 1819 note. That was all that needed to be said; everyone knew what was going on. A recent, purported slave insurrection had resulted in the arrest of a number of alleged conspirators in May, several since executed and others severely beaten. Wary of another uprising, town leaders increased oversight of the city's blacks. Augusta's white Baptists were thus called upon to provide some oversight of the city's black Baptist church which, with a membership of some 600, was the largest in the city. The resulting alliance between Baptists white and black may have spared Springfield's members from heightened racial animosity during late 1819 and early 1820.[75]

As race relations deteriorated in the city, Augusta completed and the United States government occupied the Augusta Arsenal, the latest of a series of military structures built in the decades following the American Revolution. Located on the bank of the Savannah River, the arsenal had originally been envisioned in 1793 by U.S. President George Washington. Unfortunately, due to the structure's unhealthy location on the river's edge, "Black Fever" soon decimated those manning the arsenal. Other periods of deathly illnesses followed the 1819 opening of the facility, necessitating the eventual relocation of the structure. In 1826 construction commenced on a new site, land now occupied by Augusta University on Walton Way.[76]

During the latter months of 1819 Brantly accepted the rectorship of the Richmond Academy, effective in early 1820, and agreed to preach to Augusta's white Baptist congregation. Refusing to assume the title of pastor or accept a salary, he determined to grow the church to the point of constructing a building and supporting a pastor. Against the backdrop of Augusta's population growth, industrial expansion, economic opportunities, and racial unrest, the Baptist congregation thus found renewed hope in the person of William T. Brantly. In turn, Brantly found personal joy. Shortly after his arrival in Augusta he married a local, Margaret Joyner.[77]

Sadness, however, visited the congregation in the death of Abraham Marshall on August 15, 1819, who at the time was yet pastoring the Kiokee Baptist Church. The venerable Baptist leader bequeathed to future generations a spiritual legacy that remains to the present day in the life of the Kiokee Baptist congregation, the First Baptist Church of Augusta, and other churches. Many of his descendants yet live in the area, some members of the Kiokee congregation.[78]

Routine matters, too, characterized the life of the church. Meeting house or not, members were expected to be present for worship services, as Polly Holt learned. "Sister Holt has been seen [visited] and promised to attend more regularly," note church minutes of November 27, 1819. In Augusta and beyond, repeated failure to attend church services stood as a sin worthy of expulsion. Holt apparently followed through on her promise to rejoin worship services.[79]

The year 1820 dawned with, still, only four white church buildings in Augusta—those of the Episcopalians, Roman Catholics, Methodists, and Presbyterians. Under Brantly's leadership, however, the Baptist congregation prepared to move forward. On the twentieth of the first month of the year Brantly led the church to formally reorganize itself in a special service. Following the meeting, Basil Manly of South Carolina, a former student and current friend of Brantly's and a future leader in Southern Baptist life, offered words of encouragement to those present.[80]

The optimism proved well-founded. Following previous failed attempts to obtain land, Brantly suggested that the congregation look to "the extreme western limit of the town." There lay the city's former horse racing track, home to "the sport of kings." The pastime of well-healed citizens, horse racing probably posed little temptation to the Baptists of Augusta. Making arrangements with the owner, Mrs. Sarah Jones, they purchased the lot for $1,500.[81]

Redemption of the land came next. The congregation hired John Lund as architect, his previous jobs including St. Paul's Church and city hall. A cornerstone ceremony including a Masonic procession (many Baptist pastors of the day being Masons) took place on February 12 at the site of the old racetrack on the southwestern corner of Greene and Jackson streets, one block off Broad Street. In "the presence of a number of spectators," Rev. Brantly gave "an appropriate address" and offered "an impressive prayer," while the Presbyterian pastor, Rev. William Moderwell, voiced the closing prayer. An inscription on a silver plate buried with the cornerstone read: "This cornerstone, deposited by the trustees of the Baptist Church in this city, is consecrated to the worship of the Triune God, to the promotion of one faith, one baptism."[82]

As construction of the meeting house began, the congregation prepared itself spiritually. By April 9 twenty-five members comprised the "Baptist Church of Christ" in Augusta. A church constitution was adopted on May 6, and the summer months witnessed the first baptismal services in the church's short history.[83]

Among those baptized in the river waters was Ann Lamar Milledge, widow of former Governor and U.S. Senator John Milledge, namesake of the state capital of Milledgeville. Milledge, one of the largest planters in the Augusta area, had willed his estate to Dr. John Milledge Galphin, nephew of his first wife, Martha Galphin Milledge. Milledge's baptism signaled that the Baptist faith could appeal to persons who moved in Augusta's upper strata.[84]

And just what did these Baptists of Augusta believe? Unfortunately the May 1820 church constitution and a revision in April 1821 have been damaged with the passing of time. From what can be gleaned, however, the 1821 constitution stressed the faithful witness of scripture and the necessity of personal commitment to Jesus Christ as savior, required believer's baptism by immersion, and took seriously sin and church discipline.[85]

Ambitiously, church members wished to construct a building "which would compare favorably with any church then existing in town." Yet despite continued growth in membership—at least four persons being added about this time—the church did not have the means to fund such an extensive building project. Again, William Brantly stepped to the forefront.[86]

As rector of Richmond Academy, Brantly enjoyed good relations with the Presbyterians, many of whom sent their children to the academy and "were both wealthy and numerous."[87] Serving as a bridge between the established Presbyterians and the up-and-coming Baptists, Brantly raised funds from his Presbyterian clients totaling nearly $10,000. The remaining funds and pledges came from Baptists in Augusta and beyond. Locally, Augusta Baptist contributions took the form of pledges and pew rents. According to one account, however, few church members "were able to contribute anything towards the erection of the building, but their brother Baptists throughout the State, with their proverbial zeal and liberality, came to the rescue."[88]

Despite, or perhaps due to, the relatively poor fiscal fortunes of the Baptists of Augusta, the congregation valued piety above wealth even during the construction of their meeting house. For the little band of believers, members' money was less important than their faithfulness to church attendance as admonished by the Bible in Hebrews 10:25. Some Augustans may have scratched their heads upon learning that the small Baptist congregation in December of 1820 threatened to expel members who were "in the habit of absenting themselves from the public meetings of the church." Fortunately, by March 1821 many of those guilty of non-attendance had accounted for their absences and promised to begin attending again.[89]

On May 26, 1821 a long-anticipated moment finally arrived: the dedication of their first meeting house. "The Church met in the new church in this place built for our worship," congregational clerk Joshua Key wrote of the important day. A dedication ceremony took place amidst "a crowded House & an attentive congregation." Members expressed gratitude for "God's Goodness and mercy towards us in erecting so comfortable a building." Basil Manly, having come down from South Carolina for the occasion, preached an afternoon sermon. Among those baptized in the river that day were Elizabeth and Margaret Ware, sisters of Augusta's current mayor and later Georgia's first senator, Nicholas Ware. And to the joy of all, Brantly formally accepted the pastorate of the congregation now numbering 66 members.[90]

Almost 90 years after the founding of the Georgia colony downriver at the mouth of the Savannah River, a white Baptist meeting house finally stood in the city of Augusta.

Stability and Respectability

A sanctuary secured, the Augusta congregation enjoyed enhanced standing in the city and among Georgia Baptists. With greater respectability and prominence came more responsibility.

One year following the dedication of the church building, pastor Brantly in 1822 represented the Greene Street congregation in the formation of the statewide General Baptist Association (in 1827 renamed the Georgia Baptist Convention). Gathered in Powelton, Hancock County, delegates elected Brantly assistant secretary of the association, a position he retained for the next four years. Commitment to cooperative mission work and educational endeavors undergirded the organization comprised of local churches and regional associations.[91]

Also in 1822 the Augusta congregation temporarily took under its wing the declining Red Creek (Abilene) Baptist Church located west of the city. In March "Dr. Brantly visited Abilene, preached, and baptized four blacks, namely: Violet, Sukey and two others, names not recollected, belonging to Marshall Keith. Ned belonging to same was baptized last summer."[92]

Blacks, Baptists or otherwise, were deemed of little importance by white churches of the South, their names inconsequential. Clues to Southern church racial structures lie within the ambivalent summary of Brantly's visit to Abilene. State laws in much of the South prohibited black slaves from joining churches without their masters' approval. Many slaves, therefore, attended the churches of their owners, often by compulsion. Within the confines of the church sanctuary, however, they were allowed a degree of spiritual autonomy. In theory they were the spiritual equal of whites. Although having more rights within the church than without, in reality they yet remained of lesser standing in congregational life, unable to fully express themselves.[93]

Augusta's white congregation, though, demonstrated a more charitable spirit, perhaps due to the absence of slave members, an unusual scenario for Baptist churches in the antebellum South. The lack of black members can be attributed to the apparent absence of planters among the church's membership, as well as the strong presence of the nearby black Springfield Baptist Church, one of few independent black congregations in the entire South.[94]

Native Americans, recently pushed further westward, comprised the other notable minority people group in Georgia. From a safe distance many of the city's residents contemplated the "taming of the ferocity" of the "savage" with the Christian gospel. In November 1822 three converted Indians, two Cherokees and a Delaware, spoke at the white Baptist church. Before a curious crowd of onlookers they stood "as the trophies of grace and the advocates of Jesus and his religion," wrote one observer. "Who could refrain from feeling at such a sight? There was the relenting savage calling for the interposition of christian benevolence to rescue his suffering countrymen. There was heard the voice of the gospel from mouths to which our former associations had assigned the horrid grim of fury and the yell of murderous resentment. Let christians hence learn that their labour is not in vain." The appeals of the domesticated savages opened the door for enhanced missionary efforts.[95]

The presence of the Native Americans in Augusta also stood testimony to another recent transformation of epic proportions. Prior to the 1790s Baptists, many adherents of Calvinistic theological teaching that posited individual salvation as the arbitrary will of God regardless of human actions or beliefs, avoided missionary activity. Some prominent ministers refused to preach the gospel to known sinners, fearing that God might be offended if the gospel were heard by one he had predestined to hell. English Baptist ministers Andrew Fuller and William Carey in the 1780s, as previously noted, challenged the status quo, declaring that God desired the preaching of the gospel to the "heathen" in foreign lands. Carey became a missionary to India in 1793, and in the decades following, many Baptists in England and America embraced missionary work, the latter forming the aforementioned Triennial

Convention in 1814. Other Christian denominations also embraced mission work during this time.[96]

By 1823 foreign missionary work in exotic locales excited many Americans, as evidenced in Augusta when the local newspaper reported on the death of William Ward, a Baptist missionary in India alongside Carey.[97] The Baptists of Augusta may not have been as exotic as Carey and Ward, but they did try to raise their visibility through numerous advertisements in the *Augusta Chronicle* that year. The ads notified everyone that the pews in the Baptist church were now free for all—no pew fee required. All were welcome to attend.

Thanks to Brantly, the Baptists enjoyed good relations with other congregations. When the civic leaders of Augusta in November 1823 set aside a day for "Public Thanksgiving for the blessings conferred on our citizens," the Baptists joined the Presbyterians and Methodists in the observance.[98] Augusta of the early nineteenth century periodically observed such days in November, although Thanksgiving would not emerge as a national holiday until the 1860s.

Baptists shared many of the same theological convictions as the city's other Christians, particularly in regards to the Trinity, an ancient and complex theological formulation of the three embodiments of God: Father, Son, and Holy Spirit. However, Unitarianism, a theology focused on the unity and oneness of God, rather than the threeness of the Trinity, claimed many adherents in Northern states. Brantly in February 1824 preached a sermon titled "Trinitarians Rational," attracting many non-Baptists to the Sunday service. The discourse impressed listeners enough that it was subsequently published in booklet format and sold at the local bookstore.[99]

Perhaps in order to attract Methodists and Presbyterians, Brantly set aside certain Sundays for "publicly dedicating children to the Lord." While infant baptism could not be accommodated by Baptist churches, child dedication at least afforded some comfort to non-Baptist families accustomed to infant baptism.[100]

The return of a charter member in 1824 occasioned congregational-wide rejoicing. On April 11 "Joseph Phillips applied for restoration to the church after having absented himself from the church for nearly four years and joined the Methodists. His acknowledgments were approved of by the church and he restored to fellowship."[101]

Dr. William H. Turpin, owner of a thriving drugstore, took note of the ascendant Baptist congregation. "Many religious discussions" with Brantly convinced him to join the church, whereupon he was baptized July 11, 1824. Likely the wealthiest member of the congregation, Turpin's generosity assisted the ministries of the church and of broader Baptist life, paralleling his expanding business fortunes. An incorporator of the Augusta Savings Bank in 1827, Turpin also became commissioner of the Georgia Railroad Company (1833), an incorporator of the Jackson Street Ice Company (1837), and an incorporator of the Augusta Machine Works (1850).[102]

Against the backdrop of a handful of notable Augustans settling into the Baptist pews on Greene Street, the congregation in June 1824 nominated two new deacons, Edward Martin and L. B. Holloway, to assist Dr. Brantly in the leadership of the church. To no one's great surprise, two years later William Turpin joined the ranks of deacons.[103]

For all the excitement and progress of 1824, the year closed on an unexpected note. The church minutes of December 9 succinctly expressed the congregation's sorrow upon learning that its pastor was casting his eyes northward. "Brother Brantly communicated his intent of leaving this church and going to Philadelphia. The thought of losing him was deeply and sensibly felt by the church." The First Baptist Church of Philadelphia, birthplace of America's first national Baptist denomination and now the largest Baptist church in the nation, hoped that Brantly would succeed the recently departed pastor, Dr. Henry Holcombe, a mentor to Brantly. To the relief of the Augusta congregants, their pastor declined to accept the call of the Philadelphia church. During a visit to Philadelphia, Brantly had learned that "the church was disturbed to a serious extent by some differences upon doctrinal subjects."[104]

Having refused the call of the Philadelphia church, the charismatic Brantly continued attracting prominent additions to the church. In May 1825 Mrs. Hannah D'Antignac, wife of Revolutionary war officer Capt. John D'Antignac, joined the congregation. The following month one of Augusta's leading physicians, Dr. Milton Anthony, converted to the Baptist faith and was baptized. A founder of the Medical Society of Augusta, Anthony sought improvements of the city's medical standards. Aided by the society, in 1826 he pursued the formation of a medical school, his efforts in 1828 garnering a state charter for the Medical Academy of Georgia.[105]

Structural changes accompanied membership growth. In March 1825 local businessman Eli Mustin accepted the position of clerk, a position he would hold for forty-six years. The church also voted to move communion services from quarterly to monthly, hired its first sexton, "Brother Bell," and elected William Turpin as treasurer.[106]

First Baptist Church Philadelphia, however, did not give up on Brantly. In late 1825 the Pennsylvania congregation resolved its internal controversy through the withdrawal of certain members. Again, the members contacted the Augusta pastor. Satisfied with the church's soundness, Brantly accepted the congregation's call. On April 2, 1826, came a moment many dreaded: "This day our Beloved Pastor & Brother Rev. Wm. T. Brantly requested a letter of dismission for himself...to the 1st Baptist Church in Philadelphia which was granted."[107]

Brantly, however, remained in town for a few more weeks in order to attend the annual gathering of the Georgia Baptist Convention, hosted for the first time by the Greene Street church. During the gathering he read an essay, "Rules for Interpreting Scripture." Noting that Brantly "wielded a weighty, and judicious influence in Georgia," Georgia Baptists expressed their appreciation of his leadership.[108]

While a sad affair for church members, Brantly's move was far from a setback for the Augusta congregation. Vibrant and thriving, the church anticipated a prosperous future.

Within the City and Far Beyond

By the time of William Brantly's departure the Georgia Baptist Convention fared well, its fortunes bolstered by a rising interest in missions and education.

Some 150 miles to the southeast of Augusta and near the coast stood the private, religiously-influenced Sunbury Academy. Established in 1788, for the next three decades the school had been presided over by Rev. Dr. William McWhir, a Presbyterian, Irish native, graduate of

Belfast College, notable scholar, and strict disciplinarian. In 1821 another Presbyterian, Irishman, and Belfast-trained scholar arrived at the academy as a teacher of languages. James Shannon, however, did not long remain a Presbyterian while in Sunbury, converting and being baptized into the Baptist faith in 1823.[109]

At the Sunbury Academy Shannon labored in a fervent missions environment. With the school playing a central role, Liberty County between the years 1800 and 1840 produced more than fifty home and foreign missionaries. Perhaps the emphasis on the missionary enterprise factored into the young man's decision to join the Sunbury Baptist Church. Regardless, by 1826 Shannon felt called of God to become a pastor. Shortly before William Brantly announced his resignation in Augusta, Shannon secured at least two letters of reference from Liberty County, one from the pastor of Sunbury Baptist. Upon Brantly's leaving, both of these letters presumably made their way to the deacons of the Augusta congregation. Brantly, having ministered alongside Shannon on several occasions, likely put in a good word for the Irishman. One month following Brantly's departure, the Augusta congregation called Shannon as its second pastor. In so doing, the church acquired a leader whose interests included discipline, missions, and education.[110]

Shannon's propensity for discipline may have heightened during his time at the Sunbury Academy, but if so, his concerns were not out of place within the context of a Baptist congregation. Reflecting most Baptist churches of the era, the Baptist church on Greene Street expected members to live upright lives. Drunkenness, card-playing, profanity, and sexual impropriety were among the personal sins especially frowned upon in Baptist life of the South.[111]

Contrasting widespread Baptist ambivalence about alcohol (other than inebriation), with Shannon's blessing the Augusta congregation passed a resolution disapproving of members who visited "dram shops . . . for the purpose of drinking." In addition, some members crafted a resolution opposing Masonic fraternities, a position clearly at odds with Baptist sentiment at a time when many clergy and laity alike were Masons. Facing much opposition within the congregation, the resolution was easily defeated.[112]

Moral fervor notwithstanding, church records during Shannon's three-year pastorate provide few details concerning various accusations of personal misconduct among members. Not so regarding church absenteeism. Either way, disciplinary cases resulted in the formation of a committee to investigate the matter. Upon questioning, the alleged offender typically asked for forgiveness or provided evidence of innocence, whereupon the church discontinued discipline proceedings. Occasionally, however, repentance was not expressed and forgiveness not extended.

Among a number of expulsions of church members, Sister Mary Foster was removed from the church for some unnamed conduct on September 24, 1826. A month later on October 17, 1826 the congregation decided, for reasons unstated, that a certain member was not really a Christian: "Our Sister Sabrina Gardner was this day excluded from this church, she having deceived the church by a false statement, by which we were induced to receive her."[113]

Sin also existed outside the congregation. In the minutes of July 12, 1828 members expressed remorse at the church "being in a backslidden condition" and voiced alarm "at the great and increasing problems of iniquity in our City."[114] Perhaps the oblique reference in part reflected Baptists' disdain for horse racing, a sport in which gambling was front and center.

Although some members were expelled and the congregation expressed disapproval of sinners outside the church, the Baptist community grew nonetheless. On March 10, 1827 fourteen persons were baptized. Within a space of two weeks that month some twenty-nine persons joined the congregation either by baptism or by transfer of membership. In July a revival among the Baptists of Georgia began in Eatonton, Georgia under the preaching of Adiel Sherwood and spread throughout the state. Over the course of several months between 10,000 and 20,000 people were converted, including 4,000 at one time. One of two additional ministers who preached to great crowds during the revival, James Shannon also effected many conversions. The season of revival continued for about fifteen years and impacted many communities, Augusta included. As Shannon's tenure in the city drew to a close in 1829, church membership had risen to 128 and three young men—"Brothers" Goodman, Atwood, and Law—had been licensed to preach.[115]

The increase in church membership paralleled a second emphasis of Shannon's, that of missions. At Sunbury Academy the former instructor had witnessed many of his students embrace missions, and in Augusta the pastor of the Baptist church found a congregation enthralled with missions, both foreign and home. In these early days of Baptist mission work, congregations and individuals supported missionary endeavors directly, and sometimes through associations or newly-developing state conventions. Locally, Augusta's Baptists supported education for poor children through the Augusta Free School Society.[116]

Education, a third characteristic of James Shannon's pastoral years in Augusta, reflected a continuation of his years of teaching at the Sunbury Academy. In 1827 Shannon addressed the Georgia Baptist Convention and garnered support for an institution of higher learning, later Mercer University. Preaching again at the 1829 convention, Shannon "made a profound impression upon the people," according to one participant.[117]

Missions and education intersected in the 1827 arrival of an Augusta branch of the then-three-year-old Baptist General Tract Society (later the American Baptist Publication Society), headquartered in Philadelphia. Perhaps William T. Brantly, now a pastor in Philadelphia and working with the Society, fostered the organization's opening in Augusta, an occasion welcomed by his former congregation with a day of fasting and prayer. The Society's Augusta branch sold 15,000 religious pamphlets the first year, attracting the attention of officers in Philadelphia. Baptist legend Luther Rice, Society founder and fund-raising agent of both the Society and the Triennial Convention, visited Augusta in 1828. From the city's Baptists he elicited a donation of $140. He also found a lasting friend in the person of William H. Turpin, the Turpin house becoming Rice's "Georgia home."[118]

Evidencing a decade of growth and expanding influence, the Baptist church on Greene Street stood as a vibrant part of the city's spiritual life. On July 4, 1829 members of Christian churches throughout the city gathered at the Baptist church to commemorate the nation's independence, with Shannon and other ministers addressing the crowd.[119]

James Shannon, however, sought a return to the world of higher education. Resigning the pastorate, he departed Augusta in November 1829, the remainder of his career focused on academic life. Between the years 1840 and 1859 he served as president of three different colleges, most notably the University of Missouri (1850-1856). During this time he also converted from the Baptist faith to that of the Disciples of Christ (A.K.A. Campbellite).[120]

New Institutions, Big Ambitions

Sweden's Carl D. Arfwedson, touring the United States, said of Augusta in 1830: "Of all the towns in the Southern States, none, with the exception of New Orleans, had a more agreeable exterior and inspires the stranger at first with a stronger idea of comfort and wealth than Augusta." About the same time, travel writer James Henry Buckingham of Cornwall praised Augustans for their kindness.[121]

Although an April 1830 fire destroyed hundreds of buildings, fortuitously sparing the Baptist church on Greene Street, the city rebounded with determination. October 1 marked a monumental achievement as the Medical Academy of Georgia opened, with the name quickly changed to the Medical Institute of the State of Georgia. Improvements to the Savannah River continued, and plans were made to build a railroad between Augusta and Charleston.[122]

Against this backdrop, on February 13, 1830, the Greene Street Baptist congregation called its third pastor, Charles Dutton Mallory. Serving as pastor until 1835, the Virginia native, when not preaching, focused much of his attention on education and missions. Under Mallory's tutelage the church established a formal Sunday School, a new institution in American Baptist life focused on the spiritual education of young persons. In addition, the congregation ordained lay leader C. F. Sturgis to the ministry as a missionary among the Cherokee Indians, the first member of the congregation to serve as a missionary. And when missionaries from Burma visited the congregation, church members gave generously, "one lady placing in the basket a carefully sealed package, which proved to be all of her jewelry."[123]

Also during this time a young man named William Milton Tryon joined the Augusta church. Born in 1809 and a native of New York, the young Baptist was licensed to preach by the congregation in December 1832, afterward enrolling at Mercer Institute in Penfield (now Mercer University in Macon). Following brief stints with the Georgia Baptist Convention and several churches in Alabama, Tryon and his family moved to Texas, the second missionary appointed by the American Baptist Home Mission Society to the state. There he met Robert E. B. Baylor, and the two drafted the charter for a new Baptist institution of higher learning. Each suggested that the institution be named after the other. Tryon's request prevailed. Baylor University was created in 1845, with the former Augustan serving as president of the board of trustees.[124]

Mission work in distant places, while thrilling many Baptists of the 1830s, did not diminish local efforts. Historically, many Baptist congregations initially formed as arms or missions of an established church. Alongside the growth of Augusta, some members of the Greene Street church in 1831 requested permission to leave and form a congregation across town, on the east side of the city. While a few questioned the wisdom of such a venture, permission was granted and a new congregation formed, likely the Calvary Baptist Church.[125]

Other church matters during Mallory's years as pastor were more routine, but nonetheless indicative of wider Baptist life at the time. The church revised its constitution in 1832. Church expenses included the sexton's salary; oil, wicks, and globes for lamps; "aid" for "2 sisters in affliction"; communion expenditures; and the stabling of the horses of visiting preachers. Mallory received $700 for his services in 1833. In addition, discipline cases remained a staple of church life. An unnamed male church member in April 1833 confessed that he "went to the circus," a worldly entertainment frowned upon by many Baptists. The offender repented for bringing "reproach upon the cause of Christ." The following year "Bro. Sanders Walker...was excommunicated on the charge of habitual neglect of our meetings for worship and business."[126]

Outside events sometimes impacted the whole of church life. When a cholera epidemic swept through the city in the summer of 1832, the church held a fast day. Sunday meetings were suspended through October in order to prevent the spread of the contagion. The epidemic eventually subsided, although Augusta remained susceptible to outbreaks for many years.[127]

Despite the ever present prospect of disease due to the nearby river and wetlands, Augusta prospered. The Charleston and Hamburg Railroad reached Hamburg across the river from Augusta in 1832, while the following year construction on the Georgia Railroad between Augusta and Athens commenced. Along with the railroads came new commercial activity, including the 1834 construction of the Richmond Factory on Spirit Creek ten miles distant, the first textile mill in the area. From raw cotton the mill produced plain clothing for slaves.[128] With cotton acreage in Georgia growing dramatically and powering the Southern economy, many more textile mills soon opened.

Meanwhile, economic tensions escalated across the river as a federal tariff restricted cotton profits. Exports to Britain dropped, and in 1832 South Carolina's elite planter class threatened to withdraw its state from the Union. State legislators requested that Georgia join them in nullifying the federal tariff, the first step on the road to secession. In response the federal government increased to 600 the number of soldiers stationed at the Augusta Arsenal, as U.S. President Andrew Jackson prepared to forcefully collect the tariff in South Carolina.

An August 18, 1832 public meeting in Augusta addressed the growing Nullification Crisis. Henry Mealing, prominent citizen and charter member of the Greene Street church, attended. Following deliberations Augustans voted against nullification, with Mealing among the more prominent voices. Augusta's decision helped convince the state to stay out of the fray, forcing South Carolina to ultimately accept a compromise with the federal government.[129] Where other members of the Baptist congregation stood on the issue is unknown. Differing opinions may well have existed. Freedom of conscience, after all, remained central to Baptist life.

Progress and challenges in both church and city thus marked Charles D. Mallory's pastoral tenure. His ministry transcended Augusta in the 1832 publication of *Memoirs of Elder Edmund Botsford*, a South Carolina Baptist leader of the eighteenth century. Pastoral duties, however, commanded most of his time, until health issues, perhaps exasperated by the city's climate, led him to think about "some other field of labor." Upon his resignation in November 1834, Mallory agreed to remain in the pulpit while the church sought a new minister.[130]

Following Mallory's announcement, the congregation created a Pastor Search Committee headed by William Turpin. Within weeks the committee contacted one of the most well-known and successful Baptist pastors in all of America—none other than William T. Brantly.[131]

Since his departure from Augusta to the First Baptist Church of Philadelphia, the elder Brantly's ministerial successes had been remarkable. Under his leadership some 600 persons were added to the rolls of the Philadelphia church. He also taught in a local Baptist college, was a popular revival preacher, and served as president of the Baptist General Tract Society. From 1827 to 1833 he served as editor of the Washington-based *Columbian Star* Baptist newspaper, later renamed the *Christian Index* and relocated to Washington, Georgia under the editorship of Jesse Mercer.[132]

Thus it was no surprise that William Turpin, one of Augusta's most industrious and successful businessmen, contacted William Brantly, one of America's most successful and industrious Baptist ministers, about returning to Augusta. But it may have been a surprise, if a pleasant one, that Brantly responded positively. On February 7, 1835, "Brother Turpin informed the Church that he has heard from Bro. Brantly & he may be expected to come, he was to resign the Pastoral care of the Church In Philadelphia Lord's day January 25th & to leave Philadelphia [for] the South about the 1st of April." For Brantly's part, health concerns may have contributed to his decision to return to the South.[133]

Amid great expectations Brantly arrived in Augusta in March and asked the church to call a special business meeting. The March 30, 1835 meeting, however, took a most unusual turn. In an awkward exchange Brantly informed church members that he would be unable to fulfill his "pledge to return to Augusta and assume the pastoral charges" of the congregation. Church minutes are vague, indicating that Brantly voiced "many reasons" for having a change of heart.

Brantly's request shocked those present. Following discussion, members voted not to release Brantly from the contract to which he had previously agreed. Binding in the eyes of God, a promise between Christians could not be easily broken. Now the congregation faced the difficult task of effecting a mutual resolution in the spirit of Christ.

This was perhaps the most difficult task the young church had yet encountered, other than that of acquiring land and erecting a meeting house. Refusing to release Brantly from his pastoral contract, "The members present, understanding that Bro. Brantly has some [?] embarrassments, and that his leaving the City of Philadelphia without their entire sentiment would produce to him great uneasiness, they resolved to make an effort for his relief, and to meet tomorrow afternoon, to ascertain what can be done." The following day the congregation voted to inform Brantly of its decision and provide him with a copy of the minutes of March 30 and "any other statement of facts" that he might desire from the church.[134]

The month of May arrived with the Greene Street congregation yet in limbo. On May 3 "Brother Mallory preached his farewell sermon from the last verse in Rev." After the morning worship service the church went into business meeting and granted letters of dismissal to "Bro. & Sister Mallory." Minutes after releasing the current pastor from his position, "A letter from Rev. W. T. Brantly was read before the church & on motion Resolved that we postpone action till our conference meeting next Saturday."[135]

Postmarked from Philadelphia April 22, the letter portrayed Brantly as caught in the untenable position of having signed a contract with Augusta Baptists without having been released from his Philadelphia duties. To leave the First Baptist Church of Philadelphia without a letter of dismissal would complicate the transfer of his church membership back to Augusta. Caught in a predicament of his own making, he could see no easy way out. In desperation Brantly pleaded for the mercy of his former congregation: "My beloved Brothers & Sisters pity and forgive your once devoted pastor and now affectionate friend and brother in the Lord."[136]

Gathering yet again in a business session on May 9, the Augusta church made the best of a rather tense situation, resolving "that in consequence of Elder Brantly's uncompliance with his contract to [take] charge of this church as expressed in letter of April 22nd last past that the church" release him "with the blessing of God."[137]

Suddenly, the future of the church seemed unclear. A committee, quickly formed to find a supply preacher, wrote the pastor of the First Baptist Church of Beaufort, South Carolina "an urgent letter of invitation to assist us." Brantly had pastored the Beaufort congregation prior to assuming the Augusta pastorate in 1820. The South Carolina congregation was now led by lawyer-turned-minister Richard Fuller, a former student of Brantly's. Upon further reflection, the Augusta congregation "by a unanimous vote" asked Fuller to become its new pastor. Worship services, meanwhile, were suspended and replaced with informal gatherings on Sunday afternoons. The reply from Fuller finally arrived, declining the church's invitation.[138]

Next the church, once again by unanimous vote, extended a call to John Kerr. Formerly pastor of the First Baptist Church of Richmond, Virginia, Kerr counted among the state's Baptist leaders. His positions included that of president of the Board of Managers for the Virginia Baptist Seminary and the Virginia Baptist Missionary Society. Kerr, like the two previous candidates, also declined the church's offer.[139]

Despite the Augusta church's connections South and North, months passed before a pastoral candidate accepted the congregation's call. In the meantime, the church hosted the 1835 annual meeting of the Georgia Baptist Association, with former pastor Charles Mallory serving as pro-tempore officiator during the meeting.[140]

A Unique Partnership

Settling into a period of time without a pastor, the Greene Street Baptist Church in 1835 found itself caught up in an ongoing chain of events that would ultimately distinguish the congregation from other Baptist churches of the South.

An 1831 slave uprising in Virginia, the Nat Turner rebellion, thereafter heightened oversight and suppression of the South's slave population. Many Southern states passed laws forbidding the education of black persons. Georgia did so in 1833, banning the teaching of blacks (whether slave or free) "to read or write either written or printed characters."[141] State leaders hoped this would sufficiently keep blacks in check.

Northern abolitionist organizations, however, proliferated following the Nat Turner rebellion. By early 1835 some Augustans deemed the activities of the anti-slavery organizations of significant concern. In July the postmaster of Hamburg, South Carolina, across the river from Augusta, intercepted an "incendiary" abolitionist pamphlet distributed by Northern churches. Weeks later the editor of the *Augusta Chronicle*, A. H. Pemberton, asserted that the Springfield Baptist Church should be abolished because "such churches are fruitful nests of mischief without the least promise of good." Pemberton further opined that "negroes" should be required to attend white churches. The Springfield church, an autonomous black congregation, remained an anomaly. Throughout the South, blacks otherwise attended white-led churches or worshiped separately, but under the direct supervision of whites.[142]

Springfield's Baptists, however, had an ally. Within days of his pronouncements, Pemberton, informed that the Springfield church was supervised by the city's white Baptist church on Greene Street, retracted his criticism of the city's black Baptists.[143]

Having established at least a minimal relationship in 1819, the two Baptist congregations following the tension-filled summer of 1835 expanded their joint efforts. In December the Springfield congregation requested that the Greene Street church take them under "watch care," in effect a partnership arrangement designed to dull ongoing racial tensions in the city. Obtaining the blessing of the Georgia Baptist Association, the Greene Street Baptist Church in 1836 accepted Springfield's invitation, in the process paving the way for the black congregation to become a member of the Association.[144]

The expanded relationship between the two churches, initiated by the independent black Baptist congregation, was possibly the most progressive interracial cooperation among antebellum Baptists of the South. The unusual arrangement of a white-only congregation protecting the autonomy of a black-only congregation provided space for Springfield Baptists to remain leaders among black Baptists of the South. The absence of planter members in the Greene Street congregation may have fostered the cooperative spirit. Regardless, this unique biracial partnership, albeit paternalistic, empowered the Baptists of Greene Street to maintain a witness of racial cooperation even when unexpected events pressured the church otherwise.

Winds of Change

While strengthening ties with the city's black Baptists, the congregation's pastoral search came to an end in December 1835 when William J. Hard, a former professor at Mercer University and teacher in Augusta, accepted the church's call. In the interim an addition to the congregation's constitution required the use of ballots to decide future elections of pastors, deacons, and committee members. Perhaps some members' voices had not been fully heard in the recent pastoral search processes. Regardless, the move strengthened the church's Baptist identity in terms of democratic decision-making. In an ironic twist, the same month of Hard's acceptance, the congregation received into membership Henry Robinson, a licensed preacher.[145]

Under Hard's leadership the congregation enhanced and expanded its relationship with the Springfield congregation, while internal matters of discipline, sermon delivery, theology, missions, and temperance characterized the remaining years of the decade.

Discipline, a major concern of the church since its inception, loomed large in 1836. During the year various members were charged with faulty theology (not believing in Satan or eternal punishment), attending horse races, participating in balls, lapsing into intoxication, and failing to attend church services. The congregation also intervened to settle a personal matter between two female members. And in a case highlighting common differences between the informal preaching found in many rural churches and a more educated clergy in city churches, the Greene Street Baptist Church expelled Henry Robinson due to his unrepentant criticisms of pastor Hard for writing and reading his sermons. Robinson had also condemned the pastor for performing an improper marriage (the couple eloped).[146]

Most disciplinary matters took place on familiar ground. Theological controversies over the doctrine of eternal punishment, however, were less common. Nonetheless, some Christians, pointing to the absence of the word "hell" in the Hebrew and Greek languages of the Bible, questioned eternal punishment.[147] Baptists, historical advocates of freedom of conscience, were free to question even such basic matters as the afterlife, but not all felt comfortable doing so.

Alongside a belief in the "everlasting punishment" of the wicked, the church's constitution echoed a traditional, post-millennial view of the "knowledge of God" as progressing throughout the earth. Reflecting a common interpretation of the biblical book of Revelation, "Satan" would soon be "bound" and the kingdom of God would reign on earth for "a thousand years," after which God would return and judge the righteous and wicked.[148]

The missions landscape of Baptist life in the 1830s was also not without controversy, evidenced by an anti-missions movement that split many congregations during the decade. Within recent years, in fact, the Georgia Baptist Association had lost some member churches that insisted missionary work should only be conducted directly by local congregations, and not associational or national organizations. William J. Hard moved quickly to ensure that the Augusta congregation remained on the side of cooperative missions work, in 1836 establishing two special missions offerings each year to be sent to the association.[149]

On a different front, some Baptists of America were on the leading edge of a growing alcohol abstinence movement. Northern Baptists embracing abstinence did so from the conviction that alcohol threatened families and society, while Baptists of the South did so more from the perspective of personal purity. Not all Baptists of Augusta embraced the fledgling abstinence movement at this time. Hard, however, made known his opposition to alcohol, throwing his support behind the formation of the "Total Abstinence Society" in 1836. During his pastoral tenure several members were excommunicated for drunkenness.[150]

In other areas of church life, the congregation formed a Sunday School Society under the leadership of C. F. Sturgis, newly returned from his missionary work among the Cherokees. The church elected Bennett Harris as a deacon, and pastor Hard began leading the church in acapella singing—the congregation apparently having few, if any, hymn books.[151]

The church continued to grow under Hard's leadership, with many new members added to offset those dismissed, excommunicated, or deceased. Hard led the congregation to print 200 copies of the church's constitution and confession of faith for distribution, more than enough for a church of 127 members as of October 1838.[152] Presumably this reminder of the church's procedures and beliefs assisted the congregation, new and old members alike, in navigating the many disciplinary issues and new developments during the second half of the decade. In addition, the documents were likely provided to prospective members.

Increasing numbers of children in worship services, meanwhile, proved to be both a blessing and a challenge. In August 1837 the church requested that pastor Hard remind parents of "the propriety of keeping children under their own eye during worship."[153]

On a more personal level, William J. Hard during his pastoral tenure married Ann Turpin Walton, a niece of William H. Turpin. Nonetheless, the pastor's relation with some church members apparently deteriorated over time. A July 1838 reference to difficulties between pastor and congregation offers no details. Although the church refused in July 1839 to accept Hard's resignation, the pastor referred to an "unhappy condition" with no clear explanation.[154]

Compounding the church's internal struggles, yellow fever swept through the city in 1839. For two months the church closed its doors. During this time several church members lost their lives, including the prominent doctor Milton Anthony, co-founder of the Medical College, who died on September 19 while ministering to the sick. In the words of the church's early historian Isabella Jordan, Anthony's "splendid life was sacrificed that others might live." Another chronicler said of Anthony: "He was a man of the most exemplary character, of great ability in his chosen profession, enormous industry, and a patriot of the highest type."[155] A plaque later placed on the first floor of the college building paid tribute to Anthony's religious faith:

> In memory of Milton Anthony, M.D., Founder of this College. A martyr to humanity and to the duties of his profession, during the fatal epidemic of 1839. Cheered by Religious Faith through the Griefs and Trials of his life, he passed from the cure of the sick to the sleep of the just, amid the tears and blessings of the poor. True to his own favorite maxim that a virtuous will is almost omnipotent, he overcame by study the defects of education and, patiently toiling to eminence, bequeathed

to posterity a noble example of genius and industry, animated and directed by Patriotism and benevolence.[156]

Perhaps some church members considered the epidemic an act of providence. When the city flooded the following year on May 28, 1840 and the church roof caught fire, members with Calvinistic leanings might reasonably have wondered if God was trying to get the church's attention. Fortunately—providentially?—several alert persons doused the flames, avoiding extensive damages to the meeting house.[157]

The city's economy, on the other hand, suffered a serious blow in the loss of some 1,000 bales of cotton. The fluffy stuff, by now comprising more than 50 percent of U.S. exports, had become the primary engine of the South's economy.[158] Perhaps no city in the South was more dependent upon cotton than Augusta. The city's unique and important place in the South's economy held both promise and peril for the city on the river and the Baptists who called Augusta home.

Smooth Sailing, Distant Clouds

In early 1840 the Augusta congregation accepted William J. Hard's resignation. The minister returned to the academy, first at Mercer University and later, back in Augusta, as a founder of the Augusta Female Institute.[159]

Once again the church sought a pastor with experience in the world of education. And once again the Brantly name rose to the forefront. This time, however, the church extended a call to William T. Brantly Jr., the son of the church's first minister and a recent graduate of Brown University. Upon receiving word that the Augusta congregation desired his services, the young man quickly accepted the call.[160]

Augusta's new pastor was licensed to preach but not yet ordained, so the congregation scheduled an ordination service for December. Program personalities included prominent Baptists and local ministers. The elder W. T. Brantly, renowned North and South and now serving the First Baptist Church of Charleston, preached the ordination sermon. Adiel Sherwood, author of *A Gazetteer of the State of Georgia* and the most prominent Baptist minister in the state, gave the charge to the younger Brantly. Richard Fuller, a young minister, formerly a student of Brantly's, and destined to be one of the leading Baptist ministers of the century, gave the closing address to the church. Local program participants consisted of Juriah Harris, pastor of the Kiokee Baptist Church, and C. F. Sturgis, an ordained member of the Augusta church.[161]

Typical of a Baptist ordination service, Brantly gave witness to his personal Christian beliefs. His testimony reflected the positions of many Baptists of his time. Like most Baptists, Brantly affirmed the religious and spiritual authority of scripture, but not textual perfection, nor literal truth in all matters upon which it touched. The Bible, he declared succinctly, is "the only rule of faith and of practice." So, too, he agreed with most Baptists in voicing his belief in the Trinity. But going against the grain of many Baptists of the South, Brantly came down on the side of theological Arminianism, or free will, declaring, "I believe the salvation of all to be a possible thing." Many other Baptist pastors in Georgia and beyond were, by contrast, decided Calvinists, convinced that God before the foundation of the world had predestined some persons to be saved, and others to hell—and nothing a person could do would negate his or her predetermined afterlife. Salvation, for Calvinists, was possible only for the elect.[162]

Corporately, Brantly expressed his views of the church body. "I regard the Christian Church as a company of believers, banded together to promote the glory of God, in their own spiritual improvement, and in the conversion of the impenitent," he noted in his statement of belief. "The officers of all such churches are: Pastor and Deacons. The ordinances are: Baptism and the Lord's Supper." Brantly thus gave voice to long-held Baptist principles of local church autonomy, the Lordship of Christ, regenerate church membership, and symbolic ordinances.[163]

Brantly's generous theology agreed with his congregants. Echoing his father's tenure, the young pastor's early years in the pulpit proved successful. April 18, 1841 in particular stood out as "a day which will long be remembered by this church. Twenty-five willing candidates were baptized in the Savannah River between 3 and 4 o'clock in the afternoon by our pastor." Other converts, perhaps desiring a more formal ceremony, received baptism in the church's newly-completed indoor baptistry located under the pulpit. On November 7 the congregation dedicated a Sunday School building.[164]

Under Brantly's pastorate the church in 1841 abandoned a staple of Baptist local church life: the annual election of a pastor. Some congregations tended to select a different member of the congregation to preach each year, while others (like the Greene Street church) routinely re-elected the current pastor. Regardless, annual pastoral votes in Baptist life were on the wane.[165]

Meanwhile, Augusta of the early 1840s witnessed economic transition due to regional developments. South Carolina's nullification crisis had led some Georgia businessmen to focus on textile production in an effort to diversify local economies beyond raw agricultural products. By 1840 the state boasted fourteen cotton factories, earning the nickname, "The Empire State of the South." Richmond County claimed several of the factories, albeit none in Augusta.[166]

Unfortunately, a cotton surplus in the South led to a regional depression. Desperate farming families moved to towns and cities in search of work. Augusta witnessed an influx of impoverished rural folk at a time when jobs were few. City leaders faced the twin challenges of providing jobs for newcomers and preventing an exodus of citizens.[167]

During this critical time in the life of the city, Greene Street Baptists rejoiced to see one of their own lay leaders, Martin Dye, win election as Augusta's mayor—twice: from 1841 to 1842, and then again from 1843 to 1846. Recognizing the economic crisis at hand, Dye in his first mayoral term co-founded the "Home Industrial Society," a successful effort to employ women who needed to support their families. Of a far-longer reaching consequence, he also presided over the relocation of the office of the Georgia Railroad Company from Augusta to Marthasville (later Atlanta). Even more importantly, within Dye's second term initial construction of the Augusta Canal began in 1845 as a project designed to provide power for the construction of city factories. Civic and business leaders alike hoped the canal would bring greater prosperity and growth to Augusta.[168]

The year 1844, however, brought sadness to both church and city. In the fall the elder William Brantly, pastoring in Charleston, fell victim to paralysis. The Charleston congregation requested that the Augusta church allow Brantly Jr. to succeed his father as pastor, but Augusta's Baptists, while saddened "at the hopeless condition" of Brantly Sr., "could not feel it in their duty to release Dr. Brantly." Accordingly, the younger pastor brought his father to live with him in Augusta, where the latter passed away on March 28, 1845.[169]

In regional Baptist life, the Augusta congregation in September 1844 sought permission for dismissal from the now-greatly expanded and ever geographically distant Georgia Baptist Association in order to "unite with an association nearer to us." The process took two years, with the church finally joining the Hephzibah Baptist Association in July 1846.[170]

Yet there were much greater winds of change blowing in Baptist life in Georgia and throughout the South, winds that bore dark clouds of distrust and division. The South's largest and most successful congregations depended upon the material wealth of their planter members. Slave labor often constructed and financed church buildings. Pastoral salaries depended upon the riches earned from such labor, as did funding of mission enterprises.

Methodists in 1844, disagreeing over slavery, voted to divide North and South. Methodists of the South turned to Augustus Baldwin Longstreet, pastor of Augusta's St. John's Church, to compose the declaration of protest against abolitionism among Northern Methodists. The parting of ways came in Louisville, Kentucky in 1845, and in relatively peaceful fashion.[171]

Peaceful hardly characterized the division among Baptists, however. Baptists of the North by the early 1840s reached a point where many in good conscience could no longer condone the enslavement of human beings. Although anti-slavery societies grew more prominent among Northern Baptists, the Triennial Convention in 1841 refused to make either slavery or abolitionism a test of fellowship and elected as president William B. Johnson, an Edgefield District South Carolina planter and co-founder of the missionary organization. Nonetheless, the slavery-abolitionist rhetoric heated up in the next few years. Johnson, offended by the rising abolitionist tide, resigned from the presidency of the convention in 1844. Tensions reached a fever pitch the same year in October when the board of the American Baptist Home Mission Society of the Triennial Convention refused to appoint as a missionary a Georgia Baptist slaveholder. Long angry at being called sinners by many of their brethren in the North, Baptist planters in the South condemned the

Home Mission Society. The Georgia Baptist Convention quickly reprimanded the ABHMS, the GBC's actions in turn affirmed by the Virginia Foreign Baptist Missionary Society.[172]

From late 1844 into the spring of 1845 the heated discourse between Baptists of the North and South escalated. Georgia Baptist leaders demanded equality for slaveholders within the ABHMS. Joseph Baker, editor of the *Christian Index*, unable to make up his mind as to what exactly should be done, in December finally voiced the possibility of a geographical division from the North. With the dawning of the new year, Baker's suggestion gained steam. By April 1845 most deemed necessary a separation between anti-slavery and pro-slavery factions.[173]

Augusta's Baptists, while vested in the slave economy, remained on the periphery of the fierce debate. A September 1844 letter published in the *Index*, likely written by the aged and ill William T. Brantly Sr., spoke against separation from Baptists of the North. Having no enslaved members, and few planter members, congregational finances depended less directly upon slave labor than did many First Baptist churches of the South. In addition, the congregation maintained an ongoing relationship with the independent black Springfield Baptist Church. Finally, Augusta's white Baptists yet maintained an excellent relationship with the American Baptist Publication Society and the American Baptist Home Mission Society, with William Turpin arguably the organizations' greatest supporter in the state of Georgia.[174]

In and around Augusta, however, larger realities loomed. Near the small city of commerce and industry encircled by plantations in Georgia and across the river in South Carolina, dark clouds gathered across fertile cotton fields.

4

An Unexpected Legacy of a Church Set Apart

Adjacent to Augusta and sharing a border with the Savannah River, the prosperous South Carolina county (or "district") of Edgefield represented the economic identity of the Deep South at large. "The climate is simply delicious, neither too cold nor too hot. The soil is excellent and produces cotton in perfection," noted a nineteenth-century observer. From this district the Nullification Crisis, the state's first attempt to secede from the Union, occurred in the early 1830s. Ten years later ever greater numbers of slaves toiled on large plantations, their stolen labor financing the education of their masters' sons at elite schools, the sons then returning to Edgefield to practice law and participate in politics, collectively making African slavery ever more profitable. Local ministers blessed the cycle of ill-gotten wealth with a robust biblical apology for the South's "peculiar institution."[175]

In Edgefield from the profits of cotton arose the first Baptist college in the South and the first private institution of higher education in South Carolina, a collaboration of Baptists in the state and across the river in neighboring Georgia. William T. Brantly Sr., then pastoring the Greene Street Baptist congregation in Augusta, represented Georgia Baptists in the planning of the institution that opened in 1826. Christened Furman University, the school bore the name of the recently-deceased Richard Furman, a towering South Carolina Baptist minister, president of the state Baptist convention, and a leading advocate among white Baptists of the South of slavery as God's will for the black race.[176]

William B. Johnson, a wealthy planter and co-founder of Baptists' national Triennial Convention, succeeded Richard Furman as president of the state Baptist convention. Arguably the most powerful Baptist in the nation, he moved to Edgefield in 1830 to pastor the town's Baptist church. Then in 1844 Johnson, serving as president of the Triennial Convention, threw caution to the wind. Angrily resigning from the national organization, he embarked upon an entirely new crusade that would reshape both denomination and nation.[177]

Abolitionist views were evil and contrary to scripture, Johnson had for years warned his Northern Baptist friends. But instead of heeding his words, they had turned their back on the Bible and tarred Johnson, a wealthy slaveowner, as a sinner. Now they would pay the price for their betrayal.

In January 1845 Johnson left Edgefield and traveled southward. In Georgia, Florida, and Alabama he visited with Baptist leaders. Voicing his opposition to the Triennial Convention's abolitionist sentiments, he advocated for a Southern, pro-slavery, missionary-focused Baptist convention. Apparently his supplications fell upon receptive ears. Many of the leading Baptists of all three states, after all, were themselves planters.[178]

An article appearing in the March 14 edition of the Georgia Baptist *Christian Index* reinforced Johnson's message in the Deep South. An account of the recent refusal by the Triennial Convention to appoint an Alabama slaveowner as a missionary further riled planters. "One thing is certain," the statement from the board of the Triennial Convention noted defiantly, "we can never be a party to any arrangement which would imply approbation of slavery"[179]

As Johnson campaigned, Virginia Baptists, predominant among Baptists of the South but thus far hesitant to support regional separation, finally weighed in. The state's Baptist paper, the *Religious Herald*, on March 13 published an article from the board of the Virginia Baptist Foreign Mission Society, an extension of the Triennial Convention, condemning abolitionist Baptists and unequivocally calling for a gathering of concerned Baptists of the South. "Augusta, Geo." the Virginians noted, would be "a suitable place"—but far from the best. "While we are willing to meet our Southern brethren in Augusta, or any other place which may be selected," the article declared, "we should heartily welcome them in the city of Richmond."[180]

Augusta? Virginia Baptists had not mentioned this previously. Even the Baptists of Augusta were unaware of their sudden prominence.

Johnson quickly sprang into action, persuading Georgia's Baptist leaders to support a South-wide gathering in Augusta. Notified that his church had been volunteered to host the meeting, Brantly consented. On March 20 the Georgia Baptist Executive Committee issued a statement approving "the sentiments and resolutions of our Virginia brethren" and noting that they had "ascertained" the permission "of the Baptist Church in Augusta" in "inviting our brethren of the Southern and Southwestern states...to meet in Augusta on Thursday before the 2nd Lord's Day in May next."[181]

Just like that, the die was cast. The first Southern gathering of Baptists would be held at the Baptist church on Greene Street, and there was little time to get ready.

A Question Long Unanswered

Why Augusta? Historians Baptist and secular, local and national to this day have not adequately explored this most basic of questions.

First Baptist Richmond, founded in 1780, stood as one of the leading Baptist churches in America. The best Baptist minds called Richmond home, Virginians were quite sure, a number of whom worked in already-established denominational organizations. While only proper that the newly-envisioned Baptist convention of the South be established in Richmond, the genteel Virginians could make no such demands. That would be too forward and ungentlemanly. Suggesting Richmond alongside an obviously unacceptable alternative would, however, be courteous and respectful while achieving the desired end.

But which alternative?

Suggesting the next logical location, the First Baptist Church of Charleston, South Carolina, would not be advantageous to the Virginians. Founded in 1696, the congregation was the South's oldest Baptist church. Harboring great wealth and connected by rail and sea, the city of Charleston rivaled Richmond in prominence. Although Virginia gentlemen looked with disdain upon Charleston's profit-driven planter class, the church would be favored by Baptists of the Deep South.[182]

So the Virginians ignored Charleston and instead mentioned Augusta, a town of which they apparently knew little. John Kerr, previously president of the Virginia Baptist Foreign Mission Society, in 1835 had summarily dismissed a call to pastor the Greene Street congregation, not even bothering to visit the city. Jeremiah B. Jeter, principle author of the *Religious Herald* article mentioning Augusta, in his writings there and otherwise indicated no familiarity with the town. *Religious Herald* editor William Sands pronounced Augusta "pleasant," albeit "very dusty" and in decline. Both Richmond and Charleston boasted three times the population, and Savannah twice, that of Augusta, a town yet suffering from the lingering cotton depression and home to relatively few planters. Long existing apart from the mainstream South, Augusta hovered awkwardly between the clashing Virginia and Charleston traditions. Some critics dismissed Augusta as a Yankee town, to the annoyance of leading citizens.[183]

In the Virginians' minds, perhaps Augusta served as both an obvious non-choice and a nod to William B. Johnson. The Edgefield pastor, leading the charge for a Southern convention, lived nearby. Along Augusta's Broad Street Johnson sold his cotton, and he may have spoken of the town in casual conversations of years past. Perhaps Johnson in recent weeks had verbally suggested holding the gathering near his hometown. After all, the 1844 slavery-driven division of Methodists in a New York conference took place under the guidance of Augusta's Methodist pastor, Augustus Longstreet. But what better stage for Johnson to display his leadership than in Richmond, the center of Baptist life in the South? The flamboyant Edgefield planter, pleased at the recognition of his efforts, would surely jump at the opportunity.

Except that he didn't. What exactly transpired in Johnson's mind is unknown, but upon learning of the Virginians' overtures he quickly urged Georgia Baptist leaders to invite Baptists of the South to Augusta. Then he turned to William Brantly Jr., who knew nothing of the plan. If Johnson told Brantly of his reasoning for recommending the church as host, the Augusta pastor never recorded the conversation. Nor did the church's first historian know. "Just why so small a city should have been selected has eluded the best research men of the denomination," Isabella Jordan noted in her later years during the 100th anniversary of the 1845 meeting. Perhaps, she offered, Augusta "though smaller than many other Southern cities, was widely known for its intelligent interest in religious affairs."[184]

Securing Brantly's approval, Johnson on behalf of Georgia Baptist leaders and the Greene Street Baptist Church hurriedly circulated a formal invitation for Baptists of the South and Southwest to gather in Augusta and discuss the formation of a regional convention.

Upon learning of Johnson's forwardness, the Virginians must have been stunned that they had been outmaneuvered. Nonetheless, Jeremiah Jeter determined that Johnson would not have the last word. Of this the Virginian was certain.

A Pivotal Moment in Baptist History

One could reasonably argue that the May 8-12, 1845 convening of Southern Baptist elites in Augusta represented the second most important moment in the history of the denomination in America, the first being the establishment of Baptists in America in 1638 in Providence, Rhode Island. For more than 200 years after their founding, theological and ecclesial differences had sometimes sorted Baptists of America into differing camps, yet had failed to disrupt a generally transcendent and broad-based national fellowship. This time, however, the disagreements in the Baptist family were driven by ideology and culture, to which theology and ecclesiology remained subservient.[185]

Ironically, the Augusta Baptists, like many other Baptists throughout the South, may not have realized the significance of the upcoming meeting. Perhaps they were not even certain it would really transpire. Ambivalent, too, were Baptists of Mississippi, Tennessee, Florida, Kentucky, Louisiana, and North Carolina, who expressed little to no interest in the gathering. Not until April 23, two weeks prior to the scheduled conference, did the Augusta congregation spring into action, determining that "In anticipation of the contemplated convention to be held in our city on Thursday 8th May three brethren...were appointed a committee to provide for the accommodations of Delegates. A committee was also appointed...to make provisions for the horses of the Delegates." On April 30 the committees reported to the congregation that they had helped arrange lodging for 130 delegates and that horses of the visitors would be stabled at the rate of 37 ½ cents daily.[186]

A flurry of activity followed. The congregation postponed a scheduled May 10 meeting. On May 7 the church ran an ad in the local newspaper instructing arriving delegates "to report themselves upon their arrival, to a Committee who will be in waiting at the Lecture Room of the Baptist Church, to designate the lodgings which have been provided for them." A number of local homes were counted among the lodging options. Augusta businessman and Baptists' own William H. Turpin made available his "hospitable mansion." Other businessmen welcomed the visitors for economic reasons. The Georgia Railroad and Banking Company and the South Carolina Rail Road Company offered special rates, with the former setting aside a special passenger car for delegates.[187]

And come they did, 153 of 327 from Georgia, and all but a few from Georgia, South Carolina, or Virginia. The Virginia delegation traveled to Charleston by steamer, experiencing a "violent storm."[188] From Charleston to Augusta, rail cars offered smoother going.

Wednesday evening, May 7, featured a special worship service on Greene Street in the structure one visitor described as "a commodious brick edifice." None other than William B. Johnson stood in the pulpit and delivered the keynote address. Delegates had been called together to "render the glory of God" in "all their actions," Johnson emphasized. Separation from abolitionists would be necessary to preserve biblical and moral integrity.[189]

Thursday morning the conference began. Again in the pulpit, Johnson presided over devotional exercises. Afterward, host pastor William T. Brantly ascended to the pulpit yet shrouded in black in remembrance of his late father. Upon calling the business session to order, he returned to his seat and observed opening formalities, including his honorary appointment to a "committee to ascertain and report the delegates to this meeting." Reports followed, the first declaring with certainty that slaveholders would no longer be appointed by the Triennial Convention.[190]

Declaring themselves "lovers of the Bible" and faithful to the "Word of God," the delegates thereafter proceeded to officially separate themselves from the Triennial Convention and establish a new organization to accommodate the wealth of planters in the funding and sending of missionaries. In a seemingly predetermined manner, they elected Johnson as president. The organization took the name Southern Baptist Convention and adopted a constitution provided by Johnson. Delegates established boards for foreign missions and domestic missions, the task of missions constituting the sole initial purposes of the SBC. In a nod to the Virginians, the gathered elites elected Jeremiah B. Jeter as president of the Foreign Mission Board, to be headquartered in Richmond. Marion, Alabama, in the Deep South received the nod as headquarters of the Home Mission Board. The organizational structure reflected a more unified approach for missionary funding than that of the Triennial Convention from which Baptists of the South separated.[191]

On the other hand, delegates stayed with the familiar by passing a constitution referring to the SBC as an alternative "Triennial Convention." Meetings were to be held every three years, with an option for more frequent meetings as "called by the President." Determining the Augusta meeting to be organizational rather than triennial, delegates voted to hold the first triennial event the following year in Richmond, the Virginians thus claiming their own victory in regards to formative gatherings of the Southern Baptist Convention.[192]

Whether or not they understood the underlying subtleties, seven of Augusta's Baptists attended at least one of the conference sessions. In addition to Brantly the seven consisted of: businessman John A. Barnes; deacon, merchant, and current Augusta mayor Martin M. Dye; long-time clerk Martin Hill; farmer Naphthali Byron Moore; merchant William H. Stark; and deacon and merchant Isaac W. Whitlock. Other than Brantly, most apparently drifted in and out of the sessions as their time allowed. Conspicuously absent among the roster of delegates was William H. Turpin, vice-president of the Philadelphia-based American Baptist Publication Society, a Northern Baptist agency with a branch in Augusta and viewed with suspicion by many leading Baptists of the South.[193]

If they were the least bit perceptive, the Augusta delegates realized they stood apart from the other Baptists of Georgia who participated in the formation of the Southern Baptist Convention. One Georgia delegate observed that those assembled "included many of the most able and best men found among our Southern Baptists." The characterization was no idle chatter. Their fellow Georgians whom Augusta Baptists hosted were a far more privileged lot than typically sat in the pews of the Augusta church. The *average* Georgia Baptist assembled in Augusta owned more than twenty slaves, a staggering number six times the state average for white males. Ownership of twenty slaves qualified one for the elite status of planter. Only sixteen of the assembled Georgia Baptists, or about 10 percent, owned no slaves, compared to 75 percent or more of Georgia's white citizens at large. By way of contrast, two of the Augusta delegation owned no slaves (Brantly and Martin Hill), only three owned more than five slaves (Dye, Byram/Byrum, and Stark), and none were planters.[194] In addition, their congregation had no slave members.

Not a one of Augusta's delegates were among the 73 men elected to an official position within the newly-formed Southern Baptist Convention. Nor were any members of the Greene Street church thereafter represented in any official capacity in the life of the denomination until pastor Joseph G. Binney attended the 1853 session in Richmond as a representative of the Georgia Baptist Association.[195] Few if any businessmen had the time, as did planters and pastors, to attend such lengthy meetings.

Different from the other delegates Augusta's Baptists may have been, the hosts nonetheless received praise from the visitors in the form of a resolution. "We earnestly supplicate that God's mercy may descend in rich effusions and more than repay in spiritual blessings the efforts of our friends to render our stay among them so agreeable."[196]

The meeting closed with the singing of "Blest Be the Tie That Binds." Afterward William B. Johnson composed a written address to the public explaining the reasons for Southern separation. Baptists of the North shouldered responsibility for the break, Johnson insisted. "Fanatical attempts have been made, in some quarters, to exclude us of the South from christian fellowship," he noted. But Northern Baptists "have failed to prove," he insisted, "that slavery is, in all circumstances, sinful." One known Northern Baptist foreign missionary, Johnson's address noted, had stooped so low as to remit "money to the United States to aid in assisting the slaves 'to run away from their masters.'" In response to the evil of abolitionism and in affirmation of "the extension of Messiah's kingdom, and the glory of our God," Johnson informed the world, the Southern Baptist Convention had been formed.[197]

Northern Similarities, Southern Sensibilities

The events of May 8-12, 1845, monumental in the Baptist story, represented an affirmation of a maturing missions movement on the one hand, but the rejection of foundational Baptist identity on the other. Of the latter, Southern Baptists' turn away from human freedom and equality reflected uncritical cultural accommodation of black slavery and signaled the unraveling of the United States of America.[198]

Members of the Augusta Baptist congregation, however, had less existential concerns on their minds. One week after the departure of the Baptist divines, on May 17 the church's Horse Committee noted that the livery stable bill remained unpaid. Upon learning in August that the newspaper ad remained outstanding, the church formed another committee to take care of the matter. Other than these two notations, church records are silent concerning the aftermath of the May gathering.[199]

Some church members may have resented Southern Baptist leaders' harsh rhetoric against Baptists of the North. Although Georgia Baptist divines in the fall of 1845 condemned the American Baptist Publication Society for publishing literature written by abolitionists and asked the Society to refrain from sending such material to the state, Turpin remained the organization's vice president for four more years. In addition, the Society maintained its long-standing presence in Augusta.[200]

William H. Turpin's voice mattered. In 1846 the Augusta congregation voted to expand its building. The church added more pews and constructed a belfry. Turpin gifted the church with a bell, eliciting the gratitude of members: "Resolved that the recent magnificent present from our Brother W. H. Turpin merit from us the members and worshipers of the Baptist Church a united and cordial vote of thanks. That the tones of the delightful Bell with which he has been pleased to furnish our new Dome, will ever [?] the most grateful remembrances of the generous Donor."[201]

While Turpin's influence ensured the congregation's continued connection to the Baptist world of the North, the church maintained its relationship with the independent black Springfield Baptist Church. On January 10, 1846 the congregation was asked to assist with "a difficulty in the Springfield African Church about a pew," perhaps a referral to pew rentals. Springfield's relationship with the Greene Street congregation helped protect black Baptists from racial animosities, perhaps including members of Springfield's daughter congregation, the Thankful Baptist Church established in 1840.[202]

In addition to fostering partnerships with Northern Baptists and black Baptists, key church laymen sought to advance the city's economy. Thomas W. Miller, businessman, city mayor (1850-1852), and Greene Street Baptist layman, in 1845 spoke of "the cold damp of commercial death" settling upon the formerly prosperous city. Fortunately, the construction of the Augusta Canal, designed to generate water power for cotton mills and other factories, soon led to a new golden age. Within two years new and varied commercial enterprises and industries flourished, bringing new jobs to Augusta. Former city mayor, Greene Street Baptist deacon, and SBC delegate Martin Dye was one of four commissioners to procure subscriptions of stock in establishing the Augusta Manufacturing Company and organizing the Augusta Factory in 1847. Among the largest in the state and a regional marvel, the city's first textile mill became such a tourist attraction that the company created a side business selling tickets to visitors. Some 200 workers, poor women and children previously unemployed, produced 32,000 yards of cloth a week by 1849.[203]

Other mills soon followed, including the Granite Mill, a flour mill built by James Coleman in 1850 during Miller's mayoral tenure. In addition, two flour mills opened and a raft of new factories produced hard goods large and small, collectively reducing dependence upon Northern manufacturers.[204]

That the city stood as an anomaly to the plantation economy of the Deep South did not escape the attention of elite planters. By 1849 some white Southerners worried that Augusta's manufacturing economy threatened the viability of the peculiar institution of slavery. Nonsense, the *Augusta Chronicle* declared. The city's black population already worked in many trades, so why not utilize slaves in the factories alongside white wage laborers? The *Chronicle* wrote glowingly of "Augusta mechanics who are turning out beautiful Steam Engines, locomotives, carriages and a thousand other articles are doing more for the South than all its sectional politicians put together."[205]

Northern commercial similarities aside, the city's Baptist church on Greene Street retained a Southern identity in matters of discipline. In December 1847 the congregation admonished two female members for violating a church prohibition against visiting the theater, while "Brother Branyan informed the church that he has been guilty of drinking in excess within a few days, that he very much regrets it" and would not do it again. All three were allowed to retain their membership.[206]

Pastor Brantly, meanwhile, felt a new calling. To the sadness of many, he resigned from the church in August 1848 to take a position at the University of Georgia. In response to Brantly's leaving, the church composed a farewell letter to the former pastor that thus ended: "And now we must say farewell—what more can we add save a prayer that God may help you in the discharge of your present duties, and that his wisdom may lead us in the path in which we should go."[207]

The Augusta congregation, however, struggled to find a new path forward. Revs. Nathaniel Greene Foster (1849) and Charles B. Bennett (1850-51) briefly filled the pulpit, the former (previously a lawyer) uncomfortably and the latter plagued by ill health that led to his death. During Bennett's periods of illness William T. Brantly Jr. frequently returned to fill the pulpit.[208]

Signs of progress gradually emerged. In August 1849 the congregation discussed the "Subject of having an Organ placed in the Gallery of our Place of Worship," but "owing to the smallness of our numbers of members present no action was taken by the church." Yet the 230 members soon paid off the church's debt, paving the way for the purchase of an organ and employment of an organist. Professional music thus became a new part of the Greene Street Baptist worship experience.[209]

The Unusual Case of Joseph Binney

A period of stagnation marked by limited progress thus preceded the arrival of Boston native and church friend Joseph Getchell Binney. Formerly the pastor of the First Baptist Church of Savannah, Binney had more recently served as an American (Northern) Baptist missionary in Burma. Prior to sailing for Burma in 1843, Binney had visited, at the invitation of William T. Brantly Jr., the Greene Street Baptist Church, lodging with William H. Turpin.[210]

While Binney's mission work met with success, his wife Juliette's health deteriorated, leading to a return to the States in 1850. Several brief pastoral stints in the North did not improve her health, at which time the couple accepted an invitation from Turpin to return "to Augusta to spend the winter." The visit led to an invitation to pastor the Augusta congregation, and Brantly preached the sermon at Binney's installation service in February 1852.[211]

The irony of calling a Triennial Convention missionary as pastor was surely not lost on the congregation. Seven years earlier the church had hosted the South-wide gathering that condemned and separated from the Triennial Convention, yet the man in the pulpit represented that very body and, as church historian Anna Jones more than 100 years later summarized, "infuse[d] his enthusiasm for foreign missions into the very heart of the church and did such a thorough job of it that First Baptist Church is to this very hour completely dedicated to the cause of foreign missions."[212]

So enthused with their pastor were the Augusta Baptists that, when Juliette's improved health led Binney to resign in July 1853 in order to return to Burma, only to waver while in Boston awaiting departure, the church asked him to return and offered to increase his salary. While grateful for the offer, Binney regained confidence that he should return to Burma. Yet at the very last minute, with the family's belongings already aboard the ship, he changed his mind again, due in part to lingering concerns about his wife's health. Two months after resigning his second missionary appointment, and three months after having left Augusta, Binney returned to the Augusta pulpit.[213]

In the meantime, in 1852 the church addressed issues indicative of a Southern economy primarily benefiting elites. Although whale oil now vied with gas for lamp lighting, the church determined that oil lamps remained too expensive. Raising pew rents, the following year the church borrowed money to make repairs to the sanctuary, temporarily meeting in the Masonic Hall.[214]

The church's businessmen could only do so much for a congregation lacking the abundance of financial resources enjoyed by many First

Baptist congregations of the South peopled with wealthy planters. Savannah's First Baptist congregation had constructed a new sanctuary a mere thirty-three years after the church's founding.[215] Now in its fourth decade, the Augusta congregation struggled to raise money to pay for essential property repairs.

While the congregation moved forward slowly, Joseph Binney, unbeknownst to church members, eyed new opportunities. Prominent in Baptist life, Binney found himself courted by several Baptist educational institutions. In June 1854 Columbian College in Washington, D.C., bestowed him with an honorary Doctorate of Divinity. Shortly thereafter the Theological Institution at Fairmount near Cincinnati, Ohio, appointed him as president. He reluctantly declined, the church none the wiser.[216]

Then in August yellow fever once again struck Augusta. One writer described it as "being on board a burning ship, every one thought of his own safety and of those dependent on him. In two hours after it was known that two deaths had occurred nearly simultaneously in different parts of the city, every one who could do so was fleeing for his life."[217]

Just about everyone, that is, except for Joseph Binney. Even as he cast about for other career opportunities, the Augusta pastor remained committed to his church and city. Residing in the countryside during the night, each day of the epidemic Binney returned to town from 8 a.m. to sunset to visit the sick and dying. Although some church members protested, he opened church doors each Sunday. Some who attended one Sunday were dead by the next, and Binney often helped with the funerals. He caught the fever but survived, albeit with temporarily debilitating effects. In a gesture of great appreciation for him, the congregation hired a pastoral assistant during the winter months, George D. Boardman, future pastor of the First Baptist Church of Philadelphia.[218]

Having faithfully, and with his very life in danger at times, served the Augusta congregation for some three years, in the spring of 1855 Joseph Binney accepted an appointment as president of Columbian College. He departed from the Augusta church on good terms and in 1858 returned to the mission field in Burma. Upon his death during an 1878 voyage, his burial took place in the Indian Ocean.[219]

From High Times to the Lowest Point

Following Binney's departure the Augusta congregation called yet another pastor with Northern connections, albeit this time "North" meant Canada.

J. E. Ryerson, a native of St. Catherines, Canada, arrived in 1855 during a city-wide religious revival. An effective and persuasive speaker, Ryerson's pulpit presence fostered overflowing crowds and weekly baptisms. In 1856 church membership reached 280.[220]

The numerical growth continued throughout much of Ryerson's tenure. The congregation yet consisted solely of white members, although a "few Colored persons" sometimes attended services. In 1858 the church appointed Levi M. Carter as a city missionary charged with further enlarging the church's presence in the city among mill workers. So successful a preacher and evangelist was Carter that he soon asked for his own building. In response, the church created a "Committee on Building a Second Place of Worship." The committee reported in September that, in light of "the large attendance in the present house" and the "impossibility" of accommodating the growth in "our present place of Worship," a second "place of Worship was needed." Paternalistically, the church constructed a small chapel in the vicinity of Martin Dye's Augusta Factory. Initially known as Kollock Street Chapel, the mission ministered to mill workers and later became Second Baptist Church.[221]

And still the revival continued. The influx of new members led the Greene Street congregation in 1859 to debate requiring potential members to have "religious conversations" with the church prior to their "application for membership."[222] The debate proved inconclusive.

Under the Canadian's leadership the Augusta congregation also enhanced its heretofore casual relationship with the Southern Baptist Convention. With Turpin no longer an officer of the Northern American Baptist Publication Society, the church increased support of the Southern Baptist Publication Society, hosting the Society's 1856 annual meeting. The same year the congregation founded the city-wide Augusta Church Missionary Society and in 1857 hosted the annual meeting of the state's Georgia Baptist Convention.[223]

Newfound vitality, however, did not come without attendant controversies. Notes of discord temporarily breached the church's harmony. During 1857 an anti-instrumental faction gained an upper hand, leading the congregation to "dispense with the use of the organ and with the services of a choir for twelve months." Following a few months of a capella music, however, the church voted to bring back the organ and choir, which have remained to the present day.[224]

No sooner had the musical disputation been put to rest than greater troubles brewed. In November 1857 church member P. P. Bond offered an effusive apology for the sin of intoxication. "I have sinned against God and brought a reproach on the cause of Christ," he wrote to the church. "I feel deeply mortified and humbled and I hope God has heard my prayers that I might resist temptation and for the future live the life of a Christian," he pleaded. Evidencing forgiveness in the face of repentance, the church took no disciplinary action.[225]

Other instances of intoxication among the membership occurred the following year, not all confined to males. Then in September 1859 came a bombshell. The church received a letter of resignation from pastor Ryerson, a missive that in turn triggered charges of "intoxication" and public indecency. Six church members had been aware of the misconduct, but "in mercy to Bro. Ryerson (whom they wished to save)" had not told others, instead determining to try and help their pastor. Evidencing Calvinistic theology, the church attributed Ryerson's misconduct to the "Providence" of God. The church accepted Ryerson's resignation, but refused his request of a letter of dismissal. Without such a letter, Ryerson would have difficulty joining another Baptist church.[226]

In October the pastor confessed, but the next month disputed certain of the charges. The dialogue between the various parties spilled over into the following year, leading to a charitable, if weary, final parting of ways between the congregation and Ryerson in January. Finally granting a letter of dismissal, the congregation bid Ryerson "God speed in the work of preaching the Gospel."[227]

Secession and War: The View from Greene Street

The year 1860 thus dawned with the church on Greene Street in disarray. But so, too, was the entire American nation as civil war loomed, a fate sealed in the Augusta Baptist church house in 1845.

On the cusp of war, Augusta's Baptists realized the challenges confronting their congregation. In the face of a schism among members, a committee appointed to bring healing to the church reported in January that "difficulties appear to be so complicated that they are unable to devise any plan which they are willing to recommend." There was no pastoral leadership. Finances were tight. The possibility of a split hovered over all. And in the midst of the difficulties, long-time member Ann Milledge passed away. Yet despite the church's troubles, the Augusta congregation by this time was regarded "as one of the most important [churches] in the denomination in the South."[228]

Hoping to heal the divisions and move past the struggles, the congregation once again sought the services of a prominent pastor, this time in the person of Patrick Hues Mell, a leading minister and educator among Georgia Baptists. As had a number of Baptist statesmen in years past and to the disappointment of the congregation, Mell declined, the church not perceived as important enough.[229]

Under these adverse conditions the church turned to another Northern native, Vermonter Adoniram Judson Huntington. A graduate of Yale and Brown universities, former professor at Columbian College, and more recently a pastor in Farmville, Virginia, Huntington accepted in September 1860 the call to pastor the Greene Street Baptist Church in Augusta.[230] He likely knew Joseph Binney from his time at Columbian, yet another extension—albeit once removed—of the Brantly family's continuing influence upon the congregation.

Huntington arrived in a city then comprised of some 12,500 persons as the nation faced its greatest crisis ever. Abraham Lincoln's election as United States president in November 1860 proved to be the final straw for elite Southern planters and their allies, powerful and influential men who collectively controlled statehouses, local economies, and religious institutions. They called Lincoln the "black president," certain that he would abolish the "peculiar institution."[231]

South Carolina took the lead in seceding from the Union on December 20, 1860. Sentiment in nearby Augusta ran strong, as revealed in a January 1, 1861 editorial in the Augusta *Daily Constitutionalist*:

> If there be any who look forward to a Southern Confederacy as the dearest ideal of greatness, who hope to see her banner assert the freedom of the white, and the proper servitude of the black, wherever the breeze of any land expands it above the universal sea; who wish to be free from all unity with those Abolitionists who set their puny wisdom above the laws of God and the decrees of the Constitution—VOTE FOR SECESSION.[232]

Elite planters dreamed of a glorious Southern empire. Despite divided public sentiment in Georgia and a questionable popular vote, the state seceded on January 19. Although many Augustans criticized secession, a city-wide celebration led to "a magnificent scene—the glare of myriads of lights lighted up the city with dazzling brilliancy," intoned the *Daily Constitutionalist*. Cries of "Joseph E. Brown, the champion of the South!" were heard. (Brown, Georgia's governor, was a Southern Baptist.) In the evening "fire companies formed in procession, and marched into Broad street, with banners, torches, and transparencies, and preceded by the Augusta Brass Band, which discoursed some of its sweetest strains along the way." On January 24, Augusta's federal arsenal surrendered to state forces.[233]

February witnessed the establishment, to great fanfare, of the Confederate States of America, a union eventually including eleven Southern states. The war commenced when South Carolina fired upon the United States' Fort Sumter on April 12, 1861. Lincoln responded by calling for volunteers to join the U.S. Army to put down the "Southern Rebellion." The Confederacy then moved its capital from Montgomery, Alabama to Richmond, Virginia in order to place pressure upon the nearby U.S. capital of Washington, D.C.[234]

Many white Georgians recently opposed to secession united behind the war effort. Nineteen Richmond County companies of troops marched off to war by February 1862, including some members of the Greene Street congregation. Meanwhile, Augusta emerged as a critical resource for the Confederacy. A center of manufacturing in the South, the city provided industrial war-time support, including the 1862 establishment of the Confederate Powder Works, the largest such structure in the South. In addition, Augusta's rail infrastructure helped transport soldiers to points north, east, and west, even as the city established the Georgia Relief and Hospital Association.[235]

Religion played an important role in support of the Confederacy. The story of Southern Baptists during the American Civil War is now recognized as more complex than historians long assumed, and is a microcosm of the larger dynamics of the war. Churches in Georgia did not approach the war uniformly. While virtually all local churches bid farewell to and supported their men who marched off to war, congregational responses to the great conflict varied. Some discussed the war openly, others indirectly, and still others never mentioned the war in church records.[236] The Augusta Baptist congregation engaged the war more than most on levels local and South-wide.

On November 9, 1861 some Baptists recently arrived from New Jersey requested membership but were unable to produce appropriate documentation of their faith due to "not being able to obtain letters of dismission on account of the War now existing." Accepted as members without proper credentials, others from Virginia, Savannah, and Charleston followed during the war years.[237]

In a strange twist, in December 1861 Presbyterians of the South gathered at Augusta's First Presbyterian Church and, voicing pro-slavery views while condemning abolitionism, formed a new denomination.[238] For Augusta's Baptists, the event likely brought back memories of 1845. Combined with the national Baptist split and the role the city's Methodist pastor played in crafting separation documents for national Methodists, the Presbyterian gathering reinforced Augusta's surprising, central role in the drama of major Christian denominations separating North and South over the issue of slavery. In addition, in November 1862 Augusta's St. Paul's Church hosted the first General Council assembly of the Protestant Episcopal Church in the Confederate States of America, yet another Southern denomination birthed in reaction to the politics of slavery and secession.[239]

Southerners and Northerners alike clearly and frequently pointed to slavery as the cause of the war, largely the extent of their agreement during the war.[240] Southern Baptist newspaper editors, preachers, and other leaders routinely proclaimed slavery as God's will for the black race and trumpeted the Confederate nation as God's kingdom on earth, obliquely setting aside their faith heritage of church-state separation. Northward, Baptist writers and preachers condemned the Southern slaveocracy and expressed confidence that God would lead the United States to victory over the immoral practice of human slavery. All the while Baptists of both sides claimed allegiance to the Bible and freedom. Southern Baptists insisted a literal reading of the Bible mandated black slavery, even as Baptists of the North offered contextual biblical interpretations emphasizing human equality, freedom, and love as God's higher will for all humanity.[241]

Leaders of all the South's major Christian denominations— Presbyterian, Methodist, Episcopal, Reformed, Lutheran, Disciples, and Baptists—united in support of the Confederacy. In March 1862 they demonstrated solidarity by sending representatives to Augusta for the founding of the Bible Convention of the Confederate States of America. Greene Street Baptists' venerable William H. Turpin attended as a delegate. Delegates elected A. J. Huntington as a manager of the new organization. In response to "the slavery agitation" within the American Bible Society, delegates directed the organization to initiate the South-wide publication and circulation of "Holy Scriptures, without note or comment."Afterward, the Greene Street congregation collected weekly offerings to purchase religious reading material for Confederate soldiers. W. J. Hard, formerly the church's pastor and now a Confederate chaplain, distributed the literature to soldiers.[242]

Meanwhile, in the absence of many male church members who were off fighting in the army, the women of the Greene Street Baptist Church rose to the forefront. Uniting with white women in Augusta's other churches, they "served hot coffee (made of parched corn, rye and chicory), and biscuits to the soldiers passing through Augusta, going to the front. They also met the trains bringing in the wounded, attending them to the hospitals, where they acted as volunteer nurses."[243]

Biblical convictions aside, many churches of the South suffered during the war years, their pews depleted, doors too often closed on Sundays, and in many instances meeting houses damaged or even destroyed. Even so, some not in the path of troop movements and battles witnessed periods of revival as home-front residents sought God's help and assurance in times of great tribulation.[244]

The Augusta congregation, striving to carry on as usual despite the national crisis, experienced both difficulties and blessings. Local mission work continued. In April 1862 the Augusta Baptist Missionary Society met at First Baptist. Huntington declared as "cold and lifeless" the "condition of the church" in September 1862. Yet two months later in the face of an upturn in attendance the congregation voted to hold a second Sunday service. Further evidencing revival in the city, the Kollock Street Baptist Church matured into an independent congregation pastored by James H. Cuthbert, formerly minister of the prominent First Baptist Church of Philadelphia, the same church that William T. Brantly Sr. had earlier served upon departing the Baptist church of Augusta.[245]

Although Union armies steadily pressed deeper into the South, the city of Augusta remained distant from battlefields and federal troops. Perhaps viewing Augusta as a safe place, the Southern Baptist Convention returned to the Greene Street Baptist Church for its 1863 meeting. From May 8-12, delegates—overwhelmingly ministers—conducted business and addressed war-time conditions. A. J. Huntington and William H. Turpin attended as local representatives. The times were difficult, foreign mission efforts at a standstill. In the midst of distant "carnage and desolations of war" delegates voted to focus the convention's missionary efforts on the Confederate Army, asking churches to supply army chaplains, missionaries, and colporteurs (sellers of Bibles and other Christian literature) for ministry to and evangelization of soldiers. Delegates declared the war "just and necessary," pledged fidelity to their Southern nation, called upon home-front Baptists to "give diligent attention" to the "moral and religious training" of children, and lamented "the privations of those reduced to poverty by the war."[246]

Augusta's Baptists understood the "privations" referenced by the visiting ministers and denominational leaders. Due to Union blockades of Southern ports, rampant inflation plagued the city, the price of many food goods out of reach of ordinary citizens. In 1863 the Greene Street congregation raised the pastor's salary by $500. Grieving women sewed uniforms for soldiers. And as the year wore on, more and more churches, including the Greene Street church, temporarily served as hospitals for wounded Confederate soldiers. Following the Battle of Chickamauga in September 1863, hundreds of wounded Confederate soldiers filled the sanctuary, while the church lot briefly served as a detention camp for federal prisoners.[247]

Nonetheless, an economic bright spot shone in the city, a legacy of Augusta Baptists' Martin Dye, the city's former mayor and enterprising businessman. With the South cut off from finished goods from Europe and the North, the Augusta Factory provided much-needed textile products. A "gold mine" during the war, the mill employed many women and children whose husbands and fathers served in the Confederate Army.[248]

Augusta's industrial might, however, could not save the South. By 1864 the Confederacy reeled from mounting battlefield losses. Refugees first trickled, then streamed into Augusta. Federal armies advanced southward, marched into Georgia, and pressured Atlanta. From January 1864 onward the Greene Street Baptists received displaced Atlantans into their membership, including the family of their former pastor, William Brantly Jr., then pastoring Atlanta's Second Baptist Church. Following the fall of Atlanta to federal forces on September 2, 1864, a guest preacher, New York native John Lansing Burrows of Richmond, Virginia, preached to the Augusta congregation on September 11. Titled "Nationality Insured!" and utilizing the text Jeremiah 18:1-10, Burrows' sermon declared that although God was currently punishing the Confederacy for the nation's sins—"selfish greed of wealth," "Sabbath profanations," "grovelling drunkenness"—He would yet grant victory over the United States if Southerners repented and returned to God. As in all other known sermons preached in white Baptist pulpits of the South during the war, the enslavement of blacks did not count as a sin.[249]

Published by the *Baptist Banner* newspaper, the title page of Burrows' sermon broke with tradition by referring in print to the church as the "First Baptist Church, Augusta," rather than the Greene Street Baptist Church.[250] From this point forward, First Baptist became the church's typically referenced name as Greene Street faded into the background and then fell into disuse.

Although Union General William T. Sherman spared Augusta on his March to the Sea and Burrows' assurances of divine intervention offered hope to the members of First Baptist, God did not favor the Confederacy. Federal battlefield victories continued, and the Union presence in the South rapidly expanded. Confederate soldiers deserted in massive numbers, returning home to take care of suffering families. By early 1865 many Southerners considered the war to be lost.[251]

Even as the Confederacy crumbled, the First Baptist Church of Augusta took a number of actions in support of the stricken nation. Members continued the collection of funds for distribution of religious literature to soldiers. After the Confederate capital of Richmond fell to federal forces, Augusta's Baptists voted to host the "next annual meeting" of the Confederate Bible Society (a meeting that never took place). The same day former pastor William J. Hard, now a lay member of the church and serving during the war as a Confederate chaplain, "stated to the church that several Soldiers in the Hospital in which he is working as chaplain, have lately professed conversions." Hard requested that deacon Martin Dye and others "visit at the Hospital any who are candidates for Baptism & if satisfied, recommend them for membership to the church." Some were baptized and joined the church in May, while an earlier soldier convert of Hard's, John Shepherd, joined First Baptist in November.[252]

A Revolution Unfinished

By war's end much of the South lay in ruins, including hundreds of churches. Despair and joy mingled bitterly. Hundreds of thousands of men had died on distant battlefields. With great relief families welcomed home surviving soldier husbands, sons, and brothers, many maimed, sick, or mentally shattered. Post-war church records rarely speak of their families bearing the burdens in stoic resignation, as did Baptists of the Greene Street congregation.

Perhaps overwhelmed by the present harshness and imminent future challenges, Adoniram Judson Huntington resigned from the pastorate shortly after the war, noting his desire to seek "some other field of labor" where he might "accomplish a great amount of good." He soon returned northward to the faculty of Columbian College in Washington, D.C.[253]

Yet all was not lost, or even very different. True, following generations of enslavement, African Americans celebrated newly-arrived freedom in the months following the war. All too soon, though, disillusion set in among freedmen as white citizens of the South determined to prevent their ex-slaves from achieving any meaningful measure of success. Even before the war's end elites, glossing over the earlier Southern consensus of slavery as the cause of war, crafted the beginnings of a "Lost Cause" narrative of a righteous "Old South" of noble whites and faithful, happy slaves; "states rights" in defense of Southern honor as the cause of the war; and superior United States military and industrial might overpowering heroic and saintly Southern soldiers and officers. The historical revisions preserved the status of white supremacy and black servitude, establishing an ideological basis for resisting legal equality granted to African Americans via the Thirteenth, Fourteenth, and Fifteenth amendments to the U.S. Constitution.

America's quest for freedom and liberty for all would remain long unfinished.[254]

5

A New South Congregation

Wave after wave of Northerners washed over the South in the months and years following the war. Soldiers, preachers, teachers, missionaries, philanthropists. White and black. Young and old. Religious and secular. Altruistic and opportunist.

Soldiers occupied the South's cities to ensure that white citizens respected the freedom granted to their former slaves. Carpetbaggers followed, Northern transplants with agendas. The opportunists sought personal profit. Adventure lured others. Many, though, from a sense of higher calling came to help provide education and job training for African Americans, to the disdain of Southern whites.

In Augusta the Northerners experienced a unique Southern city. Spared the ravages of war, the city of commerce and industry projected an atmosphere not altogether unlike that of the North. Here federal forces found a somewhat more agreeable welcome than most elsewhere, their coins and banknotes eagerly sought by local businessmen. While Atlanta lay in ruins, Augusta's merchants in the summer of 1865 padded their pockets in lucrative fashion. By the end of the year the city remained in far better condition than many other cities of the South.[255]

Against the background of a troubled city yet prosperous, the First Baptist Church transitioned into an emerging new world layered in antebellum white supremacy, fledgling freedoms for African Americans, white poverty, and the daily presence of federal occupation. Most Southern churches watched as black members left and formed their own autonomous congregations. Many churches, long dependent upon the riches of labor stolen from slaves, suffered sudden impoverishment. The Green Street congregation, absent black members and with few planter congregants, suffered lesser economic loss. Although hardships among church families led to a decline in attendance at business meetings and cold winter months without heating in the sanctuary, the church moved forward, hopeful of better times.[256]

Early Post-war Transitions

Seeking renewed stability following the war, the Baptists of Greene Street turned to a familiar, nearby face: James H. Cuthbert, pastor of the Kollock Street Church, the previous mission arm of the Greene Street congregation to mill families that had formed as a congregation in 1860.[257]

A native of Beaufort, South Carolina and nephew of renowned Baptist minister Richard Fuller, Cuthbert had pastored the historic and prestigious First Baptist Church of Philadelphia before moving to Augusta, thus following the earlier trajectory of the elder William T. Brantly. One writer described Cuthbert as "earnest and impressive, reminding one frequently by his appearance and the tones of his voice of Dr. Fuller. As a man, Dr. Cuthbert is among the few who are without stain or reproach."[258]

The February 1866 death of William Turpin marked Cuthbert's early months in Augusta. Among the most notable members of the congregation, Turpin's death commanded considerable attention in church records. "Sacred to the memory of Wm. H. Turpin," church minutes lamented of the "beloved and respected Deacon of the First Baptist Church, Greene Street, Augusta, who fell asleep in Jesus on the Eighth of February 1866 aged nearly 76 years. He was Baptized in the Savannah River in July 1824 by Revd. Wm. Theophilus Brantly." Church minutes of the July following included a long tribute to Turpin, of which copies were subsequently sent to the Georgia Baptist *Christian Index* and the Virginia Baptist *Religious Herald*, the deacon having been a native of Virginia. Turpin was "the chief dependence of this church for nearly twenty years," the memorial noted. "Spiritually he was one of its main supports." The same had been true financially.[259]

Other challenges followed. Cuthbert became ill during the summer and missed several weeks of services. Discipline cases, on the decline during the war years, again became commonplace. In April 1867 "Bro. Stoneman presented himself as one who had brought a reproach upon the cause of Christ, by intemperance, which he greatly deplored, expressed the hope that God had forgiven him & asked the forbearance of the church toward him, promising to try and watch against sin for the future." Although he did not expressly ask for forgiveness according to church records, Stoneman was forgiven and "declared to be in good standing in the church."[260]

An unusual discipline case unfolded in 1868 when "Bro. Lathrop" faced charges not only of "the intemperate use of intoxicating drink," but also of doctoring financial books and stealing from a local store. Although initially clearing him of any wrongdoing "from the charges festering," the church reversed course and regretfully excluded him, apparently because Lathrop did not bother to respond to the charges. Many other church discipline cases took place during the 1860s and early 1870s. William J. Hard, prior to his death in 1874, often visited the accused to seek reconciliation.[261]

Subtly hinted at within post-war church minutes is the fading importance of church discipline. Not asking for forgiveness (Stoneman) nor even bothering to respond to accusations of wrongdoing (Lathrop) indicated a loosening of the church's grip upon member behavior. Across the South and North alike in the late nineteenth century this pattern played out as the social stigma long associated with congregational expulsion confronted an emerging world in which civic institutions replaced churches as arbiters of matters moral and criminal. In addition, urban congregations in particular became more concerned about member retention than the fine points of moral and doctrinal purity. By the end of the century, church discipline became more a memory than a reality in many Baptist congregations. The post-war records of the Augusta church reflect this gradual but definitive movement away from church discipline, including the use of toned-down language in instances of members leaving the congregation for a church of a different denomination.[262]

Meanwhile, economic hardships, death, and issues of member morality all preceded a post-war low in May 1867. "On Lord's Day afternoon the 12th of May when Providentially no one was present, a large portion of our House of Worship fell in," church minutes record. Vacating the sanctuary for the remainder of the year, services moved to the Masonic Hall. Unable to pay for the repair work, the congregation appealed to both fellow Augustans and Baptists outside the city for assistance. Thankful for the "great liberality" of those who were not church members, the ceiling was repaired and services resumed in the church house in January 1868.[263]

Yet in the midst of trials, glimpses of hope and renewal emerged. Regular prayer meetings in 1866 implored God's guiding hand. Reflecting a concern for the children of deceased soldiers shared by Southern Baptists at large, Cuthbert took it upon himself to preach a children's sermon one Sunday each month, in addition to Sabbath (Sunday) School sessions. The church also received a gift of a small collection of books for Sabbath School use. A family from Virginia joined the congregation. In August a formerly expelled member (William M. Lawrence) requested and received readmission.[264]

The same month the congregation honored Hamilton H. Hickman for his faithful service as a deacon. Hickman, an up-and-coming businessman and investor, soon became a church trustee. From 1868 to 1899 he served as president of the Graniteville Mill across the Savannah River, and in the 1880s and 1890s held other prominent titles within Augusta's business community. During Hickman's trustee years, the board often met in his office.[265]

Also within the larger community of Augusta, James T. Bothwell, church layman and local judge, in the summer of 1866 convened a meeting of local freedmen to determine if they would be willing to pay taxes to construct a school for their children. Eventually a school was established.[266]

Returning to an earlier concern regarding the faith credentials of new converts, in October 1867 the church appointed a Committee on Examination (comprised of the pastor, deacons, "and four other brethren") to visit with "candidates for Baptism" prior to their "being presented to the church for membership." In January 1868 the congregation elected four new deacons: Eli Mustin, Zachariah McCord, John W. Meyer, and William M. Jackson. The election of J. J. Pearce followed in 1871.[267]

Visiting ministers sometimes ascended the pulpit of First Baptist Augusta, as did Savannah's First Baptist pastor, Sylvanus Landrum, in May 1867. One of few coastal Southern Baptist ministers who remained in the pulpit throughout the Civil War, including during federal occupation, Landrum stood as a statesman among Georgia Baptists.[268] Perhaps the veteran pastor encouraged his Augusta brothers and sisters to press onward despite meager resources and stagnant membership.

Around the time of Landrum's visit two absentee members requested that the church remove their names from the membership roll, prompting the formation of a committee to examine the roll book for other non-attending members. One year after the investigation of church membership began the congregation declared "no longer in fellowship with us" several members who had "united with churches of different denominations from ours."[269]

Others, however, joined the church. Most prominent among new members during the second half of the decade was James C. C. Black, a Kentucky native, Confederate veteran, lawyer, and future city leader, Georgia legislator, and member of the U.S. House of Representatives. Black joined First Baptist in 1867, evidently believing the church had a great future. In the coming years he became the most influential layman within the congregation, a leading shaper of the church.[270]

For members new and old, the Bible remained central in church life. Nonetheless, few internal records referenced sermons or biblical passages. An exception is July 1868, when church minutes noted that the pastor read a "portion of the Book of Revelation" prior to a business meeting. The following month the church revisited doctrinal issues, adopting a revised confession of faith and church covenant. Even as the church focused on proper doctrine, members also voted to forgive and readmit into membership Clara Butler, previously excluded in 1849. An underlying concern throughout the decade, the church's finances benefited from the implementation of weekly offerings. [271]

Amid progress mixed with challenges, James Cuthbert's resignation in 1869 elicited both sadness and warm memories. The passing of Eleanor J. Green, baptized by Brantly Sr. in 1825, signified the fading of personal memories of the church's early years.[272]

Into the New South with a "Cheerful, Loving Piety"

A long campaign to oust Northern political oversight characterized 1870s Augusta and the South at large. Ending the final vestiges of Reconstruction in 1877, white Southerners regained political control. Augusta's industrial infrastructure, including an expansion of the Augusta Canal, reinforced the city's status as one of the largest inland cotton markets in the world. Emerging new markets and the establishment of a public education system also characterized the decade.[273] First Baptist Church, in turn, shared in the city's politics, prosperity, and civic growth.

From St. Joseph, Missouri in late December 1869—and coinciding with Augusta's early efforts to annul federal supervision—arrived Dr. James Dixon as the congregation's new pastor. Although unanimously called as pastor, Dixon's family had Canadian roots and seemingly little ministerial experience.[274]

Dixon with his veiled past arrived at a time when Augusta's leaders were busy curtaining off the harsh realities of Southern history. Pushing aside public memories of slavery, they celebrated a heritage of honor and chivalry. Confederate generals and soldiers became saints. While Dixon's arrival stirred the ecclesial embers of First Baptist, a visit to the city by war hero Gen. Robert E. Lee on March 30, 1870 fanned the flames of white Southern pride. The fire burned a bit brighter when Confederate president Jefferson Davis graced the city the following year, the same year that 20,000 spectators attended a mock medieval joust complete with riders dressed as knights, a festival celebrating a glorified "plantation civilization" and prominently featuring the Ku Klux Klan.[275]

The Confederate Memorial Movement furthered the transformation of Southern memory. Led by wealthy women, local chapters of the movement throughout the South honored deceased Confederate soldiers by re-interring their bodies and constructing community monuments in their honor. A contingent of Augusta women in 1870 determined to erect a monument in their city. Simultaneously some women of First Baptist trained their efforts on advancing the financial interests of their church. Whether honoring the South's dead or raising money for church, white women increasingly assumed more prominent roles in the post-war South.[276]

African-American citizens, meanwhile, busied themselves with efforts to improve the future of their own race, assisted by some members of First Baptist. Although many white citizens viewed with suspicion the recently-formed and then-struggling African-American Augusta Theological Institute housed in the basement of the Springfield Baptist Church and employing (Northern) American Baptist instructors, James Dixon on behalf of First Baptist provided assistance. Working with William Jefferson White, a local pastor and leading black educator, and "a few members of the white Baptist convention of the state" [Georgia Baptist Convention, or GBC], the "Genial, eloquent, aggressive" Dixon helped the school locate a new president, Joseph Thomas Robert. Formerly pastor of the First Baptist Church of Savannah, Robert's astute leadership saved the institute from near collapse. Georgia Baptists soon joined with Northern Baptists in employing two students as home missionaries. Later the Institute moved to Atlanta and became known as Atlanta Baptist Seminary and, finally, Morehouse College.[277] Without the support of Dixon and the GBC, Morehouse College might not exist today.

Heightened racial tensions throughout the 1870s only minimally intruded into the church building. Like many white churches, First Baptist employed a black church sexton, or janitor. "Old Sandy," whom church historian Isabella Jordan described as "the most imposing and thoroughly aristocratic negro who ever walked down a church aisle," remained dutifully subservient. But under unusual circumstances on October 7, 1876 the church received, upon the recommendation of James C. C. Black, its first "colored" member in the person of Luke Mattox. Feeling called to the ministry yet at odds with local black Baptist leaders, Mattox persuaded First Baptist to grant him a license to preach, whereupon he was dismissed on good terms by the congregation to use his gifts among Augusta's black Baptists.[278]

The year 1871 proved to be an especially notable year for First Baptist. Under the revival preaching of the Rev. George Needham of England, scores of young people were converted and baptized into the church, many of whom remained members for decades. The installation of a hot-air furnace provided a more comfortable worship experience. Curtis Chapel, named after D. L. Curtis and constructed near the west end of Broad Street, extended the church's community footprint. Upon Eli Mustin's resignation as clerk the congregation presented him with a gold-clasped Bible.[279]

Controversially, an attempt by some to "break fellowship with any member who keeps a Liquor Saloon or Barroom" ended in failure, an outcome Abraham Marshall would have applauded. Faith heritage notwithstanding, many Baptists of the South now gravitated toward a strong anti-alcohol position. Although at least a few members of First Baptist Augusta found involvement with alcohol "inconsistent with the teachings of the New Testament," traditionalists overruled prohibitionists.[280]

Apart from the church, controversy arrived in Augusta in 1873 in the form of 200 Chinese workers employed in widening and deepening the Augusta Canal. Following the completion of the project, some of the Chinese immigrants settled in the city on a permanent basis.[281] Soon, their story would intersect that of First Baptist.

Amid transitions in both church and city, James Dixon's popularity became detrimental. Such was his renown that by 1873 and to the concern of the congregation, the First Baptist pastor spent a considerable amount of time speaking in other churches and at educational commencements. His absences from the church mounting, deacons in 1874 also determined that their pastor was "wholly inadequate with the value of money." Rumors of personal debts surfaced, later tied to losses in speculation in cotton futures. Called to appear before the congregation to explain his absences and finances, Dixon resigned the pastorate. Moving to Indiana, he eventually left Baptist life.[282]

Following Dixon's unhappy departure, the congregation in early 1875 called M. B. Wharton as pastor. Coming from the pastorate of the Walnut Street Baptist Church in Louisville, Kentucky, Wharton's tenure at First Baptist Augusta proved brief due to ill health. During his tenure of less than one year, however, the church added a number of new members, sold the parsonage on Campbell (9th) Street, and remodeled the church building. By January 1876 Wharton was back in Louisville, this time as an agent of the Southern Baptist Theological Seminary. Health issues apparently resolved, afterward he served for three years as United

States consul to Sonneberg, Germany, then as editor of the Georgia Baptist *Christian Index*.[283]

Upon Wharton's departure the First Baptist congregation periodically met with the First Presbyterian Church, reflecting a "beautiful expression" of "fraternal feeling" in the words of Isabella Jordan. In addition, ongoing participation in the regional Hepzibah Baptist Association provided an ever-present anchor in stormy times. Financially, the congregation sold the pastorium and used the proceeds to pay down some of the church's debt.[284]

Thereafter the congregation took a new tack in securing a pastor. Rather than seeking an established minister, the church in 1876 called a twenty-three-year-old young minister and Georgia native then pastor of the First Baptist Church of Shreveport, Louisiana. The son of Savannah's First Baptist pastor Sylvanus Landrum and college classmate of two Augusta church members, William Warren Landrum arrived at his first pastorate feeling poorly qualified, yet with promise and possibility.[285]

Landrum's youthfulness came with impeccable educational credentials, including degrees from Mercer University, Brown University (Rhode Island), and the Southern Baptist Theological Seminary. The young pastor emanated a warm-hearted religion and generosity of spirit. During his Augusta pastorate he became known as "a good preacher and pastor, and a man of more than ordinary abilities. He hates controversy, has great faith in the power of gospel preaching and the efficacy of a cheerful, loving piety, and his highest ambition is to be a consecrated and successful minister of Jesus Christ." Isabella Jordan said of Landrum: "He was beloved by the entire congregation, both old and young," and during his tenure a "great peace and harmony" prevailed in the church.[286]

Landrum arrived about the same time that a *Chicago Tribune* correspondent referred to Augusta as a town of "enormous aristocratic pretensions." Describing an emerging New South, the writer noted that the attentions of white citizens "seem to be altogether entwined around the dead past, and a dead ancestor is more to them than all living men and women especially if they do not belong to their own particular and exclusive set." Celebrating the end of Reconstruction in 1878, white Augustans unveiled and dedicated a Confederate monument. Freed from

Northern oversight, Augusta and the rest of the South pursued long desired agendas of economic development and racial separation.[287]

As Southern identity calcified, Augusta's First Baptist Church sought to identify its own members. The 1879 publication of a church "Manual" included, for the first time, a printed listing ("Roll") of church members. Previously confined to church minutes, the list was made available to all members. The committee responsible for the list asked for "the indulgence of members for any mistakes or omissions which may occur." Keeping track of "those persons who have removed from the City, or whose whereabouts were unknown," presented an ongoing challenge. The committee noted its intention of publishing the Roll on an annual basis.[288]

Financially, the church's debt in 1880 stood at $1,316, having gradually declined during the previous years, thanks in no small part to the fundraising efforts of the women of the congregation and the quarterly collections of offerings. Unwilling to add further to the debt, the congregation that year voted to delay painting the church fence and purchasing hymn books. Two years later, however, finances improved enough that the church abandoned the tradition of pew rents, declaring the practice to "violate equality of members."[289] The reference is to the historical Baptist principle of all Christians standing equal before God—otherwise known as the "priesthood of all believers."

Improving finances allowed the remodeling of the sanctuary. Private donations funded the purchase of a new organ in 1877. Custom built by the New York company Jardine & Son, upon its installation the builder joined local musicians in an inaugural recital program. In 1881 the congregation's Ladies' Sewing Society paid for new upholstery for the entire church.[290]

Furthering Baptist work throughout the city, in 1879 First Baptist conferred to the Curtis Baptist Church the lot of land on which it was located plus the remaining balance of funds from the David L. Curtis fund. Two years later William Landrum provided assistance on behalf of First Baptist in organizing the Berean Baptist Church (later Crawford Avenue Baptist Church) in the mill community of Harrisburg. The new church ministered to the families who worked for the Sibley and King mills. In September 1883 leaders of Berean Baptist reported on their failed efforts to "erect a church building" due to the "inability" to raise adequate funding. The mill workers appealed to First Baptist "to apply the money's arising from collections for Home Missions to the mission work at Berean Baptist." In a business meeting chaired by mill president Hickman, First Baptist granted the request.[291]

The First Baptist congregation also remained involved in the life of the city's black Baptists, in 1879 assisting in the formation of the Union Baptist Church in partnership with the Augusta Board of Education. Like other black churches in Augusta, the congregation's sanctuary, in addition to being a historic place of worship (the building formerly a mission church of First Presbyterian Church) on 11th and Greene, became a community center for African Americans. Within their autonomous congregations, black Augustans co-mingled spiritual matters with social uplift in defiance of a world that treated them as second-class citizens and offered minimal encouragement for betterment.[292]

In addition to city ministries that bridged socio-economic and racial divides, the First Baptist congregation supported the missionary work of the Southern Baptist Convention (SBC), at that time still recovering financially from the economic devastation of the Civil War and post-war years. A portion of church offerings supported missionary efforts, both foreign and home. The church also contributed to mission work within the state through the Georgia Baptist Convention.[293]

Progress, however, mingled with sadness as within four years two of the most central figures in the history of First Baptist Church passed away. Death first befell layman and local businessman Eli Mustin in 1878. The passing of Mustin, 60 years a church member and for 40 years clerk, led former pastor William Brantly Jr. to compose a moving tribute to his friend. The Madison, Georgia *Madisonian* newspaper called Mustin "a man of many noble traits of character, of large influence and greatly beloved by his fellow citizens." In addition, Brantly Jr.'s death in 1882, while pastor of the Seventh Baptist Church of Baltimore, Maryland, led the Augusta congregation to pass resolutions noting that till the end he remained "universally and cordially beloved," and that "feelings of sorrow at his removal from earth are comforted by the assurance of the Gospel which he preached and whose glorious promises he is now realizing in the presence of the Saviour."[294]

Transition continued as current pastor William Landrum led the congregation to put its official documents in order. Under his tenure the church republished its Articles of Faith and Covenant and Rules of Order, and an updated Church Roll.[295] A capable administrator, Landrum prepared the congregation for a future in which SBC city churches would function professionally and efficiently.

Augusta, too, became a model of efficiency and prosperity. In the early 1880s the city took possession of the Augusta Canal, recently enlarged in 1875-76. A flurry of new business construction ensued, including a host of mills and factories. Sibley Mill, the most significant, opened in 1881 boasting to be "the finest single mill building in the world." First Baptist layman James Verdery was counted among the mill's founders. In addition, new banks, rail connections, and sewers served the expanding city, whose boundaries were expanded in 1883.[296]

With the expansion of business came a new invention: the electric light. Introduced in Augusta in 1881 in the Globe Mill, electricity within a year illuminated Broad Street at night. As in other towns large and small throughout America, Augustans greeted the arrival of electric street lighting with curiosity and awe. Conquering the darkness of night that had for all of human history limited the full potential of human activity, electric lights transformed the nation. Augusta stood apart as the first town in the South to acquire full illumination by electricity.[297]

William Landrum led First Baptist into this exciting new era of city-wide growth and prosperity, only to resign in October 1882 due to the ill health of his wife, Ida. "Young, vital and enthusiastic" and loved by the congregation, "serious heart trouble" necessitated Ida to try a new climate. Regretting the departure of Landrum and his wife to Richmond, sadness soon gripped the congregation in learning of Ida's death. In an era of the South when remembering the dead was a part of life, First Baptists' young women memorialized their friend by forming the Landrum Society, an organization devoted to beautifying the church. In honor of Ida Landrum, the society donated a Chickering grand piano, a brass reading desk, and two silver communion plates.[298]

Following Landrum's departure, the Baptists on Greene Street invited William Adams, the pastor of the city's First Presbyterian Church, to temporarily and "at his pleasure to conduct the evening services at this church," and bring along with him "the Presbyterian congregation."[299]

Now a prominent church with key laymen and a finger upon the pulse of the New South, the congregation sought a new leader capable of taking the congregation to yet greater heights.

A Most Diverse, Unusual, and Impressive Journey to Augusta

By 1883 the First Baptist Church of Augusta could point to a long record of pastoral stories, many exceptional and some rather unusual. Perhaps the recently deceased William T. Brantly Jr., the congregation's longest tenured minister (1840-1848) and host pastor in the formation of the SBC, was the most beloved minister in the church's history to date. Or maybe Jr. shared the honor with his father William T. Brantly Sr., the church's first pastor (1820-1826). Then again, Brantly Sr.'s later convoluted and aborted attempt to return to the Augusta pastorate from the pulpit of First Baptist Philadelphia may have tarnished his image. On the other hand, Joseph Binney's pastorate (1851-1855) surely qualified as the most unusual, his years in the pulpit marked by furtive attempts to lure him to the world of Baptist higher education, repeated changes of mind about returning to the foreign mission field, and his amazing and dangerous ministry among yellow fever patients in 1854.

Such a notable and memorable congregational past notwithstanding, the arrival of Lansing Burrows in October of 1883 changed everything. In fact, his life's route to Augusta was more diverse, unusual, and impressive than any of his predecessors.

Born in Philadelphia (the same Pennsylvania city intertwined through much of the church's history), Burrows moved to Richmond, Virginia as a young lad, where his father pastored the city's First Baptist Church. Enrolling in Richmond College, young Burrows then transferred to Wake Forest College (North Carolina), only to see his studies interrupted by the war. Enlisting in the Confederate Army, he obtained the rank of sergeant prior to his capture in 1864 and subsequent imprisonment at Fort Delaware.[300] That same year Burrows' father, John, then pastor of Richmond's First Baptist Church, as previously noted, preached a guest sermon at First Baptist Augusta, following the fall of Atlanta to Union forces.

Obtaining his undergraduate degree between enlistments, Burrows after the war was ordained to the Baptist ministry in Kentucky and pastored in Missouri. The Midwest, however, proved but a brief stop along a most uncharacteristic sojourn back North. Whereas few Confederate veterans harbored any inkling of moving to the North following the war, Burrows accepted a pastorate in Bordentown, New Jersey; earned a Master of Arts degree from Princeton University (New Jersey) and a Doctor of Divinity degree from Madison University (Hamilton, New York); and pastored First Baptist Church of Newark, New Jersey and First Baptist Church of Lexington, Kentucky.[301]

A lesser Northern-born and educated, Confederate Army veteran, Southern Baptist-turned-Northern (American) Baptist-turned-Southern Baptist minister might have then labored in obscurity in the hills of Kentucky. Not so with Lansing Burrows, who, thanks in part to his father's influence, hosted the annual SBC gathering in his First Baptist Church, Lexington in 1880; was appointed SBC statistician in 1881 and voted SBC secretary in 1882; became a vice president of the Home Mission Board in 1882; and in May 1883 was chosen to "preach the Convention sermon" the following year.[302]

In its birthing in 1845, the Southern Baptist Convention had in effect imposed itself upon William T. Brantly Jr. and the Augusta congregation. Among the corresponding delegates of 1845 was John Lansing Burrows of Pennsylvania, representing the American Baptist Publication Society, which hoped to maintain friendly relations with Baptists of the South. The post-war Convention, well along the road of recovery from the terrible war for which it was partially responsible, returned to Augusta in October 1883 in the embodiment of Lansing Burrows, son of a former Northern Baptist leader now renowned among Southern Baptists.[303]

The arrival of Burrows signaled an entirely new era in the life of the First Baptist Church.

A Pastor Well-suited

Lansing Burrows was a coup, the statesman long sought by the Augusta congregation. James C. C. Black chaired the "Committee on Pastoral Relations" that recommended Burrows. Upon his acceptance of the church's call, the congregation undertook a self-examination. The businessmen of First Baptist understood and appreciated Burrows' emphasis on statistical analysis. Church membership stood at 416, a respectful if underwhelming figure. Thanks to years of fundraising by the women of the congregation, church debt stood at a mere $130. A first-rate pastor, however, would necessitate greater effort on the part of the congregation. Expressing great anticipation and perhaps hoping to please the new pastor, the church soon voted to purchase a pastorium. In addition, the church appointed a committee "to prepare and have hung in each of the hotels framed invitations to strangers and all others to attend divine service at this church."[304]

For his part, Burrows quickly assessed the situation, noting, in his opinion, "an alarming low state of Christian activity in the church." In the face of this unfortunate state of affairs Burrows scheduled revival services. Soon, crowds filled the sanctuary. Many professed faith in Christ and joined the church. As if the fires of revival were not enough, shortly after the six weeks of services drew to a conclusion the sanctuary went up in literal flames, due to a faulty basement furnace. A fire engine doused the flames, but the resulting water damage made the destruction all the worse, requiring a "complete overhaul," for which the church's insurance paid. The congregation met in the opera house during repairs.[305]

What did the members of First Baptist think of their new pastor and his early whirlwind of revival activity? "With clear comprehension, unabated earnestness and living faith, Dr. Burrows by eloquent discourses from the pulpit, interesting talks in prayer meeting and by personal contact among the members roused a lovely and profound interest in the work proposed. The outcome of these efforts was a reawakening among the entire church." With excitement in the air, in 1884 an enthusiastic congregation extended an invitation to the Southern Baptist Convention to return to Augusta in 1885.[306]

Although an inclusive persona drove church membership upward, doctrine yet mattered. In December 1883 the church "excluded" Elizabeth M. Hull "on grounds of a denial of the faith." Expressing charity, the following month Burrows prayed "for the restoration and conversion" of Hull and other "excluded members." The pulpit also mattered, evidenced the same year in the installation of a memorial pulpit to T. W. Coskery and his wife.[307]

Burrows knew that an ascendant congregation required appropriate funding. Whether in mission efforts or pertaining to church salaries, ministries, and other expenses, church finances needed an overhaul. In October 1884 Burrows said aloud what perhaps others were thinking. Calling for more equity in "raising the revenue of the church," the pastor declared that about seventy persons "carried the financial burdens of the church and it could not longer remain in this condition." The church "should confront this matter," Burrows told congregational leaders. A church-wide "obligatory" meeting presumably impressed upon members the need for all to contribute financially to the church.[308]

Having raised the bar of the church statistically, denominationally, and financially, Burrows set about steering his flock more deeply into the currents of Southern Baptist life, currents that increasingly included women.

A Convention, City, and Church Reshaped by Women

Southern white women yet occupied a confined space in Southern culture. Subservient to men and denied careers outside the home, women often found ways to utilize their talents within a restrictive environment. The war years provided opportunities for women to form support organizations for soldiers, whether in sewing groups, hospital work, temperance efforts, or other activities. Often, churches hosted their gatherings. Following the war, temperance advocacy remained at the forefront for some post-war Southern women, both within and without church life. In addition, many rallied around Confederate soldier memorial efforts.

Women's advocacy also trickled into post-war Southern churches via another route: missions. Brought to a virtual standstill (other than within the Confederate Army) during the Civil War and Reconstruction years, mission efforts afterward benefited from the work of women. By 1875 Southern Baptist leaders formally acknowledged women's role in raising missionary funds within their subservient status. "The native earnestness, the loving sympathies, and the intuitive tact of women most happily qualify her as a valuable auxiliary in this work," convention minutes noted that year.[309]

In a patriarchal South, women's work on behalf of missions remained a local church phenomenon until the mid-1880s. Even so, their collective contributions mounted and leaders of the SBC increasingly feared that women's missionary work reflected a larger women's rights movement. An 1884 convention debate (of which only men were allowed to participate) over the matter of women's missionary work resulted in a refusal to appoint a female superintendent of women's work.[310]

At least some Southern Baptist men disagreed with the outcome of the debate. A Virginia Baptist *Religious Herald* commentary declared the need for "more effective means for stimulating and systematizing the liberality of our Southern women." The "women love organization and work well together. It remains for our wise men to formulate some scheme that will effectually utilize our Southern women," the editorial ascertained.[311]

Lansing Burrows understood the need for churches to embrace the work of women in appropriate roles, having for years openly advocated that women teach children at home and in Sunday schools.[312] In the Augusta pulpit he found willing allies for the expansion of women's roles into the realm of the missionary work of Southern Baptists.

The timing proved impeccable. As 1885 dawned, conversations about women's work swirled nationally in Southern Baptist life, conversations sure to continue as First Baptist Augusta hosted the denomination's annual conference. Within First Baptist were skilled, motivated women ready to rally their congregation and denomination behind a new and worthy cause.

As in most Baptist churches of the South in the late nineteenth century, women were prohibited from serving as ministers, deacons, or trustees. Memories of Martha Stearns Marshall forgotten or willfully ignored, women had few leadership opportunities. Although collectively comprising about 75 percent of the Augusta congregation's membership, since the middle of the century women's contributions remained largely confined to domestic duties such as sewing clothing for the poor and draperies for the church. Perhaps most visible was the Dorcas Ministry. The church's Dorcas women by the 1880s met weekly "in the large double parlors" of the Burrows home, around the invalid Mrs. Burrows. In comfortable surroundings and by the dozen or more they socialized, sewed, knitted, and otherwise busied themselves in the crafting of personal items for needy citizens of the city.[313]

In addition the women of First Baptist periodically raised funds for church debt relief, a publicly undervalued role nonetheless reflecting the importance of women regarding congregational finances. Women also raised funds for city missions. While men, including Rev. James Patterson, prominently led the way in the October 1884 formation and subsequent operation of a City Mission Board charged with preaching the gospel in "weak points in the city," women played an important but muted support role in securing funding for the ministry.[314]

The City Mission Board may have been established with the coming of the Southern Baptist Convention in mind, as were other developments. Four months prior to the convention gathering, the First Baptist Church in January 1885 appointed pastor Burrows as "general chairman" of a committee tasked with the "entertainment" of the convention. Signaling the importance with which Burrows, an officer of the SBC, viewed the annual gathering, he promptly appointed six sub-committees: Finance, Hospitality, Hotels & Boarding Houses, Transportation & General Correspondence, Special Correspondence & Assignments, and Public Comfort. No women sat on the committees.[315]

During this time of organizational growth, typed documents began appearing in church records—the typewriter having become popular in America the previous decade. Burrows in March 1885 "emphasized the growth of the church in years with accumulated records and valuable papers" and suggested "The dignity of the church demanded" the purchase of a safe.[316]

The dignity of the church also demanded a more substantial role for women. Weeks before the gathering of the SBC, Burrows organized the church's Woman's Foreign Missionary Society (WFMS) in the home of Isabella Jordan. Jordan was elected president, Mrs. H. H. Hickman vice president, Adele Verdery secretary, and Mollie Bothwell treasurer of the society, a local organizational forerunner of national Woman's Missionary Union (WMU).[317]

The very act of forming the society reflected the constrained realities of the time. Burrows organized the society because women were not yet empowered with such responsibility. To ignore patriarchal custom would have invited unhelpful criticism. Church records list the married officers by their husbands' names, indicative of the cultural norm of women's subservience to husbands. Although single adult women were considered inferior to married women, they were known by their first names and enjoyed greater legal rights.[318]

Within the missionary society women exercised both sisterhood and greater autonomy denied in denominational life. Southern Baptists as a denomination voiced interest in distant lands, yet the men leading the Foreign Mission Board were unable to secure, or unwilling to devote, adequate funding. Local WFMS groups financially aided missionary activity, providing leadership where men failed.[319]

On the other hand, two prominent men stood behind the leading officers of the Augusta church's Woman's Foreign Missionary Society. William M. Jordan, "a well known and highly esteemed cotton merchant," was the husband of president Jordan. A partner in the cotton firm of Sibley & Jordan, he was a leading layman of First Baptist. Hamilton H. Hickman, husband of vice president Hickman and president of the Graniteville Mill, was likewise a respected businessman and leading church layman. Prominent among the city's women by virtue of their husbands' status, Jordan and Hickman brought to their missions passion both social currency and access to personal bank accounts.[320]

Meanwhile, preparation continued for the annual Southern Baptist Convention, the third hosted by the First Baptist Church of Augusta (the first in 1845, the second in 1863). Twenty-three men served on a committee tasked with "entertaining" delegates. Burrows commended the ladies' Sewing Society for "having been instrumental in raising the funds necessary and furnishing the labor of overseeing the work of completely carpeting the audience-room," perhaps a reference to the sanctuary.[321]

Local news reports spoke glowingly of the upcoming meeting of the "respected and powerful" SBC. Extensive coverage in the *Augusta Chronicle* included a condensed version of the proceedings of the historic 1845 gathering.[322]

The SBC convened on May 6, 1885. Patrick Hues Mell, the now-legendary Southern Baptist who a quarter century earlier turned down the pastorate of the Augusta church, presided as president. An article in the *Chronicle* commended Mell as "a perfect parliamentarian" who demonstrated "a remarkable achievement of leadership" during the meeting.[323] Lansing Burrows, as convention secretary, represented Augusta. Although now typically known as the First Baptist Church, printed convention material again referred to the church as the "Greene Street Baptist Church.[324] Church minutes sometimes did likewise.

In addition to Burrows, First Baptist Augusta delegates included deacons James C. C. Black, H. H. Hickman, Charles Z. McCord, J. S. Patterson, and D. R. Wright. Black formally welcomed the delegates on behalf of First Baptist. The entirety of the Augusta delegation included representatives from a number of the city's Baptist churches, congregations that began as mission efforts of First Baptist. On the first day of the convention Augusta delegates were collectively appointed to constitute "a Committee on Religious Exercises," or devotionals.[325]

The religious nature of the gathering aside, perhaps more than any other convention meeting since the war, the 1885 meeting evidenced controversy. While polite and orderly, the disagreements concerned women's roles in the organization.

The convention yet restricted officer positions and delegate status to men only, to the growing dismay of many women whose local church efforts funded as much as one-third of the convention's mission work. The prior convention's refusal to appoint a superintendent of women's work rankled faithful females, who this time around asked to be counted as official delegates. The men refused, but did agree to appoint a committee for further study of the matter. None of the delegates from the hosting church received placement on the committee.[326]

Also of interest, Lansing Burrows' thorough and lengthy statistical report revealed that an unusually high number of "colored associations" were affiliated with Southern Baptists. Burrows' report indicated that more than half of Georgia's Southern Baptists were black.[327] Not yet having formed a viable national convention, some black Baptists, while worshiping apart from whites in local churches, found white Baptist denominational structures helpful in terms of modeling educational and mission enterprises. An early and ongoing relationship between First Baptist Augusta and the independent Springfield Baptist Church, resulting in the latter's affiliation with the otherwise white Georgia Baptist Convention in the 1830s, may partially explain the phenomenon of black associational involvement in Georgia Baptist denominational life.

As in 1845, no delegates from Augusta's First Baptist congregation, Burrows excepted, were appointed to official convention positions. As businessmen, many of the church's leading men lacked time to formally engage in national Southern Baptist life in a leadership capacity. Nonetheless, Hickman and James T. Bothwell represented First Baptist (alongside Burrows) in a number of future SBC conferences, with Hickman in 1898 serving as a convention vice-president during the annual session in Norfolk, Virginia.[328]

The *Augusta Chronicle* considered the 1885 convention important enough to print, in a special weekly edition of the newspaper following the event, the entire proceedings. Afterward, the First Baptist Church published "a card of thanks to all who assisted in the entertainment of the recent Southern Baptist Convention."[329]

Making a particular impression upon the women of the First Baptist Church were the numerous references during the convention sessions to foreign mission work in China, the nation primarily occupying the attention of Southern Baptists' missionary efforts since the convention's inception. Pastor Burrows may have further spurred their interest. His father, John Lansing, had at the 1881 SBC meeting chaired a report on "The Chinese in California" in which he recommended the appointment of an unnamed Baptist "sister" then working among the state's Chinese population.[330]

Following the SBC gathering, the Augusta church's Woman's Foreign Missionary Society raised funds for the purchase of a bell for a new chapel in the town of Chin Kiang, North China, and for support of Matthew Yates, a missionary serving in China.[331] Then the women examined the mission opportunities in their own city.

Long gone from Augusta were most of the several hundred Chinese laborers hired in the 1870s to work in the construction of the Augusta Canal. Only a few remained. According to the 1880 census, ten of Georgia's seventeen resident Chinese residents lived in Augusta, operating eight grocery stores. By 1900 the Chinese population grew to forty-one, collectively owning twenty-nine grocery stories and eight laundries.[332] These few enterprising individuals filled a niche in a racially-polarized, increasingly segregated town by providing goods and services to black citizens.

The leaders of the church's Woman's Foreign Missionary Society in 1885 perceived a missions opportunity among the twenty or so estimated Chinese residents of Augusta. Mrs. Stokes Walker, formerly serving as a missionary in China with her husband, encouraged Mrs. Isabella Jordan to consider starting a Chinese Sunday School. Mrs. A. Smith Irvine, a new church member from Baltimore, was familiar with a similar ministry in Boston.[333]

While white women in Baptist life were not allowed to teach men (white or black) under normal circumstances, there appears to have been less opposition to the instruction of Chinese men, a largely hidden and undervalued segment of Augusta's population whose business successes caused resentment on the part of many white merchants. At a time when many "Chinese remained behind closed doors in fear for their safety," the First Baptist congregation and the mayor of the city sought to alleviate their fears.[334] The subsequent Chinese ministry of the church represented yet another manner, in addition to partnerships with black Baptist congregations and lower class mill village mission churches, in which the First Baptist congregation bridged racial, ethnic, social, and economic divisions in the city.

Augusta's Chinese may have been initially surprised to see two white Baptist women, riding in a buggy pulled by an old white horse, traversing their neighborhoods and visiting their places of business. The scene evoked church memories of Abraham Marshall riding his white horse in Augusta almost a century earlier. But most of the Chinese likely knew nothing of Christianity, much less Baptists. Invitations to an afternoon "Sunday school" at the First Baptist Church garnered little enthusiasm. Only one responded that first Sunday in November 1885, perhaps out of curiosity, or maybe to polish his rudimentary English skills. The Bible lessons, taught in English, were translated into Mandarin and Cantonese. Slowly, others came. In time one, Chung Yung, converted to Christianity and became the first Chinese to join the church, "a faithful member until death." By the end of the century Augusta's Chinese citizens felt more secure in the city. A number of men attended the Chinese Sunday School, eventually conducted by a large volunteer staff of fourteen persons, primarily women.[335]

Sometimes unexpected events intruded into the church. In 1886 an earthquake struck Augusta during a worship service. The rumbling tremor shook the building, causing panic. As worshipers crowded the aisles in an effort to get out of the building, organist Annie Capen rushed to her instrument and "struck the familiar chords of 'Nearer My God to Thee.'" N. L. Willet, an eyewitness to the event and the future husband of the organist, said of that moment: "I never saw a big congregation so near a disastrous panic, and I never saw a big panic so marvelously and ingeniously averted. My own thought at the time, as I joined the organ in singing, was that I believed that the tall walls of the church would probably fall in the next minute or so, but that I felt I would rather go down in the crash with a song on my lips."[336] Apparently the church building survived with minimal damage.

Annie Capen also played a role in implementing a congregational celebration of Christmas. Historically shunned by many Baptist churches as a pagan or popish holiday, Christmas observances did not appear in Southern Baptist churches until the 1880s. First Baptist Augusta apparently first observed the holiday in 1885, gathering for the singing of Christmas songs. The same month Lansing Burrows preached at the building dedication of the new African-American Tabernacle Baptist Church. The congregation would soon become one of the leading black Baptist churches of the South.[337]

Within First Baptist Augusta and the denomination at large, Southern Baptist women following the 1885 SBC meeting steadily pressed for more missions involvement. In 1888, at the urging of Annie Armstrong of Baltimore, Maryland, and against the wishes of some men who feared their wives might usurp their leadership, women attending the annual SBC gathering in Richmond, Virginia formed the national

Woman's Missionary Union. The official statement announcing the new organization noted that women members were "desirous of stimulating the missionary spirit and the grace of giving, among the women and children of the churches, and aiding in collecting funds for missionary purposes, to be disbursed by the Boards of the Southern Baptist Convention."[338]

First Baptist Augusta's Woman's Foreign Missionary Society soon became a formal local chapter of the national organization. Taking the lead in raising funds for Southern Baptist missionary work, women increasingly played a more prominent role in the life of the convention and local churches. Mary Emily Wright, sister of Isabella Jordan, served as a national WMU officer and president of the Georgia WMU in the early years of the organization. Wright lent both her organizational and writing skills to the organization, editing the Georgia Baptist *Mission Messenger* newspaper, establishing what became the national WMU prayer calendar, and writing, with Lansing Burrows, a book about WMU: *The Missionary Work of the Southern Baptist Convention*, published by the American Baptist Publication Society in 1902.[339]

China served as the beginning point for WMU nationally and locally. The women of First Baptist also raised funds to support mission work in Mexico and Havana, Cuba. Periodic appeals from pastor Burrows to the whole congregation for special mission offerings ensured the involvement of the entire church body in contributing to both the Foreign and Home Mission boards of the SBC.[340]

The church's focus on missions included growth in city ministries. Through the City Mission Board, First Baptist Augusta provided financial assistance to many struggling congregations, including churches previously started by the Greene Street congregation. Missionary work also extended into neighborhoods. In a basement room of her mother's home, Mary Emily Wright in 1890 started a weekly Sunday afternoon ministry of religious instruction to African-American children living nearby. For nine years the Gingerbread Mission continued, so named because Wright gave gingerbread to the children each week.[341]

Also in the 1890s church women formed a Sunbeam Band for mission education for children. The women's widespread and contagious energy and enthusiasm led the Augusta congregation in 1891 to support a foreign missionary. Selecting Rev. William H. Sears, a Missourian serving in North China, James T. Bothwell and John Phinizy joined the women of the church in providing financial support. Bothwell and Phinizy "each agreed to do without cigars for a year," contributing the money thus saved to Sears.[342]

The missions collaboration between pastor Lansing Burrows and the women of the First Baptist congregation during the last fifteen years of the century instilled in the church a missionary fervor and involvement that remains to the present day.

Professionalism and Efficiency: Golden Years of a City Church

Ambitious and determined, Lansing Burrows never seemed to tire in leading the First Baptist Church to new heights. In this respect, the pastor and the congregation parted ways with the city, which in the 1890s dissolved into a quagmire of politics and stagnation brought about by Gilded Age excesses, anti-corporatist populist politics, and underlying anti-Catholic, anti-black hatred. Three prominent church laymen were involved in public service during this time, in some instances seeking to bring about a semblance of justice for the disadvantaged at a time when justice grew increasingly rare.

First Baptist layman William C. Chapman in 1890 unsuccessfully ran for mayor. James C. C. Black reached his political zenith by winning Augusta's U.S. congressional election of 1892 as a Democrat. Five years later a populist uprising turned him out of office. Racially, early Jim Crow laws late in the decade forced greater separation of the races, leading to a system of apartheid and denying blacks the right to vote. In 1897 the Richmond County School system discontinued the public high school education of African-American students by shutting down Ware High School, invoking a lawsuit against the school board by a group of prominent black businessmen. Superior Court Judge Enoch H. Callaway, a deacon of First Baptist, ruled in favor of the plaintiffs and against the closing of Augusta's black high school. The U.S. Supreme Court decision that ultimately resulted, *Cumming v. Richmond County Board of Education*, overturned Callaway's ruling and effectively gutted the "separate but equal" ideology of an 1896 court decision (*Plessy v. Ferguson*) defining legal public accommodations for blacks, thus allowing Richmond County to deny high school public education for African Americans. *Cumming* remained in place until overturned by the more well-known *Brown v. Board of Education* in 1954. Judge Callaway, in effect, tried but failed to put a brake on the march of Southern apartheid.[343]

In the midst of the political and social turmoil, commerce and industry advanced while baseball, football, horse racing, theater, and extravagant expositions entertained the masses. Lansing Burrows, meanwhile, focused primarily on the higher calling of the gospel. Symbolizing the coming of age of a denomination and a church, the pastor of First Baptist employed his professional skills, utilized the newest publishing technologies, and enhanced the work of church committees.

Advanced publishing techniques allowed Burrows to create and publish a Baptist newspaper under his byline and the auspices of the church. From 1887 to 1892, *Helping Hands* rolled off the presses a number of times yearly. As professionally crafted as any state Baptist newspaper, the publication contained Bible lessons, profiles of Baptist leaders, Baptist news South and North, coverage of other denominations, humorous short items, stories about First Baptist, and much more. Dozens of local businesses advertised in the newspaper, testimony to the church's ties to the business community. Circulation apparently included many subscribers apart from church members. The cheerful, ecumenical, and instructional nature of the paper reflected Burrows' own personality and inclinations.[344]

While *Helping Hands* proved to be an excellent promotional, publicity, and educational tool, Burrows frequently turned to specialized and creative church committees to manage increasingly complex congregational affairs. Long a part of Baptist churches, committees in the late nineteenth century underwent a professional makeover, a reflection of modern business practices. Formal, narrowly-focused, and well-ordered, a new generation of church committees helped urban churches deploy members with the right skills to expand congregational membership.

"His whole pastorate was a time of soul-winning," church historian Jordan later wrote of Burrows. "[S]o fast were the young people being received into the church" that the pastor created a committee "to instruct and train young converts." These young men and women represented the future of the church. The committee tasked with educating them consisted wholly of women: Mrs. A. Smith Irvine, Mollie Bothwell, and Mary Wright, aided by Burrows. Two young men from this era, William Richards and J. Sumner Rodgers, were ordained by Burrows and became pastors.[345]

Committees proliferated during Burrows' tenure as pastor. In 1888 alone he led the congregation to establish six new committees to oversee significant ministries of the expanding church: Sunday School, finance, poor of the church, church property and repairs, music, and new members.[346]

Growth in membership, evidenced in both Sunday School and worship services, presented challenges and opportunities for the Finance Committee. Church debt mounted in 1889. Determined to eradicate the red ink, Burrows enacted a "Plan of Financial Operations." Supervised by the deacons, the plan involved the crafting of an annual budget and the expectation that all members would contribute to the finances of the church, based on "the circumstances and abilities of each." A church-wide assembly held the first Sunday afternoon in November brought members together to plan for the future of the congregation, afterward becoming an annual event." Even though the financial picture brightened, a continued shortfall in 1893 led to a decision to postpone the installation of electric lighting. On the other hand, the congregation voted the same year to assume costs related to music, which had heretofore been obtained by special fundraising.[347]

Some persons, however, could contribute but little toward finances. With women far outnumbering men, including many poor widows, the church voted to acquire a city cemetery (now Magnolia Cemetery) lot for indigent members.[348]

In its eighth decade and considerably older than most members, the church building also needed attention. As early as 1892 Burrows suggested that the sanctuary be remodeled. On the occasion of his tenth anniversary in the Augusta pulpit in 1893, Burrows looked beyond the mere absence of electricity and, in a sermon titled "After Ten Years," again spoke of the need to remodel the church, recommending the addition of a columned facade like that of the Church of the Madeleine in Paris. Church members, however, envisioned greater changes in the form of rebuilding rather than remodeling. Despite a lack of financial resources to do so, the congregation unanimously voted to replace the sanctuary and created a building committee in February 1896.[349]

Meanwhile, Calvary Baptist, a small mission congregation earlier established by First Baptist, disbanded and turned over its property to First Baptist. The former church facilities found use as a Sunday School mission, until the property was sold during World War I. On a more positive note, First Baptist assisted in the securing of a place of worship for Woodlawn Baptist Church on 15th Street.[350]

Against the backdrop of membership growth, expanded committees, financial challenges, church property concerns, and mission church involvement, Burrows implemented changes to the leadership structure of the church. Traditionally, a nominating committee recommended new deacon candidates for the church's approval. Signaling a new era of direct congregational elections, in 1892 John C. Lee and A. Smith Irvine became the first two deacons chosen by popular vote.[351]

Other men also shaped the church during the last two decades of the century. J. Cuthbert Shecut, an educator involved in the creation of the city's public school system in the 1870s, served as secretary of the City Mission Board. James T. Bothwell, in addition to involvement in missions fund-raising, served as a deacon and Sunday School superinten- dent. Fred T. Lockhart created a "floating Sunday School" that met on a canal barge in conjunction with the mill village Berean Mission (later Berean Baptist Church). D. R. Wright, a local businessman, served faithfully as a deacon for thirty-nine years. Both Wright and William M. Jordan passed away in 1891, the latter following an extended period of illness.[352]

Yet more than any other person in the post-war era, Lansing Burrows transformed the First Baptist Church of Augusta. In October 1893 the congregation passed a remarkable resolution of appreciation for Burrows, noting:

> [F]or the first ten years he has been a faithful pastor to his flock. His eloquent sermons have been elevating and instructive, setting forth in a clear manner the word of God and have furnished food for our souls. He has not only lovingly ministered to our spiritual wants in the pulpit and prayer meetings, but has been a friend to the poor, has visited the

sick, comforted the dying and buried our dead. . . . he has our confidence our love and affection, and we esteem ourselves fortunate indeed in having him as the shepherd of our flock.[353]

It would be hard to imagine a more resounding affirmation of pastoral ministry. Lansing Burrows' enthusiasm, energy, efficiency, and excellence during his first ten years in Augusta set the stage for a church membership engaged and excited during the remainder of the decade.

A "Knight" for Freedom of Thought: Lansing Burrows and Walter Rauschenbusch

Beyond remarkable successes on the local level, Lansing Burrows' influence brought First Baptist, once again, into the national spotlight.

Perhaps among the most ecumenical Baptists of the era, Burrows' involvement in Baptist life extended to that of American (Northern) Baptists. While serving as the secretary of the Southern Baptist Convention, he also held the title of recording secretary of the American Baptist Education Society (ABES). Founded in 1888 in Chicago, the society sought "the promotion of Christian education, under Baptist auspices, in North America," birthing the University of Chicago in 1890.[354]

Furthermore, from 1882 to 1912 Burrows served as a leader in the Northern-centric Baptist Congress, "a pioneering Baptist intellectual think tank and forum for theological, social, and ethical discussions and debates among members of Baptist churches." The "most vital avenue for the expression of Baptist intellectualism of its time" according to one Baptist scholar, the Congress met annually to, in its own words, "promote a healthful sentiment among Baptists through free and courteous discussion of current questions by suitable persons." The Baptist Congress, in short, was the annual venue where progressive and liberal Baptist thinkers addressed the pressing issues of the day affecting Christianity and church life.[355]

Through the American Baptist Education Society and the Baptist Congress, Lansing Burrows became friends with one of the greatest Baptists of the era: New York City pastor and social gospel advocate Walter Rauschenbusch. A liberal American Baptist, Rauschenbusch also served as secretary and treasurer of the Baptist Congress. Burrows' involvement with Baptist intellectuals such as Rauschenbusch resulted in the Baptist Congress' first meeting held in the Deep South, hosted by First Baptist Augusta from December 5-7, 1893. Appointed vice president of the gathering, Burrows chaired a local committee comprised of his church's most capable laymen: James T. Bothwell, Frank R. Clark, John P. Dill, Hamilton H. Hickman, John W. Hillis, Carlton Hillyer, A. Smith Irvine, John C. Lee, R. M. Mixson, Joshua S. Patterson, John Phinizy, Henry C. Roney, William J. Rutherford, James Paul Verdery, James B. Walker, and Thomas R. Wright. Georgia governor William J. Northern served as president of the Congress.[356]

In the First Baptist sanctuary Rauschenbusch addressed one of the great questions of the Gilded Age: "The Church and the Money Power." Referencing Jesus, the Bible, and early and modern history, Rauschenbusch spoke of church and wealth as enemies, warning his fellow Baptists to oppose anything that would "enslave the church to the money power." Other topics addressed by presenters included "Emotionalism in Religion," "Shall Our Young People be Organized for Christian Work?", "Ethical Versus Forensic Conceptions of Salvation," "What Constitutes Valid Baptism?", and "The Indwelling Christ."[357]

Lansing Burrows closed the meeting by speaking of his church:

> I wanted to see in these historic walls this Baptist Congress of America. I do not know how long they will stand. They have already stood for three-quarters of a century, rocked by earthquake, scorched by fire, swept by flood, and yet they stand for the fourth and fifth generations of those who founded the church to come and worship God within. In these pews, half a century ago, sat the men who organized and formulated the policy of that Convention which has grown so large, that we who saw its small beginnings almost dread to see it come again. But all of you, brethren, of diverse opinions especially, we wanted you to come and show us how, though differing in various modes of thought, you can disagree and yet be bound together in brotherly affection.[358]

Expressing disappointment that so few "Southern brethren" had attended and chagrin that some Baptists of the South dismissed the gathering as "composed of soreheads and cranks," Burrows voiced his commitment for freedom of thought. Echoing his Baptist heritage, he noted that the suppression of religious dissent in the South "smells of the middle ages." "I wish every man to have the conscious power of cherishing his own opinions and his own interpretations of God's word, and to exercise his own privilege of judgment, without incurring the sneers or coldness of others," the First Baptist pastor declared. "I should like myself to be a knight in a new crusade—against the disposition to wound and mortify and crucify for the sake of opinion. I would have men to be free in their thoughts."[359]

Upon voicing his thoughts, Burrows concluded the gathering with participants singing "Blessed Be the Tie That Binds," after which everyone shook hands. That afternoon the delegates visited the Augusta Exposition, and in the evening "a banquet was given in honor of the Congress, at the beautiful Hotel Bon Air, by the citizens of Augusta, where the visitors learned still more to admire and love their brilliant and warm-hearted hosts."[360]

The Augusta Legacy of Lansing Burrows

Augusta's Baptists. Southern and Northern Baptists. Conservatives and liberals. Young and old. Men and women. White, black, and Chinese. Everyone seemed to like Lansing Burrows.

Among the most progressive white Baptists of the South, Lansing Burrows defied neat labels at a time of expanding conservatism in the region's political, social, and religious structures. No one else in the Deep South dared host a gathering of leading liberal and progressive Baptists of the North. The 1893 gathering of the Baptist Congress represented a hope that Baptists of the South might put aside, or at least tone down, animosities dating to the formation of the Southern Baptist Convention and prior.

Even so, the Confederate veteran remained a son of and apologist for the Old South. The chaplain of Augusta's Confederate Survivors' Association, in 1896 Burrows sorrowed over the loss of the South's "Golden Age." He maintained white Southerners had been in the right to fight to preserve African slavery, the source of their wealth, riches that in turn became their undoing. The Confederate nation was of God, the army the most religious ever. "Men went into battle equipped with Bibles and bearing on their lips the strains of old familiar hymns. Their generals ascribed their victories to the favor of God, and honored Him while they dictated their dispatches to their superiors. Upon their banners they inscribed their trust in God; and when they failed they bowed in marked submission to Him." In these remembrances Burrows glossed over frequent, war-time complaints among Baptists of the South that the Confederate Army was in reality a den of sin and vice, with many regiments having no chaplains.[361]

The last four years of Burrows' ministry at First Baptist Augusta, while as notable as his earlier years, are obscured by a fire that destroyed church records dating from 1895 to 1915. Local newspaper accounts indicate that Burrows successfully maintained the internal tension between Old South ideology and ecumenical openness while nurturing his congregation. In 1897 he preached in the city's African-American Thankful Baptist Church. The same year an Augusta newspaper article referred to Burrows as "one of the ablest preachers in the South." In 1898 one account described as "splendid" the church's choir. On March 7 of the same year Burrows preached "a most eloquent sermon on home missions," while on June 6 morning worship took the form of "children's services." With their pastor out of town the last Sunday of July 1899, church members simply called off services, rather than trying to find someone to fill his rather large shoes.[362]

For a period of time in 1898, however, events to the south generated unease and disruption in church and city. On February 15, 1898 the U.S. Battleship *Maine* exploded, the incident soon plunging the United States into a brief war with Spain over the latter's island colonies in the Pacific. A number of the men of First Baptist joined other locals in volunteering to fight. Burrows served as chaplain of the volunteers, traveling with them to a staging camp in Tampa, Florida. In August, Spain capitulated, giving victory to the U.S. in the form of control over Spain's former Pacific colonies. Augusta's men in uniform returned home as heroes.[363]

Statewide in the late 1890s Lansing Burrows remained popular among Georgia Baptists, serving as a vice president of the Georgia Baptist Convention and appointed to a committee to rewrite and revise the organization's constitution. In 1898 First Baptist Augusta hosted the state convention.[364]

Lansing Burrows' resignation from the Augusta pastorate in 1899 occasioned great "personal bereavement," resulting in a congregational "Resolutions of Regret," a "Testimonial" to his positive impact upon the church, and a "beautiful gift" on his last day in the pulpit. From the longest tenure of any First Baptist Augusta pastor at that time, Burrows assumed the pulpit of the First Baptist Church of Nashville, Tennessee. Two years later Mrs. Burrows died following years of rheumatism and arthritis. Over the course of the next two decades Burrows remained as statistician for the Southern Baptist Convention until the time of his death in 1919, serving as the SBC president from 1914 to 1916.[365]

From Burrows' long and inclusive ministry First Baptist Augusta emerged a renewed church. Challenges remained and a new century beckoned, but the future looked bright.

6

Rebuilding, Rising, Reforming

The twentieth century in America dawned like no other. As the sun set on the expansion of the Western frontier, from the East new and fiery rays of populist reforms probed the dark corners of humanity. Protestant morality and technologically-driven modernization together fueled change in politics, society, business, and religion. Conservatives and liberals alike held aloft the badge of "progressive." States and cities from coast to coast searched for ways to improve the lives of ordinary citizens. From Washington, D.C. in the first decade of the century, newly-elected President Theodore Roosevelt absorbed the nation's mood by shaping anti-trust policies, establishing business regulations, formalizing the conservation movement, and expanding military might in order to secure world peace. Running for a third presidential term in 1912, Roosevelt, fearful of the progressive agenda losing steam under his successor William Howard Taft and determined to hold back the tide, in one of his most memorable speeches shouted: "Fearless of the future; unheeding of our individual fates; with unflinching hearts and undimmed eyes; we stand at Armageddon, and we battle for the Lord!"[366]

Battlefield particulars, however, varied from North to South. Northern leaders spearheaded economic, industrial, and social reforms designed to solve the ills of urbanity. White politicians of the largely rural South steered a trajectory far more conservative. On the ground in Augusta and South-wide, upper and middle class citizens led the way. White Protestants steeped in a theology of personal salvation, and hence individual responsibility, framed reform as the betterment of individual persons. To quell the unrest of poor whites they devised uplifting policies such as public education, prison reform, regulation of child labor, and social services. Ongoing harsh measures against blacks, from strict segregation to lynchings, heightened racial anger and confrontation.

Neither did many white Protestants of the South approve of religious diversity. Roman Catholics and mainstream Jews they only grudgingly tolerated, while more exotic faith groups such as Greek Orthodox Catholics and Russian Orthodox Jews—both sects newly-arrived in Augusta—elicited even less interest.[367]

Unable to make inroads into the white Protestant South, Roosevelt lost his apocalyptic battle to the Democratic candidate, New Jersey governor Woodrow Wilson. Born in Virginia and reared in Augusta, Wilson swept the South in the 1912 presidential election. His résumé reflected the relatively cosmopolitan nature of early twentieth-century Augusta, a place where Northerners found themselves quite at home. Manufacturing and industry empowered the local economy in a fashion similar to that of Northern locales. Banks, law firms, and a thriving business scene more reflective of the urban North than the rural South bespoke of much wealth in the city. The leading Baptist pulpit, that of the First Baptist Church, had long been occupied by pastors from the North or with Northern ties, while prominent businessmen were counted among the church's leading laypersons.

By the late 1880s in the midst of the Gilded Age, Augusta's elites realized, if only partially at the time, that the combination of a Northern-like economy and mild Southern weather appealed to well-to-do Northerners who wished to live in comfort during the winter months. Florida offered the best winter climate, but acceptable weather and closer proximity to the North advantaged Georgia in a pre-automobile era. Already, the Jekyll Island Club off the coast of Georgia, opened in 1888, attracted many of the world's wealthiest families such as the Morgans, Rockefellers, and Vanderbilts. Sailing their private yachts southward each winter, in the spring they returned to their residences and offices in the North.[368]

A second and third tier of wealthy Northern families also emerged from the Gilded Age, a clientele that the enterprising builders of the Bon Air Hotel, established in 1889, sought to attract. Built on a hill above Augusta in Summerville, a community of wealthy Augustans, the elegant hotel offered the finest of amenities in a mild winter climate. Popular recreational activities during the hotel's first decade included horseback riding and bicycling. Electric street cars on rails provided easy access to downtown Augusta, three miles distant. The combination of location, fine lodging, excellent food, and casual recreation resulted in a thriving business by century's end. First Baptist maintained an open invitation for hotel guests to attend worship services. Many responded.

Displaying a nimble entrepreneurial acumen, the city's tourist industry marketed to Northern trends. In 1898 the *Augusta Chronicle* noted a loss of interest, among Northern snowbirds, in horseback and bicycle riding. The "fad with those who rode only for pleasure died the death of all such passing novelties," the paper intoned. In the place of pleasure riding a novelty to Augustans enraptured Northern visitors: golf. The "only reason the game is known at all is due to Northern enthusiasts. To them a season without golf is what a barbeque without meat is to a Southerner."[369]

Opened in 1897, the Bon Air Golf Club originally consisted of nine holes and a club house for use by hotel guests and upper class locals. Professional golf instructors from Scotland soon arrived, as did automobiles, collectively attracting all the more wealthy tourists and winter residents. Among notables who became winter fixtures were business magnate John D. Rockefeller and President William Howard Taft. Newspaper coverage followed both. A popular magazine article summed up what happened next. After Augusta "was discovered by John D. Rockefeller . . . other millionaires learned of the beauty and solitude of Augusta and flocked there in great numbers, and real estate took wings. Winter hotels, winter cottages, winter golf links sprang up like Jonah's gourd." Augusta reigned foremost in Georgia as "a glad-hander to rich tourists." The golf "links make the heart of the tourist glad, and the people of Augusta suffer every winter from enlarged craniums, due to the many nice things said about the town, its beautiful women and its lovely children."[370]

Against this backdrop First Baptist exerted great influence within the city. Leading layman and attorney James C. C. Black in 1901 became the first president of the city's newly-formed Augusta Bar.[371] Benefits to the church accrued from Augusta's Northern-inspired prosperity and destination status included new members, prominent guests, and yet more connections with Baptist life of the North. The construction of a grand new sanctuary seemed only fitting.

A New Sanctuary in a New Century

Upon Lansing Burrows' departure from the pastorate in 1899, the congregation, well along in early preparations and fundraising for a new sanctuary, wasted little time in seeking a successor. Following a pattern well established by now, members looked northward. Also reflective of prior pastoral searches, they turned to a friend of their recently-departed pastor.

A native of Wilmington, Virginia, graduate of Crozer Theological Seminary in Pennsylvania, and recently pastor of the Franklin Square Baptist Church in Baltimore, Dr. Sparks W. Melton attended annual Southern Baptist Convention meetings alongside Burrows. Thanks to Burrows, few Southern Baptist churches exceeded the Augusta congregation in terms of organization and efficiency, traits to which "the brilliant eloquent" Melton brought "zest and inspiration." Mere weeks after Melton's arrival in April 1900 the church formed a Building Committee and began a two-year process of formulating plans and obtaining financial estimates for the project.[372]

Five of the church's prominent businessmen comprised the Building Committee: Paul Mustin, Frank R. Clark, Albert J. Twiggs, Jere T. Smith and James B. Walker. Successful men, many or perhaps all had homes (some seasonal) in Summerville or beyond. Twiggs, a local contractor, a decade later constructed a levee for the city of Augusta. All stayed in town during the hot summer months of 1900 through 1902 in order to closely monitor the planning and construction of the new sanctuary.[373]

As the new sanctuary took shape, Melton strove to follow in the big footsteps of his predecessor. As preacher, pastor, and denominational leader, he fared quite well. Isabella Jordan remembers Melton as loved by church members "old and young alike," and among the older families, "not only as a pastor, but as a dear son." The *Augusta Chronicle* frequently spoke glowingly of his sermons. Yet the capable pastor and pulpiteer also harbored strong opinions. In the annual Baptist World Congress gathering of May 1900 in Richmond, Virginia, Sparks W. Melton offered a blistering rebuttal of "far-reaching tendencies connected with Protestantism of this century—the rise and growth of ritualism, tractarianism, or sacerdotalism, or the high church movement," borrowed from the Roman Catholic Church.[374] Like many other Southern Baptist leaders in this era of Protestant hegemony, Melton perceived a threat to American Christianity from an immigration-fueled, expanding Catholic presence.

Nonetheless, First Baptist maintained good relations with other local Protestants. Customary "Union" meetings of downtown churches— Methodist, Presbyterian, Christian, and Baptist—took place in the summer months. Some Presbyterians took an absence from their church in November 1900 to hear Madison C. Peters, a famous New York Presbyterian preacher recently converted to the Baptist faith, speak from the First Baptist pulpit. During the 1904 centennial celebration of the First Presbyterian Church, the First Baptist congregation passed "a set of resolutions expressive of cordial fraternity," bidding "Godspeed to their sister church." On December 29, 1907, Howard T. Cree, "one of the most prominent of Disciples members" in the South, the pastor of Augusta's Christian Church and future secretary (executive) of the Interchurch World Movement, preached at First Baptist.[375]

Denominational activity on the part of First Baptist, meanwhile, continued unabated. Melton attended annual SBC meetings, as did Mary Emily Wright as a representative of the church's Woman's Missionary Society.[376]

During the waning days of the old sanctuary, on September 9, 1901 members gathered to pray for U.S. President William McKinley, shot three days prior by an assassin while in New York. McKinley died four days later, and on September 15 First Baptist hosted a citywide service in memory of the president, attended by more than 1,000 persons. In November the church hosted an eight-day citywide Sunday School "teacher's institute," followed by a protracted revival, including an evening "mass meeting" for men. In December the church choir presented a Christmas musical program.[377]

Pastoral goodwill, denominational activity, Protestant camaraderie, and special church events aside, the excitement of a new sanctuary remained uppermost in the minds of the members of the First Baptist congregation. The women of the church held numerous fundraisers over the course of the year 1901, including a summer "moonlight excursion," a fall "handkerchief bazaar," and a winter "apron bazaar." At a cost of

$60,000, the church selected the South Carolina architectural firm of Wilson and Edwards to draw building plans. Willis F. Denny, leading architect, had earlier designed the city's Albion Hotel.[378]

Anticipation mounted in 1902 with the June 2 selection of contractor C. L. Rounds to construct the new sanctuary. Rounds began work quickly, within ten days removing most of the interior furnishings, pews excluded. Sunday, June 22 marked the last worship services in the sanctuary that had served the congregation faithfully since 1820. In the presence of a large gathering, pastor Melton preached and presided over the Lord's Supper in a celebratory morning service, while the evening program featured special music and a historical sermon by Rev. J. H. Eakes, pastor of the St. John Methodist Church, who spoke of the history of the Baptist congregation. Both joy and sorrow marked the occasion, with many tears shed as members walked out of the sanctuary for the last time.[379]

Demolition began the next day. Down came the 1846 bell, later remolded into a tablet in memory of Dr. William H. Turpin, its donor. The walls followed, then the recovery of the cornerstone. A silver plate dated February 12, 1820 read: "This cornerstone, deposited by the trustees of the Baptist Church in this city, is consecrated to the worship of the Triune God, to the promotion of one faith, one baptism." Included with the plate were a 1798 dollar coin, 1818 quarter, 1802 dime, and 1807 penny.

Upon complete demolition of the building, on September 9 several hundred members gathered again at the corner of Greene and Jackson for laying of a new cornerstone. Those assembled sang "Praise God From Whom All Blessings Flow," after which Dr. Melton gave an invocation. Another hymn followed, then scripture reading by Melton and prayer by Rev. R. L. Motley, pastor of the Curtis Baptist Church, formerly a mission church of First Baptist. Hamilton H. Hickman, one of the most prominent lay leaders in the church's history and now the oldest living member, turned the first shovelful of dirt. A choir sang "Christ Our Cornerstone" prior to the depositing of the new cornerstone containing a copper box donated by H. T. Graham. The box's contents consisted of a few coins, several Augusta newspapers, a church manual, a few other small items, and a new silver plate with the names of the pastor, trustees

(Hickman, James C. C. Black, W. J. Rutherford, T. R. Wright, J. C. Lee), various committees associated with the construction of the new sanctuary, church treasurer (John Phinizy), architect (W. T. Denny), and contractor. Melton again spoke, followed by the singing of "All Hail the Power of Jesus' Name" and a benediction by Methodist pastor Eakes.[380]

For more than a year following, the First Baptist congregation held worship services in the Tubman High School auditorium. Workers finished the "lecture" or Sunday School room by the end of December 1902. In early January the "great iron girders" needed to support the sanctuary's dome and roof swung into place. A new organ followed in early fall, two "memorial windows" in September, and new "handsome walnut-pews" in November. Also in November, a large gathering took place in the lecture room and a preview of the sanctuary elicited the "greatest of enthusiasm."[381]

During the construction Melton shared the pulpit with a variety of guest speakers, mostly fellow preachers, many from the North, but at least one a local baseball player. A. Paul Bagby, third baseman of the Augusta Tourists minor league baseball team and an aspiring seminarian, assumed the role of pastor of the church for a month during Melton's summer vacation. His presence in the pulpit evidenced the growing popularity of baseball in the city, a sport not yet widely respectable, and criticized by many Baptists of the South. The following year one of baseball's greatest players ever, Ty Cobb, launched his playing career in Augusta.[382]

Missions support continued in 1903, led by church women who opened a "lunch room" at 812 Broadway in February to raise funds. In October the Woman's Missionary Society held a meeting in the church's new lecture room. The following month, James C. C. Black delivered a lecture "for the benefit" of the Ladies Aid Society.[383]

The fitting of the last of the new sanctuary's two Tiffany stained glass windows took place on December 3, 1903. Three days later the magnificent new sanctuary opened for a dedication service, a day on which the other downtown churches closed their doors in honor of First Baptist. Services took place at 11 a.m., 3:30 p.m., and 8:30 p.m. Overflowing crowds marveled at the grand domed roof, arches, and stunning stained glass windows. Joining Melton in the pulpit for the morning service were former pastors Lansing Burrows and William W. Landrum, with Burrows preaching a sermon titled "Strength and Beauty Are in His Sanctuary," based on Psalm 96:8. In the afternoon Henry G. Weston, president of Crozer Theological Seminary and one of Melton's professors, preached from the new pulpit. Many local ministers also took part in the afternoon and evening services, while the First Baptist choir starred in the latter service. It was, unquestionably, a day to remember in Augusta, Georgia. A week of services in the new church sanctuary followed, and the year ended with satisfaction and excitement on the part of the members of the city's downtown Baptist church.[384]

Northern Influences and Southern Sensibilities in Church and City

The most visible Baptist presence in and around the city of Augusta remained at the corner of Greene and Jackson. There in a new, majestic, columned, domed Beaux-Classicism styled house of worship hundreds of prominent citizens heard beautiful music and stirring sermons in Sunday services marked by dignity and professionalism. The sanctuary in the early twentieth century stood proudly in the midst of the diverse city life along Augusta's "finest residential street." At 412 Jackson Street across from the church a high-end clothier offered "craftmanship of the highest order." Nearby at 408 Jackson stood the "Weng Fong Laundry," a Chinese business. Behind the church James H. Warren, a leading black businessman, operated a fruit stand. City parades often began in front of the church. The pages of the *Augusta Chronicle* frequently contained notices of prominent weddings held in the beautiful sanctuary.[385]

Many other Baptist churches dotted the landscape of the city and surrounding suburbs, most having originated as missions of First Baptist. One such congregation, the Kollock Street Baptist church in a working class neighborhood, challenged the racial status quo in August 1903. From the pulpit that month Rev. Osa Gilbert criticized a recent lynch mob in Statesboro, leading some white Augustans to accuse him of advocating racial equality. However the leaders of First Baptist may have reacted to the controversy, Gilbert's prophetic voice echoed an earlier era when the Baptists on Greene Street repeatedly defended the city's enslaved population and, after the Civil War, lent a hand to black educational efforts. Following Gilbert's comments, in November 1903 Sparks W. Melton came to the public defense of a beaten "negro" citizen.[386]

Other concerns also occupied the minds of Augustans in the months following the completion of the church's new building. In late 1903 and early 1904 some sixty children in the city perished in a spate of fires, many caused by the haphazard nature of electricity of the time. The deaths so saddened the public that Melton referred to them during a Sunday evening service in January. Grief again visited church and city one month later in the passing of Hamilton H. Hickman, prominent congregational leader and Augusta businessman. June witnessed the passing of Mary A. Bouyer, the oldest member of the church at that time. In addition, the pastor's wife, Laura Melton, during the decade experienced a long illness and was faithfully attended to by the women of the congregation.[387]

On a more pleasant note, the church's new facilities played host to numerous conferences and community events throughout the decade. In February 1904 the Georgia Young Men's Christian Association held its annual meeting in church buildings. The Hephzibah Baptist Association gathered in church parlors the following month. In October 1907 the church hosted, in the Sunday School rooms, an "informal reception" for students of the medical college.[388]

A February 1904 sermon titled "Make the Best of Your Life" seemingly represented the optimism brought about by the new sanctuary and reflected among middle and upper class Augustans. The church's "Lend A Hand" ladies club held an Easter "egg hunt" for the city's "little ones" in 1904 at the courthouse, at a time when few Baptist churches celebrated Easter. The following month the church hosted "one of the largest of the Sunday School picnics of the year" in Augusta. On November 27 "an agreeable surprise awaited those who attended the First Baptist church in a sermon by Dr. Roland D. Grant, the celebrated lecturer." One of America's most prolific lecturers at the time, Grant, a Baptist minister and member of various mountaineering and outdoors clubs, spoke at the church during a national tour recounting his adventures in Yellowstone National Park. More regionally-focused, John William Jones, well-known Confederate chaplain during the Civil War, presided over "memorial services" held at First Baptist on June 3, 1907 as part of city-wide ceremonies held in memory of former Confederate president Jefferson Davis.[389]

On the other hand, by 1907 many members of First Baptist no longer publicly viewed alcohol optimistically, as that March the church hosted the Anti-Saloon League, the leading lobby organization of a growing, national Prohibition movement. The same year the Georgia legislature passed a Prohibition bill, effective January 1, 1908. South Carolina, however, did not immediately follow suit. Speaking from the pulpit in December 1907, Melton urged Augusta's city council and Chamber of Commerce to "lift up their voices against the North Augusta Dispensary," a business selling alcohol immediately across the river in South Carolina. Located near the North Augusta Bridge, the Dispensary's spirits were easily accessible to Augustans. Ecclesiastically, by January 1908 First Baptist adopted "unfermented wine" in communion services as a replacement for the traditional fermented beverage. By 1920 most Southern Baptist churches replaced wine with grape juice.[390]

When not in the pulpit of First Baptist, Melton, in great demand, traveled widely. In May 1904 he spoke during the anniversary gathering of the Northern Baptist Convention in Cleveland, Ohio, while in June of the same year he toured the Northeast "preaching in several of the most prominent churches" in the region. January 1906 found Melton preaching in New York. Closer to home, in 1907 the Hephzibah Baptist Association chose the Augusta pastor as its new moderator.[391]

A continued staple of church life under Melton's pastoral tenure, revivals generated much enthusiasm in the new and enlarged sanctuary. The events featured numerous popular speakers, including former pastor William W. Landrum, and brought new members into the church.[392]

Fiscally, the First Baptist congregation paid off the church's debt in November 1905, followed by the construction of a "stone fence" around the church's property. Difficulty, however, befell church and city alike in the form of floods in August 1908. The church and Melton's house sustained damage.[393]

During a decade of growth and excitement the congregation's ministries expanded. The church hosted Chinese New Year celebrations for the city's "Christianized Chinese" and provided financial aid to members of the Chinese community who suffered losses due to the 1908 floods. In September 1908 the congregation established a local Baptist Young People's Union (BYPU). Representing Southern Baptists' new emphasis on ministry to young adults, the BYPU served as a forerunner of local Sunday evening educational programs and formal collegiate ministry within the denomination.[394]

On the heels of the extraordinarily effective and efficient Lansing Burrows, Sparks W. Melton's pastorate thus witnessed further congregational advances. Having led the congregation to new heights, Melton in November 1908 resigned from First Baptist Augusta to become pastor of Freemason Street Baptist Church in Norfolk, Virginia. There he served exceptionally for the next forty-four years, in his latter years referred to as "the dean of all Baptist preachers in the state of Virginia."[395]

In return, Virginia sent one of its prominent native sons to First Baptist Augusta: Dr. M. Ashby Jones, son of the recently-deceased John William Jones, famous Confederate chaplain and previously a guest speaker at the Augusta church. Jones arrived in early 1909, an opportune time. Augusta now stood among the most prominent and wealthy cities of the South. A winter home for many rich and famous Northerners, the city's diverse economy thrived.

Among the most famous of Americans at the time, U.S. president-elect William Howard Taft visited his winter rental home in Augusta about the time of Jones' arrival, rubbing shoulders with John D. Rockefeller, who routinely wintered at the Hotel Bon Air. The wealthy businessman often attended services at the African-American Tabernacle Baptist Church to hear Dr. Charles T. Walker, as did Taft in January 1909. Known as "the black Spurgeon" and arguably the most famous African-American preacher in the early twentieth century, Walker served as both minister and educator. Rockefeller financially supported Walker and his efforts to educate blacks through the Walker Baptist Institute, an organization also endorsed by many of Augusta's white ministers, including Ashby Jones.[396]

Rockefeller, Taft, and Walker signified Augusta's elite status, as did First Baptist, a congregation that included many of the city's leading citizens. Although Rockefeller sometimes attended Walker's Tabernacle Baptist, there are no verifiable first-hand accounts of the businessman worshiping at First Baptist.[397] Georgia governor-elect Joseph M. Brown, on the other hand, attended First Baptist on January 10, 1909 as the guest of deacon and judge Enoch H. Callaway.[398]

In this high-powered environment M. Ashby Jones quickly assumed the role of the city's new leading Baptist voice. He made no distinction between temporal and spiritual in terms of ministry. Within weeks Jones delivered a community high school commencement address, and in October he spoke to the city's Colored Y.M.C.A. Following a congregational Christmas music program in December, Jones preached on the subject of "Mary the Mother," in addition to delivering a second Christmas sermon to the city's Masons. Weeks later he served as the speaker of the annual (Robert E.) Lee Memorial Association gathering, including a service at First Baptist.[399]

Against the backdrop of white citizens annually celebrating the old, slavery-based South, ongoing and deteriorating race relations intersected church and city in a choreographed but tension-filled atmosphere. In August 1909 James C. C. Black spoke at a Negro Education Rally at the Haines Normal School, a private educational institution founded by Augustan and prominent African-American educator Lucy Craft Laney. Black joined mayor Joseph Cumming, in addition to Charles T. Walker and other leading black citizens, in encouraging black citizens to better themselves through education. "By request" Jones addressed "Our Relation to the Negro" from the First Baptist pulpit in a February 4, 1912 sermon, and directly addressed black citizens in July 1913. In March 1914, at the invitation of Walker, the First Baptist pastor delivered the "formal address" during a special cornerstone service for a new Tabernacle Baptist church building, then two months later delivered the commencement address to the graduating class of the Walker Baptist Institute.[400]

If Charles T. Walker was the nation's leading black Baptist preacher, Edgar Y. Mullins, president of the Southern Baptist Theological Seminary, arguably held the same title among white Baptists. In February 1910 the seminary president added to the list of luminaries parading through Augusta, speaking at First Baptist. The same month Ericsson Bushnell, prominent church singer from New York and a guest of Rockefeller at the Bon Air, in "splendid voice" sang a solo at First

Baptist. Former pastor Melton, too, received royal treatment when he returned to preach in Augusta in June.[401]

Meanwhile, within the walls of First Baptist education remained a congregational priority. In February 1910 the Woman's Missionary Society led the church in coordinating an educational emphasis on home missions. A church service in June honored graduates of Tubman High School and Richmond Academy, the latter having ties with First Baptist from the moment of the church's establishment in 1817. And in the midst of a political controversy concerning a city-wide compulsory public education bill, Jones lent his voice affirming the matter in a July 1910 sermon.[402]

In a Baptist world known for seriousness of faith and Christian responsibility, entertaining events on the church calendar provided a measure of levity. Annual Sunday School picnics at First Baptist Augusta brought much merriment, as did Christmas plays, including the production "The Sorrows of Santa Claus."[403]

Sadness, however, visited the Bothwell families in Jones' early years. In September 1909 one of the church's leading women and mission advocates, Mary J. Bothwell, passed away, followed four months later by the death of relative and leading layman, the Hon. James T. Bothwell. The congregation also grieved over other deaths, including at least one most unusual. At the request of the church's Chinese mission Sunday School, First Baptist held a Christian funeral for Chinese businessman Sam Kee, murdered in his store on September 17, 1910.[404]

Through worship, celebrations, politics, and bereavement, the congregation moved forward. Appreciative congregants purchased a parsonage on Greene Street for their pastor in August 1910. The following December the congregation elected four new deacons: Z. W. Carwile, Paul Mustin, James T. Bothwell Jr., and Dr. A. J. Kilpatrick. James C. C. Black remained chairman of the deacon board, which also included holdovers Enoch H. Callaway, T. Harry Garrett, A. Smith Irvine, John Phinizy, J. C. Lee, George W. Wright, and J. C. Shecut.[405]

The church's deacons all boasted impressive résumés. Other than Black and Smith, they came from old Augusta families. Former U.S. Congressman Black and Judge Callaway were leading attorneys in the city and known throughout the South. Mustin, Bothwell Jr., Lee, and

Phinizy were all businessmen, the latter in the wholesale pharmaceutical business and vice president of the Georgia Railroad and Banking Company. Garrett, already a well-known educator, in 1916 became principle of Tubman High School. Educator Shecut was the first principal of the North Augusta Elementary School. Carwile and Irvine ranked among notable agricultural professionals in the state of Georgia. Kilpatrick served as a medical doctor and instructor at the Medical College of Georgia. Wright, also a medical professional, became chairman of Augusta's Hospital Building Committee.[406]

Prominent men of exceptional capabilities, most of the church's deacons served in leadership positions related to the annual Baptist Congress of November 1910, meeting at First Baptist Augusta for the second time (the first being in 1893 in the original sanctuary). Mustin, Phinizy, Wright, and Carwile joined Ashby Jones in comprising the Congress' "Local Committee." Representing First Baptist, Jones opened the conference that included many of North America's leading Baptist intellectuals, including New York minister Harry Emerson Fosdick. Among the presenters were Black and Callaway, two of three program personalities neither ministers nor theologians. Both, however, were accomplished speakers, having filled the pulpit of First Baptist Augusta on a number of occasions, with Callaway also a published author.[407]

In welcoming delegates "on behalf of the Baptist churches of Augusta," Black celebrated the Congress as "a body, if not the only one, as I understand it, where one can speak what he feels and thinks." Complementing the largely-Northern audience and often interrupted with laughter from those assembled, Black in his speech demonstrated the great oratory skills characterizing his long career as politician and attorney. Callaway, in turn, delivered a lecture on Christianity and criminology, during which he commended Christian principles as preventing individuals from pursuing lives of crime, yet also clearly voiced the historic Baptist principle of church-state separation. "The Christian kingdom is a spiritual kingdom," the former judge noted, "operating through the hearts of and lives of men and women, and has no connection whatever with the earthly kingdoms and governments established by man, save and except as its principles influence the character of individual members of society."[408]

The conference ended with a prayer that God would use the minds of all those present for the advancement of God's kingdom, and that God's love would "cover the earth" with blessings. Afterward First Baptist Augusta treated its guests to a Southern banquet at the Albion Hotel, sending their Northern friends home with minds and stomachs alike satisfied.[409]

Three months later the most well-known Baptist in the nation, Rockefeller, returned to his Hotel Bon Air room in Summerville, a community annexed into Augusta in 1912. Shortly after Rockefeller's seasonal departure, First Baptist deacon and Sunday School superintendent John Phinizy, speaking before many of the city's prominent businessmen at a YMCA event, gave "a very interesting address...on 'The Bible in the Business Life.'" The address "was very appropriate, and it was fully enjoyed by all present."[410]

A Powerful Pulpit and a Looming War

In addition to wealthy winter dwellers including Rockefeller, the year 1911 witnessed a number of other celebrities in town. In January Booker T. Washington spoke to an audience of city leaders, including James C. C. Black. Well-known socialist Eugene Debs lectured to some 1,000 persons in the opera house across Greene Street from First Baptist. In November New Jersey Governor Woodrow Wilson visited his boyhood home on Augusta's 7th Street. While in town he met Ty Cobb, now a superstar for the Detroit Tigers and a resident of Augusta. Wilson witnessed Cobb's stage debut in the play *The College Widow*.[411]

The annual rhythms of church life—acclaimed preaching, professional worship music, inspiring Sunday School classes, recreational activities, service clubs, civic clubs, social gatherings, WMS, missions emphases, revivals, special concerts, holiday observances, participation in denominational meetings, periodical joint services with other Protestant churches (sometimes at Lake View Park on Lake Olmstead), and the like—marked the early years of the century's second decade, with some notable exceptions.[412]

In June 1911 men were encouraged to attend worship services minus hats and coats, while in October a number of persons "were painfully stung when they climbed to the cupola on top of the First Baptist church to make repairs to the roofs. Thousands of yellow jackets had made their home in the belfry and they resented" the human interlopers. Of a much greater pain were the deaths of deacons J. C. Shecut in December 1911 and A. Smith Irvine in January 1913. The April 1912 sinking of the ship *Titanic* occasioned a "special memorial service" for the victims, including a "powerful sermon" by Jones "upon the *Titanic* disaster." Among *Titanic* victims was Major Archibald W. Butt, Augusta native and a presidential aid to both Roosevelt and Taft. In 1914 the 15th Street Archibald W. Butt Memorial Bridge was named in his honor. Of congregational relevance was the official recording of the church's deed in 1916, an oversight during the purchase of the church lot nearly 100 years earlier.[413]

A time of joy immediately preceded Christmas 1912 in the unveiling of memorial church windows dedicated to the late James T. Bothwell and Mary D' Antignac Walker. One month later Jones brought the church's "male members together for an informal discussion of church work" at the Bon Air, an "enjoyable evening" including a banquet attended by some fifty persons. Many of the same men likely were present for an April 1913 sermon by Jones lauding the Order of Commercial Travelers, a social and fraternal organization "for commercial travelers, city salesmen, and merchandise brokers." On the other hand, for wives "Home Making" received special attention in a series of 1913 sermons of the same title preached by Jones. In March of the same year men, women, and children alike enjoyed a presentation by Faddoul Moghabghab, a Lebanese pastor and author of *The Shepherd Song on the Hills of Lebanon: The Twenty-Third Psalm Illustrated and Explained.*[414]

Befitting a prosperous city, the activities of the church reflected a congregation of considerable wealth, a large portion invested in missions work in the year 1913 through the funding of three of the city's Chinese Christians as missionaries to Ping Tu, China. In December of the same year the congregation joined Baptists nationwide in observing the 100th anniversary of "the arrival in India of Adoniram Judson and his wife, Ann Hasseltine Judson, the first Baptist missionaries, and the first American missionaries sent to foreign lands." Around this time some local Chinese women began attending the church's Chinese Sunday

School class, previously the domain of male students only. During the decade the Sunday School was credited with helping Chinese escape persecution, along with fostering in the public eye a more positive perception of the local Chinese community.[415]

As had his predecessors, pastor Ashby Jones frequently traveled northward during his pastoral tenure at First Baptist. Among many notable engagements, in May 1913 he preached the commencement sermon at Crozer Theological Seminary in Philadelphia.[416]

Locally, at a time when periodical flooding of the Savannah River ranked among the top concerns of city leaders, the First Baptist pastor in a September 14, 1913 sermon voiced support for a levee to prevent future flooding. Asserting the taming of the river as necessary for the progress of the city, he spoke of the project as God's calling to Augusta's men. Businessman and church member Albert J. Twiggs, who would soon win the contract to build the levee, likely sat in the pews that day.[417]

Whereas city leaders largely expressed agreement regarding the need of a levee, upon some other matters Augustans offered differing opinions. In a May 3, 1914 sermon titled "The Church and the State," Jones waded into the debate over the issue of holidays in public schools. True to his Baptist heritage, the pastor of the city's leading Baptist church declared that public schools, as state institutions, had "no right to designate a religious holiday."[418] Two years later he preached another religious freedom sermon. Titled "The States and Religious Institutions," the discourse criticized a proposed state legislative bill that would have allowed discrimination against Roman Catholics.[419]

While men yet commanded sole possession of leadership positions in church and city, the growing women's suffrage movement spilled over into the life of First Baptist in November 1913. Addressing the controversial subject in a formal debate, the congregation's newly-formed Young People's Club led the way forward, building upon the advocacy work of Woman's Missionary Union.[420]

Controversial, too, became the war waging in Europe and eventually known as the Great War. Some seven months following the beginning of localized conflicts in Europe, Ashby Jones, at the suggestion of the national Church Peace Union, preached a sermon in February 1915 "celebrating the 100 years of peace between the English-speaking nations." Remaining vestiges of a once-firm, broad Protestant under-standing of an already-advancing millennium of peace on earth framed the context of the Peace Union and Jones' sermon. Ironically, the European conflict escalated that very month as German submarines plied British waters. In June the Baptist pastor specifically addressed the developing events in Europe and "the issue which has arisen between Germany and the United States," a reference to the sinking of the *Lusitania*, of which Jones condemned.[421]

The attention of Augustans turned to their own troubles when a raging fire consumed almost two square miles of downtown on March 22 and 23, 1916. Racing to Augusta by train, firemen from Waynesboro, Atlanta, Macon, Savannah, Columbia, Charleston, and Greenville could not prevent the massive blaze from destroying some 746 buildings and leaving homeless about 3,000 citizens. First Baptist escaped damage, but church records from the past two decades, stored apart from church buildings, were consumed in the fire.[422]

War, however, remained on the front burner. A June 25, 1916 sermon by Jones returned to the theme of war in focusing on "what lessons we have learned from the great European conflict now being waged" and the realization of "the absolute dependence and interdependence of indi-viduals and nations upon each other." The following December Jones preached on the topic of "A Nation at War in a World of War: Have We a Right to be Thankful?"[423]

The globally-spreading war posed challenges for America's govern-ment, communities, and congregations. A unified response eluded politi-cians. President Woodrow Wilson in 1915 launched a "preparedness" defensive movement to build up U.S. naval and land forces, a step many Americans perceived as an indication of Washington's plans to join the war effort. Many common folk interpreted the military buildup and looming declaration of war as driven by corporate interests using fear tactics to exploit husbands, fathers, and sons for commercial profit. The-ologically, many clergy and churches, struggling to reconcile a gospel of peace with the world's first global warfare, yet remained averse to send-ing American forces into foreign trenches. For or against, Americans, including the 747 members of First Baptist Church Augusta, increasingly realized the inevitability of war.[424]

From the pulpit to a full house, Jones on April 1, 1917 preached a sermon titled "Defending the Flag," using Mark 8:36 and Psalm 37:5-6 as his text. Voicing civic loyalties, he called the Stars and Stripes the "great symbol of brotherhood" and extolled patriotism and the sacredness of sacrifice for country. Brushing aside his earlier peace sentiments, the "modern pacifist" Jones dismissed as "the grossest and crudest materialist" focused on self-advancement rather than national good. The Red Cross, meanwhile, prepared to send medical assistance to Europe for the relief of the wounded on both sides of the great conflict. On April 6, 1917, the day that the U.S. declared war on Germany, the *Augusta Chronicle* announced a meeting of the Red Cross to be hosted by First Baptist. The community gathering of April 11 featured former President William Howard Taft, seasonal Augustan and chairman of the national Red Cross Central Committee.[425]

Two weeks after Taft's speech First Baptist hosted a "Red Cross Rally," another of many wartime Red Cross events held at the church. In a July 8 sermon Ashby argued that Wilson's rationale for fighting the war for the "rights of others" reflected the lone Christian justification for war, while Georgia Governor Thomas Hardwick's opposition to war represented a "political interpretation" that dampened the "enthusiasm of our boys preparing to go to France." Later Jones, from the pulpit of the Bethel African American Episcopal Church (on the corner of Campbell and D'Antignac streets) "for the benefit of colored Red Cross work," presented a "grand lecture" acknowledging "the Negro" as "a Citizen of the United States," albeit with limited rights.[426]

In the midst of cheerleading for the war, Ashby Jones in August 1917 suddenly resigned from the pastorate of First Baptist Augusta, having recently accepted a call to pastor Atlanta's Ponce de Leon Avenue Baptist congregation.[427] Jones' resignation and subsequent departure came as soldiers arrived at the city's Camp Hancock, a National Guard mobilization and training camp named after Winfield Scott Hancock, the late United States officer who at the Battle of Gettysburg repulsed Pickett's Charge, the pivotal Confederate offensive that, if successful, could have changed the course of the Civil War.[428]

The church responded to the presence of Camp Hancock by opening a "reading and writing room" for soldiers. "Night after night," as recounted by church member and historian Isabella Jordan, the room "was crowded with splendid khaki-clad men from Pennsylvania, while men and women of the church moved among them with cheerful smiles and sympathetic words, serving refreshments and in varied little ministries making these boys feel that they were indeed our boys."[429]

Those last words written by Jordan bore special significance. Hancock, a bane of the Confederate States, had been a Pennsylvanian. The scene in the reading room served as a national snapshot of how the Great War brought together soldiers from the North and the South five decades following the Civil War. The Northerners had become "indeed our boys." At the same time, many young men and women of the church enrolled in the Army or Navy and prepared for deployment to Europe. Within a city long welcoming of Northern businessmen and tourists and a congregation harboring a heritage of pulpits with Northern connections, remaining regional distinctions faded away for a common cause under the flag of the United States of America.[430]

Conflict, Challenges, and Celebration

Disappointed at Ashby Jones' leaving, the First Baptist congregation nonetheless wasted little time in acquiring his replacement. Following a suggestion by Jones, the church by the first of October called Dr. William Vines of Charlotte, North Carolina. While a Southerner by birth (Tennessee), Vines' résumé, like that of so many previous Augusta pastors, included education and pastorates both South and North. The latter included a degree from the University of Chicago (founded by seasonal Augustan John D. Rockefeller) and a pastorate in Brooklyn, New York. His theological training did not include Southern Baptist institutions, and Augusta represented his furthest venture southward to date.[431]

Vines assumed the Augusta pulpit as hundreds of the city's men and women trained to fight in or otherwise support the war. Some eighty-five men and women from First Baptist eventually served, whether abroad or at home, between 1917 and the conclusion of the conflict in June 1919 at the signing of the Treaty of Versailles. Four families—the Gary, Winges, Willis, and Wilson families—each sent three sons into military service.

No members of the church are known to have lost their lives in the war.[432]

During the somber and anxiety-filled months of war, life at First Baptist Augusta consisted of a mixture of regular church activities supplemented by ministries to soldiers and participation—especially by members of the Woman's Missionary Society—in Red Cross, Salvation Army, and Syrian and Belgian refugee relief efforts. Many of the young girls of the church joined the Patriotic League, a wartime service organization fostering loyalty and service to community and country, of which First Baptist hosted local meetings. In February 1918 the congregation's Sunday School teachers presented a "service flag" to the church in honor of members serving in the military, while the WMS held a day of prayer in April for soldiers and the war. Throughout the spring and summer the church hosted a number of special services for soldiers, in addition to hosting many civic and patriotic functions throughout the war years. The general excitement of the war in 1917 bled over into the heart of church life, expressed in an increase in Sunday School attendance during the year.[433]

Meanwhile, church secretary Annie Shumate resigned her church position to become secretary of the Soldier's Welfare Committee. The departure of Shumate led the congregation, upon the suggestion of Vines, to establish a new position, that of pastor's assistant.[434] Considered a professional post rather than clerical, the church by moving in this new direction reflected the growing importance given to formal religious education by large, urban Baptist congregations.

To fill the pastor's assistant position, First Baptist turned to the recently-formed Baptist Institute for Christian Workers. Located in Philadelphia, the school served as a training ground for men and women interested in religious education, whether in a local church or organizational setting. The church selected young graduate Dorothy Lehman. Arriving in Augusta in June 1918, she quickly "won all hearts," according to Isabella Jordan. "Possessed of an unusual winsomeness, indefatigable energy, and the truest consecration of her high calling," Lehman worked with "Sunday School, BYPU, Sunbeams, and every other department of church life." She later married George Sumerau, future chair of the board of deacons, and remained a member of First Baptist for many decades.[435]

Lehman's war-era service on the church's staff represented a movement away from volunteers serving in certain leadership capacities and in favor of a broader, more robust ministerial staff. Having thus embarked in this new direction, the church staff would only grow in size and scope over time.

The latter months of 1918 proved especially challenging. A raging influenza epidemic swept throughout the city and the world, shutting down local public gathering places in October and much of November. Absent worship services, many church members ministered to the community through volunteer work with the Red Cross and at the emergency hospital at Camp Hancock. By late November the clouds of war cleared following the signing of armistices and the cessation of fighting, while the local lifting of health bans brought a return of worship services to Augusta's churches. Simultaneously, however, William Vines resigned to assume the pastorate of the First Baptist Church of Norfolk, Virginia.[436]

Following a series of guest speakers in early 1919, in July the congregation upon the suggestion of former minister Ashby Jones called as pastor Dr. Edward L. Grace, a little-known minister and recent chaplain with American forces in France and Germany. Grace arrived as Augusta welcomed returning veterans with a celebratory gala. At this time church membership stood at 867, new members joined the church monthly, and church life included a robust WMS and social services ministries, the latter a result, to no small degree, of wartime opportunities.[437]

Grace's arrival coincided with a high degree of post-war patriotism in the nation and locally. America's military might had saved the world. The nation's ideals of freedom and democracy, long a beacon of light from afar, now shone brightly across the globe. Coupled with his wartime service in Europe and the prominence of the city's leading Baptist pulpit, the pastor's voice carried much weight in Augusta. Grace, speaking at a community event, advocated for patriotism and "Americanization." It is "our duty," he insisted, "to make a distinctly American atmosphere everywhere." Many first- and second-generation immigrants and Negroes remained illiterate and ignorant of "American ideals," needful of education and a second chance. Infrastructure, too, needed transformation. "To make people love America, we must make America loveable," he declared, calling for the beautification of the nation's cities, highways, and institutions. Weeks later on November 9, 1919 "unusually large congregations" celebrated Armistice Day, taking place two days thereafter.[438]

While Grace advocated for an ascendant America, sadness descended upon the congregation with the passing of former pastor and prominent Southern Baptist leader Lansing Burrows, architect of the church's rise to greater prominence in the late nineteenth century. The congregation published a lengthy "Memoriam" in "grateful and loving memory" of Burrows' life and ministry of seventeen years leading First Baptist. Having spent much of his career helping the Southern Baptist Convention become more efficient and prosperous, Burrows would have been pleased that at the time of his passing the First Baptist Augusta congregation voted to support the denomination's newly-formed "75 Million Campaign" effort to raise funds for all of the missions and ministries of the SBC. Although the campaign ultimately fell short of its financial goals, the effort in 1925 birthed the Cooperative Program, the SBC's unified funding vehicle that remains to the present day.[439]

In an American atmosphere celebratory of freedom and democracy, the Southern Baptist Convention moved onto the national stage to a greater degree than ever following the conclusion of the Great War. In addition to the boldness of the 75 million campaign, the SBC publicly and effectively advocated for freedom of conscience and religious liberty for all, trumpeting to the world the three-century Baptist heritage of freedom. Prominent Southern Baptist pastor Dr. George W. Truett of the First Baptist Church of Dallas served as a leading spokesperson for Baptist freedom principles. In September 1919 Truett spoke at First Baptist Augusta. In May 1920 a large delegation of men and women attending the annual SBC gathering in Washington, D.C., heard Truett deliver his most famous address, one of the most celebrated Baptist speeches of the century. From the steps of the nation's Capitol, Truett spoke of Baptists' historical commitment to "freedom of conscience" and "absolute religious liberty" for all, of Baptist ecclesiology as "pure democracy," of the need for more Christian schools to further the spread of Christian principles, and in support of national Prohibition (enacted earlier that year). In short, America's victory in the war validated the freedom ideals of Baptists. From Augusta, Georgia to Washington, D.C., Baptists represented the best of America. The 1920 election of Warren G. Harding as president of the United States, the first Baptist to achieve the nation's highest office, added an exclamation point to the ascendancy of the once persecuted sect.[440]

Back in Augusta, the freedom-loving and growing congregation of Baptists on Greene and 8th (formerly Jackson) streets experienced exciting transitions. Enthusiastic response to the 75 million SBC campaign led to creation of a financial board, while Sunday School expanded and in 1920 the church staff enlarged yet again with the addition of a "Director of Educational Work," Furman graduate Eric W. Hardy (later president of the Junior College of Augusta). The same year the church purchased two adjacent lots (814 and 816 Greene Street, the homes soon renovated for classrooms) and elected five new deacons: James G. Belding, Charles G. Houston, T. D. Jones, O. B. Stoughton, and Marion S. Symms (also Sunday School superintendent). Membership growth accompanied the expansion of staffing and facilities, reaching the 1,000 mark in March 1921.[441]

Another transition corrected an old oversight when the church voted to legally change the name of the congregation from "Trustees of the Baptist Society in the City of Augusta and County of Richmond" (adopted at the time of the congregation's founding in 1817) to "First Baptist Church of Augusta."[442] The formalization of the church's name paved the way for the congregation's 100th anniversary celebration of May 8-11, 1921, corresponding with the May 1821 dedication of the church's first building. Former pastors William W. Landrum, Sparks Melton, and Ashby Jones joined Mercer University president Rufus W. Weaver on the program. A portrait of William T. Brantly, given to the church by his granddaughter Louise Brantly Morehead, was unveiled. T. Harry Garrett gave a presentation titled "History of the First Baptist Church." The celebratory capstone was the publication of Isabella Jordan's book, *A Century of Service, First Baptist Church, Augusta, Georgia*, a volume dedicated to "The Women of This Church."[443]

Outsiders in 1821, Southern Baptists South-wide and locally by 1921 were consummate insiders. With religious dominance came temptations foreign to Baptists past, however. In his 1920 Washington, D.C.

speech George W. Truett had focused on the need for Christian education in America, while careful not to equate religious instruction with public schools. From the First Baptist pulpit Ashby Jones earlier shared the same sentiments. Yet in a February 1921 address Edward L. Grace spoke *for* religious instruction in public schools, indicating his belief that it would soon transpire.[444]

While Grace's post-war sermon favoring the intertwining of religion and public schools reflected shifting winds in Baptist life of the South, Augusta, too, experienced transitions. The completion of a twelve-mile levee in 1919 afforded the city adequate protection against the flood-prone Savannah River. Many Augustans welcomed the 1920 creation of the League of Nations, the first international organization devoted to world peace. Following the enactment of the Nineteenth Amendment to the United States Constitution granting women's suffrage, in 1921 women voted in a city election for the first time and the medical college enrolled its first woman student. The same year Charles T. Walker, pastor of Tabernacle Baptist Church, passed away. Rockefeller from his summer home in New York paid homage to Walker. James C. C. Black, representing both the city of Augusta and First Baptist, preached Walker's eulogy before a biracial audience including the mayor and city council.[445]

Thus for both church and city, the early post-war years witnessed, on multiple levels, the dawning of a new era. Following a brief national recession in 1920-21, America's economy quickly expanded and further fueled post-war patriotism. Emerging progress in the spread of faith, peace, freedom, prosperity, and human rights generated excitement, stirring hopes near and far.

The path ahead looked promising.

7

An Upward Trajectory in Unsettled Times

Post-war America reveled in amazement at the magical world unfolding before its eyes and ears.

Automobiles, now commonplace and allowing travel with much greater ease, spurred business profits, entertainment options, and church attendance alike. In the skies, airplanes mesmerized the earthbound. A flying circus in the summer of 1922 drew some 50,000 Augustans who watched in horrified joy as a stuntman changed planes midair. The same year a demonstration of radio technology left citizens marveling over invisible waves traveling through the air that somehow produced sound. On a far more practical and earthy level, agricultural technology solved the problem of boll weevils, the bane of cotton growers. On the ground and in the air alike, technology not only amazed, but also transformed daily patterns of life and, for some, ushered in a decade of prosperity.

Cheer and money alike arrived in the January 1924 opening of the new Bon Air Hotel as a Vanderbilt property, the replacement of the original structure responsible, four decades earlier, for boosting Augusta's tourism industry. In a unique and exciting confluence of events in March, the world's greatest baseball player and the most prominent Baptist returned to Augusta in grand fashion. Ty Cobb came home to highlight a spring training game between his Detroit Tigers and the Toronto Maple Leafs, a minor league team. Mr. and Mrs. Warren Harding visited Augusta, she to watch the game, and he to play golf at the Bon Air Country Club. Crowds greeted Harding at a city banquet at the Partridge Inn. Few likely knew the president was a Baptist. Perhaps this was for the best, as problems plagued his administration.

Despite Harding's shortcomings, economic prosperity washed across Augusta and the nation, the boom times spurring the city forward. Large-scale land speculation in Augusta made news in the *New York Times*. New hotels sprang up, civic groups raised large amounts of money to run national ad campaigns promoting Augusta, the city's first woman lawyer opened shop, the local golf scene expanded with the opening of Forest Hills Golf Club in 1926, air service arrived via Daniel Field in 1927, a new baseball stadium was built, and "talking" movies arrived. Alongside the hive of activity enabled by the free flow of money, anti-Catholic fervor in Augusta politics subsided. Racial inequality and injustices, however, remained unabated.[446]

On balance, the times were great for the Baptists at the corner of Greene and 8th.

Visions Local, National, and Global

What a difference a century had made. Some 100 years of shaping, molding, and advancing congruent to broader changes in knowledge, technology, culture, and society produced a 1920s church with general contours that would largely span another hundred years.

Weekly services took place on Sunday mornings, Sunday evenings, and Wednesday nights. Thoughtful, informed sermons characterized the pulpit. Some of the city's best musicians led Sunday worship and special music events. Sunday School otherwise highlighted Sunday mornings, and Baptist Young People's Union Sunday evenings. Reflecting a motto of "A Church with a Welcome for You," various and robust programs provided for the spiritual needs of persons of all ages, from kindergarteners to senior citizens. The Woman's Auxiliary, a large social, prayer, and fellowship organization, hosted frequent programs. Plentiful recreational opportunities (foremost the fielding of a team in a local Sunday School basketball league) and entertainment events dotted the church calendar. Easter, Mother's Day, Independence Day, Halloween, Thanksgiving, and Christmas occasioned special services and activities, including pageants and concerts during Easter and Christmas seasons. Weddings counted as joyous occasions, funerals as sad yet often celebratory events. Revivals remained a special time of year, often netting new members. Evangelistic emphases and neighborhood prayer meetings also attracted newcomers. Missions activity included ministries to impoverished locals, offerings for home and foreign missions, and occasional presentations from visiting foreign missionaries.

Congregational social and service clubs, typically gender-specific, provided fellowship, fostered friendships, and bound together city and church. Noonday lunch and prayer meetings at the church became commonplace. Civic organizations such as Rotary Club, Boy Scouts, (Woman's) Federated Clubs, and Young Men's Christian Association, along with school commencements, utilized church facilities and intersected the religious and civic life of Augusta. Ministers and leading lay persons participated in denominational life at the associational, state, and national levels, with First Baptist periodically hosting associational and state Baptist gatherings, including annual statewide Sunday School conventions, the latter attended by more than a thousand persons. Joint gatherings with other downtown churches took place from time to time. Unlike in the nineteenth century, discipline cases were rare. A pattern of pastors spending much of the summer on vacation and preaching tours gave way to one-month pastoral leaves. During Edward L. Grace's absences, deacons James C. C. Black, Enoch C. Callaway, and John Phinizy often filled the pulpit, while former pastors Ashby Jones, William M. Vines, and Sparks W. Melton returned to Augusta from time to time to preach on Sunday mornings or evenings.[447]

A significant part of church life in the twenties, worship, alongside the pulpit, served as the most regular and visible manifestation of the congregation's faith. Taking seriously the ministry of worship, First Baptist invested heavily in offering a first-class experience. In practical terms, this meant employing quality worship leaders and obtaining suitable equipment with which to work. R. A. Irvine provided "very efficient and faithful service" as organist through the teens and into the early twenties.[448]

Central to the church's life were women. "Empowered" described the status of American white women in the third decade of the century, a characterization apt, with certain qualifications, of the women of Southern Baptist congregations. Church and city social events, as well as local and national missions activities, remained central to the female members of First Baptist, while newer roles rose in prominence and importance. Locally, although not allowed to serve as ordained ministers, Southern Baptist women seized upon other opportunities afforded by women's suffrage. Within the larger political and social world they fervently joined the conversation as guardians of Christian morality, a traditional woman's role in Southern evangelical circles now expanded and enlarged by suffrage.

Missionary advocacy and support took center stage in the 1922 appointment of Lucy Wright as a Southern Baptist foreign missionary, a first for the congregation. A special service in honor of Wright included the presentation of a Bible from the pastor and deacons and an address from Wright regarding her "hopes and ambitions" as a missionary. The ladies of the church also hosted a party for Wright. Not long after she sailed to China, the church created a new young people's group: the Lucy Wright Baptist Young People's Union (BYPU). Wright's commitment to foreign missions proved exemplary. The pride of First Baptist Augusta and complementing the church's local Chinese Sunday School ministry, for the next forty-two years Lucy Wright served in China as a medical missionary, first as a nurse and then as superintendent of Warren Memorial Hospital in Hwangshaien, Shantung Province. During her four decades on the missionary field, Wright maintained regular correspondence with her home church.[449]

The heightened prominence of woman's work in society and culture evidenced itself in the 1923 annual meeting of the Hephzibah Baptist Association, hosted by First Baptist. Eight members of First Baptist attended the gathering as delegates: Dr. and Mrs. Edward L. Grace, John Phinizy, Charles G. Houston, C. D. Johnston, Dorothy Sumerau, Mrs. W. A. Adkins, and W. H. Sturman. John Phinizy moderated the gathering of September 27-29 that highlighted the remarkable achievements of Baptist women. The Report on Women's Work declared that "The fundamentals of the Woman's Missionary Union are individual and united prayer, Bible study, soul winning, enlistment, mission, study, organized personal service, systematic and proportionate giving." But there was more. Unleashed by women's suffrage, Baptist women sought to make a difference in the city, state, and nation. Referring to present conditions in America as "this day of unrest," the report addressed pressing national issues. "The women of the Mission Union declare themselves on the side of all forces for righteousness, in the world; mission fundamentals; patriotism, national Prohibition, Sabbath observance, sacredness of the home, maintenance of the family altar, high womanly ideals of speech, dress and children; public health, Christian education and Christian Americanization."[450] This language maintained womanly themes while positioning Baptist women as actors in men's spheres of politics, civic morality, and patriotism. The framing of "Sabbath observance" as a civic duty, rather than individual voluntarism, stretched Baptists' traditional commitment to church-state separation, a heritage fraying in a nation increasingly celebratory of the cultural and social dominance of white Protestants.

More reports followed, the central missives fleshing out activities to which the women of First Baptist felt strongly committed. The Report on Missions spoke hopefully of the opportunities presented by a post-war world, and boastfully of the accomplishments of Southern Baptist missionaries. "The world war produced a mental attitude and soul hunger throughout the entire world, which has proved peculiarly receptive to our Baptist message," associational delegates affirmed. Southern Baptists "stand on the fringe of their great Foreign Missionary task. We have touched more nations at more points than any other denomination and have thus assumed greater responsibilities . . ."[451]

Alongside thinly-veiled Christian nationalism and openly-voiced missions triumphalism, the Report on the State of Religion and Temperance steered Baptists' attention to an evil that posed challenges both to national righteousness and global evangelism: alcohol. While rejoicing that Prohibition had "forced a great many people to become temperate in the consumption of liquor" and done "a great deal toward making our country the greatest nation on earth," the report lamented that "the law itself can do nothing without the moral support of the people. And we are not supporting it. The blackest crime against humanity of which the church of God is guilty, is its indifference regarding the monster evil which indifference has given license to it, and caused its boldness to defy the law, and to become a menace to the peace and happiness of our people by sending this vile poison into communities over the protest of its best citizens." Illegal liquor traffic produced "drunkenness, poverty, corruption, sickness, wounds, disease, rape, dishonesty, perjury, domestic infelicity, national degradation, sin, death and damnation." But victory was near. "Marvelous progress has been made, the enemy is routed and on the run. Let each of us throw his full strength into the charge, and when final and complete victory comes as it will, we can join in the shout [of] victory and deliverance."[452]

The drumbeat of Prohibition continued in ensuing years. A "preacher's meeting" held at First Baptist in 1925 advocated for "a local survey of prohibition conditions in and around" the city. Two years later, a lecture at the church by nationally-renowned Prohibition advocate "Pussyfoot" Johnson generated widespread approval. A Prohibition convention held at First Baptist in 1928 attracted more than 1,000 persons.[453]

Prohibition, however, had a dark underbelly: race control. In practice, the anti-alcohol crusade, especially in the South, provided an opportunity for whites to assert further control over already marginalized African Americans. James Clay understood only too well Augusta's racial dynamics. For years he sat daily in front of the First Baptist Church, "under the bla[z]ing summer sun and on the coldest days of winter," a "pathetic" but "familiar figure to all" who passed by. Like other African Americans, he was not allowed to attend white church services, a reality he readily accepted. A blind beggar, he patiently, respectfully, and silently solicited money amidst white prosperity.

Prior to having lost his sight, Clay worked as a cook at the country club, one of the better jobs to which the city's blacks could aspire. Now in his beggarly state, white citizens considered him "a wonderful example of patience; he was never heard to murmur or complain" about his physical condition or abject poverty, and "an example to many in his gratitude for the least word of kindness and his appreciation of everything that was done to help him." For his proper subservience and deference, upon his death on November 21, 1924, James Clay was hailed by a newspaper writer as "one of the best known colored men in Augusta."[454]

Southern Baptist church missionary and advocacy efforts rarely extended in any significant degree to minorites in America. First Baptist Augusta had long done more than most congregations in establishing and growing a vibrant Chinese ministry and occasionally lending a helping hand to black citizens. Many years would pass, however, before some denominational leaders would rediscover that Christ's teachings of human equality applied to the very least of persons in their midst.

Concerns, Controversies, and Celebrations

Perhaps inspired by the missions and ministry advocacy of the women of the church and association, Edward L. Grace in late 1923 and early 1924 preached a sermon series on "Women of the Old Testament." Women of the congregation remained involved in local advocacy ministries and clubs and supported the work of city social workers, whom they periodically recognized with receptions. Many engaged in social and educational pursuits. During the second half of the twenties, for example, the Woman's Missionary Society (WMS) of First Baptist hosted literary meetings with regularity.[455]

Civic and social concerns also found a voice in the pulpit of First Baptist and beyond in the person of Edward L. Grace, who followed his early twentieth-century predecessors in periodically delving into issues apart from church matters. A sermon in 1923 addressed "Law Enforcement," an area of ongoing tension in the racially divided city. The same year Grace delivered an address at the Walker Baptist Institute, while from the First Baptist pulpit in 1924 he preached a sermon on war.[456]

In no small part due to civil, moral, and social concerns throughout America, and against the backdrop of an ascendant fundamentalist movement ardently opposed to scientific thought that challenged traditional Christian beliefs, the early part of the decade witnessed growing temptations to bond together church and state. Since the late nineteenth century, critical, scientific studies of the Bible that discounted biblical literalism, alongside evolutionary science that denied the validity of biblical creation interpretations based on a twenty-four-hour rendering of the "days" of creation, had fostered a growing backlash by a new grouping of American Christians who referred to themselves as "fundamentalists." Making inroads into Baptist life North and South, fundamentalists by the 1920s sought to seize control of the Southern Baptist Convention (SBC). Evolution, controversial within and without Christianity, provided a public platform for fundamentalists. Framing evolution as irreligious and anti-American, Baptist fundamentalists opposed the scientific theory in denomination and nation.[457]

Southern Baptist leaders, meanwhile, remained moderately conservative and generally voiced a qualified acceptance of evolutionary thought as scientific truth that offered no contradiction to the truthfulness of the Bible. Edgar Young Mullins, president of the Southern Baptist Theological Seminary (1899-1928) and Southern Baptist Convention (1921-1924), represented this middle ground and led efforts to resist a fundamentalist takeover of the SBC.[458]

The controversy escalated as the Southern Baptist Convention convened in 1924 in Atlanta. Edward L. Grace, John Phinizy, and Isabella Jordan represented First Baptist Augusta at the gathering, Jordan the guest of Governor and Mrs. Clifford Walker. Mullins, author of an essay titled "A Safe Position for Baptists on Science and Religion or Evolution," sought to rally Southern Baptists to a moderate position. Alongside the conference proceedings, George W. Truett, speaking from Atlanta and in the larger context of calls by some to outlaw the teaching of evolution in public schools for religious reasons, called any move towards the union of church and state "spiritual adultery."[459]

Grace returned to the pulpit of First Augusta with much to ponder. Reflecting the national conversation about evolution, biblical creation, and public schools, the fall months witnessed a statewide controversy among Southern Baptists of Georgia in the October 1924 forced resignation of Mercer University biology professor Dr. Henry L. Fox. A proponent of evolution, Fox also raised the ire of Mercer's board of trustees and leaders of the Georgia Baptist Convention by embracing a non-literal interpretation of the Bible, allegedly denying the deity of Christ, inspiration of scripture, and Jesus' virgin birth. In a December sermon Grace declared to his Augusta congregation that the professor's "religious thinking had no temple," that is, it resided outside the purview of Christianity in placing human reasoning above the Bible. Seemingly speaking to the larger implications of evolutionary science, Grace insinuated that America needed to "put God into our national life."[460]

Generating national headlines, the evolution controversy reached new heights when in early 1925 the Tennessee legislature passed the Butler Act, a law prohibiting the state's public school teachers, including university professors, from teaching "any theory that denies the Story of the Divine Creation of man as taught in the Bible, and to teach instead that man has descended from a lower order of animals."[461] Fundamentalist Baptists cheered, overlooking the breach of church-state separation.

Shortly thereafter the SBC gathered for its annual conference in Memphis from May 13-17. Edward L. Grace attended, representing First Baptist Augusta. There he witnessed a minority voting bloc of fundamentalists determined to force the convention to denounce perceived biblical liberalism and openness to scientific evolution. Southern Baptist leaders, led by Mullins and seeking to preserve peace within the denomination, reached to the past in Baptist history and suggested that the body adopt a confession of faith. Essentially a summary of what a given group of Baptists generally believe at a given point in time, a confession in Baptist life neither annulled individual freedom of conscience nor violated local church autonomy. Voluntary faith statements, however, had at times in Baptist history served the purpose of succinctly summarizing common tenets of various Baptist groups. The confession that emerged and was adopted at the 1925 convention served as a revision and update of the 1833 New Hampshire Baptist Confession, a statement of beliefs commonly but not universally utilized in Baptist life in America. The 1925 "Baptist Faith and Message" statement spoke of the Bible as authoritative, yet avoided any particular interpretation, embraced a moderate view of the social gospel and, despite a failed effort by fundamentalists otherwise, remained silent on the issue of evolution. Collectively, the confession positioned the SBC as a moderately conservative organization in which fundamentalists, if they so wished, were welcome. Despite conciliatory efforts, many fundamentalists soon voluntarily left the convention and formed various independent Baptist organizations.[462]

Days following the Baptist gathering, John T. Scopes, a Dayton, Tennessee high school teacher, challenged the Butler Act and on May 25, 1925 was indicted for teaching evolution. The June trial in Dayton drew scores of reporters from near and far and mesmerized the nation. Well-known lawyers William Jennings Bryan (prosecuting) and Clarence Darrow (defending) squared off, effectively putting on trial a literal reading of the biblical creation account. Eight days of trial proceedings later, the jury found Scopes guilty and levied a small fine. Darrow appealed to the Tennessee Supreme Court, which ruled against him, including a denial that the Butler Act violated the separation of church and state. The same court, however, refused to prosecute Scopes, closing the saga by effectively deeming the Butler Act irrelevant. In addition, the sensational national coverage of the trial depicted fundamentalists as backward and comical, contributing to a retreat, on the part of fundamentalists, from the public eye. Even so, for the next three decades a number of state anti-evolution laws remained in effect, and school textbook publishers generally avoided the inclusion of evolutionary science.[463]

Many members of First Baptist Augusta followed the proceedings of the Scopes saga. Opinions diverged. Mere weeks after the trial, deacon Enoch C. Callaway, preaching in a sister Baptist church, offered his thoughts in a "highly instructive and most edifying discourse on science and religion." Callaway voiced his opinion concerning human evolution, declaring that:

> I cannot think that Moses' account was tradition merely. It was too true. People meet me and talk to me about this question of evolution, of whether man has descended from a lower order of animals. It is perfectly absurd. I believe in science and, to a certain extent, I believe in evolution. The Bible says that God created man in His own image. That does not mean, however, that God has a body and hands and feet like a man has. But [it] means that God put into man His Own Spirit and the fact that man had breathed into him the Spirit of God makes him a child of God. Moreover, man is the only one of all the animals that God created in His own image. He did not thus create the cow, the dog, or the horse. The fact that man had breathed into him the Spirit of God differentiates him from all the other animals.[464]

A number of local Baptists reacted much differently. The Augusta Fundamentalist League formed in the summer of 1925 for the purpose of opposing evolution, claiming among its members many local Baptist churches and ministers, but neither First Baptist nor Edward L. Grace.[465]

While the evolution and attendant fundamentalist controversies generated much discussion in Baptist life concerning the nature of biblical inspiration and truth, First Baptist Augusta remained committed to the broad concept of scriptural authority. A. T. Robertson, New Testament scholar from the Southern Baptist Theological Seminary and proponent of interpreting the Bible literally, addressed the congregation in July 1925. On October 28 of the same year the church hosted a "celebration of the 400th anniversary of the translation of the Bible into the English language."[466]

A celebration of another kind took place in January 1926 as the congregation remembered with affection former pastor and recently-deceased William W. Landrum. Deacon James C. C. Black prepared "a most beautiful tribute" in memory of Landrum in a special memorial service. More tragic was the death of young Joseph Harrison Thomas, age seventeen, who died from electrocution, one of many deaths in the early decades of the century caused by widespread faulty electrical wiring.[467]

One of the stranger incidents in the church's history took place on July 2, 1926 when an upset wife—not a member of First Baptist—killed her husband in front of the church. The First Baptist janitor testified in court. A jury determined that Mrs. Lillian Lindley McKie "shot her husband to death on the 800 block of Greene Street, while he sat in his automobile, and it was proven that she sat in the door [of the church] for more than an hour, where she could see her husband, on the opposite side of the thoroughfare, and that she killed him shortly after he appeared and got under the steering wheel of his machine. No eye-witnesses to the actual shooting were produced, all witnesses testifying that they saw the defendant immediately before or after the shooting." She was sentenced to death.[468]

Strange happenings aside, Edward L. Grace, having steered his congregation through the heat of the fundamentalist controversy, announced his resignation from the pulpit on Sunday morning September 25, 1927. In a special called business session his resignation letter was read and accepted, and his eight years of leadership praised as a time of great growth. Following several weeks of goodbyes, at the end of October the Grace family moved to a new pastorate in Richmond, Virginia.[469]

With or without a pastor, First Baptist maintained an imposing presence in the city thanks to prominent, forward-thinking members. Church deacon and mayor of Augusta at the time of Grace's resignation, Raleigh H. Daniel, recognized the potential of nascent air travel. In an era of optimism, his vision exceeded that of many of his fellow citizens. Defying naysayers, he led the way in acquiring a 300-acre field for development of an airport. A formal dedication and plaque marked the October 28, 1927 opening of Daniel Field. The Augusta yearbook of 1928

noted, "Purchase of the landing field will give Augusta all facilities needed to make it one of the leading airports in the Southeast."[470]

While Daniel led the city, fellow deacon Enoch C. Callaway, in
addition to denominational dignitaries, helped fill the pulpit following
Grace's resignation. The church's seasonal Christmas cantata, "On to
Bethlehem," provided a sense of continuity in the absence of a pastor.[471]

Judge Callaway rejoiced when fellow deacon and church trustee
James C. C. Black won re-election as president of the Augusta Bar
Association in April 1928. The lone leader of the organization since its
inception in 1901, Black was celebrated as "a man who has stood for the
highest ideals of the profession" and "for many years [has been] the outstanding figure of the legal profession in Augusta." Apart from his work
as a lawyer, Black for a remarkable seven decades served as a central figure in the life of First Baptist, "his daily life...a light shining before men
to the glory of God," standing in the community "for whatsoever was
right, was just, was according to the law of God and for the good of his
fellow beings." Mere months later, James C. C. Black passed away October 1, 1928, his death bringing great sadness to the church and city alike.
The church held a special memorial service in February 1929.[472]

Meanwhile, in August 1928 a young minister named Frederick E.
Smith, pastor of Calvary Baptist Church in Alexandria, Virginia, filled
the Augusta pulpit. Apparently he impressed the congregation, as the
church in September unanimously voted him as the new pastor.[473]

Smith assumed the helm of a large congregation popular in the
Augusta community, featuring robust programming for all ages while
maintaining strong connections to the denomination. The church updated its motto to "An Open Door—a Hearty Welcome." A wide variety of
weekly and special activities characterized the life of First Baptist—men,
women, and children alike. The weekly "Men's Bible Class" in the winter
of 1929, led by John Phinizy and desirous of even more members, held "a
membership and attendance campaign." So numerous were youth the
same year that special events were held for ages 12-14 only. Royal
Ambassadors, missions education for boys, appeared in church programming in the late twenties. First held in 1928, "Family Day" became
an annual event.[474]

Missions remained important to congregational identity and represented the church's strongest denominational bonds. The church supported foreign, state, and local mission work through annual missionary days, offerings, and weekly events. The Woman's Missionary Society led such efforts, keeping informed of the changing dynamics of missionary opportunities. A March 1929 program titled "The New Negro, a missionary challenge," reflected such awareness. A Harlem-based, national phenomenon, the New Negro Movement dismissed the servile model of the "Old Negro" and advocated political equality, an end to segregation and lynching, and, when appropriate, armed self-resistance. The most prominent leader of the group was Alain Locke, a Harvard-trained professor of philosophy and author. A number of other educated African Americans, from poets to blues singers to businessmen, lent their voices and talents. For the women of First Baptist, the New Negro Movement presented challenges to mission work among African Americans.[475]

New, too, were two astounding technologies yet in development and destined to transform the nation: radio and television. Atlanta had introduced radio to the South in 1922, while the world's first television station, WRGB in Schenectady, New York, went on the air in 1928. A December 15, 1929 *Augusta Chronicle* newspaper headline proclaimed "Television Progresses." While fascinated with the prospects of both radio and television, Augustans enjoyed neither of their own at this time. Radio would soon arrive, but two decades would pass before the establishment of television in Augusta.[476]

Amid the excitement of emerging technology, the American economy stumbled in 1929. A June 30 sermon by Smith titled "The Sacrament of Failure" unknowingly presaged a national economic downturn. In September the congregation sent a letter of support to the Home Mission Board in the wake of embezzlement committed by the organization's treasurer, a crime that took place at the pinnacle of America's financial hubris and hampered the work of the HMB for many years.[477]

On October 24 the stock market crashed, the beginning of the end of a decade of great prosperity. Four days later a WMS program at First Baptist titled "Money and Missions" encouraged investment in eternal matters.[478] Spiritual maturity notwithstanding, somber days lay ahead for the Baptists at the corner of Greene and 8th.

Difficult Times

At first the financial pressures from the aftermath of the stock market crash strained, but did not break, America's institutions and families. As industrial production slowed, wealth plunged, and job losses mounted, the nation hummed along, albeit nervously.

In Augusta, talk of the downturn echoed from Greene Street to the golf links. During the winter months wealthy Northerners vacationed at the Bon Air as usual, their money bolstering the local economy. Among the visitors was a world-renowned literary scholar, educator, author, and preacher.

Yale University English professor William Lyon Phelps loved golf so much that his yard included a private eighteen-hole course. In the winters he golfed in Augusta. Like so many other famous visitors of years gone by whose lives were lived in or intersected the church world, Phelps while in Augusta in the winter of 1930 spoke from the pulpit of the First Baptist Church. A full church house listened enraptured to a talk about the parables of Jesus. Phelps returned to Augusta for a number of years following, preaching at First Baptist each winter.[479]

Augusta's resort industry, however, grew increasingly isolated from America's city streets. Bank failures first surfaced in the fall of 1930. By the end of the year some four million Americans were out of work. Northern visitor Charles E. Barker, formerly President Taft's physician and now a renowned speaker on the Rotary and Christian circuits, in January 1931 spoke at First Baptist. His topic, "The Road to Happiness," offered a personal salve in the face of unfolding national despair.[480]

As hopes dwindled on the streets of Augusta, residents with sufficient money tuned into the city's first radio station, WRDW. Opened on July 6, 1930, the first broadcast consisted of sermons at St. John's Methodist Church.[481] Other churches soon visited the radio studio. On February 8, 1931 Marion B. Symms, First Baptist Sunday School superintendent, gave an on-air presentation titled "Scouting and Its Relationship to the Church." At the time, Boy Scout troops routinely attended church services.[482]

Even as First Baptist turned to radio as a way to reach a larger audience, some Augustans turned to alcohol in an effort to cope with financial despair. For the women of First Baptist, long crusaders against alcohol, the mass arrests and incarceration of drunks in the winter of 1931 brought unwelcome tidings of the ineffectiveness of Prohibition. In May of the same year Frederick E. Smith attended the annual Southern Baptist Convention in Birmingham, Alabama, where a resolution brought by Baptists of Georgia requested that the convention undertake greater efforts to enforce Prohibition.[483]

Nonetheless, alcohol provided scant relief as Augusta's citizens struggled economically. In an unanticipated turn of events, golf came to the rescue of some when golfing champion Bobby Jones announced in July 1931 that he would build "his ideal golf course" in the city. Construction began within months, and the Augusta National Golf Club opened in 1932. Two years later the club debuted the Augusta National Invitation Tournament, otherwise known as the Masters.[484]

Despite citywide struggles, stability characterized First Baptist. From worship service to Sunday School, mission activities, civic issues groups, young people's gatherings, social events, college and school banquets, music concerts, holiday pageants, and weddings and funerals, church life carried on. In one instance the church even hosted a rather exotic event.

Commercial air flight brought distant lands ever closer. Greater accessibility to biblical lands fostered mounting interest in the region. In the spring of 1931, members of First Baptist and other Augustans gathered in the sanctuary to listen to fascinating lectures on Palestine by the exotic Princess Rahme, a Syrian princess with a degree from the Baptist Theological College of Chicago who claimed to trace her lineage "back through Biblical records."[485]

Closer, too, was China, a nation to whom First Baptist maintained deep ties. The church's Chinese Sunday School helped birth the Chinese Benevolent Association in 1929, a citywide effort to provide assistance to the city's growing Chinese population. Augustans Woo Leong Tong and Woo Lat assisted in Chinese Sunday School leadership. On July 27, 1931 the church hosted John Lum, a missionary from China who came "to teach the Chinese children who were born in this country something about their land." The same day the church baptized seven Chinese converts. By 1933, First Baptist featured a Chinese Quartet.[486]

Holidays also occasioned opportunities for ministry. In the spirit of the Halloween season in 1931, the Sunday prior to the holiday Smith preached on "Deadly Virtues," while the Sunday after he spoke on the subject of "Ghosts." The next month in a message to the Rotary Club the First Baptist pastor noted that "Thanksgiving must be a thing born of the spirit and soul rather than a particular day set apart by proclamation." Spirit, soul, and thankful memories alike, mixed with sadness, visited the congregation in the passing of longtime lay leader Enoch C. Callaway, his body dead but spirit free.[487]

The nation's spirit and soul, trembling and troubled, sank to new lows. In 1932 stocks plunged, the Gross National Product tanked, and unemployment soared above 20 percent. A pervasive somberness hovered in the sanctuary. While pastor Frederick E. Smith attended the annual SBC meeting in St. Petersburg, Florida in May, the Richmond County superintendent, Lawton B. Evans, preached on "The United States and the Present World Crisis" from the pulpit of First Baptist.[488]

Fear gripped the SBC gathering, driving Southern Baptists further away from their historical commitment to voluntary faith within a secular state. "Christian citizenship," a promotion for Christian colleges at the convention declared, "is necessary in order to establish the principles of Christianity in law and government." Southern Baptists' support for laws avoiding commercial activity on the Christian Sabbath effectively emasculated the historical Baptist position that government should treat Sunday as any other day of the week. National Prohibition, a "Christian principle," Southern Baptist leaders viewed as a civic necessity, while indicating that Baptists should not vote for presidential candidates opposed to Prohibition. Motion pictures and gambling also came under indictment. Amid what amounted to a full-fledged moral crusade for the Christianizing of government and culture, a report on the preservation of Baptist history failed to recall the denomination's foundational principles of freedom of conscience, religious liberty for all, and church-state separation. On the other hand and with more than a trace of irony, the mission reports called for religious liberty for Christians in foreign lands where other religions, or no religion, enjoyed government favoritism.[489]

Imagining the United States as a formally Christian nation doubtlessly provided solace for many who suffered financially. In his evening sermon of January 15, 1933 Frederick E. Smith encouraged his congregants to choose success over failure, while one week later he spoke of the common ground shared by those in the sanctuary. A sermon in February evoked the nation's Christian heritage as a roadmap to a better future. In December, though, the nation's perceived Christian underpinnings hit a major blockade in the repeal of national Prohibition. Georgia and a few other states abstained. The following Sunday Smith warned against "the authorized sale of alcoholic beverages in the city of Augusta." For two more years the state kept Prohibition laws on the books, to the approval of many church members. On at least one occasion Smith attended courthouse cases involving defendants charged with "excessive" use of alcohol, where he offered prayers for the accused.[490]

As Prohibition faded and the recession turned into the Great Depression, newly-elected U.S. President Franklin Delano Roosevelt took office in March 1933. Unemployment peaked, industrial production plunged to the lowest in many years, and bank failures mounted into the thousands. Tens of millions of citizens lived in hunger, many sleeping on the streets. Within days of taking office Roosevelt led Congress to pass the Emergency Banking Act, shutting down banks for four days in order to shore up monetary reserves. During the bank closure thieves broke into the safe of Augusta's First Baptist Church. In a sign of just how bad things were, the robbers netted less than three dollars.[491]

The Banking Act was just the beginning. Afterward came a flurry of legislation and programs, collectively known as the New Deal and designed to restore national financial stability, create jobs, and establish a safety net for America's most vulnerable. Some programs, such as the Works Progress Administration and Social Security Act, generated suspicion in certain Christian quarters. Joining conservative politicians opposed to government efforts to provide relief for the impoverished, many Christian business leaders and ministers, opposing government intervention, compared Roosevelt's social programs to socialism and communism. America, they insisted, was a Christian nation founded upon the hard work and thrift of individuals. For the remainder of the decade the controversy played out in the nation's local papers, including in Augusta. Roosevelt's "Fireside Chats," periodically broadcast over radio and offering assurances of progress in addressing the nation's woes, elicited Frederick Smith in July 1934 to discuss with congregants the questions posed by the president. Later Smith waded into presidential politics by making a "cryptic utterance" seemingly implying that Louisianian Huey Long, often viewed as a clownish politician, might not make a bad president in light of the circumstances.[492]

Amid Depression-era fears and political turmoil, the year 1933 marked Georgia's 200th anniversary. Bicentennial celebrations offered a respite from troubles and travails. First Baptist, along with other city congregations, participated in the celebratory events.[493]

Augusta's Baptists also experienced a second season of celebration, joining Baptists from across the state in recognizing Mercer University's 100th anniversary, for which Frederick E. Smith served as a regional chairperson.[494] Uncertainty nonetheless loomed over the festivities. Continued financial support of Mercer from the Georgia Baptist Convention remained in question, a prospect addressed in November during the annual state convention, hosted by First Baptist Augusta. Worried and grim-faced, delegates debated the future of the state's five Baptist colleges: Mercer University, Bessie Tift College, Shorter College, Norman Junior College, and Brewton Parker College—institutions collectively attended by a number of young persons from First Baptist. Delegates reluctantly chose to primarily support Mercer, suggesting that the remaining schools each implement their own fundraising campaigns. On a more cheerful note and reflective of Mercer's long-time ties with the Augusta congregation, the university awarded Smith an honorary doctorate of divinity.[495]

The church, meanwhile, carried on as best as it could with worship, Sunday School, Woman's Missionary Society, youth ministry, Vacation Bible School, baptisms, social events, denominational participation, revivals, and other events and programs. Roscoe McGahee faithfully ushered on Sunday mornings. Organist and choir director Robert T. Watson directed the church's music ministries. In April 1933 a church youth, Webb Norman, won the statewide Georgia Baptist B.Y.P.U. speaker's contest. A June 11 sermon titled, "A Matter of Morale," by Smith advocated for a positive attitude among congregational members. A subsequent sermon on "Job" stressed the need for perseverance in the midst of affliction, while in September a sermon titled "Money and Work" offered reflections on that which many Augustans fervently wished to have more.[496]

Ministry, missions, and faith identity remained important. In 1933 Marion Symms retired as Sunday School superintendent, following twenty years of making a "great contribution" to the "children of Augusta." Smith in 1934 preached a refresher on Southern Baptist origins, reminding the congregation of its missionary roots. A source of great pride to the congregation, Frank Phinizy, son of John and having grown up in First Baptist, as a young man served as a missionary to India, his work attracting the attention of Southern Baptist leaders. Never forgetful of career missionary Lucy Wright, in May 1936 the Woman's Missionary Society raised money and purchased an x-ray machine for the hospital in Hwangsien, China, of which Wright served as superintendent of nurses. The gift came only months after Mary Verdery, the last remaining charter member of the Woman's Missionary Society, passed away.[497]

Financial hardships did not prevent a variety of guest speakers, preachers and otherwise, from visiting First Baptist during the decade. Foremost among women visitors was Kathleen Mallory, the corresponding secretary (director) of national Woman's Missionary Union. Also from Southern Baptist life, J. B. Lawrence, executive director of the Home Mission Board, preached in May 1935. Other visitors included the noted history and culture lecturer Herbert Yeuell, who entertained those present with a discourse on the history of Germany's 300-year-old Oberammergau Passion Play.[498]

During the first half of the decade the Smith family members continued their annual summer vacations, often to the North Carolina mountains. In 1935, however, a matter of contention arose between the pastor and some church members. Smith's unusual request for a year-long reprieve from the pulpit to visit and study in the United Kingdom may have generated some opposition from church leaders. Nonetheless, the Smith family departed in October 1935 aboard the ship *Queen Mary*. Her maiden voyage having been only four months prior and despite the Great Depression, the vessel reigned as the most luxurious ship in the world. Captive of the public imagination and catering to the rich and famous, the ship contained five dining room areas complete with lounges, two swimming pools, two cocktail bars, a grand ballroom, squash court, and hospital. "The Fred Smiths Sail into a Land of Romance," the local newspaper said of their high sea adventure that took husband, wife, and daughter to Scotland.[499]

With many of the church's families yet struggling financially, perhaps some grumbled about their preacher vacating the pulpit for an extravagant and prolonged family vacation. Church records note that during Smith's absence a committee of three lay persons—"Mrs. O. C. Lee, Prof. T. H. Garrett, and Mr. S. O. Houck"—assumed responsibilities for finding persons to fill the pulpit. The inclusion of a woman on the committee reflected the growing significance of women in America and represented a progressive congregational stance. The committee quickly turned to former pastors Sparks W. Melton and M. Ashby Jones to fill the pulpit. Both spoke frequently. Jones in a January 1936 evening service returned to one of his favorite themes in delivering an "intimate and comprehensive discussion of the personality and ideals of Gen. Robert E. Lee."[500]

While the congregation moved into the holiday season, a letter written by Smith from London and offering "unofficial observations" merited publication in the *Augusta Chronicle*. On a sad note, Benjamin P. Jordan, noted Sunday School teacher, passed away days prior to Christmas. The absence of a pastor during times of death and celebrations of marriage was certainly noticeable.[501]

An annual visitor in the person of Yale University professor William Phelps returned to the pulpit in February 1936. In March Augustans learned of the departure of Mrs. Gertrude Cullum, wife of department store owner St. Julian Cullum, to visit the Smiths in Scotland. Two months later Dr. Smith served as a guest speaker half a world away at the Dublin Baptist Church.[502]

For whatever reasons, discontent grew among church members during the spring and summer months. By the time the Smiths returned in August and the church's pastor regaled locals with tales of the elegant *Queen Mary*, the congregation stood upon the precipice of a split. A contingent of members advocated for the ouster of Smith. In the heat of the controversy six deacons offered their resignation. In September the congregation narrowly voted to ask Smith to resign for unspecified reasons, but by a large margin refused to accept the deacon resignations. In addition, the congregation terminated the Pulpit Supply Committee with appreciation, the work of the committee deemed finished. In October the church passed a resolution expressing "deep appreciation" for Smith's nine-year ministry, "testifying to his fine Christian Character" and wishing he and his family "God speed." By November the Smith family was en route to Greenville, Mississippi in lieu of a new pastoral call.[503]

Even as the First Baptist congregation struggled to remain intact, or perhaps because of the pastoral conflict, certain changes took shape in church life in late 1936. In September the church changed its tagline to "In the Center of Augusta," publicly communicating its geographical location rather than focusing on the word "welcome." Deacons authorized repairs and updates of church facilities, including window and heating system repairs, along with a review of the church's membership roll and constitution. Deacon Paul Mustin, having survived the earlier vote of confidence, was elected chairman of the Finance Committee in November. The newly-formed Pastor Search Committee of fifteen included a number of the deacons who earlier had offered to resign, in addition to two of three members of the earlier Pulpit Supply Committee and seven women. Mrs. J. O. Greene rallied the church's young people.

Former pastor Ashby Jones returned to supply the pulpit through the holiday season. Weeks before Christmas the congregation explored the possibility of purchasing a new organ, with deacon Marion Symms, having also survived a vote of confidence in September, named as chairman of the Organ Committee. Upon acquiring the instrument, a special recital took place in March 1937. Collectively, these actions of the pastorless congregation served to move the church forward while healing internal wounds incurred during the Smith controversy.[504]

A Growing Church in a Suffering World

Renewed and determined, First Baptist Church wasted little time in seeking a new pastor. Six months passed before the search committee and deacons settled on a consensus candidate in April 1937. Dr. Paul Caudill, a native of Dockery, North Carolina and young professor at the

Southern Baptist Theological Seminary of Louisville, Kentucky, visited to meet the congregation. Perhaps due to the recent troubles at First Baptist, Caudill asked a number of questions of the congregation before making his decision, including if he would be "free to preach the full gospel according to the Word of God."[505] Caudill represented an emerging wing of Southern Baptist thought more conscious of the social ministry side of the Gospels that Northern Baptist Walter Rauschenbush in 1893 had spoken of from the church's pulpit. Assured of his freedom, he accepted the call.

The church's newest pastor, splendid organ, missions-minded members, benevolence, illnesses, and alcohol occasioned headlines in the months following. A notable Greek scholar, Caudill proved a capable pastor and soon assumed, as had his predecessors, the role of the city's public Baptist leader. Meanwhile, a young, visiting music phenomenon from Illinois named Virgil Fox attracted many Augustans to the concerts he gave on the church's organ. Fox later became one of the greatest organists of the century. The church's women, including Fern Caudill, took their turn on center stage in March 1938 as some 2,000 attended the Jubilee Celebration of the Georgia Woman's Missionary Union, hosted by First Baptist. Yet big, celebratory events could not mask poverty within the congregation, and special offerings were used to minister to "needy Christians" of the church. Affecting all classes, a summer 1939 outbreak of infantile paralysis (polio) led the city to temporarily ban children from church. Alcohol, too, remained a concern, evidenced in the showing of a "temperance picture" (movie) titled *The Beneficent Reprobate*.[506]

Caudill's early years in Augusta coincided with growing American uneasiness about a self-proclaimed religious and moral German movement recently evidencing signs of sinister intentions. Adolf Hitler, the German chancellor, in 1928 had declared on behalf of the Nazi movement, "We tolerate no one in our ranks who attacks the ideas of Christianity...in fact our movement is Christian." Claiming faith in Jesus and often praising Germany's traditional Christian heritage, Hitler in the ensuing years set about elevating the state to the status of religion. Nazi enactment of legislation enshrining in German society conservative morality, national unity, personal discipline, Aryan racial purity, anti-communism, discrimination against homosexuals, and military might led many German Christian leaders and denominations to support Hitler's movement. Upon the invitation of German Baptists and Hitler, the Baptist World Alliance, including American delegates, convened in Berlin in 1934. Frederick E. Smith, pastor of First Baptist Augusta at the time, criticized the nationalist views of the "Reich church" as clashing with the historic church-state separationist principles of the Baptist faith, yet supported the Berlin gathering and encouraged participation (he did not attend) as a way to demonstrate courage to the Nazis. Smith's comments notwithstanding, many white Americans applauded Hitler's moral, racist, and anti-communist agenda. Berlin also hosted the 1936 Olympics. America and most other nations participated, albeit some with reservations. Still, many world citizens downplayed Nazi aggressions. Yet by the time First Baptist in April 1938 hosted a German music group presenting an Easter cantata, German and American doubts about Nazism were on the ascendancy.[507]

The First Baptist pastor sought to balance his anti-war views alongside growing public awareness of Hitler's campaign of hatred against Jews. As the U.S. government mounted an arms buildup in the face of Hitler's expanding military offensives, Caudill in February 1938 reiterated his belief in the "futility of war," declaring that women's suffrage served as a buffer against military conflict. Yet in November at the Georgia Baptist Convention the Augusta pastor criticized Hitler for persecuting Jews, noting that "Christ, a Jew, died that he might create a band of brotherhood between all races."[508] Nonetheless, brotherhood between black and white in America seemed no closer.

Against the backdrop of global anxieties, in September 1939 Germany invaded Poland. Hitler refused to heed demands from Britain to withdraw, igniting another world war. Amid the yet-distant conflict, First Baptist grew and moved forward, breaking ground on a "badly needed" educational building on Telfair Street in November, of which the dedication and opening took place September 8, 1940. The church's Christmas pageant of December 1939, titled "The Bells of Peace," capped a year of anxieties by celebrating the Prince of Peace.[509]

Congregational hopes and advances, meanwhile, paralleled the end of America's Great Depression. The New Deal had worked. An advertisement in the January 7, 1940 edition of the *Augusta Chronicle* summed up renewed American optimism: "Money—whenever you need it." The discovery of an 1841 dime during construction of the First Baptist educational building reminded members of a simpler world before cars and airplanes. The hosting of yet another world-renowned organist, Claire Coci, added further emphasis to the dawning of a new age of prosperity. The fortunes of Southern Baptist institutions at large also soared, with First Baptist fully participating in national, regional, and state denominational activities and opportunities, including WMU, Baptist Training Union (BTU), Baptist Young People's Union (BYPU), Brotherhood, evangelism emphases, annual SBC gatherings, periodic group retreats to Ridgecrest Conference Center in North Carolina, and the 1939 meeting of the Baptist World Alliance in Atlanta. Baptist higher education, too, remained important. Mercer University president Dr. Spright Dowell preached at First Baptist Augusta in April 1940.[510]

Nonetheless, the specter of war drew ever closer. As the church hosted Georgia Governor J. Cleve Allen for a special dinner in September 1940, Germany dropped munitions on London, intent on reducing the city to rubble. The same month the U.S. government instituted the Selective Training and Service Act of 1940, requiring all men between the ages of 21 and 45 to register for the draft.[511]

Against the backdrop of a vast and growing war across the ocean, a 1941 *Augusta Chronicle* feature story about First Baptist Church portrayed a growing and vibrant congregation with a global reach. "Living a full religious life as a member of the First Baptist church here means far more than merely attending a service or two on Sunday," the article emphasized. "The church offers a schedule of daily activities for almost every age group" and "Every effort is made to have the church serve as a religious, recreational center for its members." In addition to "fine sermons and special music on Sunday, daily prayer services are now being held in light of present world conditions. The Rev. Paul Caudill, pastor, believes that only through fervent prayer can a righteous peace be achieved." In a newly-emerging world of modern technology "An activity which is attracting much attention to the First Baptist church are the regular Sunday night broadcasts over radio Station WRDW. Known as the Baptist Youth Hour, this program is scheduled at 6 p.m. Numbers of young people are getting excellent experience through participation on this program." Leadership included both men and women. "Special classes for church members who want to improve their religious thinking are usually in progress at the First Baptist Church. On Tuesday, Wednesday, and Thursday nights, instruction is at present being offered in 'What Baptists Believe.' Miss Wooten is in charge of this instruction."[512]

Special events in 1941 included a church-led annual School of Missions, for which Lucy Wright returned to Augusta as an instructor. A special "outdoor service" took place in late spring. Denominationally, Caudill was elected president of the Georgia Baptist Sunday School Convention. Organist Robert T. Watson's election to a seat on the city council reflected the prominence of First Baptist in the life of the city. Caudill's selection as the commencement speaker at Georgia State College in Milledgeville spoke to the larger influence of religion in public life.[513]

Religious influence, on the other hand, had limits. Caudill and a number of other Augusta ministers took exception to the city's plan to register prostitutes. The church by 1941 broadcast Sunday sermons over the radio, but radio station WGAC censured a September 1941 message by Caudill about prostitution. The station manager, reflecting public expectations of the day, explained that "our code of ethics forbids us to use the air for discussion of subjects that would not be in good taste for discussion in a family group including small children." He continued, "We do not feel that it would be in good keeping with our ethical code to allow discussion of prostitution on the air, and we have banned all mention of the local vice controversy for this reason."[514]

The Second World War

Censorship aside, war ultimately proved a greater concern for Augustans than prostitution. In early 1941 a yet neutral America began providing military equipment to Britain. Simultaneously, activity on America's military bases increased and a number of individual Americans voluntarily left the states for military service with the Allies, waging war on the Axis powers of Germany, Italy, and Japan. In October the First

Baptist Church of Augusta invited local service men from Camp Gordon to a midweek prayer service. A soldier registry in the church vestibule collected contact information so that servicemen could receive invitations "to dinners, meetings, socials, and all activities."[515]

Then everything changed with the unanticipated and seemingly unprovoked Japanese attack upon the Hawaiian military base of Pearl Harbor on December 7, 1941. Public war wariness instantly transformed into anger. The United States declared war on Japan the following day, and on December 9 First Baptist held a special prayer service.[516] Two days later Germany and Italy declared war on the U.S.

Military deployments quickly began. Patriotism, gloom, and joy mingled awkwardly during the Christmas season. Casting aside previous anti-war sentiments, Caudill wrote in the church bulletin: "With the world literally aflame in the brutal throes of the most colossal war that man has known, with our nation caught in the vortex of that conflict; with our boys, one by one, leaving in answer to their country's call; with the light of brotherhood and love all but blacked out. . . . Christians must dedicate all to Him." In November 1942 the church's "Week of Prayer for Foreign Missions" took on the added perspective of a world literally aflame.[517]

All across America young men poured into military ranks, including eighty-two church members by June, a number rising to 190 by March 1943. Caudill met and prayed with each departing service member and his or her family at the train station. Through the remainder of the war, Mrs. W. Y Seymour, church secretary, remained busy mailing church materials and letters to uniformed personnel, 669 persons total. The pastor and congregants individually corresponded with and prayed for the men and women overseas, while a number of special prayer services took place throughout the war. Unveiled in the summer of 1942, a memorial plaque in the vestibule served as a constant reminder of members serving overseas, while special honors memorialized those who lost their lives in the line of duty. Among those serving was Chaplain D. P. Jenkins, who baptized twenty-five soldiers in the Mediterranean Sea, all of whom became members of the church in absentia. Locally, many women of First Baptist volunteered for the Red Cross, while the church established a ministry to soldiers at Fort Gordon and held services at the Richmond County jail and the Government Quarantine Hospital.[518]

Throughout America government and industry retooled in support of the military effort, as reflected in new taxation, spending, and research priorities, along with rationing of goods and commodities. Many professional baseball players donned military uniforms and crossed the ocean. Augusta National suspended play after 1942, the groundskeeper raising turkeys and cattle on the greens.[519]

Augusta joined many other cities in periodic evening blackouts, a practice designed to prevent theoretical enemy aircraft from seeing city targets. Churches were not exempt. In October 1942 the city council fined First Baptist "for failure to co-operate during Augusta's first blackout Friday night." Robert Watson, city council recorder, "set a penalty against the First Baptist church where he is organist at $50 and costs. A small light had been inadvertently left burning at the church, and the air raid warden on that block, also a member of the church, had made the case."[520]

As labor and transportation affected the growth and movement of food, the U.S. government asked families to grow gardens of fruits and vegetables. First Baptist sponsored a spring "Victory Garden" contest. The summer of 1943, in turn, led to a weeks-long season of spiritual growth and revival in the face of worldly uncertainties, resulting in many new members. Caudill from the pulpit addressed problems of race, other current national ills, and post-war plans. Racial injustice in America remained a serious problem, even as black and white soldiers alike served in Europe against the violently racist Hitler regime. Caudill did not challenge the social and political status quo, instead declaring Christ as the answer to the multitude of ills facing the region, nation, and world.[521]

During this time Caudill received his Ph.D. from the Southern Baptist Theological Seminary, an accomplishment viewed with pride by the congregation. Of the church he noted, "We are destined to become a large church, and will as long as we hold up Christ as our ideal." Summer revivals bore evidence of his bold words. By the end of the year membership exceeded 2,000 for the first time.[522]

Local missions, too, advanced during the war years. In the face of Augusta's large Chinese population the mayor in April 1942 proclaimed

"China Week." That October the Southern Baptist Convention relocated China missionaries Mr. and Mrs. M. W. Rankin to Augusta, where for the duration of the war they worked alongside the First Baptist Chinese Sunday School in ministering to locals. In August the church elected eight new deacons, including Paul Jue, superintendent of the Chinese Sunday School since 1935 and among the first Chinese deacons in Southern Baptist life.[523]

More transitions visited the church in the passing of two of the church's more prominent lay leaders in 1943, Paul Mustin in May (age 85) and John Phinizy in July (age 78), followed by the February 1944 resignation of Paul Caudill. Great success had attended Caudill's seven-year pastorate. During his tenure Caudill ministered to rich and poor alike and served on civic boards, his presence in the community and pulpit leading to congregational growth. He departed to pastor the First Baptist Church of Memphis, Tennessee with much gratitude on the part of his Augusta flock.[524]

In the months following, S. L. Stealey, professor of church history at the Southern Baptist Theological Seminary, briefly served as interim pastor, with former minister Dr. Sparks Melton also returning to fill the pulpit on occasion. T. Harry Garrett, W. M. McElmurray, and H. R. Creamer attended the annual Southern Baptist Convention meeting in nearby Atlanta. There they heard a resolution addressing "the increasing acuteness of the race problem within the nation, and especially in the South." Composed by a committee of progressive denominational leaders, it called upon Southern Baptists "to do everything possible for the welfare of the [black] race, both economic and religious and for the defense and protection of all the civil rights of the race."[525] African Americans had yet to be granted civil rights in the South, but circumstances were slowly moving in that direction.

Across the ocean the course of the war changed on June 6, 1944, known as D-Day. Some 160,000 Allied troops landed on the beaches of Normandy in occupied France, beginning an offensive against Nazi Germany that proved to be the turning point of the great conflict. Fierce fighting in the summer and fall months led to a string of Allied victories, halting German advances in Europe.

As the distant tide of the war turned, First Baptist in August 1944 called a new pastor, Albert Warren Huyck, a Wisconsin native. Whereas the congregation maintained long ties to the Southern Baptist Theological Seminary in Kentucky, the first and leading academic seminary in Southern Baptist life, Huyck became the first graduate of the Southwestern Baptist Theological Seminary in Fort Worth, Texas to serve in the Augusta pulpit. Southwestern had a reputation of graduating great evangelistic preachers. First Baptist, touting itself as "a tower of spiritual strength" since 1817, needed an evangelistic-minded pastor to maintain church growth following Paul Caudill's remarkable ministry.[526]

War developments and a flurry of church activity characterized Huyck's early months. Soldiers of the Tenth Armored Division stationed at Camp Gordon, some members of First Baptist, voiced thanks for the church's ministry as they departed to the battlefields of Europe. As the faraway deaths of young men mounted, church bulletins memorializied church members who gave their lives for their country. Working with the United Nations' Relief and Rehabilitation Administration, the women's Dorcas ministry collected emergency clothing for Europe. Training Union Director Martha Tanner resigned to attend the Woman's Missionary Union Training School in Louisville, Kentucky in preparation for missionary service in Africa. Vera Atkins, newly-graduated from Southwestern Seminary, became the new pastor's assistant. Nickels R. Beacham came aboard as new choir director.[527]

Christmas 1944 witnessed rationed yuletide and prayers for service members. Allied forces engaged in a major offensive, the Battle of the Bulge, against the Germans. The enemy's retreat in January elicited joy. American service members soon began returning home. Following the unexpected death of President Franklin Roosevelt on April 12, 1945, mere weeks before peace talks began, the church adopted a resolution— and mailed a copy to new President Harry S. Truman—promising prayer for the world and asking world leaders to seek "Divine Guidance."[528] Hitler committed suicide on April 30, and Germany surrendered one week later. Japan capitulated on September 2, bringing to a formal end the greatest war in the history in the world. The planet sighed with relief.

Grief over the loss of loved ones also marked the end of the war. First Baptist Augusta lost eleven members: Wayne A. Barnes, Paul T.

Chance, D. Buist Downing Jr., Jack C. Fortune, J. D. Harvey Jr., Richard F. Halford, Weyman C. Martin, Albert T. Montgomery, J. N. Routh Jr., Preston Towns, and Charles A. Turner. Their names are enshrined on a bronze memorial plaque in the church.[529]

In the weeks and months following the war, the United States honored Russia's pivotal help in defeating Axis forces. Renowned world lecturer Charles A. Wells, speaking at First Baptist in September 1945, proclaimed Russia as "the neighbor of the world." Two months later the church participated in Russian relief efforts, shipping "108 kits of staple food, first aid supplies, toilet articles, and other needed commodities to the Russian War Relief Headquarters in New York." In between a revival led by evangelist Gypsy Smith resulted in overflowing crowds. Huyck called upon the congregation to "begin again" in the church's daily living and programming.[530]

Grand New Heights

Alongside the closing of a terrible chapter in world history, a new and exciting era in Southern Baptist life dawned. The 1845 formation of the Southern Baptist Convention at First Baptist Augusta presaged a national civil war, one with far more American casualties than World War II. The centennial anniversary of the SBC, also held at First Baptist, celebrated denominational advances and heralded the coming of age of Southern Baptists, now numbering more than five million persons.

Southern Baptists from throughout the South gathered at the corner of Greene and 8th from May 6-9, 1945. City leaders celebrated the monumental occasion. Marion Symms chaired the church's Centennial Committee. Symms, Harry Jernigan, and Ralph Griffin compiled "A Brief History of the First Baptist Church" for delegates. Isabella Jordan Whitney wrote for the *Christian Index* a historical essay of the church's first 125 years. The church's Historical Committee, comprising T. Harry Garrett, Mrs. John (DeLacy) Phinizy, Mrs. John B. Whitney, Marion Symms, and Mrs. George Sumerau, arranged for the creation of a bronze historical marker. Presiding over the radio broadcast unveiling of the marker were Mrs. James T. Bothwell representing First Baptist Augusta, and Mrs. T. B. Corbett, granddaughter of William B. Johnson, nineteenth-century Edgefield First Baptist pastor and first president of the Southern Baptist Convention.[531]

Looking also to the future, between April and July 1945 the church licensed three young men to preach: Roy Ryan, Robert Geer, and Ellison Jenkins—with Geer later ordained. A new Building Committee in the fall prepared the church for the construction of yet another education facility. In 1946 the deacon board expanded again and the church hosted the annual Georgia Baptist Sunday School Convention. Martha Taylor graduated from Woman's Training Union school and departed for the mission field of Nigeria. An enlarged church staff of seven included Huyck, Edith Hayes (educational director), Mrs. B. K. Barnes (secretary), Grace Murphy (assistant secretary), Robert J. Watson (organist), Fred W. Bowdidge (choir director), and Lucy Wright (missionary to China).[532]

The pace of progress accelerated in 1947. Sunday School, Woman's Missionary Union, youth ministry, Chinese ministry, and the board of deacons all expanded. Highlights of the year included a revival crusade, the revising of the church's constitution, resumption of services of parental dedication of children to the Lord (a practice of founding pastor Willliam T. Brantly), purchase of two adjacent properties for expansion, and financial support of the Calhoun Street mission earlier established by Edwin Napier, recently ordained to the ministry. Worship services, broadcast on radio station WBBQ, blanketed the city.

Growth perhaps softened the sadness of the passing of two prominent laymen, T. Harry Garrett (1946), chairman of the Music Committee, and C. D. Johnson (1947), former superintendent of the Chinese Sunday School. The two men represented many of an older generation, men and women alike, whose faithful service helped lay the groundwork for the church's growth in the 1940s and following.[533]

The benefits reaped from the combined leadership and commitment of Garrett, Johnson, and hundreds of other devoted church members were enabled by a chain of events apart from their control. The advances of First Baptist Augusta and many other Southern Baptist churches in the 1940s, the most rapid decade of growth thus far, involved global conflict. Though terrible, World War II triggered the greatest mass migration in American history. Some 57 percent of Americans changed residences, 21 percent across state lines. Sixteen million moved to military bases. Tens of millions relocated from farms and small towns to work in city-based defense industries, joining the ranks of the middle class. The percent of Southerners living in urban areas skyrocketed from about one-third to almost one-half.[534]

The successes under pastors Paul Caudill and Warren Huyck, in short, owed much to the congregation being in the right place at the right time. An urban area with industrial capacity, land for expansion, and proximity to a military installation marked the right place. World War II and the subsequent Cold War against communism—the latter initiated in 1947 as the U.S. government came to see former ally Russia as a national enemy—provided the right time. The combined forces produced massive economic growth for certain metro areas, including Augusta. In many instances other urban churches of the South also benefited from this convergence of factors, especially First Baptist congregations. Thousands of churches collectively rode the rising wave of demographics and reaped the financial benefits of a thriving economy. The Southern Baptist Convention surged in response.

Financial prosperity fueled, and Sunday School channeled, institutional growth. Now common throughout Southern Baptist life, Sunday School served as the common and primary entry point for recruiting new church members. Whether in churches large or small, urban or rural, many Southern Baptists read and studied from the same evangelistically-intensive, carefully-constructed, and theologically-welcoming literature produced by the convention's Sunday School Board. By the late 1940s the Sunday School training course for teachers consisted of forty-eight books. Not every local church teacher had time to read them all, but in 1948 Mrs. O. A. Lazenby became the first at First Baptist Augusta to do so. Revivals, too, attracted new members, including a citywide 1948 Billy Graham crusade and a 1949 church revival led by Wayne Dehoney and George Beverly Shea.[535]

Nonetheless, national unease remained. New homes, nice cars, and larger bank accounts did little to quell a rising tide of nuclear fears among an expanding middle class. In late August 1949 the Soviet Union conducted its first atomic test, joining the U.S. as a nuclear power and causing panic in America. Weeks later Billy Graham, a Southern Baptist, in

Los Angeles opened his first large, multi-denominational crusade. Speaking to the fears of the hundreds of thousands who attended and the tens of millions who read accounts in newspapers and magazines, Graham changed the course of America.

"Western culture and its fruits had its foundations in the Bible, the Word of God, and in the revivals of the seventeenth and eighteenth century," he declared. "Communism, on the other hand, has decided against God, against Christ, against the Bible, and against all religion. Communism is not only an economic interpretation of life—communism is a religion that is inspired, directed, and motivated by the devil himself who has declared war against Almighty God."[536]

Reverberating from Los Angeles to Washington, D.C. to Augusta, Georgia and all points in between, Graham's words, on the heels of the Soviet atomic tests, ignited a national religious revival unlike any previous. Little matter that Graham incorrectly attributed Christianity to the nation's founding, thus denying his own Baptist heritage that contributed to America's establishment as a secular nation. The world, for the first time, faced the prospect of global annihilation. The godless Soviet Communists now possessed the capability of destroying the United States at a moment's notice. The only power higher than nuclear was God, and to God Graham pointed America.

In response to the Soviet atomic tests the U.S. government redoubled efforts to stockpile nuclear weapons, including the construction of the Savannah River nuclear facility adjacent to Augusta and across the river. In the wake of anti-communism fervor elevated to feverish levels by Billy Graham, a U.S. senator from Wisconsin, Joseph McCarthy, began a ruthless campaign to root out communist sympathizers in America. For years McCarthy and his supporters violated Americans' First Amendment rights of freedom of conscience and speech. Graham, now the leading Christian voice in America, supported him throughout, to the point of denouncing the eventual senatorial censure of McCarthy.[537]

In this highly-charged, ideological environment families by the tens of thousands moved to Augusta to work at the Savannah River facility. Church membership swelled, by 1950 reaching 2,357, with 1,817 enrolled in Sunday School and a second Sunday morning worship service added. In March 1951 alone the church welcomed 53 new members.

Flush with money from tithes of members old and new alike, the same year the church signed a contract to build a new educational building on Telfair Street for $303,000. A new parking lot accommodated the growing number of automobiles. The church voted to petition the mayor "to clean up" the downtown "dives." A remodeled sanctuary reflected new prosperity, and a spate of building acquisitions on the church's city block helped accommodate enlarged programming. Church staff expanded, including the hiring of a full-time, professional minister of music, Earl Holloway, and the adoption of graded choirs. Some 200 voices united in December 1952 for an impressive presentation of "Christmas Music in Candlelight." Woman's Missionary Union enrollment approached 300, Lottie Moon missions offerings reached new heights, and the Chinese Sunday School grew to such a degree that the Southern Baptist Home Mission Board assigned a missionary worker, Emily Goon, to First Baptist. Beyond the block, First Baptist started three new mission churches: Bothwell Lee Memorial Mission (1949), Clark Mission (1949), and East Boundary Mission (1953). Area-wide, the congregation at Greene and 8th led in the formation of a new Baptist association, the Augusta Association. Further out still, dozens of young members graduated from high school and enrolled in Baptist colleges and universities around the South in order to train for the ministry, including the pastor's son, Albert, who attended Furman University.[538]

Near and far, the stirrings of revival gave hope that America could successfully face great challenges. First Baptist Augusta took this hope to heart. Despite the national threat of nuclear war and the local departure of a number of families due to the completion of the construction of the Savannah River Plant, thousands of jobs remained and excitement and enthusiasm pulsed through a congregation vibrant and expectant.[539]

8

Overcoming Challenges in a New Era

"It couldn't be better," proclaimed a 1950s advertisement for Coca-Cola. Shaped by corporatist optimism in the face of a booming national economy, the public narrative of the decade of the fifties masked a nation in chaos. White, successful-looking men and women smiled at America from advertisements, while *I Love Lucy* elicited laughs from television viewers. Yet in reality the decade unfolded as if it were a bottle of shaken, warm Coca-Cola opened by an unsuspecting consumer.

Never-before-seen threatening clouds of global nuclear conflict hovered above long-standing, pent-up moral crises. Generations of racial apartheid collided with renewed legal efforts to enforce constitutional human equality, heightening the violence and terrorism long perpetrated against African Americans. A white Protestant worldview of morality forged in the early twentieth century slammed into emerging post-war ideologies untethered from accepted societal norms. Free-flowing economic capital shredded financial constraints of the 1930s, empowering corporations, elevating middle-class America, enshrining the modern age of technology and convenience, and imprinting consumerism as patriotic duty and personal success. War became business, and commerce the new soul of America.

The multi-directional and jarring transitions bred a mixture of tensions and opportunities, fears and hopes, caution and excitement never before experienced. America, Augusta, and Southern Baptists would never be the same again.

A Pastor for the Times

In 1953 Dwight D. Eisenhower succeeded Harry S. Truman as president, the Korean War came to an ambiguous end, the Cold War escalated as the U.S. tested its first hydrogen bomb, sports came into American homes on television sets, and sex came out of the closet when

Playboy magazine hit the newsstands. President Eisenhower visited Augusta twenty-eight times, so often that the Augusta National Golf Club built a house for him. If he paid attention to the city when not golfing, the president noted the construction of the four-lane Gordon Highway bisecting downtown to accommodate the rapidly growing number of automobiles, as well as Augusta's march ever outward toward the surrounding suburbs. During the decade the nearby Savannah River Plant settled in for the long haul, the city's population swelled, and Augustans grappled with new racial, social, and civil realities brought about by the 1954 *Brown v. Board of Education* decision that struck down segregation.[540]

Rising on the swelling tide of international threats and domestic upheavals, civil religion reached new heights in America. Led by Billy Graham, communist-fearing white Protestant United States legislators quickly set about tearing into the "wall of separation" between church and state as envisioned by early Baptists and enacted by the nation's founders. Truman in 1952 established an official and evangelical-oriented National Day of Prayer. Weeks after his presidential swearing-in ceremony, Dwight Eisenhower was baptized at Graham's insistence. Congress and President Eisenhower in 1954 rejected the secular nature of the 1892 Pledge of Allegiance, written by Baptist minister Francis Bellamy, by adding the words "under God" to the pledge. The following year the words "In God We Trust" were added to currency, and in 1956 the phrase became the official national motto. During this time some legislators attempted to add an amendment to the Constitution declaring America a Christian nation. A proposed constitutional amendment read in part, "This nation devoutly recognizes the authority and law of Jesus Christ, Savior and Ruler of nations, through whom are bestowed the blessings of Almighty God." Congress never acted upon the amendment.[541]

Regardless of the national benefits of civil religion in the 1950s, the "blessings of Almighty God" found manifestation at the corner of Augusta's Greene and 8th streets. On Sundays, Mondays, Tuesdays, and Thursdays of many weeks, First Baptist activities began in the morning and ended late in the evening. Sundays consisted of early morning worship (8:45 a.m.), Sunday School (9:50 a.m.), morning worship broadcast on WAUG 1050 radio (11:15 a.m.), Chinese Sunday School (4 p.m.), Lucy Wright Young Woman's Association Meeting (5:30 p.m.), Training Union (6:45 p.m.), and Evening Worship (8 p.m.). Other weekly activities included multiple Woman's Missionary Society events, women's circle group meetings, Bible studies, children's meetings, choir practices, a deacons meeting, and Wednesday evening prayer service. Easter day, a special occasion in the church calendar, was filled with as many as five services. An annual "Youth Week" featured more than 100 "officers," participants presumably many times more. The nursery grew so fast that members were asked to loan extra baby beds to the church. A small blurb in a church bulletin in March 1953 explained the busyness: "A church, like a vehicle, runs most smoothly when it bears a heavy load."[542]

Standard fare throughout larger Southern Baptist congregations, many of these activities, down to the time of day, reinforced a denominationally-driven, programmed, homogenous approach to church life. Viewed from the outside, First Baptist Augusta attested to a coming of age of American Christianity. A historically business-influenced congregation, First Baptist Augusta within the Southern Baptist world functioned in exemplary fashion in an urban Southern market now attuned to orchestrated religious rituals, professional Christian education, and ascendant civil religion.

Church doors represented the threshold from the outside world into the sanctuary. Expanding the congregation's share of the Augusta marketplace meant enticing newcomers to enter the sanctuary. So many Augustans responded that it became increasingly difficult, among the thousand-plus who attended services each Sunday, to discern members from visitors. A church bulletin from the decade explained a simple, clever way to identify newcomers based on the fact that members received postal mailed copies of the bulletin prior to Sunday services. "Our ushers do not know all the members of this big church. When you enter the door, rather than anyone to feel slighted, a bulletin is handed to you. If you are a member of First Baptist, and have read the bulletin, won't you please just say, 'No thank you.' The ushers will then know that you are a member. Such graciousness will make it possible for every visitor present to have a bulletin."[543]

First Baptist Church bulletins, too, served as portals to an imagined national morality. The March 15, 1953 edition noting the burgeoning alliance of Christianity and White House doubtlessly elicited nods of approvals. "In the World of Religion," the bulletin proclaimed, "President Eisenhower has advised religious leaders that he does not approve of the consumption of liquor at the White House, and has issued an order banning drinking by members of the White House executive staff during business hours or at any time while at their offices." The same year a bulletin praised Eisenhower for launching the "Religion in American Life (RIAL) Campaign, stressing the theme, 'Light Their Life With Faith – Bring Them to Worship This Week.'" Another 1953 bulletin hewed a different way. Echoing Baptists' heritage of religious liberty for all and church-state separation, it praised "basic human rights" granted to all Americans.[544]

Viewed from the inside, First Baptist of the early and mid-1950s met the moral expectations and spiritual needs of many Augustans. A majestic sanctuary each Sunday created, from ceiling to stained glass windows to carpeted floors, an atmosphere of hushed and thoughtful reverence. The Christian faith preached, sung, and taught within the sanctuary and attendant buildings offered a gospel message that at times comforted, and in other instances challenged, members and visitors alike. Ambitious and exhaustive church programming bathed the entirety of one's being, if one so desired, in the light of scripture, Christ, and fellowship. Successes were readily evident, as each Sunday witnessed the addition of new members, sometimes dozens.

From Augusta and throughout the South, the world of Southern Baptists rode so high and promising that few on the inside could have imagined that the denomination had reached its institutional pinnacle. The worlds of local church and denomination came together at First Baptist for a memorable revival in March 1953 featuring the president (J. D. Grey) and the director of the music department (Hines Sims) of the Southern Baptist Convention. The same year First Baptist joined the SBC in preparing for a convention-wide campaign to enroll "A Million More in '54" in Sunday School. Decades would pass before the spiritual headiness of the times truly sank in. In the early twenty-first century Southern Baptist analyst Ed Stetzer said of the fifties: "The peak of growth for Southern Baptists was 1954. When population growth is factored in, we have been in decline ever since."[545]

In this heady era Albert W. Huyck on April 19, 1953 suddenly resigned from the pastorate of the Augusta congregation. Under his leadership church membership had mushroomed from some 2,000 to about 3,000. In announcing his resignation in order to assume the pastorate of the smaller but up-and-coming First Baptist Church of West Palm Beach, Florida, Huyck praised the Augusta church and implied that it needed a pastor of greater capabilities. The church bulletin that very day contained similarly upbeat words: "Such a glorious future ahead if we have the vision and the will to get ready!" Two weeks later in the bulletin Huyck was praised as "one of the finest and most capable Pastors that ever served this or any church."[546]

Undaunted by the loss of Huyck during these turbulent yet exciting and promising times, First Baptist quickly turned to a young minister and Baylor University graduate who could easily have starred in Coca-Cola commercials. An international sports star and Baptist evangelist, twenty-six-year-old Robert Jackson Robinson, a Fort Worth, Texas native and "man of unusual scholastic achievement and pleasing personality," represented the intersection of scholarship, sports, and religious revival—a powerful combination at a pivotal moment in the nation's history. His path to Augusta threaded through the Baylor Student Revival Movement, collegiate basketball stardom, selection as the 1947 recipient of the Jack Dempsey Award as America's outstanding athlete, a 1948 Olympic gold medal on the U.S. basketball team, the offer (and refusal) of a professional basketball contract, and the leading of revival services at more than 1,000 churches around the globe—including a Boston Billy Graham crusade in 1950. As if this were not enough, "Jack" shared a common thread woven throughout the entire history of First Baptist: a connection with Philadelphia, Pennsylvania. From the city's Temple University Robinson had earned a graduate degree in theology.[547]

Jack Robinson's first message at First Baptist, immediately following a prior speaking engagement at the Baptist World Youth Congress in South America and delivered at a Wednesday evening service on August 5, 1953, elicited great excitement. More than a thousand people attended, "crowding the auditorium, many standing in the vestibule, on the

steps and outside in the driveway where a loudspeaker had been set up."
That night the Robinsons, Jack and Charlotte Furrh (from Mineral
Wells, Texas, a graduate of Texas Christian University, and a former
beauty queen), transferred their church letters from the Grambrell Street
Baptist Church in Fort Worth, Texas.[548]

The Robinsons' arrival coincided with an intentional decision on the
part of First Baptist to remain downtown even as the sparkle and excitement of the suburbs captured the imagination of prosperous families and
businesses. A church bulletin article titled "The Challenge of the Church
Located in the Heart of a City" insisted that "Every city needs a great
downtown church where people from all walks of life pass through a door
marked 'Whosoever will, let him come.' It makes for a cosmopolitan
congregation and a mighty challenging program." Churches "in the
neighborhoods" met a need, but "most of the great churches in our cities
are downtown. All roads lead to the downtown church."[549]

Many city leaders, too, remained convinced of the centrality of
Augusta's downtown. A newspaper article about Broad Street described
the avenue near First Baptist as "market place, playground, civic center…
the heart of Augusta."[550] Time would soon enough prove entrenched
beliefs as mere wishful thinking, but for the moment the city's yet pre-
eminent Baptist church shone brightly in the addition of one of
America's most prominent young ministers.

First Baptist Augusta expected much from the new pastor, and
much from the church's 3,000 members. Of the latter, a church bulletin
at the beginning of summer 1953 encouraged members to resist taking
weekends off "in favor of the lakes, the links, and the likes," including
bass fishing and automobile trips. A subsequent bulletin announced,
"Take a vacation—but not from God!" Special, tongue-in-check yet serious words were directed to Sunday School teachers and officers: "Nothing short of an earthquake or death" should keep them away from weekly
meetings. The year-around faithfulness of all members, including participation in an October four-day "Church-Wide School of Stewardship"
culminating in a "Victory Sunday," would help ensure that the church
reached an unprecedented $198,000 budget in 1954.[551]

Even so, the church allowed Jack Robinson to temporarily preach
part-time as he finished his Doctorate of Divinity degree from South-

western Baptist Theological Seminary in Fort Worth, Texas. Denominational speakers filled the pulpit for most weeks, preaching messages of evangelism, godliness, and faithfulness. During Robinson's absence church members received reminders that weekly church attendance was more important than the new American dream of real estate, bank accounts, and new automobiles. Church bulletins reinforced the messages. President Eisenhower, the congregation was assured, attended church weekly out of "grave responsibility for this nation." "If the president can take time to attend church every Sunday, shouldn't we too?" Federal Bureau of Investigation (F.B.I.) chief J. Edgar Hoover appeared in a church bulletin, instructing members to "force" their children "to go to Sunday School and church . . . with no further discussion about the matter!" "The parents of America can strike a most effective blow against the forces which contribute to juvenile deliquency," Hoover insisted, "if our mothers and fathers will take their children to Sunday School and Church regularly." [552]

Missionary enthusiasm also coursed through the congregation. Martha Tanner, home on furlough from missionary work in Nigeria, led a Wednesday night service in April 1954, speaking of the work of the Foreign Mission Board. The same month members were reminded that Southern Baptists viewed "all nations" as their mission field, theirs the task of winning the world to Christ. An overflow crowd of more than 2,000 for Easter services, including record Sunday School attendance, reinforced local perceptions of a triumphant Baptist faith. [553]

Amid soaring civil religion and denominational confidence clothed in presumptiousness, Jack Robinson finished his studies at Baylor and moved his family to Augusta in May 1954, manning the pulpit permanently on September 13 and soon settling into a new pastorium on Overton Road far from downtown and near Augusta National. His pastoral residency secured, Robinson helmed a downturn church expanding in membership in tandem with a city and nation experiencing a suburbs-centric, post-war baby boom. Dynamic pastoral leadership alongside municipal tensions were destined to frame the immediate future of First Baptist Augusta. [554]

Scaling New Heights

Between the months of June and December 1954 change came fast and furious to the church at the corner of Greene and 8th. The East Boundary Mission some eight blocks east of First Baptist became independent, taking the name Morningside Baptist Church. Minister of Music Earl Holloway, having only recently initiated the "First Annual Church-Wide School of Sacred Music," resigned and followed former pastor Albert W. Huyck to First Baptist Church of West Palm Beach, Florida. Fellow Southwestern seminary graduate, C. Winfield Rich, for a brief time joined Robinson on staff as educational director, succeeded in 1956 by yet another Southwesterner, Carlton Carter. From Jackson, Tennessee, and also a Southwestern graduate, came Kenneth Cochrane as the new music director. [555]

The church's music ministry suffered a sad setback in the passing of organist Robert J. Watson in August 1955. During his thirty-five years of congregational service Watson had also been active in community organizations and played for hundreds, perhaps thousands, of funerals and weddings. The organ silent during Watson's funeral service, Robinson on behalf of the congregation celebrated and remembered the musician's "superlative Christian life." Thereafter the American Guild of Organists sponsored a memorial concert in memory of Watson, at which time the late organist's family presented the church with the gift of an oil portrait of the musician. Twenty-two-year-old Sidney A. Richardson of Pelham, New Hampshire soon became the new organist.[556]

In addition to personnel transitions, the church expanded the sanctuary to enlarge the choir and organ space and make the baptistery more readily visible. Sunday School departments expanded from four to six in order to accommodate overflow crowds. The Chinese Sunday School prospered. Nine new Church Training classes were added. Bulletins routinely touted the need for the latter, including an article that declared "In Baptist Training Union You Can..." "learn to speak in public," "learn the Baptist way of life and learn to discuss it intelligently and openly," "learn to pray in public," "grow as a Christian," and "strengthen your testimony so you can be a strong witness for our Lord."[557]

More church programs necessitated continued expansion of educational facilities, including the acquisition of properties at 817 and 819 Telfair Street. Financial gifts from Merial Black Carey and Katherine Black, daughters of the late influential church leader and judge James C. C. Black, helped provide for a third-floor addition to the Telfair Street educational building, the floor named Black Memorial Hall in memory of Black. [558]

Along with the changes came a breath of cool air, literally. A historical hindrance to the South's development, the region's hot climate finally met its match in the arrival of air conditioning in the post-war years. In the summer heat of August 1954 the members of First Baptist Augusta decided to install air conditioning in the church for a cool $22,500. Enthusiasm for climate change seemingly matched the excitement generated by their new pastor. Dan Matheny gushed that "Air Conditioning is another step forward in the growth of First Baptist to reach more people." "It will make our services more worshipful to the individual by creating a more pleasant atmosphere," pronounced Bridges Evans. "Our church services filled throughout the Summer will mean more for missions," declared Schulyer Clark. [559] Sweltering summer worship services stirred by the gentle swish of hand-held funeral home fans soon became tales from a past of which no one wished to return.

The missionary focus of the church, however, benefitted from more than just air conditioning. By now baked into the theological bones of Southern Baptist churches, missions, alongside uniform Sunday School literature, defined the denomination and congregation. More than any other dimension, foreign missions remained that which gripped the imagination of Southern Baptists. Long-time church member and foreign missionary Lucy Wright, having previously served as a medical missionary in China, transferred to Pusan, Korea in 1953. The following year the Lottie Moon Christmas Offering for Foreign Missions, a seasonal denominational emphases named after one of Southern Baptists' earliest and most successful missionaries to China, netted $4,452. For many years promoted solely through the congregation's Woman's Missionary Union, in 1955 the offering garnered church-wide publicity and netted more than $10,000, a sum annually surpassed in many succeeding years. Other special offerings supported home, local, and regional missionary efforts.[560]

Also central to the life of the church, revivals remained an annual fare. In a decade when "soul winning" became common language in Southern Baptist life, the congregation's 1955 spring revival added 101 persons to church rolls, while Baptist businessman and philanthropist Howard E. Butts Jr. led the 1957 revival. The church licensed more young men to the ministry: Joseph S. Dukes III in 1953 and Robert Hughes, William Roscoe West, William Parker Jr., and Guy Douglas Mattox in 1955. In 1961 the church also ordained West, who then pastored the Abilene Baptist Church of Martinez.[561]

Likewise evangelical in nature, Vacation Bible School extravagances for children and youth highlighted summers, while Royal Ambassadors (for boys) and Girls Auxiliary groups were staples of Wednesday nights and a kindergarten, taught by Mrs. Stanford Woodhurst, was added to the church roster. In the Cold War era the congregation expressed concern for both the souls and minds of the hundreds of children attending church. During the Christmas season of 1953 a poem in the church bulletin warned parents of buying guns as gifts for their sons. Titled "Guns for Christmas," the poem by C. S. Munro in part read:

> They gave him guns for Christmas—
> Gave him the lust to kill.
> Then wondered why that very lust
> Filled all his mind and will.
> They gave him guns for Christmas
> On the birthday of the One
> Who came to give us life and love
> That the Father's will be done!
> O mothers of little sons,
> Set not their hands to fight—
> Teach them to hate the things that kill—
> That love and peace are right.[562]

Reaching persons with the gospel of Christ, the overriding desire of the congregation, found a fresh and powerful expression through the addition of televised morning worship services. December 11, 1955 marked the initial broadcast, aired on WRDW-TV and the first televised worship service in the Augusta area. (Immediately considered a success and within a few years reaching some 20,000 homes, the weekly television services continue to the present, manned by Charles Moody, who has served in this capacity for six decades.) Months after the forward-looking television broadcasts began, Marion S. Symms, long-time deacon, sought to preserve artifacts of the past through the establishment of a historical alcove wherein historical artifacts and pastoral portraits were permanently exhibited.[563]

Meanwhile, pastor Jack Robinson garnered an ever greater share of accolades. In 1957 Robinson received his Doctor of Theology degree from Southwestern seminary, preached the annual Georgia Baptist Convention sermon, and was elected to Baylor University's Hall of Fame (induction to the Texas Sports Hall of Fame followed in 1966). Honored as Augusta's "Man of the Year" in 1958, Robinson also received the Distinguished Service Award from the Junior Chamber of Commerce. The recognitions reflected remarkable accomplishments. Within the first four years of Robinson's pastorate some 1,500 persons had been added to church rolls. Enrollments in Sunday School (2,044), Training Union (576), Woman's Missionary Union (517), and Brotherhood (233) stood at all-time highs and subsumed many of the church's thirty-two committees, alongside a church budget of nearly $250,000.[564] At First Baptist Augusta, early signs of Southern Baptist decline remained invisible.

An Anchor in Troubled Times

Churches exist in a state of perpetual transition, to which First Baptist Augusta of the late 1950s proved no exception. A number of long-time members passed away, including former Sunday School teacher J. J. Carswell (1955), former church treasurer Harry Jernigan (1957), and former pastor Sparks W. Melton (1957). The passing of these three and other older members during the decade represented the slow fading of institutional memory prior to World War I. On a different note, an especially tragic death visited the community in 1958 in the passing of Mrs. Julian Fiske Jr. (Carolyn Cox), a choir member and young mother who died saving her young son from a gasoline fire in the family home. The church received a set of hand bells given in her memory.[565]

A large contingent of youth members, meanwhile, represented the post-World War II trajectory of the congregation. Seeking to accommodate surging numbers of children and young people, Southern Baptist youth ministry entered into the era of professionalism. First Baptist appointed Jewelle DeLaughter as youth director on a part-time basis. Sunday School, Training Union, mission projects, choir, retreats, sporting events, Youth Sunday, and other activities and events provided opportunities for young people's faith and personal development. The Robinsons accompanied a large contingent of youth to the 1958 Baptist World Youth Congress in Toronto, Canada.[566]

Other congregational advances near the end of the decade included the addition of a meditation garden and library, given by the church's Woman's Missionary Union and the latter furnished by Mrs. Dooner in memory of her late husband, H. R. Dooner. In November 1959 the church paid off its remaining debt. The same fall First Baptist hosted the annual state gatherings of the Woman's Missionary Union and the Georgia Baptist Student Union (BSU), Southern Baptists' collegiate ministry to the swelling ranks of young people attending schools of higher education. College represented an uneasy but exciting period between youth and adulthood, influencing the future of the church's young persons. BSU provided spiritual guidance during this important time, with many collegians of First Baptist involved in local chapters of the organization. The First Baptist congregation viewed college as an opportunity "to better prepare for future responsibilities" in church life and beyond. The church's 129 members enrolled in institutions of higher education represented more than thirty colleges, universities and seminaries, many Baptist-affiliated. Most, however, attended non-Christian schools, a reflection of the twentieth century direction of higher education and a foreshadowing of a future of declining church attendance in an increasingly-secularized American culture.[567]

That which took place within the church, however, could not mask the outside world. From the pulpit Jack Robinson preached sermons that alternatively looked inwardly and outwardly. "Jack's sermons are punctuated with the now," noted one newspaper editor. "He makes it a point to keep up on current religious, political and historic trends." His sermons from 1959 to 1960 evidence the editor's observation. "When God Searches Us," "Found Faithful," and "Old Clothes and New Hearts" encouraged listeners to examine themselves. "The Danger of Drifting" warned believers to remain faithful, while "Help for Boredom" spoke to a sometimes dulling side-effect of a fast-paced and ever-changing world. "Why Immersion of Believers?" reminded members and visitors alike of the Baptist heritage of voluntary faith. "The Materialism of Christianity" warned believers against placing faith in the excesses of financial prosperity. A sermon titled "What Communism Says About Christmas" addressed the larger, ever-present challenges of communism, atheism, and nuclear warfare. Members chose as their favorite sermon in 1960 "In God We Trust," echoing civil religious patriotism embodied in legislative action of the past decade.[568]

Robinson's latter sermon came amid Protestant anxiety over the possible election of a Roman Catholic, John Kennedy, to the U.S. presidency. Caught up in civil religion and anti-Catholic fervor, many fearful Southern Baptists deemed Kennedy unsuited to hold the nation's highest office. Numerous First Baptist Church bulletins reprinted articles calling into question Kennedy's fitness for the presidency due to his religion. Embracing a stance that would have astonished early Baptists, the article scoffed at the notion that "Religion should stay out of politics." At the same time, many Baptists masked anti-Catholic sentiments by insisting that the Roman Catholic Church was opposed to church-state separation, a true charge nonetheless diluted by Southern Baptists' recent violations of church-state separation through the embrace of civil religion. Despite stoking opposition to Kennedy, following his election to the presidency Augusta church members prayed "that God will give guidance and directions to this man." Not all Southern Baptists were so magnanimous. Many from Kennedy's presidency onward worked all the harder to tear down the wall of separation between church and state two centuries earlier inspired, through blood, imprisonment, and other persecutions, by minority Baptists of colonial and early America.[569]

Other political matters elicited evolving positions on the part of the Augusta congregation. In the early sixties as some Christian denominations sought government funds to assist the educational efforts of religious colleges and universities, First Baptist joined most other Baptists across America in opposing state assistance, citing Baptists' historical opposition to church-state separation. From the same historical convictions First Baptist Augusta and most other Baptist congregations offered no criticism of several U.S. Supreme Court decisions of the same era banning government-sponsored prayer in public schools. Nonetheless, having previously compromised in other church-state matters in recent decades, many Baptists in Augusta and throughout the nation would do so again, by the 1970s willfully accepting government funds for denominational institutions of higher education, while increasingly (and incorrectly) criticizing the government for forbidding prayer in public schools.[570]

National and world concerns aside, a bulletin headline of "Our Ideal: A Great Church" encapsulated the congregation's overriding desire. One bulletin article declared that "A church cannot rise above its people. If it would be a better church in character, in attendance, in the things that money can buy, then its people must be better in character, in attendance, and in Christian giving." The article reminded members that there were "Ten Important Growth Factors in the Building of a Baptist Church to Meet the Needs of All"—Sunday School, Training Union, Woman's Missionary Society (Union), Brotherhood, a music program, church-wide visitation, mission activities, Sunday morning worship, Sunday evening worship, and Wednesday evening prayer service. First Baptist embodied all ten denominational emphases in robust fashion at the turn of the decade of the sixties, not the least being missions. In 1960 the church adopted two new missionaries to Nigeria, Dr. and Mrs. G. G. Pitman.[571]

Church members spoke of Jack Robinson in glowing terms, appreciative of the excitement, enthusiasm, and passion he brought to the pulpit and community. Several of his sermons appeared in a 1960 collection of best Southern Baptist sermons. Robinson's influence spanned the globe, including service as chaplain of the SS *Argentine* in 1961, a stint that took the Robinson family to Europe and Russia. Upon the occasion of his tenth anniversary with the church in September 1963, congregational members compiled a Book of Appreciation to the Robinsons and the church hosted a reception for the family. Daughter Charlotte

Anne occasioned family and church pride. At the age of eleven an excellent student and world traveler, in a city newspaper contest she won a twenty-volume set of World Book Encyclopedias.[572]

Although denominational ties and a charismatic pastor collectively elevated the global reach of First Baptist, troubles mounted closer to home. Following the 1954 *Brown v. Board of Education* Supreme Court ruling outlawing racial discrimination in public schools and paving the way for the Civil Rights movement and integration, the city of Augusta remained fully segregated longer than any other Georgia city. Over the objections of city leaders, a federal court in 1962 finally forced Augusta to integrate buses. Churches, however, were another matter. Like most other white Christian congregations of the South, congregants of First Baptist Augusta throughout the decade refused to allow black persons into their sanctuary. Of the Civil Rights era, Jack Robinson later recollected that "Southern Baptists were not facing this issue at all." Historians in recent decades have pointed to Southern Baptists' adamant resistance to integration as a major contributor to irreversible denominational decline.[573]

Racial isolation, for First Baptist, paralleled the city's downtown decline. As families increasingly moved to the suburbs, for modest outlays the congregation continued purchasing nearby buildings, expanding further beyond Greene Street. Demolition of the old Jackson Hotel allowed additional parking space, while other properties underwent makeovers. Soaring expenses associated with remodeling and installation of air conditioning necessitated the hiring of a full-time building superintendent— Johnny K. Crawford—collectively signaling the difficulties inherent in maintaining outdated buildings.[574]

Cultural and structural challenges notwithstanding, the congregation's membership grew all the larger, topping 3,000. The ranks of deacons and ushers, yet all men at this point, further expanded to serve the needs of the church. Perhaps none was more prominent during this era than Roscoe McGahee. A local businessman, McGahee's church service spanned the breadth of the congregation. At various times he chaired the board of deacons and the board of ushers; served as church moderator; was a member of the Finance, Stewardship, and Building committees; served as president of "The Men of the Church"; and helped found the

Crusader Sunday School Class. Of McGahee, long-time church member Robert Anderson later recalled, "Roscoe was always there to greet you with a warm smile and handshake every Sunday. He did this for almost fifty years. Everyone knew and loved Roscoe."[575]

McGahee and his fellow laymen provided leadership for a congregation expanding across age groups. All areas of church life thrived. Increasing numbers of youth led to the creation of a new staff position, that of assistant pastor and youth director, initially filled by Lynn Bishop and followed by Dan Shaddock. A robust youth program included Sunday and Wednesday Bible studies and classes, weekly fellowships, recreation, chapel choir, revivals, banquets, competitive sports teams, and annual Youth Week and youth camp, the latter held at various locations including Hilton Head Island (South Carolina), Savannah, Panama City (Florida), and Ridgecrest (North Carolina). At the same time, growing ranks of aged members brought about the formation of the Golden Years Club. Yet another constitutional revision took place, while the church budget pressed and then surpassed a quarter of a million dollars.[576]

Several other notable personal landmarks, personnel changes, and church events occurred during the early years of the sixties. R. T. Baggott in 1962 celebrated 1,000 consecutive Sundays attending Sunday School. The following year the church called O. David DeRossett as minister of music. Also in 1963 the church's History Committee undertook pre-liminary planning for a 150th anniversary celebration in 1967 by initiating a "Know Your Church" bulletin column. Formed in 1965 and chaired by Cason Bruker, the Sesquicentennial Committee spent the next two years planning the anniversary program.

Jack Robinson in 1964 led the way in the creation of a forward-looking annual evangelical emphasis known as Four Great Sundays. Held each September thereafter through 1977 and featuring notable musical artists, the annual events attracted large crowds and many new members.[577]

A pride of the congregation, long-time Foreign Mission Board (FMB) missionary Lucy Wright in 1964 announced her retirement following forty-two years of medical ministry in China and Korea. Upon returning to the states the church named her "missionary emeritus." Jackie Eubank, in turn, moved to Africa as a FMB medical missionary, while the church's annual contributions to the Lottie Moon Christmas Offering for foreign missions approached $15,000. In recognition of the church's denominational engagement and contributions, Jack Robinson in 1965 was elected to the Executive Committee of the Southern Baptist Convention. Internally, new staff members arrived: Alice and Allen Stickney (youth director and assistant minister, 1964), Sidney E. Hatfield (building superintendent, 1964, in the wake of the passing of Johnny Crawford), and Jacques M. Kearns (music minister, 1965). By 1966 fourteen persons comprised the staff of a 3,609-member congregation.[578]

These and other remarkable congregational advances and achievements came amid strong, religiously adverse social and political upheavals roiling America and reaching into Augusta. Among the more notable challenges were the advancing Civil Rights movement and Southern white resistance to the Civil Rights Act (1964) and Voting Rights Act (1965), troubling escalation of the decade-long Vietnam War, pervasive popularity of subversively-perceived rock 'n roll music among younger Americans, and a growing and rebellious youth culture that birthed the women's liberation movement and a sexual revolution—among other developments.

Precisely at this perplexing and puzzling time Augusta's First Baptist Church simultaneously looked backward across 150 years of vibrant faith heritage and gazed forward in search of a new home.

Difficult Transitions, Exciting Times

For many First Baptist members the church's weeklong "Celebration and Consecration" of late March and early April 1967 provided the greatest highlights of the year. A relay horseback ride by church deacons to the Greene Street sanctuary commemorated the eighteenth century journey of Daniel Marshall to the outskirts of Augusta, leading to his arrest by colonial authorities, reminding congregational members of the persecution experienced by their faith forebears. Other events took place in the Bell Auditorium near the church. A historical pageant written by Dorothy Lehman Sumerau and directed by Allen Symms dramatized twelve events in the 150-year-old story of the church, while a special Easter cantata also bore witness to the church's faithfulness. Former living pastors were honored in a reception. A sermon by Southern Baptist Convention president Dr. H. Franklin Paschall highlighted one evening service.

The same week, in one of the most memorable events in the church's more recent history, the world-renowned evangelist Billy Graham preached, and musician Cliff Burrows led music, at an evening service attended by an overflowing crowd. Of greater long-lasting significance, the release of a new church history volume, written by Anna Olive Jones and accompanied by a signing party, took place. The week drew to a close with "dinner on the grounds" inside the Bell Auditorium, a special music presentation by *Baptist Hour* soloist Joe Ann Shelton, the burning of remaining church indebtedness notes, and a concluding sermon by Jack Robinson in the sanctuary.[579]

A special prayer by Robinson declared of the church's heritage: "We thank Thee for her baptisms, weddings, and funerals; for her record of ministries to hungering hearts, seeking minds, and embittered souls. We pray that this ministry will continue: that the sick be visited, the captive be freed, that children be taught, that youth be given guidance, that adults be challenged, and the aged be comforted." Church historian Jones offered her observations and thoughts of the church's long journey: "...through fire, flood, and battle it has stood, a bulwark of spiritual strength...In the entire 150-year span First Baptist Church has made it a tradition to open her heart to meet the needs of her people. She has ever been generous in monetary giving, stalwart in keeping the faith, and conscious of her missionary challenge."[580]

Within days of celebrating their faith heritage, congregational members turned their attention forward. United in honoring the past, members' views of the future diverged greatly. In 1964 a group of church leaders had met in the home of Robert Norman to discuss relocating the church. A Long-Range Planning Committee resulted, and in April 1967 the committee reported its findings. An old, deteriorating, and crowded sanctuary could no longer meet congregational needs. Efforts to acquire two adjacent lots for expansion ended in failure. The 3,601-member church's current portfolio of secondary buildings lacked adequate space, requiring ever greater financial commitment for maintenance. Parking facilities were inadequate. Fewer and fewer church families lived in or near downtown.

Many long-time members, although aware of the problems, expressed emotional opposition to a recommendation by the planning committee that the congregation consider moving to a new location. Embedded in the midst of more than an entire block of church buildings, the sanctuary in particular housed the memories of generations of families of faith, powerful legacies embedded in minds and hearts and spiritual moments sealed in eternity. Why not build a new, third, larger, and grander sanctuary on this sacred site? Most First Baptist churches in America, after all, yet remained in downtown locations, many thriving.

Other members, however, envisioned the practical advantages of moving to a more expansive location central to the majority of church members, and featuring newly-constructed, modern facilities attractive to young families. Regardless, whether remaining or moving, a successful future for First Baptist required a greater financial commitment on the part of members than ever before. Facing mixed feelings among members and the inevitable prospect of massive financial outlays, the congregation made no immediate decision regarding the church's future.[581]

Nor did a resolution suitable to all church members emerge as congregational discord characterized the months following the report of the planning committee. Nonetheless, with insight from church member and real estate agent Newt Thompson, the committee identified a potential building site, thirty-two largely-wooded acres to the west of the city, situated in the midst of an area to which city planners envisioned Augusta expanding in the coming decades. Only one business, a grocery store, existed in the vicinity of the land, leading some members to balk at moving to such an isolated location. Abandoning the corner of Greene and 8th would represent the most significant church event in the lives of First Baptist members, a rooting-up of the entire tangible identity of the church's 150-year history. Not surprisingly, opposition hardened among some in the face of such a monumental undertaking. Proponents, however, believed a relocation was necessary in order for the congregation to prosper in the future. Church staff and most lay leaders were of the latter opinion. Relations between factions grew tense, casting a shadow over worship, Bible studies, and other church activities.

On May 5, 1968 came an eagerly-anticipated and memorable day. Gathering in the Bell Auditorium, members cast votes on the future of their church. Should the congregation purchase the land in question for $488,000? Upon tally of the ballots, the majority answered "yes." Afterward proponents went home that night anticipating a new future for the church, while some opponents determined to dig in their heels.[582]

What happened next plumbed the depths of Baptist polity, straining the historical unity of the Augusta congregation. Democratic decision-making, a foundational principle of the Baptist faith before democracy came to the American nation, paired with a strong sense of Christian graciousness and a willingness to reconcile had long characterized the congregation. Few Baptist churches founded in America's early years had avoided congregational splits in the many ensuing years. Augusta's First Baptist congregation, however, stood as a notable exception. So when fifteen disgruntled church members in November 1968 took the unprecedented step of launching a lawsuit and obtaining a restraining order to prevent the church from moving, a disappointed Jack Robinson, along with staff and lay leaders, faced unchartered and uncertain waters.

Amid growing excitement leavened with legal tensions, church leaders, confident that the judicial system would ultimately refuse to interfere with democratic church polity, moved forward in planning for the relocation. Evidencing the enormous scale of the undertaking, ninety church members comprised the Building Committee that met for the first time on January 20, 1969. Chaired by long-time lay leader Richard (Dick) Daniel, the committee began the task of formulating a financially feasible plan for constructing a multi-building campus on Walton Way. At the same time Robinson, Daniel, and others sought to allay the concerns of dissenting litigants. Genteel and unceasing efforts at reconciliation won over some opponents. A 1969 decision by the Georgia Supreme Court against plaintiffs, followed by judicial denials of appeals in 1970 and 1971, resulted in a win for the church.[583]

On the corner of Greene and 8th, meanwhile, weekly church life carried on much as usual, including strong attendance for worship, Sunday School, Training Union, Woman's Missionary Union, Brotherhood, youth group meetings, and other activities. Charlotte Robinson modeled the role of an ideal minister's wife, teaching young married women's

Sunday School, W.M.U., and a new members Baptist history class. She also conducted historic tours of church buildings. Among special emphases, Youth Week remained an annual highlight, while the yearly Four Great Sundays in Septembers drew large crowds to hear first-class musicians and passionate preaching.[584]

First Baptist Augusta also maintained a significant presence in larger Baptist life, a reflection in no small part of its renowned pastor. In 1968 Jack and Charlotte Robinson accompanied a youth contingent to the Baptist World Youth Conference in Berne, Switzerland. In a life-changing experience, the church's youth learned from world-renowned Christian leaders, including theologian Karl Barth, pastoral counselor Paul Tournier, and evangelist Billy Graham. Afterward Charlotte Robinson wrote a glowing accent of the experience, her article published in the Georgia Baptist *Christian Index*. Jack Robinson, now the church's longest-serving pastor, in 1970 toured the world on a preaching tour and traveled with a contingent of Baptist World Alliance leaders to Washington D.C., visiting president Richard Nixon in the Oval Office. Few equaled the Augusta pastor's prominence in national and world Baptist affairs.[585]

Back home in Augusta, the year 1970 emerged as one of the most pivotal in the church's history. Under the direction of the Building Committee, church members through a "Suggestion Opportunity '70" campaign were encouraged to provide feedback concerning their preferences for the Walton Way facilities. Many responded enthusiastically. Spilling over into the larger life of the church, members' excitement fueled a forward-looking, rousing spring revival led by James W. Middleton and Ron Owens. A telephone survey of unchurched families in the western reaches of Augusta accompanied the first sign of the First Baptist presence on Walton Way: the erecting of a "Future Home" sign. Signaling growing anticipation among members, a "smashing success" of a picnic, the first church event on the land, "attracted a crowd of more than a thousand and generated a terrific spirit of enthusiasm."[586]

Realizing the monetary challenges facing the congregation in the construction of new buildings, a planning committee in 1970 crafted a debt-retirement campaign designed to retire church indebtedness by the end of the following year. Afterward and to most church members' relief,

Superior Court Judge William M. Fleming issued a final judgment against the remaining few dissidents, declaring, "There is no genuine issue to any material fact . . . the action is hereby dismissed." The congregation responded in November by affirming a new budget, the largest in the church's history, and pledging more than the budgeted amount.[587]

The church's whirlwind year of 1970 also included the hosting of two significant denominational events. In honor of its founding in the church in 1845, the SBC Home Mission Board celebrated its 125th anniversary at First Baptist. Georgia Baptists, meanwhile, returned to First Baptist for their annual gathering. Messengers from churches across the state experienced the hospitality of which the congregation was long known. Elected president of the convention, Robinson addressed messengers, speaking to Southern Baptists' concerns over a widening distance between American youth and church against the backdrop of a nationwide youth countercultural movement and young peoples' opposition to the Vietnam War. Speaking with words of caution in the midst of his church's year of triumph, Robinson focused on generational issues dividing Southern Baptists in Augusta and beyond. College experiences increasingly led youth away from church participation. Many churched young men served in uniform in Vietnam, even as many on the home front criticized the controversial conflict. Robinson acknowledged parental and denominational angst over youth activism and troubles. Declaring that Southern Baptists should pay "more attention" to young persons, he nonetheless assured those in attendance of no "generation gap in our churches and denominations." Other state conventions reported declining baptism rates, but Robinson perceived Georgia Baptists as stable, although noting that "I think we might have to confront within five or ten years the issue of baptism."[588]

Meanwhile, the city simmered with tensions other than religious and generational. Against the backdrop of little progress toward ending segregation in the city, the killing of a black teenager in the city jail in May 1970 led to a protest at the municipal building a mere three blocks from the First Baptist sanctuary. A march southward followed. Turning into a riot, looters attacked dozens of non-black businesses, including some Chinese-owned. Some 1,000 National Guardsmen and 150 state troopers were deployed. Before the violence could be stemmed, six black men lay dead, shot in the back. In the aftermath of the rioting and deaths, Augusta formed a Human Relations Commission and in 1972 under federal orders finally integrated schools, the last city in Georgia to do so.[589]

As Augusta integrated schools, Jack Robinson yet served as president of the Georgia Baptist Convention. In his presidential address at the 1972 annual convention in Savannah, the Augusta pastor reflected upon Southern Baptists' blind spots. "Almighty God builds the Church out of the rough material of human nature," he reminded his audience. "It is evident that the Church has often been manipulative in evangelism, at times ignoring minorities and been trapped in culture, has even sometimes taken a 'flat-out' stance on the Bible, and has known all about 'the sweet bye and bye' but little about the here and now." For his part, Robinson sought to help alleviate inequities among Augusta citizens through service on the Augusta Housing Authority.[590]

Robinson's call for ecclesial, theological, and methodological revisioning against the backdrop of cultural transformation in Augusta and throughout the South pointed to an accelerating decline of the Southern Baptist Convention, state Baptist conventions affiliated with the SBC, and many local congregations. Historians since have identified both the youth counterculture and Southern Baptist opposition to the Civil Rights Movement and racial integration as quickening downward denominational trends. On the local church level from the fifties into the seventies, the continued refusal of many First Baptist churches of the South, including the Augusta congregation, to open sanctuary doors to black persons tainted their Christian witness to increasingly socially liberal younger generations.[591]

Nonetheless, as national and regional winds of cultural and social change blew across Augusta, the timing of the First Baptist move from an economically-decaying area to the leading edge of the city's growth westward offered a sense of shelter and direction that many historically-downtown First Baptist congregations of the South did not experience. Five exciting and intense years following the initial suggestion of relocation, in 1972 the congregation submitted to the architects' final recommendations for the new campus. Minister of Education Charles E. Cunningham directed the planning for the forthcoming educational facilities, the first phase of the building program. Dick Daniel maintained oversight of the entirety of the campus development. New associate pastor Sanford Kidd provided additional ministerial leadership.[592]

On the heels of the church's first worship service televised in color, February 4, 1973, a fund-raising campaign titled "Together We Build" ran from late February into the month of March. Led by Robert C. Norman, the successful six-week effort garnered $1,303,799 in pledges. Members packed the Greene Street sanctuary for a celebratory Sunday service on March 25. "Dr. Robinson asked the congregation to rise and sing 'To God Be the Glory,' saying, 'I don't think you have ever yet sung it like I want you to sing it now,' and the people responded with a spirit-filled rendition of the beloved hymn of praise." Praise and glory to God were also given on June 4 during the first formal church service held at Walton Way, a Wednesday evening prayer meeting that took place in a former gasoline station remodeled to serve as a temporary activity building. A ground-breaking service for the educational building took place on December 2.[593]

Recognizing the inspired and passionate leadership of Dr. Jack Robinson as having enabled church staff and lay leaders to lead the congregation to new heights, First Baptist on September 9, 1973 honored the Robinsons on their twentieth-year anniversary with the church. A number of Baptist dignitaries attended the celebration, including Mrs. Robert Stanley Denny representing the Baptist World Alliance, Porter Routh representing the Southern Baptist Convention, and Searcy S. Garrison representing the Georgia Baptist Convention. Charlotte remained a leader among the church's women in 1973. Elder daughter Charlotte Ann, a recent graduate of Agnes Scott College, taught at Columbia County's Bel Air School. Younger daughter Frances enrolled in Augusta College in the fall.[594]

Meanwhile, associate pastor Sanford Kidd and wife Sue felt called to the mission field. On April 28, 1974 the Foreign Mission Board of the SBC commissioned the Kidds as missionaries to Kenya, Africa. There they represented First Baptist for a number of years, faithfully prayed over and supported by the church's Woman's Missionary Union.[595]

A second staff departure in 1974 came rather abruptly. By all accounts, Jack Robinson's stature had never been higher. In the first half of the year he served as a distinguished visiting professor at Southern Baptist Theological Seminary in Kentucky, held a seat on the Executive Committee of the Southern Baptist Convention, and preached the SBC sermon at the denomination's annual gathering in Dallas, Texas. Two months after his starring role at the SBC, however, on August 18 Robinson suddenly resigned, effective immediately, from First Baptist Augusta. Voicing great affection for the church, he cited health issues as the reason for his departure. Charlotte Robinson on the day of her husband's resignation acknowledged her appreciation to the congregation, in a personal letter declaring, "You have been the kindest, dearest, and most generous people I have ever known in my life. When I leave this church, it will be with a very heavy heart. This is my home, and you are my treasured friends." Under Jack Robinson's leadership 4,968 members had been added to church rolls, 1,421 persons baptized, and 467 couples married. In the years to come the couple would engage in vibrant ministry apart from a local church setting, eventually retiring in Augusta and returning to First Baptist as congregants.[596]

In the wake of Jack Robinson's resignation, First Baptist turned to Hilton C. Garrett, recently called as assistant minister, to preach on most Sunday mornings for the remainder of the year, with guest preachers otherwise filling the pulpit. A year of turmoil and heartbreak closed with the election of new deacons, the annual Lottie Moon Christmas Offering, two performances of the Singing Christmas Tree (featuring the sanctuary, chapel, and hand bell choirs), and "A New Year's Prayer" for God to strengthen congregants' hearts "to face with courage all that may befall us along the unknown trail. Lead us in faith and hope and love. Grant us thy presence as we walk in familiar ways or engage in fresh experience."[597]

9

Freedom and Faithfulness: The Walton Way Years

Following years of envisioning, planning, and construction, on August 24, 1975 the First Baptist congregation worshiped for the last time at the corner of Greene and 8th streets. Nostalgia, hope, anticipation, and excitement marked the occasion. Among those remembering and honoring the past were dozens of descendants of early church members who had participated in the church's 1820 and 1902 cornerstone ceremonies:

- T. R. Wright
- James C. C. Black
- Enoch H. Callaway
- H. C. Perkins
- William T. Brantly
- W. J. Rutherford
- J. C. Lee
- James T. Bothwell
- John Phinizy
- Lindsay Coleman

The service closed with the congregation singing, "Blest Be the Tie That Binds." Many departed that day with a thankful sadness, never to return. "Fortunate indeed," Martha Daniel noted, were those over the years who had worshiped in the Greene Street sanctuary.

One week later on August 31 the congregation moved to 3500 Walton Way. Worshiping in the gymnasium of the activities building, church members offered praise to God for their new future in West Augusta. Thankfulness to God continued during the facilities' dedication service of October 19, a ceremony attended, among others, by Edward M. McIntyre, the mayor of Augusta; James L. Sullivan, past president of the Southern Baptist Sunday School Board; and William W. Leathers, pastor of the Kiokee Baptist Church. The congregation honored Dick Daniel for chairing the Building Committee, while Sullivan preached a message titled "Because Our God is Great."[598]

Also building westward, the city reached the church three years later with the opening of two new shopping centers, the Regency Mall and the Augusta Mall. Many downtown businesses relocated to the malls, leaving in their wake more empty buildings and urban decay downtown. City leaders and businessmen responded in the late 1980s with a downtown revitalization project along the Savannah River. Since expanded, Riverwalk Augusta features parks, an amphitheater, museums, art galleries, and hotels.[599]

Commercial development quickly surrounded the west end malls, followed by the rapid construction of residential neighborhoods. The construction of the Interstate 520 loop spurred yet more development. Perched in the midst of the bustle of activity stood the First Baptist Church, a prime beneficiary of the city's expansion.

Together

"Together We Build," a fundraising campaign begun in 1973 to finance the construction of the initial buildings on Walton Way, gave way in 1976 to a "Together We Continue to Build" campaign for the financing of a new sanctuary.[600] In a broader sense, "together" characterized the congregation that had persevered through a lawsuit, sadly bid farewell to the church's longest-serving pastor, moved far away from their historic downtown location, and eagerly anticipated an even brighter future.

Called as the new pastor of a rebirthed, expectant, and unified congregation, Arkansas native George Balentine, recommended by former pastor Albert W. Huyck, arrived in Augusta 1975, in time to lead the church to Walton Way. A graduate of Southern Baptist Theological Seminary, Balentine had taught at Palm Beach Atlantic College, written Southern Baptist curriculum, and traveled and studied abroad. His wife Mary Sue and daughter Beth quickly became involved in church activities.[601]

Evidencing the shared responsibility necessary for congregational cohesion, in 1976 a total of 280 members served on church committees. Committees included Trustees, Baptismal, Benevolence, Bereavement, Blood Bank, Christian Recreation, Committee on Committees, Evangelism, Finance, Food Service, Historical, Library/Media, Lord's Supper, Membership, Missions, Music, Nominating, Nursery, Personnel, Property, Public Relations, Pulpit-Supply, Radio TV/PA, Royal Ambassadors, Scouting, Stewardship, Student Loan, Transportation, Youth and Ushers.[602]

The church's programming and annual activities remained as they had been on the corner of Greene and 8th, a continuity providing internal familiarity and reflecting ongoing denominational ties. Even so, significant changes emerged. Perhaps most prominently, Balentine advocated for women's ordination, one of a growing number of Southern Baptist pastors to do so. In December 1975 at a gathering of city clergy he declared, "There is neither male nor female in Christ. There is no evidence that in the New Testament that women should not be ordained. Many women make outstanding contributions in missionary efforts, yet ordination is denied them."[603]

From their earliest days Baptists allowed for women ministers, yet few churches in ensuing centuries acted on the controversial subject of gender equality. Among progressive Southern Baptist churches of the 1970s, an emergence of women deacons marked the beginnings of a revival of a denominational tradition long neglected. In 1978 Dr. George Christenberry, Sunday School director, chaired a study committee on women's roles in the life of the church that advocated a change to deacon rules. A recommendation that "all resident members of the church over twenty-one years of age shall be eligible to serve as a deacon" passed on a vote of 168-80. Despite their newly-won eligibility, no women were voted in as deacons that year. Nonetheless, a new day slowly dawned as First Baptist Augusta and some other progressive Southern Baptist congregations embarked on the journey of welcoming women as equal partners in church life.[604]

The past and the present also intersected during the United States Bicentennial year of 1976, celebrated under the direction of a Bicentennial Committee chaired by Chaplain and Mrs. P. T. Raley. From June

13 through July 4 the festivities included a church-wide bicentennial picnic in a "wooded area" of the church's campus and the unveiling of a memorial plaque to the church's World War I and World War II veterans. A dramatic presentation honoring the spirit of America and titled "One Nation Under God" reflected the 1950s language of civil religion foreign to earlier Baptists.[605]

Tensions inherent in Baptists' evolving views on church and state sometimes surfaced in Sunday evening Church Training, a denominational program teaching Christian discipleship and Baptist heritage. The 1977-1978 year offered four "divisions" of courses for members: New Church Member Orientation, Church Leader Training, Doctrine Equipping Center, and Church Member Training.[606]

January Bible studies, an annual event in many Southern Baptist churches, likewise provided educational opportunities for members. In 1978 American Baptist theologian Ralph Elliott preached and taught the book of Exodus at First Baptist Augusta. In the early 1960s Elliott, then a professor at Midwestern Baptist Theological Seminary in Kansas City, Missouri, had been forced out of Southern Baptist life by a minority but vocal group of fundamentalist Southern Baptist pastors for advocating a non-literal, and hence liberal, interpretation of a portion of the book of Genesis. His views, however, were welcome in the theologically diverse Augusta congregation.[607]

Modern technology intersected ecclesiology and theology in the late 1970s. In 1976 the church published its first color pictorial directory. March 1977 marked the first edition of the *Interpreter*, a semi-monthly newsletter designed "to interpret the ongoing life, work, and witness of the First Baptist Church fellowship." The same year the church hired Lavinia Polatty as financial secretary, a position she held for more than four decades. Her tenure witnessed the expansive development of the Walton Way property, spanned multiple generations of church families, and included a technological transition from typewriters to computers. A key voice for First Baptist, Polatty helped educate many lay persons about church finances and provided a ready conversation partner with church staff.[608]

Economics apart from congregational life also shaped the church. The nearby August 1978 opening of the Augusta Mall, one of the largest retail centers in Georgia at that time, anchored the city's west end and enhanced the surrounding commercial and residential real estate market, boding well for First Baptist. Wasting no time in taking advantage of favorable demographics, in September the church organized seventy Neighborhood Prayer Parties representing the twenty-two neighborhoods wherein the majority of church members lived, "to draw us closer to one another and to God." The same month the church celebrated twenty years of television ministry. In October the church passed a new annual budget of $1.1 million. Two major church campaigns overarched this time of great opportunity. "Together We Tithe and Build" and "Together We Reach Out" pointed the way to a new sanctuary.[609]

A New Sanctuary and New Ministries

Winds of religious hostility arose in Baptist life in 1979. Fundamentalists publicly initiated efforts to reshape Southern Baptist Convention boards and agencies into their theological mold. At the same time, independent Baptist Jerry Falwell founded the Moral Majority, a national coalition of conservative to fundamentalist Christians determined to turn America into a Christian nation. The two movements shared common ground as Falwell assisted Southern Baptist fundamentalists in their quest to take over the SBC.[610]

In the October 1979 election of the church's first two women deacons, Augusta's First Baptist congregation rejected ascendant conservative theological and political correctness. Prominent members of the church and not seeking controversy, Anna (Olive Jones) Bannister and Margaret Parker remained undaunted by opposition from some who disapproved of women leaders. The same month of her election, Bannister, as church historian, directed a "Historical Panorama of Building" program, while Parker, holder of a seminary degree in biblical studies, designed stained glass windows for the church's envisioned new sanctuary. A Sanctuary Committee, chaired by Mary Emma Anderson and including Jackie Blanchard, meticulously planned the building's design, including a high ceiling designed to evoke the feel of the original sanctuary.

Martha Bell, meanwhile, penned an essay on the difficulties of building during a recession. "If today we face tremendous challenges," she wrote, "we do so with a heritage of faith that assures us that God's greatness is adequate to our every need. We face a bright future with the promises of God." Looking beyond physical facilities, George Balentine encouraged church members and Georgia Baptists at large to busy themselves with the task of evangelization in fulfillment of the New Testament command to spread the Good News of Christ's love for the world. In Augusta and beyond, numerous were the "lost," a euphemism for those persons not knowing Christ and thus bound for hell.[611]

A December 2, 1979 groundbreaking service for the new sanctuary, designed by architects and church members Stan Woodhurst and E. L. Perry, bespoke of great hopes for First Baptist. The cornerstone ceremony of November 2, 1980 elicited joy and praise for God's faithfulness. Many members joined the congregation as the building slowly took shape. Anticipation mounted with each passing month.[612]

Within and without the pulpit, Balentine provided excellent leadership during a time both hopeful and adverse. Alongside the pastor a professional and dedicated staff helped meet the needs of the growing congregation. The newest staff member, Jacob Malone, yet another Southern Baptist Theological Seminary graduate, joined the church team as minister of activities. Launching what would become a thirty-three-year career with First Baptist, Malone supervised a rapidly-growing roster of recreational and mission programs and projects.[613]

Amid the sanctuary construction project, George Balentine in 1982 accepted a new ministerial calling as president of Shorter College, a Baptist college in Rome, Georgia. He departed with the deep gratitude of the congregation that he had led from downtown Augusta to Walton Way, into a new chapter of women's leadership, and toward a new house of worship.[614]

Following Balentine, the congregation in late 1982 chose Charles Bugg as the church's next pastor. A Florida native and graduate of Stetson University and the Southern Baptist Theological Seminary, Bugg had previously pastored churches in Florida and Indiana, most recently the First Baptist Church of DeLand, Florida. The congregation welcomed Charles and Diane and their two young children, Laura Beth and David.[615]

Bugg arrived at an important period in the church's history. Central to the congregation's ministry and presence on Walton Way, the new sanctuary opened for worship on March 30, 1983. A majestic Georgian architectural style building with a semicircular Corinthian portico entrance 35 feet in radius and with columns 38 feet in height greeted worshipers. A 199-foot tall steeple crowned 41,000 square feet of floor space capable of seating 1,250 persons on the main floor and the balcony combined. Broadcast engineering facilities within the sanctuary included a studio and equipment room.

Celebration, joy, excitement, and thankfulness to God characterized the special day long anticipated. Along the interior walls beautiful stained glass windows visually portrayed the "Life of Christ and Story of Salvation" ("Gospel Window," on the south side of the building and the left side facing the pulpit) and "The Response of the World to the Life and Work of Christ" ("Epistle Window," on the north side of the building and the right side facing the pulpit). The latter included panes representing the history of the church.[616]

Following a few remaining touches, September served as an extended time of dedication of the new sanctuary. Celebration, inspiration, historical remembrance, and future visioning marked the month. Jack Robinson, now pastor emeritus, and former pastor George L. Balentine, alongside forty-eight other former staff and members, attended the Sunday, September 4 service. From Louisville, Kentucky came Southern Baptist Theological Seminary president Roy L. Honeycutt, indicative of the importance the church placed upon the institution known as the intellectual center of Southern Baptist life.

To a packed house Robinson delivered a sermon titled "What Happens in This Place?" Of the move to Walton Way the former pastor declared, "We needed to move, and it was the right time and the right place." Of the sanctuary he enthused, "I think it's a fitting and gorgeous worship setting," but "it's the people and the ministries and the programs" that are most important.[617]

Other sermons followed during dedication month, including "Remembering Our Promise" by Charles Bugg (September 11), "What Mean These Stones" by Balentine (September 18), and "Remembering Our Purpose" by Bugg (September 25).[618]

Justifiably proud of their accomplishment, First Baptist members nonetheless could no longer count upon a lovely sanctuary in and of itself to attract large numbers of new members. Yet even as many prominent Baptist churches across the South evidenced visible signs of decline, First Baptist Augusta saw continued vitality based on these 1983 figures:

- Church membership—3,489
- Sunday School enrollment—2,060
- Woman's Missionary Union—360
- "Men of the Church"—190
- Graded choir program—508

The addition of Patti Fowler to the church staff as coordinator of preschool, kindergarten, and Mother's Day Out programs enhanced family ministries. Among the best in Augusta, the church's preschool served the city at large. For church members, a new education building soon complemented the sanctuary and provided expanded accommodations for the growing congregation.[619]

Although defying demographic trends, headwinds remained, including the impact of popular televangelists. Far different from the city-wide broadcasting of worship services, televangelists gathered national followings. Rather than encouraging listeners to participate in local church life, they solicited listeners' loyalties and money. Charles Bugg addressed this problem in 1985 while speaking to the West Augusta Rotary Club. "There are people who are vulnerable—those who sit home all day, who are lonely and confused," he noted. Bugg, expressing traditional Baptist convictions, also voiced concerns about the maturing Religious Right movement that intersected with the world of televangelism. "I am tremendously afraid of the wedding of politics and religion. One day it may not be your brand of politics or religion."[620]

Bugg spoke of the growing politicization of American Christianity even as the Southern Baptist Convention and Georgia Baptist Convention drifted away from historical convictions and into the currents of the Religious Right. Faithfully attending annual SBC and GBC gatherings, he witnessed the transformation. Each summer of his Augusta pastorate Bugg returned from the annual SBC discouraged over fundamentalist gains toward control of the organization, a concern shared by many leading laypersons. Although he served on the state GBC Executive Committee and as a convention vice president, by the second half of the decade Georgia Baptist fundamentalists openly criticized Bugg's theology as too moderate. David Hudson, a Harvard Law School graduate and "one of the most articulate laypersons" in the church, addressed the GBC in defense of Bugg and traditional Baptist identity. Amid concerns about the growing theological distance between their church and Southern Baptist entities, in 1988 the congregation formed a Denominational Study Committee and began assessing what steps, if any, the church might take in relation to the SBC and GBC.[621]

On a more personal level, a family crisis and subsequent struggle impacted pastor and church alike. A mere two-and-a-half months following their arrival in Augusta, Charles and Diane Bugg learned that their son David, age eleven, had a brain tumor. Surgeries and radiation treatment followed, as did parental grief and bitterness. The church rallied around the Bugg family with support and love, creating a special bonding between pastor and congregation. As Charles Bugg later recalled, David's illness during his Augusta pastorate transformed him into a better, sensitive pastor, in turn allowing him, from his own dark experiences, to serve as a counselor to many church families facing difficult problems. Pastoral themes often found expression in sermons, some of which were collected and published in a book of sermons titled *Getting on Top When Life Gets Us Down*. The volume spoke to readers of how Christ helps persons overcome life's problems. David survived his long bout with the brain tumor, but it left him suffering from physical side effects that continued into adulthood.[622]

As pastor of the most prominent Baptist church in the city, Bugg also enjoyed an elevated status in Augusta. While involved in various clubs and a speaker at numerous civic and service events and functions, the Augusta pastor's most meaningful community involvement was his relationship with the city's Black Baptists, including the historical Tabernacle Baptist Church. With race relations yet tense in Augusta, Bugg had opportunity to minister across racial divides during his pastoral tenure.[623]

Youth ministry, meanwhile, progressed under the direction of youth minister Reece Sherman, who held the position from 1984 to 1992. Youth programs at Walton Way, service projects in the community, and annual summer camps highlighted the church's efforts to reach and disciple junior and senior high schoolers. As minister of activities, Jacob Malone's work intersected with the church youth in the planning and directing of children's and youth camps and organizing community sports leagues for Augusta area churches. Other ministers of this era included Phil Bennett, minister of education, and Andrew Menger, minister to singles.[624]

Echoing a historical pattern, a number of laypersons played leading roles in the life of First Baptist Augusta during the decade of the eighties. Thomas Blanchard, Tom Dozier, George Perkins, and Guy Jennings, among others, served as effective moderators during this time, the position second only to the pastor in terms of influence. Robert ("Bob") Norman, long-time prominent Augusta attorney, also provided key leadership. In 1986 Patricia Mangum was elected the church's first woman chair of the Finance Committee. Pat otherwise served the church as a deacon and member of the Personnel Committee. Debbie Williams organized many of the church's special events, while Martha Daniel chaired the Landscape Architect Committee charged with beautifying the church's grounds, including the addition of a memorial garden. Also crucial to the life of the church, pastoral secretary Eileen Martin enabled staff members to more efficiently fulfill their ministerial roles and responsibilities.[625]

Notable events included a 1988 celebration of the 100th anniversary of Woman's Missionary Union under the direction of church WMU director Francis Hardin. The church's WMU included more than a dozen groups and provided oversight of Baptist Young Women, Acteens, Girls in Action, Mission Friends, and Royal Ambassador programs. The first annual women's retreat took place in 1988.[626]

The church's music ministry, led by Glen C. Adkins, also expanded. The sanctuary choir toured Europe in 1989. Some 660 persons participated in 18 choirs and instrumental groups at that time. In addition to Adkins, paid music ministry staff included a secretary, part-time organist, part-time music assistant, and part-time instrumental director.[627]

Major staff changes marked the latter part of the decade. Arriving from Southern Baptist Theological Seminary, where he had served in administrative roles including assistant to president Roy Honeycutt, Rodger Murchison in 1987 assumed the position of associate pastor. Raised in a strong Baptist family in the small rural community of Coy, Arkansas, Murchison accepted Christ at the young age of ten, later attending Baylor University. From there Murchison went to Southern for his seminary degree, afterward working for the school. Recruited by Chuck Bugg and a search committee seeking to meet a growing congregational need for pastoral care, Rodger and Margaret and their son Mitchell (age five) and daughter Rebecca (age three) found a warm welcome at First Baptist. Rodger, in turn, provided a much-needed counseling ministry to the large congregation, his tenure lasting twenty-five years and including hundreds of wedding and funerals.

Murchison later in his ministry earned a doctoral degree in grief ministry at Princeton Theological Seminary, taught twice-annual grief ministry workshops in the church, and developed a national and international speaking ministry in the field of grief ministry. Rodger also became a leader in the Augusta community, serving as chairman of the Augusta Housing Authority and on the boards of Habitat for Humanity and the Ronald McDonald House. In 2011 he published a book, *Guide for Grief*, aimed at survivors and caregivers and focused on ten common questions, including, Why did my loved one die? Where are they? How long will I grieve? What about children who mourn and mourning children? Can any good come from all this loss?[628]

The Bugg family members, meanwhile, expressed gratitude for the church's care of them as Charles resigned from the pastorate in April 1989 to accept a position, ironically, at Southern Baptist Theological Seminary. There Bugg taught as professor of preaching until 1993, afterward pastoring Providence Baptist Church in Charlotte, North Carolina, and later serving as interim pastor in a number of churches and periodically returning to preach at First Baptist Augusta on special occasions.[629]

Denominational and Mission Transitions

As the decade of the nineties dawned, the theological and political controversy within Southern Baptist life reached new heights. New fundamentalist SBC leaders decried Baptists' historical freedom commitments and instead demanded that missionaries and other convention employees embrace a literal, inerrant Bible, a more recent and controversial understanding of scriptural inspiration and interpretation. In addition they rejected women in ministry and the academic freedom of seminaries. First Baptist Augusta's Denominational Study Committee, comprised of concerned laypersons and staff including David Hudson and Rodger Murchison, reevaluated the church's relationship with the SBC. On January 24, 1990 the committee issued a resolution recommending that the church continue its "historic commitment to the Southern Baptist Convention" but "Cautiously study the organization and purposes of the Southern Baptist Alliance and Baptists Committed to the Southern Baptist Convention" and "Encourage Southern Baptist Convention leadership which is inclusive of *all* Southern Baptists." The church decided to continue supporting the SBC's Foreign Mission Board, Home Mission Board, Baptist Sunday School Board, and Cooperative Program, along with ministries of the Georgia Baptist Convention. The congregation also reaffirmed its relationship with the more moderate Augusta Baptist Association. At the same time the Denominational Study Committee on behalf of the church determined to "monitor" the denominational entities and "review Southern Baptist Sunday School Board literature to make sure it affirms the doctrines of the priesthood of the believer and the competency of the soul." The committee encouraged deacons to read literature about the changes taking place in Southern Baptist life. Finally, the church affirmed support of:

1. Ordination of women
2. Commitment to missions
3. Academic freedom for Southern Baptist seminaries
4. *All* Baptists in Christian love, regardless of their differences.[630]

Amid denominational challenges First Baptist Augusta called a new pastor in April 1990. Recommended by former pastor George Balentine and a native of Hialeah, Florida, Timothy L. Owings, wife Kathleen (Kathie) Pignato, sons Nathan and Justin, and daughter Lindsey were enthusiastically received into the First Baptist family. A graduate of Palm Beach Atlantic College and with a doctorate from Southern Baptist Theological Seminary, Owings had pastored the Calvary Baptist Church in Tuscaloosa, Alabama prior to coming to Augusta.[631]

Proclaiming a focus on missions and diversity, Owings arrived at a critical juncture in denominational life. Following the election of twelve consecutive fundamentalist presidents of the SBC, ultraconservatives now claimed a majority of trustees on Southern Baptist mission boards. Mere months after the recommendations of the church's Denominational Study Committee, in August 1990 some 3,000 concerned, traditional Southern Baptists informally gathered in Atlanta to discuss an alternative funding program of missionary support. Owings, Murchison, and key lay leaders from First Baptist Augusta attended the gathering. From this meeting emerged a new, national plan for supporting missionary work, formalized in the establishment of the Cooperative Baptist Fellowship (CBF) in 1991. On March 20, 1991 the Augusta congregation became one of the earliest churches to adopt the alternative giving plan, allowing members the choice of designating a portion of their tithes to either the SBC or CBF. Although a momentous and groundbreaking step for the mother church of the SBC, many members believed the convention, not the church, had changed in terms of belief and practice. In moving away from a singular relationship with the SBC, First Baptist Augusta bore witness to the world of the primacy of Baptist principles of local church autonomy, freedom of conscience, and the priesthood of believers.

In the decades following, CBF came to function as an alternative denominational-like organization for moderate to liberal Baptists, primarily of the South. From an initial focus on missions, CBF also embraced alternative theological institutions, chaplaincy, and more. First Baptist Augusta gradually became more involved in CBF life, albeit not exclusively, than Southern Baptist life.[632]

Even as denominational upheaval buffeted the Southern Baptist Convention and impacted First Baptist Augusta, a new trend was taking shape in the Baptist world: the direct support of missionary work on the part of local churches. This emerging development in Baptist life arose from two decades of congregational youth ministries that often included annual youth camps and mission trips. In the Augusta congregation many adult members who had participated in mission trips during their youth helped transform the entire congregation's thinking about missions ministry.

Timothy and Kathie Owings, earlier having served on the mission field in Brazil, arrived at First Baptist as the church was weighing a greater focus on direct missions involvement. Phil Bennett, minister of education, and a group of laypersons had recently conducted a mission trip to Panama for the purpose of building a church, reporting favorably of their work. Mere months into his pastorate Owings preached the funeral of long-time church member Dorothy Moore, a retired school teacher who had been involved in missions education through WMU. Moore left one-third of her estate to the church. Owings recommended, and the church affirmed, the creation of the Dorothy Moore Missions Endowment from the proceeds of her estate gift. Set aside to send church members on immersion mission projects around the world, additional monies later enlarged the endowment, with the fund eventually consisting of millions of dollars. Dorothy Moore's generosity funded an expanding missions ministry, including three mission trips to Brazil led by the Owings.[633]

A focus on international and national missions, however, did not preclude local ministry and missions. Bennett led the church in the establishment of the First Vietnamese Baptist Church, an ethnic congregation that met in the Mission Activity Center of First Baptist. He also initiated church involvement in Augusta's Interfaith Hospitality Network, an organization ministering to homeless families. The Chinese Sunday School, of which Ralph Wong served as superintendent, remained a vital part of the congregation, and in 1990 First Baptist hosted a reunion of former members of the city's larger Chinese community. Many former residents returned for the special occasion, some from as far away as California.[634]

Other exciting events at Walton Way included the February 1991 dedication concert of a new Schantz Organ with a performance by Diane Bish. The same year witnessed the birth of a new music ministry program, the School of Arts; the addition of Randall Lee Germann to the staff as minister to singles; and the hosting of the Georgia Baptist Convention. On March 22, 1992 the congregation celebrated its 175th anniversary to the theme of "Heritage & Hope," a special event in which former pastors Paul Caudill, Warren Huyck, Jack Robinson, and George Balentine participated.[635]

In addition to advances on the Walton Way campus, First Baptist engaged the Augusta community. The Los Angeles riots of 1992 led Owings and Clarence Moore, pastor of Good Shepherd Baptist Church, to form "Augustans Together," an organization devoted to addressing local race relations. "It's difficult but not impossible," the First Baptist pastor noted, "to communicate the message of inclusion, respect, and love." Through Owings' invitation Gardner Taylor, pastor emeritus of the Concord Avenue Baptist Church of Brooklyn, New York, and one of the leading black Baptist preachers in America, preached at FBC Augusta on September 16, 1994, the first African American to preach from the church's pulpit. In addition, a pulpit exchange between Owings and Otis Moss III, pastor of Tabernacle Baptist Church, led to a 1999 joint worship service. "Both churches are concerned about the family, equal opportunity in society, and reaching people for Jesus," Moss stated. "And both have a strong commitment to preaching and doing the gospel with integrity and faithfulness."[636]

Owings also started an hour-long weekly evening radio show on WGAC. Titled "Religion Tonight," the program discussed religion and contemporary issues with callers. Eventually expanded to two hours, it received syndication throughout Georgia during the latter half of the decade. In addition, Owings published a book in 1998 titled *Hearing God in a Noisy World.*[637]

Timothy and Kathie Owings both took a special interest in the church's youth ministry, including attending youth camp and Kathie's teaching of tenth grade girl's Sunday School. Laypersons involved in teaching and assisting the youth included Barry Cook, Mike Toomey, Beth Mobley, the Wallace family, and others. In 1993 Jud Reasons replaced Reece Sherman as minister of youth. Under his leadership programming and participation expanded further.[638]

Concerned about Baptist identity during a decade of denominational turmoil and amid a growing trend of non-denominationalism, Owings in the summer of 1994 preached a series of five sermons on "A People Called Baptists." The topics consisted of the following:

1. Soul Competency (Ps. 42:1-5)
2. Regenerated Church Membership (John 1:12)
3. The Priesthood of the Believer (1 Pet. 2:9-10)
4. Autonomy of the Local Church (1 Thess. 1:1-10)
5. Separation of Church and State (1 Pet. 2:13-17)

Published as a booklet, the sermon series found continuing use as a way to introduce new members, many of whom increasingly came from non-Baptist backgrounds, to the Baptist faith.

Although no longer solely a Southern Baptist church, First Baptist Augusta remained committed to the best of the church's historical Baptist identity and open to reexamining denominational shortcomings of the past. From May 8-10, 1995, the 150th anniversary of the Southern Baptist Convention's founding, the church hosted a hallmark conference titled "A Time to Remember."

Sponsored by the SBC's Historical Commission and the Southern Baptist Historical Society, the conference attracted the largest gathering of Southern Baptist leaders hosted by the church other than the three SBC annual meetings of 1845, 1863, and 1885. Total attendance reached 900 in a special worship service. Charles Bugg returned to Augusta to address the assembly, imploring attendees to remember the markers and lessons of the past. Top Southern Baptist officials brought "greetings and remembrances," including Jim Henry (SBC president), Morris Chapman (SBC Executive Committee president), Jimmy Draper (BSSB president), and Robert White (GBC president). Slayden Yarbrough, interim executive director of the Historical Commission, presented "A Declaration of Repentance and Rededication" that was read by the congregation. The statement acknowledged "slavery and defense of the right to own slaves" as a priority of the SBC's founders in 1845, and pledged to "combat publicly the sins of racism and exclusion in our communities" in order that "by acknowledging and repenting of the sins of our past we will be freed to live in justice and peace in the present."

The three-day conference also included dramatic presentations of Annie Armstrong (portrayed by Freddie Neal of North Augusta Baptist Church) and William B. Johnson (portrayed by Quinn Pugh, executive director of the New York Baptist Convention). A panel discussion featured Dellanna O'Brien (executive director of national Woman's Missionary Union), Emmanuel McCall (pastor of the African-American Christian Fellowship Church, Atlanta), William Harrell (pastor of Abilene Baptist Church), Carol Woodfin (professor of history at Palm Beach Atlantic College), and Slayden Yarbrough. Collectively, conference events represented the first time that SBC officials formally and forcefully confronted and apologized for the slavery-infused founding of the convention.[639]

First Baptist took to heart the need to move beyond racial boundaries inherent in denominational life. Within a few years of the 1995 conference, two well-accomplished African-American women, Joann Carr and Annette Taylor, joined the congregation. Carr later served as chairman of the Personnel Committee and a deacon. Taylor performed as a soloist, sang in the choir, and also served as a deacon. In the ensuing years, more African Americans, including Peggy Koon, joined the congregation and became key lay persons.[640]

Inclusive and Creative

At a time when many First Baptist congregations in the South evidenced decline, the Augusta church's location, accommodating campus, large staff, and dedicated lay leaders allowed for inspiring worship services, extensive Sunday School classes, exceptional music ministry, far-reaching missions involvement, vibrant youth programming, holistic children's and family ministries, community ministries, and outreach efforts. Of the latter, the popular television ministry weekly reached a large audience beyond the church campus.

Seasonal, special music programs featured the church's choirs at Easter, Christmas, and other occasions. Owings, an accomplished musician in addition to pastoring, played an annual Christmas program on the piano. The church also made its facilities available for community music events, including the hosting of the Augusta Symphony Orchestra (later named the Symphony Orchestra Augusta, or SOA) annual Masterworks series. In 1998, Augusta native and Grammy-award-winning opera singer and recitalist Jessye Norman performed her first hometown televised performance during a PBS Christmas music special hosted by First Baptist.

Numerous other well-known personalities visited the church during the course of the decade, invited by Owings, a man of wide-ranging connections. Golfer Larry Mize spoke of "The Master," Jesus Christ, in April 1992. "Because you've placed your trust in him," Mize said in relation to the address, "you're a child of the King, and you're worth the death, burial, and resurrection of Jesus Christ." Bill Curry, football coach at the University of Kentucky and a friend of Owings, spoke in May 1994. From Baptist life, Daniel Vestal and Frank Pollard, among others, also spoke from the pulpit.[641]

A major addition to the Walton Way campus took place with the October 1, 2000 dedication of an administration annex and covered walkway adjoining the sanctuary and housing a music suite, senior adult department, and the administrative offices. Jack Patrick chaired the fund-raising committee that made the project possible. Later named the Daniel Building after Dick Daniel, the new structure served as the daily command hub of the church's campus.[642]

Other advances during the Owings pastorate included the addition of carillon bells in the church steeple, the development of a memorial garden, retirement of church debt, and the establishment of a Long-Range Campus Completion Committee (2000) chaired by church members Nick Evans and Charles Shaefer Sr. working with architect Lawrence Corley of Birmingham, Alabama. The committee envisioned the next major campus addition, that of a chapel and fellowship hall.[643]

The dawning of the new century also created opportunity for First Baptist to reevaluate the church's overarching direction and focus. One hundred years earlier in the midst of ascendant modern business practices, the congregation had embraced efficiency and professional programming as an avenue of advancement and growth. In the year 2000 the congregation turned to the growing contemporary usage of vision statements, a corporate strategy increasingly utilized by local churches. The church that year adopted a church vision statement, reading: "First Baptist Church, led by the Spirit of Christ, will grow up by becoming a more loving, accepting, nurturing congregation. The church will prayer-fully focus its energies on reaching people in the Greater Augusta area through inspirational worship services and a strong relationship-building Bible study program. We will broaden our ministries by involving our members in missions."[644]

The inclusive vision statement echoed the values of the Cooperative Baptist Fellowship, of which the church increasingly became involved, including the hosting of the 2001 annual gathering of the Cooperative Baptist Fellowship of Georgia, to the theme of "Where Baptist Still Means Freedom." The CBF gathering came mere months after former U.S. President and Georgian Jimmy Carter, a Southern Baptist for most of his life, formally left the Southern Baptist Convention. Citing the convention's "rigid" creedalism, opposition to women in ministry, and rejection of women's equality, he declared himself aligned with the CBF. Carter's move, widely covered in newspapers throughout America, evoked an avalanche of letters of support, as well as opposition, from Baptists nationwide. Edlyn Elliott of FBC Augusta wrote a letter in sup-port of Carter, noting the church's affirmation and inclusion of women ministers. But unlike Carter, the congregation also remained involved in Southern Baptist life.[645]

Also focusing on missions, the vision statement echoed the congre-gation's extensive hands-on involvement in annual mission projects ena-bled by the Dorothy Moore Missions Endowment. In one of the more memorable mission experiences near the turn of the century the church sent a mission team to the 2002 Salt Lake City Winter Olympics, part of a Southern Baptist outreach effort that included the SBC's North Amer-ican Mission Board and state Baptist conventions, including Georgia.[646]

The church's vision, inclusiveness, missions, and ministries impact-ed Augusta native Tripp Martin. Nurtured by the congregation as a child and youth, Martin afterward earned degrees from the University of Georgia and Wake Forest University, as well as a doctorate from the McAfee School of Theology of Mercer University, a CBF-affiliated sem-inary. In February 2003 the Augusta congregation ordained Martin to the ministry, the ordination council consisting of a cross-section of church staff and lay leaders, men and women alike: Owings, Allan Thomas, Wayne Hunsucker, Daisy Roberts, Jimmy McLeod, Anna Bannister, Dan Smith, Mary Lou McKay, and moderator J. I. McNair. Following ordination, Martin served as associate pastor of Northminster Baptist Church in Jackson, Mississippi.[647]

Two months later First Baptist Augusta debuted an especially crea-tive event: a C. S. Lewis Festival. A tribute to and celebration of the life and work of the renowned Christian writer of the *Chronicles of Narnia* children's fiction series and other works, the April festival followed two years of planning and work by Rodger Murchison, Wayne Hunsucker, and Debbie Williams. The festival resulted from Murchison's travels to the author's home in England and study of his life. Transformed for three-and-a-half weeks into Narnia's "the land of forever winter," in the church's activity building hundreds of children walked through huge wardrobe doors and rows of fur-lined coats into a reproduction of Nar-nia, a land filled with Christmas trees, talking animals, and an evil witch—the setting of an allegorical telling of the gospel. Visualizing the Narnia experience provided "a wonderful way to share Christ," Murchison enthused.

While children marveled at the visualization of Narnia, local pulpit exchanges focused on Lewis' life and writings, while arts performances and academic seminars also engaged adults. Lewis scholars from as far away as New York made presentations. The festival concluded with a performance by the Augusta Dance Theatre. Entirely free to the public, the event drew more than 8,000 persons. Inspired by the festival's suc-cess, the church hosted a second C. S. Lewis Festival in 2006 in partner-ship with the Church of the Good Shepherd and Reid Memorial Presbyterian Church.[648]

Against the backdrop of great progress, expanding missions in-volvement and innovative ministries under the pastorate of Timothy Owings, his thirteen-year tenure at First Baptist—the third longest among the church's pastors—came to an end with Owings' resignation in May 2003.[649]

Under the direction of a transitional team, more than two years of congregational introspection followed Owings' ministry. George

Balentine and Bruce Morgan served as interim pastors, both greatly appreciated and well loved by the congregation. Staff members Lavinia Polatty, Jacob Malone, Patti Fowler, Dede Maddox (ministry assistant to pastors), and Rodger Murchison provided leadership continuity. Among others, Robert Brand provided key lay leadership as moderator. Church historian Anna Olive Jones Bannister described the church during this time as having "a dynamic program of worship, education, mission activities, singles and benevolent ministries, television ministry, and kindergarten."[650]

An Expanding Impact, a Firm Foundation

In October 2005 the congregation called C. Gregory DeLoach III as pastor. Born and raised near Eatonton, Georgia, a graduate of Shorter College and Southern Baptist Theological Seminary and holding a Doctorate of Ministry from Columbia Theological Seminary, DeLoach had most recently pastored the First Baptist Church of Marietta, Georgia. He, wife Amy Arrington, and sons Clark Gregory DeLoach IV and Aaron Arrington came at a time when membership stood at 4,075.[651]

A preacher since his college years, DeLoach's love of pastoring was readily evident. A deep voice and inspiring sermons characterized his preaching, while a genuine love of people undergirded his pastoral care role. The congregation reciprocated. From "day one" in the Augusta pulpit DeLoach characterized the church community as "ready to love their pastor."[652]

Soon after DeLoach's arrival, former pastor George L. Balentine passed away in April 2006 in Brunswick, Georgia. The many persons who remembered Balentine's leadership in the church's relocation to Walton Way mourned his death while celebrating his life and legacy clearly visible in the thriving church campus in the heart of prosperous west Augusta. No longer boundaried by vacant land, First Baptist existed within a surrounding sea of businesses and offices, the sanctuary's tall steeple standing tall and quite visible amid the hustle and bustle of city life.

Having largely built out the church campus, the congregation during DeLoach's pastoral tenure encompassed an era in which the congregation grappled with a nationwide declining interest in institutional religion. Visible though the church's steeple, fewer and fewer Augustans found it compelling. Less relevant to the concerns and lives of younger generations, programmatic, denominational-centric programs, Sunday School lessons, and institutional-focused literature no longer solely brought newcomers into sanctuaries or generated church growth. Sunday mornings featured multiple services, yet an absence of Sunday night worship and programming reflected the realities of families overburdened with work schedules, children's sporting events, and other time constraints.

Amid a fraying of denominational loyalties, First Baptist Augusta expressed greater affinity with the Cooperative Baptist Fellowship, still a young organization and existing beyond traditional denominational constraints. The church's first pastor in the modern era with a terminal degree apart from a Southern Baptist seminary and with ministry experience largely lived within CBF life, DeLoach straddled the changing world of American Christianity. In his own words, the denominational Baptist "battle was over with" by the time the church called him as pastor. The SBC and CBF had parted ways in clearly-defined fashion, divided over issues of women in ministry, the nature of biblical interpretation, missionary philosophy, and organizational functionality. While some First Baptist members remained staunchly SBC supporters and many identified with CBF, such proclivities remained secondary to congregational unity. Others, having arrived from a different faith background, had no inherent concept of what Baptist meant. The growing lack of knowledge of Baptist identity, expressed against the backdrop of a rapidly-advancing, non-denominational culture within American Christianity, resulted in the once unthinkable scenario of some laypersons serving on staff search committees sincerely asking if being Baptist was a prerequisite for serving on the church staff. The congregation's quasi-Baptists thus shared with committed, diverse Baptists the commonalty of a singular local church transcendent of differences and acting as an anchor across varied faith traditions and divergent beliefs.

Against the backdrop of fading denominational identities, DeLoach in the summer of 2007 preached a series of five sermons collectively titled "The Baptist Story." Designed to both elucidate principles of Baptist identity and articulate the inclusive nature of the best of the Baptist tradition, the sermons reflected a historically-rooted, progressive Baptist vision for the twenty-first century. Sermon titles included:

- "Soul Freedom, Personal Integrity, and the Priesthood of All Believers"
- "Religious Freedom and Liberty"
- "Freedom and the Authority of Scripture"
- "Church Freedom and Our Autonomy"
- "Believer's Baptism and the Mark of Christ"

Of the five principles, the most exclusive was "Believer's Baptism," the historical practice of reserving baptism by immersion for persons previously professing faith in Christ. Increasingly, non-Baptists not baptized as believers perceived the requirement as unnecessary for followers of Christ. And while some Baptist churches quietly backed away from a prerequisite of believer's baptism by immersion, First Baptist Augusta remained committed to this symbolic practice as a requirement of church membership.[653]

Cultural transitions posed additional challenges. Although Augusta remained a conservative city in the Deep South Bible Belt, First Baptist of the twenty-first century confronted a fading Southern cultural norm of Sunday mornings as a time set aside for church. "We are in a very real competition of people's time on Sunday mornings," DeLoach noted of the reality of the times. "Creating that sense of identity, of belonging, is our emerging challenge." Church members by and large no longer felt compelled to be present whenever the doors of the church were open. "Fostering that real sense of church as koinonia is a challenge, and it has to happen seven days a week," DeLoach declared. Deeming occasions when the church body came together as times of celebration, he compared the past to the present. Historically, believing and behaving shaped community. But in the twenty-first century, "the front door of the church is about creating a community that is belonging, and then we understand more about the believing and behaving."[654]

Sunday worship in particular occasioned much conversation and some controversy. Traditional, hymn-focused worship fell out of favor throughout much of American Christendom in the twenty-first century.

Ironically, theologically conservative congregations tended to more readily embrace contemporary praise music, often replete with electric guitar and drum-infused pop bands favored by younger generations, while theologically progressive churches often retained traditional worship norms favored by older generations.

Striving to make worship more relevant and appealing to younger persons, First Baptist Augusta added a third morning worship service named REACH and featuring contemporary music to complement the traditional 8:30 and 11:00 traditional services. In a vote marked by controversy, the church later voted to return to two services, an 8:30 REACH and an 11:00 traditional service. REACH effectively helped the church attract and minister to younger families and singles more comfortable with popular media and casual attire, a demographic group increasingly disassociated from institutional religion. "Led by our praise band, this service of worship draws from contemporary styles of Christian music and integrates video, drama, and art to help tell the timeless story of the love of Christ for all the world," proclaimed the church's website in 2016 of the contemporary service. "REACH is characterized by a relaxed and 'come as you are' atmosphere."[655]

The formation of a "Church Health and Growth Committee" in 2010 reflected broader concerns of national and regional religious decline. Contemporary worship did not represent a singular solution to this existential problem. Seeking a New Testament biblical paradigm for revitalizing church amid an increasingly secular culture, the committee focused on "love" and community as a way forward: "1) Growing in love for our worship and mission, 2) Growing in love for one another, 3) Growing in love for neighbor." At the same time, a long-running ministry for children, Vacation Bible School, remained popular with church members and neighbors alike. In 2011, for example, 615 children swarmed over the church campus during Vacation Bible School.[656]

The Walton Way campus remained vital to the church's health and growth. Envisioned as a bridge between the Augusta community and the church's sanctuary, and between the church's past and future, the $12.5 million addition of a building comprising a 300-seat chapel and 750-person capacity fellowship hall replete with kitchen represented the final component of the master campus plan. Milton Martin served as the church's Long-Range Planning Committee chairman, and Wade Blount as the Building Committee chairman. In addition, Jacob Malone, now church administrator and known as the "Swiss Army Knife" of First Baptist, assisted in the oversight of the construction project.

The octagon-shaped Barbara Langley Storey Chapel, named in memory of the long-time church member and Sunday School teacher, opened in June 2011. Retrieved from the Kiokee Baptist Church where they had been on loan for some four decades, and restored by the Lynchburg Stained Glass Company, the antique memorial windows from the 1902-built Greene Street sanctuary occupied a prominent place in the chapel, alongside new, complimentary stained glass windows. A new cupola mimicked that of the original, 1821 church sanctuary. The color scheme reflected that of First Baptist Church, Providence, Rhode Island, the first Baptist church established in America. Under the same roof, the fellowship hall provided more seating for church and community events and included an expanded kitchen staff led by a professional chef.

One of the most memorable days in church life of the twenty-first century, the Storey Chapel and fellowship hall dedication took place on June 12, 2011. The dedication program, crafted by a Dedication Committee chaired by Janet Hudson, included presentations by guests representing three of the church's most important in-state partner organizations: R. Alan Culpepper, dean of the McAfee School of Theology; Frank Broome, Coordinator of the Cooperative Baptist Fellowship of Georgia; and Don Wheless, director of missions of the Augusta Association of Baptist Churches. A large inscription on the outside of the building quoted 1 Peter 2:5: "You also, as living stones, are being built into a spiritual house..." The event celebrated the congregation's faithfulness in the presence of Christ and pointed to a future beyond "bricks and mortar" and to "flesh and blood" ministry.

"These buildings are not just for us," DeLoach said of the facilities. "We're all part of the body of Christ, and it's meant to be shared." Wade Blount added, "This is a place where people see buildings, but if they look, they'll see lives being changed. These buildings are tools we use to get things done. There's nothing sacred about the buildings themselves. They're just the tools God has given us." Indeed, the fellowship hall quickly became the meeting place of many Augusta-area civic clubs and other organizations.[657]

A "Wall of Faith" featured a large mosaic created by Dave Welter from eleven varieties of wood, including some from the church campus. The Wall featured the names of nineteen persons whom donors wished to honor in their church gifts. The church member who originally envisioned the Wall, however, was not present to see her concept become reality.

First Baptist counted many doctors among the church's membership, a number of whom took vacation time off to do medical missions in underserved international villages and towns. Debbie Williams, wife of George, a doctor, had tragically lost her life one year prior to the Storey Chapel dedication while on a church medical mission trip to Chile. Becoming sick while flying from the United States, after landing Debbie died at a hospital in Chile. Her death devastated her family and the congregation. George returned to the states, while the mission trip continued at his request. Despite the tragedy, the church again sent a mission team to Chile the following year. "Why are we going?" Rodger Murchison rhetorically asked of the follow-up trip. "Because we share our faith in Jesus Christ as Lord this way. Some people preach sermons with words. Some people preach with actions. That's something Debbie believed in. That's what we're doing. They'll know we are Christians by our love." Transformed lives in Chile stood testimony to Williams' witness and ministry. So, too, did the Wall of Faith in the church's Storey Chapel.[658]

The untimely passing of Debbie Williams took place amid a changing missions landscape. From the inception of the modern missions movement in the 1790s through the twentieth century, missions primarily served as a way to advance the dominant Western church in a universal sense. The turn of the twenty-first century witnessed a reimagining of missions as originating not from and for the church, but rather from the very nature of God who from love desires to draw the world to him. The missionary task, therefore, centered on the living of one's daily life in search of God's activity in the world and reflecting the image of God in loving others in a holistic manner as God loves. The terminology of "missional" emerged to describe this organic concept sweeping through much of American Christianity by the time of Greg DeLoach's arrival in Augusta.[659]

Missional living evidenced itself, for example, in the church's exceptional preschool ministry to families of the Augusta community, benevolence ministry, church members' involvement in social service organizations and civic groups throughout the city, and in casual small group conversations apart from the campus. Missional also encompassed annual mission trips to national and international locations, including community relief and cleanup in Biloxi and at New Orleans Baptist Theological Seminary following Hurricane Katrina, medical missions in South America, and support of the work of the Philippine Baptist Theological Seminary. Unlike a traditional missions paradigm, no one of these could be considered more sacred or important than the others. Collectively, all of the above and more represented the redeeming work of God in the lives of humanity.

DeLoach formally advocated the transitioning of First Baptist from being a "mission-minded" church to a "missional" church in the spring of 2012. That summer the congregation created a Mission Vision Team Committee chaired by Billy Bennett and "responsible for actively seeking opportunities for FBC to be involved in mission activities both in the U.S. and around the world." The language of "seeking" near and far reflected the missional emphasis of identifying and joining the working of God. Andy Jones, having been on the church staff since 2006 and originally serving as minister to high school and college students, subsequently became minister of missional outreach. Under his leadership the church's missional activity enlarged, stretching from Georgia to the plains of the Dakotas and across oceans as church members joined the work of God near and far, including Milton Martin and DeLoach as CBF missionaries to Nepal. A capital campaign led by Perry Sentell, in addition to raising funds to retire the church's debt, also provided a new avenue of support for missional work.[660]

The working of God also included the embrace of women as equal partners in ministry. First Baptist women ordained to the ministry included Irene Bennett (2006), Martha Kate Berry Hall (2007), Christie McTier (2009), Christina Pittman (2011), and Hephzibah James (2014). In 2012 Joan Puryear served as the church's first woman moderator.[661]

In missions and ministry, traditional Baptist identity remained important. For persons new to the Baptist faith, the church offered FBC 101, 201, 301, and 401 Sunday School hour classes "for those seeking to learn more about the Baptist faith, Baptist doctrine, etc." Deacons remained central to church life. In recognition of the church's long-time, strong deacons ministry, First Baptist was chosen as one of only three Georgia congregations to co-lead a newly-created CBF network of deacons. In 2012 Rodger Murchison retired after twenty-five years on the church staff, remaining in the church as a leading layperson, including service as a deacon. "We are a better family," Murchison years after his retirement noted in a personal affirmation of the church's commitment to Baptist identity and community.[662]

A Future Hope in Christ

Gregory DeLoach with his exceptional preaching skills and love of the church skillfully led the congregation during the early years of a time marked by the challenges of ascendant non-denominationalism and the rise of the "nones," a demographic no longer associated with institutional church. Resigning in 2015 after ten years in the Augusta pulpit, he assumed a new position as president/chief executive officer of Developmental Disabilities Ministries of Georgia.[663]

Following DeLoach's departure, David Hull, retired pastor of the First Baptist Church of Huntsville, Alabama, served as interim senior pastor of an extensively-staffed church in a time of transition. In addition to Hull, the pastoral ministry team of the church consisted of Jim Walls, associate pastor; Dede Maddox, ministry assistant to pastors; Chip Reeves, interim assistant to the ministers; and Jacob Waldrip, ministerial assistant. Comprising the music ministry team were Kurt Wachtel, minister of music; Claudia Moller, children's choir coordinator; Wayne Lord, organist; Les Reagan, pianist; Tommy Payne, ministry assistant for music; and David Rose, sound engineer. The largest of teams, Faith Development, consisted of Patti Fowler, minister of weekday education; Josh Pinson, interim youth director; Kelly Garnto, interim children's director; Paul Moller, director of senior adult ministry; Leah Galey, ministry assistant for preschool and children; Lori McPherson, nursery coordinator; Susan Jones, receptionist and ministry assistant for faith development; and Elizabeth Chao, ministry assistant for students, senior adults, and missional outreach. Tim Spivey served as interim operations ministry, George Berry as activities and league coordinator, and Stephen Childress as chef. Shirley Lescantz (purchasing and scheduling), Lavinia Polatty (financial director), and Luci Worthington (director of publishing) formed the Administrative Ministry Team.[664]

As in times past, former pastors, including Chuck Bugg in 2016, returned on occasion to preach to the congregation that still felt like family.

In addition, the Sunday morning broadcast ministry of the church continued, supplemented by an expanding, 24/7 online media presence that included the establishment of a church Facebook page in 2012, the archiving of Sunday sermons on the church's website beginning in 2014, and the online publication of the congregational *Interpreter* newsletter from 2016 onward.

Exciting technological innovations, however, did not mask appreciation for the church's heritage. A 200th Anniversary Committee coordinated the 2017 celebration of the church's bicentennial led by Janet Hudson. Many other church members provided leadership for the events planned by this committee. Anniversary events marking the year-long celebration included:

- A "Kick Off" Sunday service and celebration with the introduction of an anniversary song written by Dr. Glen Adkins
- Recognition of families having three, four, five, or six generations attending FBC
- Recognition of individuals who have been a member of FBC for 50+ years, 60+ years, 70+ years, and 80+ years
- Mercer University president, Dr. Bill Underwood, and the Mercer Singers leading a Sunday service
- A service honoring the four past living ministers: Dr. Jack Robinson, Dr. Chuck Bugg, Dr. Timothy Owens, and Dr. Greg DeLoach
- An evening family Bible study, "Sharing Your Faith," for children, youth, and adults with a dessert social afterward
- A Sunday morning service recognizing FBC "Missions Through the Years" with a missions fair in the rotunda
- Hosting the annual conference of the Baptist History and Heritage Society

- Homecoming Sunday, August 20, with an 1817 "Dinner on the Grounds" and a 200-count balloons launch
- A youth anniversary concert hosted by FBC youth and inviting youth from sister churches
- A women's luncheon honoring contributions by FBC women
- A musical presentation by the children's choir telling the history of FBC
- Skits about events in the history of FBC
- A Sunday service honoring FBC trustees
- Speakers representing the SBC, CBF, and the Baptist History and Heritage Society
- A Christmas concert by David Phelps hosted in the FBC sanctuary with guests from the community
- The publication, by Mercer University Press, of a new church history written by historian Dr. Bruce Gourley

Despite the growing decline of interest in religion nationally, excitement and vitality characterize the First Baptist Church of Augusta well into the twenty-first century. Although growth in the greater Augusta area has moved further westward, the Walton Way campus remains a center of activity throughout the week. From newborns to senior adults, the campus ministers to and serves church families and the larger Augusta community. Two Sunday morning worship services meet the needs of a diverse Christian community, honoring God with song and proclamation. Dozens of Sunday School classes provide biblical teaching from a wide range of literature. A professional music ministry ranks among the best of any church. The congregation remains deeply committed to missional ministries at home and abroad.

From a storied past of historic renown, advancement, and transformation, First Baptist Augusta in its third millennium remains faithful to Baptist identity, progressive in spirit, and focused on community. The same hope in Christ that empowered the founding members of the church remains in the hearts and lives of today's congregants.

Appendices

Honorariums

Dr. Glen and Clista Adkins
From David and Janet Hudson

Dr. Glen and Clista Adkins
From J. Ben and Donna Deal

Dr. Glen and Clista Adkins
From Joe and Beth Pollock

Rebecca Olivia Adkins
From Barbara Stephens Adkins

Julian Wicklief Armstrong
From Jane Armstrong Coleman

Joshua G. Arnold
From Randy and Lisa Arnold

Shay Thompson Barber
From Billy and Sylvia Thompson

John Forsyth Bates
From the Bates Family

Paul and Catherine Bruggemann
Bloodworth and Children
From Fred and Linda Bruggemann

Nan Elizabeth Williams Bowman
From Dr. George W. Williams

Vance Bowman
From Dr. George W. Williams

Alex V. Brand
From Robert and Brenna Brand

Dr. Charles Bugg
From J. Ben and Donna Deal

Dr. Charles Bugg
From Tom Dozier

Dr. Charles Bugg
From Dr. George Williams

Roselle Dudley Burt
From Bobby and Vicky Hawes

Margaret Nix Daniel
From Warren A. Daniel

Brad, Karla, John, and Ellyson Deal
From J. Ben and Donna Deal

Dr. Tyson, Heather, and Judson Deal
From J. Ben and Donna Deal

Dr. Greg DeLoach
From Tom Dozier

Dr. Greg DeLoach
From Joe and Beth Pollock

Alison Maria Dong
From Ellen Woo Dong

Amy Jennifer Dong and
Maxwell Oliver Dong
From Ellen Woo Dong

Craig, Martha, Sarah, and Madeline Dong
From Ellen Woo Dong

Ellen Woo Dong
From her children and grandchildren

The Thomas M. Dozier Family

Anna Kay Wiggins Duckworth
From Dr. and Mrs. Wayne Wiggins

Gardner, Mathurin, and Wilkes Duckworth
From Mr. and Mrs. Mike Duckworth

Mr. and Mrs. Troy Duckworth and family
From Gloria Patrick

Alex and Andrew Elkin
From Paul and Rebecca Elkin

Alice, Jeannie, Ted, and Ann Everett
From Jean W. Everett

First Baptist Church Administrative Staff
From the Chinese Sunday School Class

HONORARIUMS

William Lawrence Fletcher Jr.
From Larry and Anna Kim Fletcher

Patti Fowler
From J. Ben and Donna Deal

David, James, Samuel, and Paul Geer
From Anita and Calvin Geer

Robin Brand Gentry
From Robert and Brenna Brand

Randy German
From J. Ben and Donna Deal

Kerry and Cathi Gough
From Anonymous

Kerry and Cathi Gough
From Len and Charlynn Collins

Grace Class Teachers:
Delores Malone, Margaret Murchison,
Betty Sharrock, and Jean Thomas
From Grace Class

Grace Girls Sunday School Class
From Betty Sharrock

Davis Griffin
From Skip and Diane Griffin

Sandra H. Griffin
From Lisa, Joshua, and Randy Arnold

Vanne Thompson Hanberry
From Billy and Sylvia Thompson

Mrs. Fey Hardy
From Skip and Diane Griffin

The Hnatt Family
From Frank and Nanci McPhail

Dot Hodges
From Marion Vann

Natalie Brooke Horseman
From Barbara Stephens Adkins

Michael and Laura Shiver Housh
From Antonio F. Shiver

Dr. Benjamin T. Hudson
From David and Janet Hudson

Brooks, Tara, and Nash Hudson
From David and Janet Hudson

Mr. and Mrs. David E. Hudson
From Warren A. Daniel

Rebecca Murchison Hughes
From Rodger and Margaret Murchison

Jake, Kevin, Hannah, and Abby
From Grandma Blackburn

Jean H. Kearns
From the Kearns Family

Beth Tanner Kroening
From Gene and Martha Tanner

Tom Lanier
From Charles E. and Jeanette S. Young

Douglas, Cara, Katherine, and Anna Lee
From Ellen Woo Dong

Harrison, Kathryn, and Claire Long
From Norman and Sandra Skelton

Jason and Katie Long
From Norman and Sandra Skelton

Louise Malone
From Delores G. and Lee and Mary Beth
Malone

The Martin Family:
Bob and Mary Ann, Marianne, Christopher,
Robin, Isaac, Chris, Elizabeth, and Zoe

Brian and Saralyn Bruggemann McDonnell
and children
From Fred and Linda Bruggemann

Jeptha Isaiah (Jep) McNair III
From Jephtha Isaiah (J. I.) and JoAnn
McNair

Matthew and Jim McPhail
From Frank and Nanci McPhail

Rex M. Mobley
From Wyman Mobley

Russell V. Mobley
From Wyman Mobley

Polly Giddens Moon
From Janet Moon Manning

Dr. Ashton J. Moradi
From Midge Powell (Grandmother)

Mitchell Burgess Murchison
From Rodger and Margaret Murchison

Dr. Rodger Murchison
From Bobby and Vicky Hawes

Dr. Rodger Murchison
From Joe and Beth Pollock

Dr. Rodger and Margaret Murchison
From David and Janet Hudson

Dr. Timothy Owings
From Jane Armstrong Coleman

Dr. and Mrs. Timothy Owings
From the Chinese Sunday School Class

Hazel Franklynn Parker
From Mr. and Mrs. William Parker

Jacob Ashley Parker
From Mr. and Mrs. William Parker

Martha Lena Parker
From Mr. and Mrs. William Parker

William Grady Parker
From Mr. and Mrs. William Parker

Mary Beth Wiggins Perpall
From Dr. and Mrs. Wayne Wiggins

Julie Rooks Phelan
From Bill and June Rooks

Caroline, Bates, Davis, and
Ann Cathryn Pinson
From Norman and Sandra Skelton

Josh and Courtney Pinson
From Norman and Sandra Skelton

Lavinia Townes Polatty
From Jane Armstrong Coleman

Lavinia Townes Polatty
David and Janet Hudson

Lavinia Townes Polatty
From Anna Kim and Larry and Will
Fletcher

Jane Rooks Poston
From Bill and June Rooks

Dot Rabun
From Marion Vann

Lee Ramsey
From Judy Ramsey

Dr. R. J. (Jack) Robinson
From Mr. and Mrs. John Buckner

Dr. R. J. (Jack) Robinson
From Tom Dozier

Dr. R. J. (Jack) Robinson
From Lee and Tim Ferrell

Dr. R. J. (Jack) Robinson
From Bobby and Vicky Hawes

Dr. R. J. (Jack) Robinson
From the Robert Jackson Walker Hawes
Estate

Dr. R. J. (Jack) Robinson
From Joe and Beth Pollock

Dr. and Mrs. R. J. (Jack and Charlotte)
Robinson
From the Chinese Sunday School Class

Dr. and Mrs. R. J. (Jack and Charlotte)
Robinson
From Jane Armstrong Coleman

Julie Armstrong Sculac
From Jane Armstrong Coleman

Allan McNair Shaefer
From Nan Hall Shaefer

Charles B. III, Maggie, and C. Brinson IV
Shiver
From Antonio F. Shiver

Key, Mary Will, and Laine Showman
From Mr. and Mrs. Chris Showman

Brooke Skelton
From Norman and Sandra Skelton

Carolee Armstrong Smith
From Jane Armstrong Coleman

Pat Smith
From Alethia E. Nowell

Mr. and Mrs. Rob Stephens and family
From Gloria Patrick

Eda Stertz
From Fred and Linda Bruggemann

B. R. and Christine Swindoll
From Jeanette S. Young

David and Stephen Tanner
From Gene and Martha Tanner

Jake and Laura Ramsey Thieben
From Judy Ramsey

Shannon Thompson
From Billy and Sylvia Thompson

Jill Rooks Turner
From Bill and June Rooks

Julie Tanner Wells
From Gene and Martha Tanner

Mark Wiggins
From Dr. and Mrs. Wayne Wiggins

Yvonne Wiggins
From Jimmy and Deborah Edenfield

Deborah Ann Williams
From Dr. George W. Williams

Lesley-Anne Dyer Williams
From Dr. George W. Williams

George Willis Williams III
From Dr. George W. Williams

Mae Woo Wong
From her children and grandchildren

Ed and Laura Young
From Charles E. Young

Memorials

Henry Bailey
From Jim and Elizabeth Beazley

Dr. George Balentine
From J. Ben and Donna Deal

Dr. George Balentine
From Tom Dozier

Dr. George Balentine
From Joe and Beth Pollock

Linda Beazley
From Tommy and Janice Williams

The John C. Bell Family
From David and Susie Bell

Dudley and Myrna Bennett
From Ronald and Virginia Bennett
and Carol Goodman

Rev. Robert Blackburn
From Mickie, Betsy, and Robert Jr.

Charles and Mary Booth
From Paul and Rebecca Elkin
and Randy and Martha Moon

Bob Brant
From Nancy Brant and family

Cason and Jane Bruker
From the Cason Bruker Bible Class

Victor Ledelle Burt
From Bobby and Vicky Hawes

Bertha Carswell
From the Joseph Carswell Family

Bertha Carswell
From Joseph K. Hardy and Camille H. Hardy

Mr. and Mrs. James Joseph Carswell
From Joseph K. Hardy and Camille H. Hardy

Mr. and Mrs. K. J. Chow
From Peggy, Gerald, and Edward Chow

Mason Clements
From Fay J. Clements

Bill Coleman
From the Coleman Family

Margaret Jernigan Daniel
From Warren A. Daniel

Mr. and Mrs. Raleigh H. Daniel
From Warren A. Daniel

Dorothy Darabaris
From Alex Darabaris

Col. (Ret.) and Mrs. David L. Davis
From Harold B. Jones and family

Yick Chong Dong
From Ellen Woo Dong

James and Gladys Ellis
From Terrell Jr. and Marilyn Redd

Kay Evans
From Alfred Evans

Dr. Theodore Everett
From Jean W. Everett

Mr. and Mrs. Julian F. Fiske
From Chip, Joy, Chiles, and Ray Fiske

Mr. and Mrs. W. F. Geer
From Calvin and Anita Geer

William Geer, Robert Geer,
and Margaret Sledge
From Calvin and Anita Geer

Edith Gibson
From Janet K. Hudson

Edith and Shellie Gibson
From Selma Horton

Annie Vaughn Giddens
From Janet Moon Manning

Jerry Gleason
From Sandra Gleason

Roscoe and Deleeta Goldsmith
From Louise Malone

Norman W. Griffin Jr. (Skeeter/DaPaw)
From Lisa, Joshua, and Randy Arnold

Myra Haig
From Fred and Linda Bruggemann

Ralph and Anne Hammett
From Lombard Jr. and Barbara Fortson

Andrea Hardy
From Skip and Diane Griffin

Mr. and Mrs. Oscar Knox Hardy
From Joseph K. Hardy and Camille H. Hardy

Jim and Gradie Harris
From David and Janet Hudson

Robert Jackson Walker Hawes
From Bobby and Vicky Hawes

Robert Jackson Walker Hawes
From David, Janet, Brooks, and Tara Hudson

Felicia JoLayne Woo Hirano
From Lynne C. Woo

Mr. and Mrs. Simpson Olin Houck
From Joseph K. Hardy and Camille H. Hardy

Mr. and Mrs. Thomas Rabb Houck
From Joseph K. Hardy and Camille H. Hardy

Robert C. Hulsebus
From Jo Hulsebus

Mr. and Mrs. Harry W. Jernigan Sr.
From Warren A. Daniel

Jean Joe
From Mae Wong

Rev. Jacques M. Kearns
From J. Ben and Donna Deal

Rev. Jacques M. Kearns
From the Kearns Family

Jack and Doris H. Lam
From their children and grandchildren

Jack and Doris H. Lam
From Mae Wong

George and Sarah Linney
From Fred and Linda Bruggemann

Frances Lowrey
From Fred and Linda Bruggemann

Harold and Bessie Malone
From Delores G., Lee, and Mary Beth
Malone

Jacob Oliver Malone
From Bobby and Vicky Hawes

Jacob Oliver Malone
From David and Janet Hudson

Jacob Oliver Malone
From Delores G., Lee, and Mary Beth
Malone

Patricia Mangum
From David and Janet Hudson

Patricia Mangum
From Mike and Emily Askew

Keith McGee
From Loretta B. McGee

Rena S. Mobley
From Wyman Mobley

Ernest, Lillie, and LaRue Monroe
From the Monroe Family

Dorothy Moore
From Fred and Linda Bruggemann

Dorroh Nowell
From Alethia E. Nowell

Inez Brown Orosz
From Dr. Judy Orosz

Charles R. Parker and Margaret Moody Parker
From Bruce and Carol Parker

Jack B. Patrick
From Gloria Patrick

Darroll T. Powell
From Midge Powell

Butch Ramsey
From Judy Ramsey

Edgar Sr. and Martha Redd
From Terrell Jr. and Marilyn Redd

Mildred Rocker
From Dr. and Mrs. Joe Olliff and family

Dr. Elwyn A. Saunders
From Marceline Saunders

Ina Guillebeau Hawes Savage
From Bobby and Vicky Hawes

Dr. Charles Shaefer Jr.
From Bobby and Vicky Hawes

Dr. Charles Shaefer Jr.
From David and Janet Hudson

Dr. Charles F. Shaefer Jr.
From Nan Hall Shaefer

Charles F. Shaefer Sr.
From Nan Hall Shaefer

Evelyn McNair Shaefer
From Nan Hall Shaefer

Dr. Charles B. Shiver Jr.
From Antonia F. Shiver

Rev. Jim Stertz
From Fred and Linda Bruggemann

Jane Strong
From the Nova Sunday School Class

Ernie Swan and Zell Bass Swan
From Mike and Jane Moxley

Preston E. Thomas Jr.
From Patricia J. Thomas

Ransom Timmerman
From Mildred Timmerman

Clara Mangum Wade
From Mike and Emily Askew

Calvin and Julia Weatherly
From Tommy and Janice Williams

David and Jenny Lind Widener
From Betty Widener Gracey

Deborah Bartley Williams
From Dr. George W. Williams Jr.

Lett and Lucille Williams
From Tommy and Janice Williams

Henry M. Wilson
From Dianna W. James

Maryann Daniels Wilson
From Dianna W. James

Mr. and Mrs. Bot Lee Wong
From Peggy, Jimmy, Judy, Kenneth Wong

Jane Chow Wong
From Mrs. Ralph Wong and family

Mr. and Mrs. K. F. Wong
From Mrs. Ralph Wong and family

Philip and Elaine Wong
From Elizabeth Wong Mark

Philip and Elaine Wong
From Mrs. Ralph Wong and family

Ralph Wong
From Mrs. Ralph Wong and family

Eugene Woo Jr.
From Lynne C. Woo

Mrs. Eugene (Amie Wong) Woo Sr.
From Ellen Woo Dong

Benevolence Ministry

Ring, ring, ring...The sound of the telephone is constant, with people asking if we can help them. Food, shelter, electricity...the needs are numerous. We volunteers in the benevolence ministry have become accustomed to these requests.

Back in the 1990s First Baptist Augusta started a ministry to give food to the hungry in our community. Church members donated food, and mission donations supplemented supplies for the food pantry. Volunteers came forward and dedicated themselves to serve.

We started small, but that didn't last long. As we grew, the numbers in our community who needed help also grew. So we opened our doors to a fixed number of families, basically, on a first-come, first-served basis. This was not enough to meet the needs, however. Families were losing their housing and living without electricity and gas and needing additional assistance. This was a little more difficult, but we stepped forward and asked God to lead us.

There had to be a plan. We initially decided to assist thirty-six families, once again on a first-come basis, giving food, counseling, and financial assistance. The difference is, we asked that our clients pay the first amount of their past-due expense and we would pay the last amount. This was a small amount, but it helped make our clients responsible for themselves. Our goal was to give each client hope.

Over the years we have grown. We started with one minister liaison, one director, and a handful of volunteers. Now, in addition to a devoted minister, we have two directors and four teams of volunteers who allow us to keep the benevolence ministry active twelve months a year. We have a budget and connections with other agencies in the area, and focus on the whole family crisis and not just food. Two of our most valuable connections are with Golden Harvest Food Bank and United Way.

Our volunteers have a number of jobs. We recruit greeters, interviewers, personal counselors, financial counselors, and food baggers. We have a purchasing agent who sees that our pantry is full.

With the help of a Sunday School class we give a Bible to each client and present the gospel and pray with him or her. We also offer free legal advice. We provide Thanksgiving and Christmas meals to families and a Christmas store where clients can purchase gifts for their children for a nominal fee. We have been able to increase the amount of funding for families and have received grants from United Way for special situations. Volunteers answer the phone each Monday morning to make appointments for clients who need financial assistance, and our two directors keep the office open every day to receive calls and special requests, mail checks, update the database, make calls to creditors, etc.

The benevolence ministry has grown to become one of the most respected missions in the area. Our goal is to assist each client in a way that adds dignity to his or her life and gives a hand up to a better quality of life. God has been faithful to provide for us. We pray that our little mission will be a blessing to many more people in the future—both those in need and our volunteers.

Terri Bennett

English as a Second Language Ministry

Augusta has a rich history of diverse language groups within its population. In addition to various businesses either owned or operated by foreign countries, the city is home to the Fort Gordon army base on which the Signal Corps operation is located. Several countries send people to Fort Gordon for training. The Medical College of Georgia also attracts many research scientists and post-graduate students from a number of countries. Our city has opened its arms to refugees from several countries over the years, with members of their extended families often relocating here too. A significant number of Chinese residents have lived in the community dating as far back as 1885 or earlier. All of these groups have benefited from the English program at First Baptist. By the same token, FBC has been blessed by our interaction with them.

In late 1975 a group of FBC ladies approached their pastor Dr. George Balentine, expressing an interest in starting an English program for residents in the community for whom English would be a second language. With Dr. Balentine's enthusiastic approval, the church enlisted Mrs. Leta Cornman, a member of a sister church and a certified literacy associate, to conduct the required sixteen-hour workshop to begin a conversational English program at FBC. Mrs. Cornman was one of the initial organizers of the literacy program under the auspices of the Southern Baptist Convention Home Mission Board in 1960. The literacy mission included conversational English along with adult reading and writing.

The training sessions began on January 13, 1976 with twelve participants in the first training session at FBC:

- Mrs. George Balentine
- Mrs. Glen Garrison
- Mrs. William Coleman
- Mrs. Jones Huskey
- Mrs. John Buckner
- Mrs. Frank McKay
- Mrs. Kerry Gough
- Mrs. P. Ulmer Savage
- Mrs. Robert Blackburn
- Mrs. George Matthews
- Mrs. Joe Overby
- Mrs. J. Eugene Pierce

Mrs. Robert Blackburn served as the first director of the program. Later directors included Mrs. Glen Garrison, Mrs. Kerry Gough, Mrs. William Atkinson, Mrs. Charles Hardin, Mrs. Robert Brant, and currently Dr. Raymond Rufo.

Mrs. John Buckner (Ruth Ann), who still teaches every Wednesday and has done so the entire forty years, will tell anyone that she has received far more blessing than she has given. Ruth Ann's students come to her in the fall speaking barely a syllable of English and leave in the spring able to have conversations, however limited, with their children's teachers and their physicians, neighbors, and others with whom they come in contact daily. Also, Mrs. Robert Blackburn (Mickie) and Mrs. Kerry Gough (Cathi) have rejoined the program following retirement from their respective jobs. They, too, tell of their joy in having been part of the founding team as witnessed by their return.

The first class in 1976 included twenty-five internationals, representing four countries, and by the end of the year forty students from a total of eight countries:

- Japan
- Vietnam
- Greece
- Brazil
- Taiwan
- Chile
- Columbia
- Pakistan

The English language program has continued uninterrupted for forty years and currently has 104 students representing twenty-four countries:

- Argentina
- Afghanistan
- Brazil
- China
- Colombia
- Costa Rica
- Dominican Republic
- Egypt
- Germany
- Ghana
- Honduras
- India
- Iran
- Japan
- Korea
- Mexico
- Morocco
- Myanmar
- Panama
- Peru
- Puerto Rico
- Syria
- Turkey
- Ukraine

While some years we have had as many as 200 registrants from thirty-seven different countries, average attendance over the last ten years has been between fifty and sixty. Numbers fluctuate as many students are temporary residents, such as military enrollees or those visiting family members, and others find employment and are unable to attend. We are blessed by all who come and are always saddened when they leave.

Although the program was designed to teach adults English conversation only, many internationals, like many Americans, have studied a foreign language with emphasis on reading and translation. Most likely those who studied conversational English received instruction from foreign-speaking instructors whose pronunciation was decidedly different than that spoken here. Consequently they may have some knowledge of vocabulary, but lack pronunciation skills. Others have had no experience with the English language. Because of the diversity of abilities, several levels of instruction are available. This diversity was discovered early on, and in the first year of the program Mrs. T. C. Bannister began an advanced class in which she taught topics such as American literature, current events, and topics of special interest to students enrolled.

Over the subsequent years as the program has grown, many other services have evolved, including cost-free childcare. Scores of FBC volunteers have come forth to share the joy of caring for the children, providing refreshments each week, serving as placement interviewers, and teaching Bible study and citizenship classes along with teaching conversational English. Since the term "English as a Second Language" has become so widely used nationally, the program has taken on that name too, affectionately being referred to as ESL.

Throughout the years many students have come to FBC practicing religions other than Christianity. It has not been a primary goal to change a student's religion, but rather to show the love of Jesus to strangers in our land, ever mindful of Jesus' words to us in Matthew 25:34-40 that when we show kindness, caring, and welcome to the strangers in our midst, we are doing so to him. We do not hide our light under a bush, however, and seek every week to share our testimonies and prayers with our students. Often during our large group time students will ask for prayers for themselves or their families in distressed countries. Amina, one of our longtime students from Syria, regularly asks us to remember her family.

We offer an English language Bible to any student who wants one, but we also provide Bibles in the students' own language. Knowing that their teacher puts much effort into the class, students often ask why we do this. The standard reply is, "God loves you and so do I." A seed has been planted by that simple response. Only God knows when that seed will germinate, but one anecdote shows that it can—and does—take root.

A few years ago Jeanette Dunagan, who had taught in the earliest days of the program but had been serving on a substitute basis in recent years, received a phone call from a Vietnamese student who had long since moved away from Augusta and with whom Jeanette had lost contact. The caller asked Jeanette if she remembered giving her a Bible many years ago, and then told Jeanette that she had just accepted Jesus as her Savior and wanted Jeanette to know what an important role she had played in her conversion by giving her a Bible many years ago.

One of the most rewarding moments in my life came when I was serving as director. I was able to provide a Japanese Bible—both Old and New Testament—to one of our Japanese Christians. She owned a New Testament but had never been able to obtain a Bible containing both Testaments in her language. As her Bible study teacher related after class, "It was like you had given her a million dollars." Of course, we had given her far more!

Teachers often become involved in the personal lives of their students by helping them find employment, housing, transportation, and other things that will help ease the difficulty of assimilating into our society. Many deep and lasting friendships have developed between teachers and students as a result.

Indeed, forty years of serving the Lord in this mission have provided far more blessings to FBC volunteers than to those whom they have served. God has been and continues to be at work in this mission.

Nancy Brant

Hearts for Heroes

Memorial Day 2005 is a day I will never forget: I met Sean. As part of the Flower Committee at First Baptist Church, it was our job to break down the large floral arrangements from the Sunday service and make small arrangements to take to members in the hospital or in a nursing home. That day a friend and I decided to take the arrangements to the uptown campus of the Charlie Norwood VA Medical Center. We had no idea where we were going or who we could give the flowers to.

As we entered the VA a lady at the reception desk told us they had just that month opened an active duty rehab wing on the third floor, so we headed there to drop off the arrangements. A nurse on the third floor said she would show us around and we could take the flowers to the rooms. First we entered a private room with a young man hooked up to numerous machines, tossing and turning and totally unaware of anything going on around him.

Sean was a 26-year-old graduate of the United States Military Academy at West Point and stationed at Fort Benning when he was in a serious accident. With multiple injuries, he was given less than a 30 percent chance of survival and most likely would never walk again if he did survive. I took Sean's hand and told him, "You will be seeing a lot of me."

I would visit Sean every week and notice minor changes or improvements. A few months after my first visit I was walking toward his room and there he was sitting in a wheelchair just outside the door. I walked over to him and took his hand and said, "I know you don't know me, Sean, but I have been keeping up with you." He replied, "Yes I do. Thank you for the flowers." What a day! Not only did Sean survive, but now he is walking. He's back home in Massachusetts with his family, driving and working.

After my first visit with Sean I told my Sunday School class, the Grace Class, about the experience and we decided immediately to start a support ministry for military personnel. I later spoke with members of the Cason Bruker Class, and they have supported Hearts for Heroes financially since that day. They've also invited the wounded warriors to their annual Christmas party.

One Sunday a gentleman from our church came up to me and said: "I just want to thank you for what you are doing. I was in Vietnam and when I came home someone spit on me." Others equated our efforts with supporting the war in Iraq and President Bush. Hearts for Heroes is not about making a political statement but about supporting our soldiers, our young men and women who are risking their lives to protect us whether they are serving in Iraq or in Atlanta.

From 2005 to 2015 we sent more than 700 "Love Boxes" to our troops overseas. The generosity of our church members has allowed us to provide for the injured soldiers at the VA hospital numerous gift cards for trips to the movies or lunch at different restaurants or bowling, golf, or other activities.

Thankfully we do not have nearly as many deployments now as in the past, but we continue to support our military. We recently hosted a marriage retreat for the wounded warriors and their spouses. They were greatly appreciative. We will continue the Hearts for Heroes ministry as long as there is a need.

Marcia Buck

Preschool and Children's Ministry

Ministry to families is a strong focus of First Baptist Church as evidenced through the preschool and children's ministry, which has had a designated minister on staff to lead this age group since the mid-twentieth century. Myra Haig, Patti Fowler, Rev. Sue Deaton Stiles, Rev. Todd Pylant, and Rev. Becca Jones have all served in this capacity.

When the church moved from Greene Street to Walton Way, separate buildings were designed and built to provide a total of twenty-four spacious classrooms. This space has been shared by both the church programs that meet on Sundays and Wednesdays and the weekday education ministry programs that meet Monday through Friday each week during the school year.

Church Programs

Sunday School provides age-graded education for children from birth through fifth grade. Elementary departments have used both the traditional Bible study model and a rotational teaching model for weekly sessions. Currently all preschool and children's departments use the traditional model.

The traditional model utilizes a director and teachers for each class. Bible study consists of small group activities and a large group hearing and discussion of the Bible story. Units focus on a theme, with supporting stories and corresponding Bible verses.

The rotational model features study of one story or Bible character for a month. Shepherds guide the children to various rooms each week where a different learning style is used (art, drama, computers, games, videos). Leaders with talents in these areas are enlisted to teach the children during the month of study.

Wednesday nights have proven to be a good time for children's age-graded choirs (age 3-grade 5), Bible skills development (grades 1-5), and missions education (age 3-grade 5). The older children's choirs prepare music to sing periodically in morning worship services, and all choirs prepare for their Christmas and spring program presentations. Bible skills include learning the books of the Bible and memorizing various Bible verses. Children have also received instruction on church history and liturgical practices. Missions education includes the study of missionaries and their places of service along with mission action projects such as the following:

- sponsoring a bike-a-thon to raise money for missions
- planning and hosting parties for senior adults in assisted living facilities
- sponsoring a fall party for special needs adults
- collecting items to send to various ministries
- caroling to homebound members at Christmas

Vacation Bible School each summer draws families from our church and also the community. Day camps and junior camps have evolved into Passport Camps and give elementary-age children the opportunity to experience a few days of age-appropriate spiritual and recreational opportunities with their peers. A fall retreat for grades 3-5 prepares children for these overnight/out-of-town events.

Special events for families include the following:

- recognizing parents of new babies in the morning worship services, delivering roses to them, and inviting them to participate in a Baby's First Christmas Brunch
- parental dedication for families of young children
- parenting seminars
- presentation of Bibles to first graders
- inquirers class for children seeking to better understand how to make a profession of faith in Christ
- mother/son and father/daughter social events in the spring
- mother/daughter lock-ins
- father/son campouts
- racer derby
- family fellowships
- fall festival/Trunk or Treat
- Family Christmas Eve service
- Easter Eggstravaganza that begins with an egg hunt and concludes with experiences of the Easter story through various stations

Many volunteers are a key part of the children's program at FBC. Teaching Sunday School, serving on Wednesday nights, helping in extended session, leading a VBS department, assisting with various special events, and chaperoning trips are all opportunities for church members to be involved in this important ministry in the life of the church.

Weekday Education Ministry

The weekday education ministry began when the church was located on Greene Street and sponsored a kindergarten. When the church relocated to Walton Way, great thought was given to the designs of the buildings and rooms to provide space for a kindergarten program. The first kindergarten class in the new facilities began in 1977.

In 1979 Sarah Prior began a Mother's Day Out (MDO) program for younger preschoolers. Through the years the program has expanded from one class to 27 classes, 12 in MDO for infants through 2-year-olds and 15 in preschool/kindergarten for 3-, 4-, and 5-year-olds.

The weekday program enrolls an average of 350 children each year and employs 40 individuals. It meets Monday through Friday from 9 a.m. to 1 p.m. and uses 18 of the classrooms in the preschool building and first floor of the children's building. The Weekday Education Committee oversees the program and is composed of church members who meet monthly to determine policies, evaluate the budget, give advice, and support the teachers with acts of kindness.

The preschool and kindergarten programs are accredited by the Georgia Accrediting Commission and seek to prepare children in all areas of their development—academic, social, physical, emotional, and spiritual. The MDO program seeks to provide a safe and loving environment for children to become accustomed to being away from home and to learn how to interact appropriately with their peers.

Through the years the clientele has become more varied in socioeconomic levels, nationalities, and home addresses in the area. More military families are seeking enrollment in the programs. Technology has become a key factor in sharing information about the ministry to those seeking to find a "school" for their child.

The weekday education ministry also sponsors a seven- or eight-week summer program for infants to children entering first grade. This program has proven to be a much needed and desired addition to summer opportunities for families in the church and community.

Even though the focus of the weekday education ministry is the preschool child, as children and their families come to FBC for these programs, they become exposed to the church and staff. Through their experiences they receive the message of love, warmth, acceptance, encouragement, and the reality of Jesus Christ. This ministry is truly an outreach of the church to the community.

Patti Fowler

History of Missions

It can be said that the long and storied 200-year history of First Baptist Church of Augusta began with a mission emphasis that continues to this day. From a group of seventeen individuals coming together and committing to pray for and with each other, to the beginnings of a Chinese Sunday School outreach to meet the needs of the canal workers, to the many ongoing ministries and mission partnerships, FBC has left an indelible footprint from the Central Savannah River Area (CSRA) to the state and beyond.

The people of FBC have always had a bent toward being a part of God's mission in the world. For the majority of our history the mission efforts have been dreamed up, established, and led by the laity. Only in recent years has there been a ministerial staff position with expressed responsibility over the arena of mission. In fact, as the Mission Vision Team discovered, most if not all of the past and present mission efforts have begun because one person or a small number of people caught a vision for what God was doing and how they could be a part. From those small beginnings each mission effort expanded to include more individuals and families as the vision for ministry spread.

Phil Bennett assumed responsibilities of the mission ministry while serving as minister of education. He was not only the ministerial liaison for the local ministries, but also organized mission trips throughout the United States and abroad. Dr. Bennett also led in the formation of the Mission Development Council (MDC), with Mickie Blackburn serving as the founding chair.

The MDC created a fundraising mechanism, "The Green Envelope," to supplement the mission portion of the operating budget through funds given for U.S. and international mission trips and for various community ministries. These monies have also been used to partially support the benevolence ministry of FBC and to fund world hunger aid agencies and the Georgia Baptist Children's Homes. Through his efforts Dr. Bennett helped to ensure that the mission endeavors of FBC would be funded for years to come.

Dr. Bennett also oversaw the establishment of the First Vietnamese Baptist Church, which shares space in our mission activity center, for its weekly Bible studies and services. Rev. Linh Luong, the congregation's second pastor, has done a great job leading the church as it seeks to reach the Vietnamese population in the CSRA. First Baptist ordained both Rev. Luong and associate pastor Rev. Khanh Le. The two congregations support each other, worship together for special occasions such as baptisms, and share table fellowship at mission banquets and other events.

Dr. Kelly Hamilton succeeded Dr. Bennett in missional leadership. Dr. Hamilton became the first minister in the long history of FBC to have "mission" in his job title rather than just in his responsibilities. This change represented a significant "high water" mark in the life of the church as it shifted away from mission as writing checks of support to mission as participation by a large segment of the congregation. There has always been a glimmer of the *Missio Dei* (mission of God) at work within and through the church, and now that light began to shine brightly again. During his tenure Dr. Hamilton established new partnerships in Ecuador and Hungary, including reconnecting with a former FBC minister of music and his wife (Glen and Clista Adkins) in their work with the Roma peoples in Pecs, Hungary.

Rev. Andy Jones served as our next minister of missions and faith development (later changed to minister of missional outreach). Under Andy's leadership and with the encouragement of our senior pastor, Dr. Greg De-Loach, an eager congregation dove headlong into an exploration of what it means to be a missional church. At the direction of the moderators the Mission Vision Team was established to study the current philosophy of mission and the existing structure by which that philosophy was to be carried out, and then to make recommendations for change to the congregation as necessary.

This group read several books related to the topic, conducted interviews with mission leaders, and brainstormed the best direction for the church to go. Andy utilized discussion groups to introduce the leadership of the mission ministry to these new concepts. Based upon these philosophies the church made intentional changes to longstanding ministries, established new ministries and partnerships, and ended others. Some of the new partnerships included the Augusta area while others were international or domestic in nature.

The church formed local partnerships with Copeland Elementary School on Jackson Road and with the Harrisburg community, appointing

Lea and Bryce Cockerham as missionaries for the Harrisburg initiative. Together they served as liaisons to St. Luke's United Methodist Church, for whom we created and staffed a children's Sunday School in order to support and train St. Luke's membership to reclaim that ministry. The Cockerhams also provided leadership to the Bridge Ministry, a partnership with New Hope Worship Center focused on reaching the homeless and working poor of Augusta. In addition Lea represented FBC by leading a team to adopt a transitional house through Action Ministries, by serving on the board of The Point (a women's shelter and ministry), and by helping many community agencies to better connect with each other and those who would benefit from their services.

First Baptist established domestic partnerships with the CBF Together for Hope initiative in South Dakota with the Lakota Indians and in Eastern Kentucky with the people of Appalachia. We also began working with Conscience International in Haiti and with Mission on the Move in Honduras through our relationship with church members and newly-appointed missionaries Ernie and Allison Sizemore.

Teams sent to these locations read *When Helping Hurts: How to Alleviate Poverty Without Hurting the Poor...and Yourself,* and make every effort to practice the principles in that book. In most instances teams also read material to raise the cultural awareness of a particular area.

Partnerships are the new normal in the world of mission. Every effort should be made to establish long-term relationships with local churches or entities that will have a more consistent presence on the ground. Whenever possible we seek to let the local organization take the lead and, in so doing, help to stop the cycle of dependency on outside groups as the ones with solutions to problems.

The missional footprint of FBC Augusta is varied and far-reaching. While God will continue to reveal the ongoing work of the Spiri, it is up to the church to observe where that work is going on and how it might participate in the work. The ultimate mark of "success," however, will not be measured by the breadth of partnership but rather by its depth. To God be the glory!

Andy Jones

251

Chinese Sunday School Ministry

In 1885 the First Baptist Church of Augusta organized a Sunday School to minister to the Chinese men in the city who had come to America in the 1860s to build the transcontinental railroad and then to Augusta in the 1870s to help widen the Augusta canal. Some locals called these 200 immigrants Celestials, or Sons of the Celestial Dynasty, because of their otherworldly, spiritual, inscrutable demeanor. They may have resembled Celestials, but they also proved to be hardworking, strong, enduring settlers who remained to form one of the oldest Chinese communities in the eastern United States.

During this time churches in the South experienced a revival in missions. With the encouragement of the new pastor at FBC, Dr. Lansing Burrows, the City Mission Board and the Women's Foreign Mission Society were organized. Feeling a "call" to share the gospel at home with their Chinese neighbors who had no contact with the church, two church women, Mrs. Isabella Jordan and Mrs. A. Smith Irvine, drove a white horse belonging to Mrs. Jordan's father around to the Chinese stores and invited the men to meet on Sunday afternoons for Sunday School. Only one man, Chung Yung, attended the first Sunday afternoon. He was later converted and remained a faithful member until his death.

Augusta's Chinese Sunday School was the second institution of its kind in the South, the first one established a short time before in New Orleans. The Augusta school became known throughout the South for its faithful mission, and soon became the model for future churches. In 1944 Augusta's young pastor, Dr. R. Paul Caudill, left to become pastor of the First Baptist Church of Memphis, Tennessee. There he took steps to develop a church, modeled after the Augusta Chinese Sunday School, that today has blossomed into the First Chinese Baptist Church of Memphis.

After World War II an appreciable number of Chinese women and children came to Augusta. In spite of rigid immigration laws and high financial costs, they were reunited with their husbands and fathers. As a result, the Chinese Sunday School prospered; generations of families joined our Sunday School. Our major goal was always to share the gospel, with Bible lessons taught in English and translated into Mandarin and Cantonese. The Sunday School met the needs of its constituents in other ways by offering a place to meet their Chinese friends and maintain their religious and cultural traditions such as lavish Christmas and Easter banquets, summer picnics, and anniversary pageants.

Numerous teachers have devoted decades of service to the Chinese Sunday School. Medora Brown taught in the school and in her home for forty-four years. She led the young Paul Jue to accept Christ and encouraged him in his growth as a Christian. She adopted him as her spiritual son, and he called her "Mother Brown." Years later Paul Jue became the first Chinese elected to the board of deacons in the South, and he also served as superintendent of the Chinese Sunday School for thirty years. His family now represents four generations of faithful FBC members.

Cora Hogon worked with the children of the Chinese Sunday School for more than forty years. She organized the Sunbeam Band for the younger ones and coordinated Girls' Auxiliary and Royal Ambassadors for the youth. She taught the children the gospel with a strong commitment to missions at home and abroad. The children presented programs singing "Jesus Loves Me" in Cantonese and sharing the gospel at local nursing homes. They even raised funds to support a leper colony off the coast of China.

Mrs. B. K. Barnes, the church's financial secretary, recalls that her most cherished service was with the young women of the Chinese Sunday School. Through her efforts the Woman's Missionary Union began the Chinese Women's Auxiliary in 1946.

H. F. LeRoy taught young people and adults for more than thirty-five years, and engaged his entire family in service to the Chinese Sunday School as teachers and mentors. Additional teachers recognized for their decades of faithful service include:

- Harry Bell
- Herman Bolton
- Myra Haig
- Margaret Lau
- Susie Roberts

- Dr. Raymond Rufo
- Mrs. W.B. Sprague
- Mrs. W.B. Verdery
- Jane Chow Wong
- Mae Wong

The Chinese Sunday School celebrates more than 130 years of service to the church and community. Six deacons, four superintendents, two ministers, and four generations of families have received their spiritual development and support from the school. Although the majority of its members are now assimilated into the larger FBC congregation, the Chinese school continues to meet on Sunday afternoons and serves the church through various ministries in missions, music, children's programs, hospitality, senior adults, and special projects. One special project was the donation of the stained glass windows in the sanctuary given in honor of Lucy Wright Parker, who served as a missionary nurse to China for forty-two years. The window is a rich symbol of the Chinese Sunday School coming full circle.

As we look to the future, we remember the honorable past and serve the present with joy, love, and firm resolve to further the gospel of Jesus Christ. When asked to reflect on the Chinese Sunday School, this is what our retired associate pastor and beloved friend, Dr. Rodger Murchison, had to say:

> I can hear it now...laughter, music, and children sharing the joy of worship. A watchword for the Chinese Sunday School is "faithful." From the most senior adult to the youngest child, [its] participants have been and continue to be so very faithful. First Baptist is a better fellowship of Christian believers because of years and years of faithfulness of the Chinese Sunday School. We all have been and continue to be very grateful for all the school has meant to our church and the larger Augusta community. To God be the glory!

Our current Sunday School teacher, Mae Wong, proudly confirms: "The Chinese Sunday School is a living testament to Mrs. A. Smith Irvine's vision of the mission Sunday School as a practical expression of the Great Commission, showing God at work in his church."

> "Go therefore and make disciples of all the nations, baptizing them in the name of the Father and the Son and the Holy Spirit, teaching them to observe all that I commanded you; and lo, I am with you always, even to the end of the age." (Matt. 28:19-20)

Dedicated in loving memory of Jean D. Joe and Doris H. Lam, faithful members of the Chinese Sunday School for 67 years

Virginia T. Lam and Mae Wong

Chinese Sunday School Honorariums / Memorials

SUPERINTENDENTS

Mrs. A. Smith Irvine
Mrs. Isabella Jordan
Mrs. Katherine Sherwood
(assistant)
Mrs. Huisler
(assistant)
Fred Lockhart
Albert Patrick
C. H. Storey
C. D. Johnston
(1928–1940)

Woo Leong Tong
(assistant)
Paul K. Jue (1940–1970)
Charles W. C. Loo
(assistant)
Philip Wong
(1970–1991)
Ralph Wong
(1991–2006)
Peggy Wong Chow
(2006–present)

DEACONS

Paul K. Jue
(1943; emeritus 1991)
Dr. Raymond Rufo
(1977; emeritus 2014)
Philip Wong
(1986)

Elaine Wong
(1996)
Roger Tom
(1999)
Mimi Tom
(2015)

TEACHERS AND TRANSLATORS

Susie Roberts
Medora Brown and Mrs. Sprague
Margaret Lau
Myra Haig
Cora Hogon
Evelyn Barnes
H. F. LeRoy
Ruby Lum Wong
(Cantonese interpreter)
Lynne Woo
(Cantonese interpreter)
Henry Lam
(Mandarin interpreter)
Jane Chow Wong
Harry B. Bell Jr.
Mae Wong

TEACHERS, MUSICIANS, WORKERS

Mrs. Airgrell
Mrs. B. K. Barnes
Georgia Eng Beam
Herman Bolton
Dorothy Bracey
Mrs. R. F. Bridas
Mrs. Horace Bridges
Mrs. H. C. Browell
Medora Brown
Joe Bruker
Mrs. Joseph E. Bruker Sr.
John Bunch
Mrs. S. J. Chandler
Allan Chang
Peter Chang
Peter Chen

Ruth May Joe Chen
Margaret Ying Chin
E. H. Clark
Mrs. S. A. Dicks
Mary Dobey
Ellen Woo Dong
Linda Woo Dong
Carrie Dorsey
Bert Eng
Mrs. Jane Eve Fair
Mary Ellen Garrett
Emily Goon
Myra Haig
Cora Hogon
Mrs. Huisler
Kate Hulse
Mary Joe Hum
Mrs. A. Smith Irvine
Anna Joe
Brian Joe
Frances Joe
Jean Joe
Mulan Eng Joe
Mr. and Mrs. C. D. Johnson
Mrs. Lula Johnson
Mrs. Ellis Johnston
Mrs. William M. Jordan
Mr. and Mrs. Paul Jue
Dale Jacqueline Lam
Doris May Lam
Mrs. Jack Lam
Virginia T. Lam
Woo Lat
Mrs. T. K. Lau
Eileen Law
Jerry Law
Christine Chew Lem
H. F. LeRoy
Madelyn Lightfoot
Fred Lockhart
Mr. and Mrs. Charles Loo
Lilliam Marsh
R. P. Marsh
Mrs. Jere Morriss
Suzanne LeRoy Mulcay
Callaway Otwell

Albert Patrick
Bertha Pearce
Jennie Pearce
Mrs. W. F. Pederson
Mrs. L. H. Peterson
Dickie Puryear
Willie Puryear
Rev. and Mrs. M. W. Rankin
Susie Roberts
Ray Rufo
Mr. and Mrs. W. F. Sample
Martha LeRoy Scheri
Prof. and Mrs. J. C. Shecut
Mrs. Kate Sherwood
Robert Smith
Mrs. C. H. Storey
William H. Sturman
Mrs. W. B. Sprague
Mrs. C. H. Stratton
Mrs. H. O. Tabb
Emily Woo Takeuchi
Martha Tanner
Lillian Rufo Timm
Ida Tom
Karen Woo Tom
Roger Tom
Woo Leon Tong
Mrs. W. P. Vaughn
Miss Edna Verdery
Mrs. W. B. Verdery
Mrs. R. J. Videtto
Mary Jane Rufo Wallace
Kate Weigle
Anna Belle White
Elizabeth Wong
Judy Wong
Mrs. K. F. Wong
Kenneth Wong
Peggy Wong Chow
Mr. and Mrs. Philip Wong
Mr. and Mrs. Ralph Wong
Mrs. Stephen Wong
Mrs. James Woo
Willie Woo
Mary Ellen Wooten

Grief Ministry Workshop

First Baptist Church Augusta is a concerned and caring fellowship always seeking to minister to the pastoral care needs of the congregation. One area of need is for those who feel the pain of grief over the death of a loved one. Beginning in the 1990s our church began to provide a grief ministry workshop for church members and others in our community.

On average about thirty-five to forty-five FBC members die each year. Also, many of our church members experience the death of friends and relatives who are not in FBC. The need for ministry to those who experience the emotion of grief is very important to our church family.

The grief ministry workshop is usually held twice a year, with the fall session scheduled in October/November near Thanksgiving and the spring session in March during the season of Lent and near Easter. We schedule the workshops near these holiday times because many people who grieve find that at holiday times their grief is more intense. Also, discussing grief issues during these holiday and holy day seasons can give new and symbolic meaning to these church calendar events.

The grief ministry is coordinated through the administrative assistant to the pastor/assistant pastor, who keeps a list of all church members who die and also non-church members who die and have family in our church. In a letter we invite surviving family members to participate in the workshop. We also promote it via emails to the church membership; articles in the *Interpreter* newsletter; flyers; notices given to local funeral homes; and radio, television, and newspaper advertisements.

Approximately fifteen to twenty people attend each workshop, with the greater number coming from the community. The church is pleased to see this ministry as an outreach to the Central Savannah River Area.

The workshop began as a six-week dialogue/conversation about many issues related to grief and then evolved into a four-week Power-Point presentation with lecture/dialogue as the format. The current workshop has retained this format but now lasts three weeks.

Currently we structure the workshop around my book, *Guide for Grief*, based on my Doctor of Ministry dissertation, "Grief and Faith: A

Study of Effect." As part of my doctoral requirements I conducted a project within the church dealing with the relationship between grief and faith. In September 1994 approximately ten church members met for six weeks to discuss grief/faith issues, and these meetings became the precursor to the current grief ministry workshop. Our pastor at the time, Dr. Timothy Owings, suggested that these meetings presented a valuable ministry opportunity and encouraged me to continue conducting them on an annual or bi-annual basis.

The grief ministry workshops have continued since 1994, with meetings held once, twice, or sometimes three times yearly. We offer a bookstore and lending library at each workshop and also make available (with permission) a roster of participants to help attendees foster continued conversation after completion of the formal sessions.

At the workshop registration table we encourage each participant to collect the following material:

- a workshop session outline
- a grief book bibliography
- articles and materials about grief
- a roster of workshop participants
- information about other grief seminars in the Augusta area

The workshop sessions begin at 4 o'clock on Sunday afternoon and usually conclude about 5:30 and include a time for refreshments. Often, because of intense participation, sessions will extend until 6 p.m.

We remind those who mourn that, as John Claypool said, "grief can be very lonely, but you don't have to grieve alone." First Baptist has discovered that ministering to those who grieve the death of a loved one can be a challenging but rewarding ministry. As a church touches the lives of families who travel down the painful and tender road of grief, we realize that C. S. Lewis, in *A Grief Observed*, was right: "Grief is like a long valley, a winding valley where any bend may reveal a totally new landscape." We pray that through these grief ministry workshops, a new revelation of God's hope and comfort and peace will be revealed.

Rodger Murchison

Stained Glass Windows

The stained glass windows at First Baptist Church Augusta are a dramatic visual story of the life of Christ and the history of the church.

Crowning the south window of the sanctuary is the Gospel Window with the theme, "The Life of Christ." This window depicts the risen and exalted Christ. He is Lord of life, Lord of the church, and Lord of all. His hope of the resurrection inspires believers to commitment and dedication to the living gospel. Adorning the north window of the sanctuary is the Epistle Window with the theme, "The Response of the World to the Life and Work of Christ."

The themes, subjects, biblical and extra-biblical research, and basic designs of the windows originated with the Stained Glass Window Sub-Committee, appointed in 1973 by Sanctuary Committee chairperson Mrs. Robert E. Anderson (Mary Emma). Members of the subcommittee included chairperson Mrs. Charles R. Parker (Margaret), Mr. Joe Taylor Jr., and Mrs. Robert E. Anderson. The First Baptist committee worked in cooperation with Dr. Henry Lee Willit, of the Willit Stained Glass Studios in Philadelphia, Pennsylvania, who prepared and installed the windows.

The windows on the north and south walls of the sanctuary are constructed in a "Palladian" grouping, a design originating with the Renaissance architect Andrea Pallado (1518-1580). A Palladian window contains three panels in which the center section is arched and larger than the two side sections.

Willet windows are fabricated of the finest glass, both imported and domestic, with the choicest mouth-blown glasses and Norman slabs. The methods of medieval glass artists are used in the treatment of hand-painted glasses by fusing them in a kiln the number of times required to make them fadeless and able to withstand centuries of exposure.

Mrs. Margaret Parker worked tirelessly for twenty years on this massive project. Many church members helped to fund this enormous endeavor. The church would not order a window from the Willet Studios until the money for that window was secured. The entire project cost more than $400,000.

In 1992 First Baptist celebrated its 175th Anniversary. As a part of that event, Dr. Timothy L. Owings, pastor, suggested that Mrs. Parker organize the themes and symbols of the stained glass windows and publish the results in a book. I assisted in helping to transform research notes and references into a manuscript and then preparing this material for printing. A beautiful sixty-four-page book, *The Risen Christ*, visually chronicles the life of Christ and the world's response to Christ through the stunning medium of stained glass.

This magnificent book includes a biblical and historical reference explaining each segment of the windows. Descriptions of the iconography used in the windows include the meaning of symbols used, the significance of colors in religious art, and biblical and historical references. Readers will experience the thrill of discovery and appreciation as the secrets of iconography and religious art are revealed. *The Risen Christ* tells the story of how the marvelous stained glass windows are a monument to the love of our church family for our Lord and his church.

A major part of the book is the memorial section listing the many members of First Baptist involved in purchasing each panel of the windows. A detailed guide designates those who were memorialized and honored and also who funded that particular panel. The book is full of gorgeous pictures of each section of the windows. It concludes with a biblical and historical reference and background portion that describes each window panel, Bible verses that tell the story of that panel, and personal profiles of Christian luminaries across the centuries. There is also a study guide to religious symbols and colors used in Christian art and displayed in these wonderful windows.

Several people in particular helped to make the book possible:

- Lavinia Polatty kept records of funds, sales, and materials.
- Bryce Cockerham created a comprehensive brochure describing the scope of the book.
- Kirk Baxley spent many hours photographing the windows.
- George Perkins, moderator, and Robert Bates, vice moderator, worked with the church to secure funding for the book's publication.

- Dr. William E. Barfield Jr. chaired a committee to market the book.
- Lydia M. Inglett managed the design of the book's interior pages and cover.

Rodger Murchison

Pastors, Trustees, Deacons, Moderators, Church Staff, Minister Ordinations

PASTORS

Dr. William Theophilus Brantly
(1820–1826)

Rev. James Shannon
(1826–1829)

Dr. Charles Dutton Mallory
(1830–1835)

Rev. William J. Hard
(1836–1840)

Dr. William Theophilus Brantly Jr.
(1840–1848)

Rev. Nathaniel Greene Foster
(1849)

Rev. Charles B. Bennett
(1849–1851)

Dr. Joseph Getchell Binney
(1851–1855)

Rev. J. E. Ryerson
(1856–1859)

Dr. Adoniram Judson Huntington
(1860–1865)

Dr. James H. Cuthbert
(1865–1869)

Dr. James Dixon
(1869–1874)

Dr. Morton B. Wharton
(1875–1876)

Dr. William Warren Landrum
(1876–1882)

Dr. Lansing B. Burrows
(1883–1899)

Dr. Sparks W. Melton
(1900–1909)

Dr. M. Ashby Jones
(1909–1917)

Dr. William M. Vines
(1917–1918)

Dr. Edward L. Grace
(1919–1927)

Dr. Frederick E. Smith
(1928–1936)

Dr. R. Paul Caudill
(1937–1944)

Dr. Albert Warren Huyck
(1944–1953)

Dr. Robert Jackson Robinson
(1953–1974)

Dr. George L. Balentine
(1975–1982)

Dr. Charles B. Bugg
(1982–1989)

Dr. Timothy L. Owings
(1990–2003)

Dr. C. Gregory DeLoach III
(2005–2015)

TRUSTEES

1949
Schuyler W. Clark
Ralph L. Griffin

1963
Russell Blanchard
F. Fred Kennedy
Robert Walton

1967
J. Hal Stockton

1971
T. Richard Daniel

1974
J. C. Harris

1975
Dan Matheny

1980
David Hudson

1989
M. Bert Storey

1991
Russell Blanchard
T. R. Daniel
Tom Dozier
David Hudson
Jim Harris
Dan Matheny
Hal Stockton
Bert Storey

1992
Russell Blanchard
T. R. Daniel
Tom Dozier
Jim Harris
David Hudson
Bert Storey

1993
Russell Blanchard
George Christenberry
T. R. Daniel
Tom Dozier

Jim Harris
David Hudson
Bert Storey

1994
Russell Blanchard
George Christenberry
T. R. Daniel
Tom Dozier
Jim Harris
David Hudson
Bert Storey

1995
Russell Blanchard
George Christenberry
T. R. Daniel
Tom Dozier
Jim Harris
David Hudson
Bert Storey

1996
Russell Blanchard
George Christenberry
T. R. Daniel
Tom Dozier
Jim Harris
David Hudson
Bert Storey

1997
Russell Blanchard
George Christenberry
T. R. Daniel
Tom Dozier
Jim Harris
David Hudson
W. L. Inglett
Bert Storey

1998
David Bell
Russell Blanchard
John Buckner
George Christenberry
T. R. Daniel
Tom Dozier
David Hudson
Bert Storey

1999
Anna Bannister
David Bell
Russell Blanchard
John Buckner
George Christenberry
T. R. Daniel
Tom Dozier
David Hudson
Bert Storey

2000
Anna Bannister
David Bell
Russell Blanchard
John Buckner
George Christenberry
T. R. Daniel
Tom Dozier
David Hudson
Bert Storey

2001
Anna Bannister
David Bell
Russell Blanchard
John Buckner
J. Doug Cates
George Christenberry
T. R. Daniel
Tom Dozier
David Hudson

2002
Anna Bannister
David Bell
Russell Blanchard
John Buckner
J. Doug Cates
George Christenberry
T. R. Daniel
David Hudson

2003
Anna Bannister
David Bell
Russell Blanchard
John Buckner
J. Doug Cates
T. R. Daniel
Tom Dozier
David Hudson

2004
G. W. Amerson
Anna Bannister
Russell Blanchard
John Buckner
Tom Dozier
David Hudson
Charles Shaefer Jr.
Bert Storey

2005
G. W. Amerson
Anna Bannister
Russell Blanchard
Byron Brown
Tom Dozier
David Hudson
Charles Shaefer Jr.
Bert Storey

2006
G. W. Amerson
Russell Blanchard
Robert Brand
Byron Brown
Tom Dozier
David Hudson
Charles Shaefer Jr.
Bert Storey

2007
Russell Blanchard
Robert Brand
Byron Brown
Doug Clepper
Tom Dozier
David Hudson
Charles Shaefer Jr.
Bert Storey

2008
Robert Brand
Byron Brown
Doug Clepper
Tom Dozier
Milton Martin
Charles Shaefer Jr.
Bert Storey

2009
Robert Brand
Byron Brown

Doug Clepper
Warren Daniel
Tom Dozier
Milton Martin
Charles Shaefer Jr.

2010
Robert Brand
Byron Brown
Doug Clepper
Warren Daniel
Tom Dozier
Milton Martin
Bill Thompson

2011
Robert Brand
Byron Brown
Doug Clepper
Warren Daniel
Milton Martin
Beth Morrison
Bill Thompson

2012
Wade Blount
Robert Brand
Doug Clepper
Warren Daniel
Milton Martin
Beth Morrison
Bill Thompson

2013
Wade Blount
Doug Clepper
Warren Daniel
Milton Martin
E. G. Meybohm
Beth Morrison
Bill Thompson

2014
Wade Blount
Warren Daniel
Wilson Haynes
J. I. McNair
E. G. Meybohm
Beth Morrison
Bill Thompson

2015
Wade Blount
Warren Daniel
Wilson Haynes
E. G. Meybohm
Beth Morrison
Bill Thompson
Bobby Turner

2016
Wade Blount
Wilson Haynes
E. G. Meybohm
Beth Morrison
Joe Taylor Jr.
Bill Thompson
Bobby Turner

DEACONS

1817–1967

Allen, Charles B.
Allen Jr., H. B.
Ammons, E. G.
Anderson, Charles E.
Anderson, Robert E.
Baker, Charles A.
Baker, Herman
Barnard Jr., Douglas
Baxter, John M.
Becker, William
Belding, J. G.
Bell Jr., H. H.
Bell, John C.
Benson III, Calvin C.
Bentley, J. Judson
Black, J. C. C.
Blanchard, Russell A.
Blanchard, William E.
Boatwright, Fred
Bolton, E. Herman
Bothwell, J. T.
Bowen, Guy M.
Bowles, Clayton H.
Bruker, W. Cason
Bruker, Joe E.
Buckner Jr., John T.
Bunch, John F.
Calhoun, James
Callaway, E. H.
Calloway, Jack
Carswell, Augustin
Carswell, J. Frank
Carswell, James J.
Carwile, Z. W.
Childress, Freddie
Christian, Clifford
Clark, John M.
Clark, Schuyler W.
Copeland, S. D.
Cox, Chiles L.
Creamer, Harry R.
Crisler, Eugene C.
Crozier, E. M.
Daniel, Raleigh H.
Daniel, T. Richard
Dill, John P.
Drawdy, Sherman
Duncan, Harvey M.

Dye, M. M.
Edwards, M. B.
Evans, George W.
Evans, L. Bridges
Fellers Jr., E. E.
Fennell, J. F.
Fiske Jr., Julian
Freeman, T. M.
Garrett, T. Harry
Geer, Calvin
Glover, Carl
Gray, Zane
Green, Jesse D.
Griffin, Ralph L.
Guest, Milton
Hammett, Wyatt H.
Hardy, Charles P.
Harris, James C.
Hickman, H. H.
Hinely, Lewis J.
Holloway, L. B.
Houck, S. O.
Houston, C. G.
Huddleston, James
Hudson, J. W.
Irvine, A. Smith
Jackson, A. M.
Janes, Lawrence J.
Jennings Jr., Guy E.
Jernigan, Harry W.
Johnson, Herman L.
Johnston, F. W.
Jones, P. K.
Jones, T. D.
Jordon Jr., Clarence
Jue, P. K.
Key, W. O.
Kidd, S. Maxey
Kilpatrick, A. J.
Koth, William E.
Krouse Jr., A. Roy
Langston, Charles
Law, McKinne
Lawton, B. W.
Lee, J. Bothwell
Lee, John C.
Lee, O. C.
LeRoy, H. F.
Ligon, Woodson

Linney, George E.
Lockhart, F. T.
Lockhart, Milledge
Martin, Edward
Matheny, C. B.
Matheny, Dan P.
Mathews, G. W.
McCord, Z.
McElmurray, Walter
McGahee, Roscoe A.
McIntosh, Claude F.
McMichael Jr., J. P.
Mealing, H. G.
Meyer, John W.
Milhous, Sam
Miller, Harry J.
Miller, Joe
Montgomery, A. J.
Montgomery, Jerome
Moody, Lester S.
Moore, N. B.
Morton, W. Troup
Mull, George H.
Murdock, James H.
Mustin, Eli
Mustin, Paul
Napier, E. Frank
Nauright Jr., John R.
Norman, Robert C.
Otwell, J. Callaway
Owens, William I.
Patrick, Roy C.
Paulk, R. C.
Pearce, J. J.
Pearce, P. E.
Perry, A. C.
Phelps, William K.
Phinizy, Irvine
Phinizy, John
Plumb, D. B.
Prestwood Jr., J. G.
Prior, Willard W.
Puckett, Sam
Pullen, Edgar C.
Rabun, J. Douglas
Rabun, Oliver
Rainey, M. W.
Reynolds, J. Aubrey
Roberts, James L.
Robertson, Silas O.
Rucker, Jule T.
Sanford, Davenport

Scaggs, Robert A.
Shaefer, Charles F.
Schaeffer, George C.
Scruggs, Chester A.
Sharpton, Julian
Shecut, J. C.
Sims, L. S.
Singleton, William
Smith Jr., J. Dan
Smith, J. T.
Smith, Morgan
Stanford, Lloyd
Stark, William H.
Steed, C. A.
Steed, W. J.
Stevens Jr., W. P.
Stewart, Virgil
Stockton, J. Hal
Stockton, R. M.
Stoughton, O. B.
Sumerau, George
Symms, R. Allen
Symms, Marion S.
Tarpley, H. M.
Taylor, Joe E.
Thompson, J. G.
Thompson, J. W.
Turpin, William H.
Veal Jr., J. Ralph
Waters, John R.
Weaver, W. M.
Whitaker, Barney B.
Whitlock, I. W.
Wren, Palmer
Wright, David R.
Wright, George W.
Woodhurst Jr., Stan
Zimmerman, R. P.

1967–2016
Adams, Harry
Alexander, Mark
Allen, Joe C.
Anderson, Robert H.
Anderson, Walter E.
Anderson, R. E.
Anderson, Donald
Anderson, W. Keith
Arnold, Randy
Atkinson Jr., Tracy A.
Atkinson, William S.
Bailey, Henry E.

Bannister, Anna O.
Barfield Jr. William E.
Barlow, Mark W.
Barnard, D. Douglas
Bateman, Julian O.
Bateman, M. Joel
Bates, Robert A.
Bates, Shea O.
Bates, Newton
Baynham, Craig
Beazley, Jimmy
Becton, James L.
Becton, Beth
Beebe, John L.
Bell, David B.
Bell, Martha
Beman III, Hal D.
Bennett, Billy
Bennett, Terrie
Benson, Calvin
Bentley, J. Judson
Berry Jr., Thomas R.
Berry, George H.
Blackburn, Mildred
Blanchard, Thomas
Blanchard, Russell A.
Bloodworth, Paul
Blount, Wade B.
Boatwright, Fred C.
Bond, William C.
Boyd III, Thomas
Boyd, Mark
Brand, Robert L.
Brant, Nancy
Brooks, Barry
Brown, Joe H.
Brown III, R. Byron
Brown, Melanie
Brown, Carl
Broyles, Larry
Bruggemann, Linda
Bruker Jr., Joe E.
Bruker, W. Cason
Buck, Steve
Buck, Marcia
Buckner Jr., John T.
Buzhardt, Steven
Byars, William P.
Callaway Jr., T. W.
Carlson, Niti
Carpenter, Michael E.
Carr, Joanne K.

Carswell, A. S.
Childress, Freddie J.
Childress, James H.
Christenberry, George
Clements, Mason
Clepper, Douglas P.
Clyatt, Clarence
Coleman, William A.
Collins, Myron D. F.
Collins, Len
Cook, C. Dan
Cook, Barry F.
Cox, Chiles L.
Crews, Ruth
Crews, David
Crisler, Eugene C.
Cronic, Eugene A.
Dail, Darrell
Daniel, Warren A.
Daniel, T. Richard
Daniel II, Raleigh H.
Daniel, N. Kenneth
Deal, J. Ben
Dekle, David P.
DeVaney, Charles A.
Dixon, Robert L.
Dorosin, Norman N.
Dorsett, Robert S.
Dozier Jr., Thomas M.
Duckworth, Michael
Duke, Emory M.
Duncan, Lynn H.
Duncan, Harvey
Earnest, Chubby T.
Elkin, Paul
Elkin, Rebecca
Eller, S. Gary
Engels, Nettie B.
Engler, Josephine R.
Engler, Harold S.
Ensley Jr., Howard
Evans, L. Bridges
Faulk Jr., F. M.
Faulk, Ann
Fellers Jr., E. E.
Fields, M. Ann
Fiske Jr., Julian
Fiske, Julian Chiles
Fletcher, W. Lawrence
Flowers, Jeff W.
Fowler Jr., William T.
Fox, Joseph C.

Frits, Beth C.
Frits, Michael J.
Frye, Jay
Galloway, Ronald F.
Gary, T. Reed
Geer, H. Calvin
Giles, David
Giles, Linda
Giles, Dennis
Gilliam, David
Gleason, Gerald L.
Glover, Lamont H.
Gough, Kerry H.
Gray, Zane
Griffith, D. Edwin
Hardin, Frances S.
Hardin, Charles R.
Hardin, Allen
Hardy, Joseph K.
Hawes, Robert W.
Haynes, Wilson
Hendricks Jr., Sam T.
Hinely, Lewis J.
Hinely Jr., Lewis
Holt, Mitch
House, Stanley C.
Hudson, David
Hudson, W. Howard
Hudson, Janet K.
Huston, Steven
Inglett Jr., W. L.
Jennings Jr., Guy E.
Jones, Jimmy
Jones Jr., William W.
Jones, LaDawn
Josephson, Allan M.
Kearns, Jean
Keel, Lester L.
Keel, David L.
Key, W. O. (Ollie)
Key Jr., William O.
Knight, Maxwell L.
Koon, Peggie
Krouse Jr., A. Roy
Kubler, Jon M.
Landon, Laurel
Langston, James H.
LeRoy, H. F.
Linney, George E.
Malone, Delores
Mangum, Patricia
Martin, Stanley E.

Martin, Robert L.
Martin, Kathy S.
Martin, Mary Ann
Martin Jr., J. Milton
Matheny, Daniel P.
McCullough, Robert
McDaniel, Lee
McElmurray, W. W.
McGahee, Roscoe A.
McKay, Frank E.
McKay, Mary Lou
McKay, Marshall
McKenzie, Donald H.
McLeod, James L.
McMichen, John E.
McNair Jr., J. I.
McPhail, Frank
McPherson, Stephen
Means, Brad
Menefee, Lee
Menger, James M.
Messick, John H.
Meybohm, E. G.
Miller, Billey M.
Mize, Charles R.
Mobley Jr., Vernon
Mobley, Beth
Mobley, Rena
Mobley, R. Wyman
Moncrief, Ronald
Moore, Fred W.
Moore, Dean
Morris, Everett
Morrison, Beth
Morton, W. Troup
Mulherin, Carol
Murchison, Rodger
Napier, E. Frank
Norman, Robert C.
O'Neal, William E.
Odom Jr., Ernest J.
Osteen, Mark
Owen, Russell A.
Paige, Peter J.
Parker, Charles R.
Parker, Margaret M.
Parker, Carla
Partl, Jeff
Partridge Jr., W. Allen
Patrick, Jack B.
Patrick, Gloria
Perkins, George E.

Pinson, Joshua E.
Pollock, Joe
Powell, Lester
Prescott, Charles
Prestwood Jr., James
Prior, Willard W.
Pullen, Edgar C.
Puryear, James B.
Puryear, Joan C.
Rabun, J. Douglas
Reynolds, J. Aubrey
Roberson, D. Bentley
Roberts, Daisy E.
Roberts, James L.
Rogers, E. Vance
Rogers, Richard
Rooks, June
Rowland, Gregory D.
Rufo, Raymond T.
Saunders, Elwyn
Scaggs, Robert A.
Schaeffer, George C.
Scott, J. Loy
Scott, Jim
Sentell III, Perry R.
Shaefer, Charles F.
Shaefer Jr., Charles F.
Shaefer, Nan
Sharrock, Betty
Showman, Chris D.
Sizemore, Thomas E.
Slaton, J. Edward
Smith Jr., J. Dan
Smith, Harold G.
Smith, Patrick G.
Smith, James C.
Smith, David E.
Smith, Sarah
Smith, Calvin R.
Sterner, Matthew B.
Stevens Jr., William P.
Storey, M. Bert
Strong, Jane
Swan, Ernest L.
Sword, Rhoda
Tanner, R. Eugene
Taylor Jr., Joe E.
Taylor Sr., Joe E.
Taylor, Annette
Testino, P. J.
Thomas, Pam
Thompson, Billy B.

Thompson, Jack
Thompson, J. Newton
Thompson, Bill
Thompson, Pam
Timmerman, Gail
Tom, Roger D.
Tom, Mimi
Toomey, Michael
Townsend, Allison
Trotter, J. Davis
Trotter, John D.
Trotter Jr., William A.
Trotter IV, William A.
Tugmon, Cathy
Turner, Bobby
Tyler III, W. Briggs
Underwood, Cone
Underwood, Ellen
Vaughan, E. Porter
Vaughan Jr., T. P.
Veal, J. Ralph
Wardlaw Jr., Wallace
Wardlaw III, Bud
Watson, Phillip B.
Watson, Linda S.
Welter, Dave A.
Whitaker, Barney B.
White, Charles
Whitley Jr., John C.
Whitmer, Philip H.
Williams, Mark B.
Williams, George
Williams, Debbie
Williamson, Brenda
Williamson, Hance
Willingham, G. Jay
Wilson, Ohlen R.
Wilson Jr., Chappell
Wingard, Scott
Wong, Philip
Wong, Elaine
Woodall, Tim
Worthington, Kurt

Emeriti
Robert Anderson
Anna O. Bannister
D. Douglas Barnard Jr.
John T. Buckner Jr.
T. Richard Daniel
H. Calvin Geer
Kerry Gough

Ralph L. Griffin
Stanley E. Martin
C. F. McIntosh
James L. McLeod
James M. Menger
Billey M. Miller
E. Frank Napier
James B. Puryear

Joan Puryear
Raymond T. Rufo
Robert A. Scaggs
Harold G. Smith
James C. Smith
Marion Symms
Joe Taylor Jr.
S. Wallace Wardlaw

MODERATORS

John Bell
(1955–1957)
Joe Taylor
(1958–1959)
John Bell
(1960–1961)
Bridges Evans
(1962–1963)
Dan Smith
(1963–1964)
Roscoe McGahee
(1965–1966)
Dan Matheny
(1967–1968)
George Linney
(1969–1970)
Bill Stevens
(1971–1972)
George Christenberry
(1973–1974)
William Trotter
(1975–1976)
Roy Krouse
(1976–1977)
Jim Puryear
(1978–1979)
William Trotter
(1980–1981)
Frank McKay
(1981–1982)
Tommy Blanchard
(1983–1984)
Cason Bruker
(1985–1986)
E. E. "Bo" Fellers
(1986–1987)
Charles Shaefer Jr.
(1988–1989)

Thomas Dozier
(1990–1991)
George Perkins
(1992–1993)
Harold Smith
(1994–1995)
J. Edward Slaton
(1996–1997)
Guy Jennings
(1998–1999)
Jimmy Smith
(2000–2001)
J. I. McNair
(2001–July 2003)
William O. Key Jr.
(August–December 2003)
Dr. Robert Brand
(2004–2005)
Milton Martin
(2006)
Cone Underwood
(2007)
Kerry Gough
(2008)
Bobby Turner
(2009)
Hugh Hollar
(2010)
Joan Puryear
(2011)
David Keel
(2012)
Perry Sentell
(2013)
David Crews
(2014)
Joe Hardy
(2015)
Larry Fletcher
(2016)

CHURCH STAFF

Associate Ministers
Lynn Bishop
  (1961–1963)
Allen Stickney
  (1964–1967)
David Turner
  (1967–1970)
Sanford Kidd
  (1970–1974)
Hilton Garrett
  (1974–1983)
Jim Stertz
  (1983–1987)
Rodger Murchison
  (1987–2012)
Jim Walls
  (2015–present)

Minister of Activities
Jacob O. Malone
  (1980–1994)

Ministers of Church Administration
David Priest
  (1996–1997)
Rocky Cannon
  (1997–2008)
Jacob O. Malone
  (2008–2013)

Educational Directors /
Ministers of Education
C. Winfield Rich
  (1954–1956)
Carlton Carter
  (1956–1957)
Wendall Sloan
  (1957–1968)
Charles Cunningham
  (1969–1984)
Phillip N. Bennett
  (1984–2006)

Ministers of Music
Earl Holloway
  (1954)
Kenneth Cochrane
  (1954–1963)

David DeRossett
  (1963–1965)
Jacques Kearns
  (1966–1984)
Glen Adkins
  (1984–1992)
Keith Burrows
  (2006–2012)
Stan Pylant
  (1993–2013)
Kurt Wachtel
  (2015 to present)

Preschool / Children's Ministers
Myra Haig
  (1952–1983)
Patti Fowler
  (1983–1992)
Sue Deaton Stiles
  (1992–1999)
Todd Pylant
  (2000–2004)
Becca Jones
  (2006–2015)

Youth Directors
Jewelle DeLaughter Fiske
  (1957–1964)
Lynn Bishop
  (1961–1963)
Dan Shaddock
  (1963–1964)
Allen and Alice Stickney
  (1964–1967)
Mary Turner
  (1967–1970)

Ministers of Youth
Larry Earnest
  (1973–1979)
Reece Sherman
  (1984–1991)
Jud Reasons
  (1992–1999)
Kelly Hamilton
  (2000–2010)
Andy Jones
  (2006–2015)
Sean Taylor
  (2007–2010)

Brian Layman
(2013–2015)
Kyle Boyer
(2013–2015)

Ministers to Singles
Andy Menger
(1986–1991)
Randy Germann
(1992–1994)
Wayne Hunsucker
(1994–2004)

Minister to Young Families
Todd Pylant
(2000–2004)

Ministers of Senior Adults
Jacob O. Malone
(1994–2008)
Keith Burrow
(2008–2012)
Stan Pylant
(2012–2015)
Paul Moller
(2015–present)

Organists
Robert J. Watson
(1920–1955)
Sidney A. Richardson
(1954–1994)
Susan Shiplett
(1994–1999)
Jeff Lewis
(1999–2000)
Pierce Dickens
(2000–2005)
Charlotte Jenkins
(2005–2012)
Wayne Lord
(2012–present)

Pianist
Les Reagan
(2006–present)

Pastor's Assistants
Hazel Dukes
(1955–1971)
Eileen Martin
(1971–1991)

Dede Maddox
(1991–2016)
Cyndi Busby
(2016–present)

2016 Staff
David Hull
(Interim Senior Pastor)
Jim Walls
(Interim Pastor)
Kurt Wachtel
(Minister of Music)
Tommy Payne
(Music Ministry Assistant)
Wayne Lord
(Organist)
Les Reagan
(Pianist)
Claudia Moller
(Children's Music Assistant)
Michael Toomey
(Contemporary Worship Leader)
Chip Reeves
(Interim Minister of Missional Outreach)
Patti Fowler
(Minister of Weekday Education)
Jennifer Huston
(Preschool/Children's Director)
Josh Pinson
(Youth Director)
Jacob Waldrip
(Ministerial Intern)
Linh Luong
(Vietnamese Pastor)
Paul Moller
(Director of Senior Adult Activities)
Tim Spivey
(Administrator)
Lavinia Polatty
(Finance Director)
Cyndi Busby
(Pastoral Assistant)
Shirley Lescantz
(Purchasing / Scheduling Director)
Luci Worthington
(Director of Publishing)
Elizabeth Chao
(Youth / Senior Adult / Missions Assistant)
Susan Jones
(Receptionist / Prayer Ministry Assistant)

Leah Galey
  (Administrative Assistant for Preschool /
  Children)
Lori McPherson
  (Nursery Coordinator)
George Berry
  (Activities Director)
Billey Miller
  (Director of Television Ministry)
Frank Whitfield
  (Custodial Supervisor)
John Dixon
  (Custodian)
Dwayne Rawls
  (Custodian)
Jessie Walker
  (Custodian)
Reggie Williams
  (Custodian)
Demetrick Harden
  (Custodian)
Stephen Childress
  (Chef)
Vanessa Symonds
  (Kitchen Staff)
Willie Woods
  (Kitchen Staff)
Laura Reed
  (Kitchen Staff)

JJ Stephens
  (Kitchen Staff)
Gary Fickhesen
  (Bus Driver)

Staff Serving 25+ Years
Mrs. B. K. Barnes
  (1940–1977)
Patti Fowler
  (1983–present)
Myra Haig
  (1952–1983)
Dede Maddox
  (1991–2016)
Jacob O. Malone
  (1980–2013)
Rodger Murchison
  (1987–2012)
Lavinia Polatty
  (1977–present)
Sidney A. Richardson
  (1954–1994)
Isaac Strom
  (1937–1976)
Robert Watson
  (1920–1955)
Luci Worthington
  (1990–to present)

MINISTER ORDINATIONS

Robert Geer
(1945)
William Roscoe West
(1961)
Allen Stickney
(1967)
Joseph Glisson
(1968)
Jacques Kearns
(1970)
Timothy Callaway
(1974)
Sanford Kidd
(1974)
John Napier Schumacher
(1979)
Rob Anderson
(1994)
Wayne Hunsucker
(1995)
Mark Kemp
(2000)
Tripp Martin
(2003)

Michael McEntyre
(2004)
Will Williams
(2005)
Irene Bennett
(2006)
Martha Kate Berry Hall
(2007)
Jeremy Echols
(2008)
Christie McTier
(2009)
Linh Luong
(2011)
Kyle Boyer
(2012)
Brian Layman
(2012)
Khanh Le
(2013)
Hepsi James
(2014)
Lang Le
(2016)

200th Anniversary Planning Committees

COMMITTEE
David C. Crews
Meg Gardner Duckworth (Mrs. Michael V. Duckworth)
Anna Kim Polatty Fletcher (Mrs. W. Lawrence Fletcher)
Dr. Franklin McPhail Jr. (Frank)
Lynn Strickland Meybohm (Mrs. E. G. Meybohm)
Dr. Rodger B. Murchison
R. Perry Sentell
William R. Thompson (Bill)
Louis S. Wall
Janet Kirkley Hudson (Mrs. David E. Hudson), chair
Joseph K. Hardy (Joe), ex-officio
W. Lawrence Fletcher (Larry), ex-officio

ADVISORY COMMITTEE
Jane Gibson Anderson (Mrs. Robert H. Anderson)
Robert H. Anderson (Bobby)
Anna Olive Jones Bannister (Mrs. T. C. Bannister)
Mildred Roberts Blackburn (Mrs. Robert E. Blackburn)
Jacquelyn Murray Blanchard (Mrs. Thomas W. Blanchard)
Jane Armstrong Coleman (Mrs. Ron Coleman)
Kerry H. Gough
James M. Menger (Jimmy)
Harold G. Smith
Sara Bailey Smith (Mrs. Harold G. Smith)

COMMITTEE CHAIRS
Ancestry
Jane Armstrong Coleman (Mrs. Ron Coleman)
Becky Leach Dozier

Anniversary Song
Dr. Glen C. Adkins

Banners
Mary Ann Dale Martin (Mrs. Robert L. Martin)

Children's Musical
Written by Margaret Reynolds Wiggins (Mrs. A. Wayne Wiggins)
Directed by Claudia Croom Moller (Mrs. Paul C. Moller)

Chinese Missions
Roger D. Tom

David Phelps Concert
Mr. Jimmy Beazley (Jim)
Elizabeth Lee Beazley (Mrs. Jim Beazley)

History Book
Dr. Rodger B. Murchison

History Dramas
Jane Armstrong Coleman (Mrs. Ron Coleman)

History in Photographs
Jacquelyn Murray Blanchard (Mrs. Thomas W. Blanchard)
Robert H. Anderson (Bobby)
Jane Gibson Anderson (Mrs. Robert H. Anderson)

Homecoming Dinner on the Grounds
Lynn Strickland Meybohm (Mrs. E. G. Meybohm)

Legal Counsel and Finance Advisor
R. Perry Sentell

Mercer Connection
William R. Thompson (Bill)

Missions Through the Years
Terrie Mims Bennett (Mrs. Billy R. Bennett, Jr.)

Multigenerational Families
Mildred Roberts Blackburn (Mrs. Robert E. Blackburn)
Gloria Davis Patrick (Mrs. Jack B. Patrick)

Photography
Hillary Bennett Odom (Mrs. Robert Odom)

Printing
Luci Worthington (Mrs. William)

Publicity
Meg Gardner Duckworth (Mrs. Michael V. Duckworth)
Anna Kim Polatty Fletcher (Mrs. W. Lawrence Fletcher)

SBC, CBF, Baptist History and Heritage Society Recognition
Dr. Franklin McPhail, Jr. (Frank)

Time Capsule
David Crews

Video Production
David Rose

Vietnamese Missions
Pastor Linh Loung

Women's Luncheon
Margaret Mitchell Murchison (Mrs. Rodger B. Murchison)

Youth Concert
Mimi Palmer Tom (Mrs. Roger D. Tom)

Consultant
Lavinia Polatty

Notes

¹DeLoach's immediate predecessor, Tim Owings, preached a similar series in the summer of 2003. See church bulletins, located in FBCA archives, of respective years.

²Margaret Parker, Rodger Murchison, *The Risen Christ* (Augusta, GA: FBC, 1992).

³For a comprehensive survey of Christian church history, see Justo Gonzalez, *The Story of Christianity*, 2 vols. (San Francisco: Harper and Row, 1984).

⁴Ibid.

⁵For a comprehensive survey of the Protestant Reformation, see John Bossy, *Christianity in the West, 1400–1700* (Oxford: Oxford University Press, 1985).

⁶For a comprehensive survey of Baptist history, see C. Douglas Weaver, *In Search of the New Testament Church: The Baptist Story* (Macon, GA: Mercer University Press, 2008).

⁷Arminianism, named after sixteenth century theologian Jacob Arminius, is contrary to the predestinarian theology of Protestant Reformer John Calvin and his followers in which only persons chosen directly by God are gifted with salvation. See Joseph Everett Early, *The Life and Writings of Thomas Helwys* (Macon, GA: Mercer University Press, 2009).

⁸See Thomas Helwys, Richard Groves, *A Short Declaration of the Mystery of Iniquity (1611/1612)* (Macon, GA: Mercer University Press, 1998).

⁹Ibid.

¹⁰See Early, *Life and Writings*.

¹¹For a comprehensive survey of New England Puritanism, see Francis J. Bremer, *The Puritan Experiment: New England Society from Bradford to Edwards*, rev. ed. (Lebanon, NH: University Press of New England, 1995).

¹²See James P. Byrd Jr., *The Challenges of Roger Williams: Religious Liberty, Violent Persecution, and the Bible* (Macon, GA: Mercer University Press, 2002).

¹³See Louis Franklin Asher, *John Clarke (1609–1676): Pioneer in American Medicine, Democratic Ideals, and Champion of Religious Liberty* (Pittsburgh, PA: Dorrance Publishing Company, 1997). In 1652 John Clarke penned *Ill Newes from New England*, a treatise expounding upon the persecution of religious dissenters in the New World.

¹⁴The "priesthood of all believers" is derived from 1 Peter 2:5.

¹⁵See Lewis Peyton Little, *Imprisoned Preachers and Religious Liberty in Virginia* (Lynchburg, VA: J. P. Bell, 1938); and John A. Ragosta, *Wellspring of Liberty: How Virginia's Religious Dissenters Helped Win the American Revolution and Secured Religious Liberty* (New York: Oxford University Press, 2010).

¹⁶Isaac Backus, *An Appeal to the Public for Religious Liberty, Against the Oppressions of the Present Day* (Boston: John Boyle, 1773).

¹⁷See Isaac Backus, *A History of New England with Particular Reference to the Denomination of Christians Called Baptists*, 2nd ed., with notes by David Weston, 2 vols. (Newton, MA: Backus Historical Society, 1871).

¹⁸See Little, *Imprisoned Preachers*, and Ragosta, *Wellspring of Liberty*

[19]See Ragosta, *Wellspring of Liberty*.

[20]See Timothy Daiss, *Rebels, Saints and Sinners: Savannah's Rich History and Colorful Personalities* (Gretna, LA: Pelican, 2002). At least two Baptists sailed on the *Anne*. Oglethorpe quietly allowed exceptions to the Anglican-only land policy, but what became of the Baptists is unknown.

[21]Edward J. Cashin, *The Story of Augusta* (Augusta, GA: Richmond County Historical Society: 1991) 9-17.

[22]See Roger K. Warlick, *As Grain Once Scattered: The History of Christ Church, Savannah, 1733-1833* (Columbia, SC: State Printing, 1987); Cashin, *Story of Augusta*, 14.

[23]Joel A. Nichols, "Religious Liberty in the Thirteenth Colony: Church-State Relations in Colonial and Early National Georgia," *New York University Law Review*, 80/6 (December 2005): 1704-1721.

[24]See C. C. Goen, *Revivalism and Separatism in New England, 1740-1800: Strict Congregationalists and Separate Baptists in the Great Awakening* (New Haven, CT: Yale University Press, 1962).

[25]Samuel Boykin, *History of the Baptist Denomination in Georgia*, vol. 1 (Atlanta: J. P. Harrison, 1881) 13; James Donovan Mosteller, *A History of the Kiokee Baptist Church in Georgia* (Ann Arbor, MI: Edwards Brothers, 1952) 69.

[26]John T. Christian, *A History of the Baptists*, vol. 2 (Texarkana, TX: Bogard Press, 1922) 209-212.

[27]Benjamin F. Riley, *A History of the Baptists in the Southern States East of the Mississippi* (Philadelphia: American Baptist Publication Society, 1898) 30. According to Mosteller (69, 108), Marshall's arrest took place under an oak tree in present-day Appling. Marshall's grave marker in Columbia County notes his arrest "was not later than 1770."

[28]Mosteller, *Kiokee*, 69-70.

[29]Ibid., 70.

[30]Ibid.

[31]Ibid., 70-73.

[32]Cashin, *Story of Augusta*, 27-35; Waldo P. Harris III, "Daniel Marshall: Lone Georgia Baptist Revolutionary Pastor," *Viewpoints: Georgia Baptist History* 5 (1976): 51-64; Thomas Ray, *Daniel and Abraham Marshall Pioneer Baptist Evangelists to the South* (Springfield, MO: Particular Baptist Press, 2006) 63.

[33]Cashin, *Story of Augusta*, 39-41, 44-53.

[34]See J. H. Campbell, *Georgia Baptists: Historical and Biographical* (Macon, GA: J. W. Burke, 1874) 55-71.

[35]Boykin, *History*, vol. 1, 259-263. Also see "The Baptist Remonstrance to the General Assembly of Georgia," 1785, in Ray, *Daniel and Abraham Marshall*, 240-243; and Reba C. Strickland, *Religion and State in Georgia in the Eighteenth Century* (New York: Columbia University Press, 1939) 164-166.

[36]Francis Newton Thorpe, *The Federal and State Constitutions, II Florida-Kansas* (Washington, DC: Government Printing Office, 1909) 789; Ray, *Daniel and Abraham Marshall*, 63, 230.

[37]William B. Sprague, *Annals of the American Pulpit*, vol. 6 (New York: Robert Carter & Brothers, 1865) 170-171, 269.

[38]Jabez P. Marshall, *Memoirs of the Late Rev. Abraham Marshall* (Mount Zion, GA: 1824) 17-52.

[39]Mosteller, *Kiokee*, 74; Ray, *Daniel and Abraham Marshall*, 33-36. Robert G. Gardner, et al., *A History of the Georgia Baptist Association* (Atlanta, GA: Georgia Baptist Historical Society, 1988) 20.

[40]Ray, *Daniel and Abraham Marshall*, 36-37.

[41]Ibid., 49, 53-55. Boykin, *History*, vol. 1, 328-329.

[42]Ray, *Daniel and Abraham Marshall*, 55-56. See also George Smith, *The Life of William Carey, Shoemaker and Missionary* (London: John Murray, 1887).

[43]Marshall established as many as thirty-nine churches in Georgia, South Carolina, and elsewhere. See Ray, *Daniel and Abraham Marshall*, 56.

[44]Three churches claim to be America's first Black Baptist congregation. Savannah's First African Baptist Church (1778) traces its roots to 1773. Springfield Baptist Church (1793) traces its roots to 1773 in Silver Bluff, South Carolina (Aiken County). The Colored Baptist Church of Williamsburg, Virginia (c. 1785) also claims roots in the 1770s. First Bryan Baptist Church of Savannah, organized in 1788, claims to be the oldest *continuous* African-American Baptist church in the United States. "Negro Churches Organized in the Eighteenth Century," in Monroe N. Work, *Negro Year Book: An Annual Encyclopedia* (Tuskegee, AL: Tuskegee Institute, 1913) 112. Ray, *Daniel and Abraham Marshall*, 55, 59-63, 239. David Benedict, *Fifty Years Among the Baptists* (New York: Sheldon, 1860) 40-41. David Benedict, *A General History of the Baptist Denomination in America*, vol. 2 (Boston: Lincoln & Edmands, 1813) 193-194. Waldo P. Harris III and James D. Mosteller, *Georgia's First Continuing Baptist Church* (Appling, GA: Kiokee Baptist Church, 1997) 215-216.

[45]"Abilene Baptist Church, Richmond now Columbia County," Georgia Baptist Church Records, Georgia Baptist History Depository, Special Collections, Jack Tarver Library, Mercer University, Macon, Georgia.

[46]Correspondence with Erick Montgomery, executive director, Historic Augusta, Inc. The 1802 Richmond Academy building remains to the present day. Following the Revolutionary War, the Anglican Church (the American expression of the Church of England) became independent of England, adopting the name Episcopalian.

[47]Charles Colcock Jones and Salem Dutcher, *Memorial History of Augusta, Georgia* (Syracuse, NY: D. Mason, 1890) 377-378. Correspondence with Montgomery.

[48]Minutes, Georgia Baptist Association, 1808, Special Collections, Jack Tarver Library, Mercer University.

[49]See William L. Lumpkin, *Baptist Foundations in the South: Tracing Through the Separates the Influence of the Great Awakening, 1754-1787* (Eugene, OR: Wipf & Stock, 2006).

[50]Leon McBeth, *The Baptist Heritage: Four Centuries of Baptist Witness* (Nashville: Broadman Press, 1987) 343-391.

[51]Minutes, FBCA, 25 March 1817. Mary Ann Mimms was the wife of Britain Mimms. Their house in North Augusta is yet standing, and is listed on the National Register.

[52]1820 U.S. Census; Jones and Dutcher, *Memorial History*, 10; Cashin, *Story of Augusta*, 71, 79, 81, 82. One hundred years following the church's founding, descendants of Henry Mealing remained on church rolls.

[53]Minutes, May 1817. The courthouse still stands as the "Old Government House" on Telfair Street.

[54]Minutes, May-August 1817.

[55]For an analysis of 19th-century Baptist church discipline in the South, see Gregory Wills, *Democratic Religion: Freedom, Authority, and Church Discipline in the Baptist South, 1785-1900* (New York: Oxford University Press, 2003).

[56]Minutes, March-August 1817

[57]Minutes, October 1817; Jones and Dutcher, *Memorial History*, 378; Isabella S. Jordan, *A Century of Service: First Baptist Church, Augusta, Georgia* (FBCA, 1920) 11-12.

[58]Michelle Gillespie, "From Household to Market: Black and White Women at Work in Augusta, 1790-1825," in Edward J. Cashin and Glenn T. Eskew, *Paternalism in a Southern City: Race, Religion and Gender in Augusta, Ga.* (Athens, GA: UGA Press, 2001) 46.

[59]Edward J. Cashin, "Paternalism in Augusta: The Impact of a Plantation Ethic Upon an Urban Society" and Gillespie, "From Household to Market," in Cashin and Eskew, *Paternalism*, 14, 46. Also see "Celebration of Georgia Bicentennial, First Baptist Church, Augusta, Georgia, February 12, 1933," 15-17, Archives, FBCA.

[60]Gillespie, "From Household to Market," 14, 47, 49, 50, 56, 57. According to the 1820 U.S. Census, of the roughly 8,638 persons residing in Richmond County, 4,831 (or 56 percent) were slaves (compared to 140 free blacks). The 42 percent of slave ownership was unusually large for the South at this time, and must be understood in the context of some slaves working in the city, in addition to many working on nearby plantations. For a survey of slave patterns in early Augusta and Richmond County, see Donnie B. Bellamy and Diane E. Walker, "Slaveholding in Antebellum Augusta and Richmond County, Georgia," *Phylon* 48 (1987): 165-177.

[61]Jordan, *Century of Service*, 6.

[62]Cashin, "Paternalism," 14.

[63]Southern wealth was primarily measured by slave ownership, and by this measure few of the founding members of the Augusta congregation were persons of wealth. According to the 1820 U.S. Census, at least six founding members owned slaves. None owned twenty or more slaves, a common measurement of large slave owner, or planter, status. Jesse Green owned eighteen slaves; Caleb Morgan (aka J. C. Morgan) owned eight slaves; Joseph Phillips (or Philips) of Burke County, Georgia, owned six slaves; Edward Martin owned four slaves; Henry Mealing of Edgefield District, South Carolina owned three slaves, as did Woodson Ligon.

[64]Baptists in America during the 19th century and alongside the larger Temperance movement gradually came to oppose alcohol usage, largely reaching a tipping point of Prohibition by about 1920.

[65]Henry R. Stiles, *The History and Genealogies of Ancient Windsor, Connecticut, 1635-1891* (Hartford, CT: Press of the Case, Lockwood & Brainard Co., 1892) 1:10.

[66]Jordan, *Century of Service*, 3-4.

[67]Minutes, October 1817, February 1818.

[68]Jordan, *Century of Service*, 9-10; Minutes, October-November 1818.

[69]Jordan, *Century of Service*, 10; Minutes, 28 February 1819.

[70]*Augusta Chronicle*, 5 April 1819.

[71]*Augusta Chronicle*, 28 July, 30 July, 18 August, 23 August 1819. The details surrounding the failure to secure land in 1819 are somewhat ambiguous, with the church seemingly rejecting both potential lots as unsuitable.

[72]Samuel L. Caldwell, *Discourse Delivered in the First Baptist Meeting House, Providence, Sunday Morning, May 28, 1865, Ninety Years After Its First Dedication* (Boston: Gould and Lincoln, 1865).

[73] Boykin, *History*, vol. 1, 115; Enoch Hutchinson, ed., *The Baptist Memorial and Monthly Record*, vol. 9 (New York: Z. P. Hatch, 1850) 311; Minutes, 22 May 1819.

[74]Minutes, June-August, 1819. Wife Martha remained a member of the congregation.

[75]Minutes, July 1819; Jordan, *Century of Service*, 11; "Conspiracy!" *Augusta Chronicle*, 10 May 1819. Later, white citizens suspected slaves were behind a November 1819 fire that caused some $50,000 in damage. In February 1820 two slaves were executed for their role in the killing of a white man. One was burned alive, the other hanged and decapitated. See Julius P. Rodriguez, ed., *Encyclopedia of Slave Resistance and Rebellion*, vol. 1 (Westport, CT: Greenwood Press, 2007) 140-141. Apart from these tensions and although various laws restricted the activities of slaves in town, many enjoyed, with the permission of their masters, freedom to move about town, worship of their own accord, and even transact business. Slaveowners in the countryside, on the other hand, often complained of their slaves spending too much time in town without express permission. See Edwin J. Cashin, *Old Springfield: Race and Religion in Augusta, Georgia* (Augusta, GA: Springfield Village Park Foundation, 1995) 16-38.

[76]See *Augusta Chronicle*, "Warfare was bad but economics fatal to arsenal," 4 July 1976.

[77]Jordan, *Century of Service*, 14; Hutchinson, ed., *Baptist Memorial*, 312. This was Brantly's second marriage; his first wife, Anna McDonald Martin, died in 1818. For more information about Brantly, see Jesse H. Campbell, *Georgia Baptists: Historical and Biographical* (Macon, GA: J. W. Burket, 1874) 208-226.

[78]William Buell Sprague, *Annals of the American Pulpit: Baptist* (New York: Robert Carter, 1860) 168-170. The author met a descendant of Abraham Marshall while visiting the Kiokee Baptist Church in February 2015.

[79]Minutes, 27 November 1819; Jordan, *Century of Service*, 11. For more information on local church discipline, see Wills, *Democratic Religion*. Following the Civil War and Emancipation, in 1886 the Springfield Baptist Church, sometimes referred to as the First African church, would have an estimated membership of 5,000, the church most likely the largest Baptist congregation in the state of Georgia; see William Hicks, *History of Louisiana Negro Baptists from 1804 to 1914* (Nashville: Nashville Baptist Publishing Board, 1915), 245.

[80]Jordan, *Century of Service*, 11-12.

[81]Ibid., 12-13.

[82]Conversation with Eric Montgomery, executive director, Historic Augusta Inc.; Jordan, *Century of Service*, 12-13, 54. Primary sources dating the cornerstone ceremony are not available. Jordan's telling of the story contains inconsistencies compared to secondary materials in church archives. Jordan dates the acquisition of the lot as 6 July 1820, and the placing of the cornerstone on, variously, 11 February 1820 and 18 February 1820 (the former of these two dates is attributed to an *Augusta Chronicle* article that she unverifiably dates as 18 February 1820), while noting that the silver plate buried with the cornerstone contains the date of 22 February 1820. In Jordan's telling, the construction of the building would probably have begun prior to the purchase of the land, an unusual scenario. It seems likely that an agreement to purchase the land preceded the formal acquisition. Contrasting with Jordan, a typed copy of a 17 February 1820 *Augusta Chronicle* dates the ceremony as 12 February 1820, a date reinforced by a 1945 *Augusta Chronicle* article also dating the cornerstone as 12 February 1820. The date of 12 February 1820 is stamped on a silver plate buried in the cornerstone. Later unearthed, it is now in the possession of FBCA.

[83]Minutes, 9 April, 6 May 1820.

[84]Jordan, *Century of Service*, 12; Cashin, "Paternalism," 13; "Will of John Milledge Richmond County, Georgia," Richmond County Will Book A, 154-155. Milledge owned 115 slaves upon his death in 1815.

[85]Minutes, April 1821.

[86]Jordan, *Century of Service*, 13; Minutes, 2 July 1820. Jordan gives the date of 6 July 1820 for the purchase of the lot. One new member was a doctor. A notation in church records indicates that clerk Joshua Key had not kept the best of records.

[87]Jordan, *Century of Service*, 13. Brantly was not only concerned with the children of wealthy families. In 1821 he helped incorporate the Augusta Free School Society, devoted to educating poor children. See Jones and Dutcher, *Memorial History*, 319.

[88]Jordan, *Century of Service*, 13. Jones and Dutcher, *Memorial History*, 367-86.

[89]Minutes, 2 December 1820; 10 March 1821.

[90]Minutes, May 1821; Jordan, *Century of Service*, 14; Anna Olive Jones, *History of the First Baptist Church, Augusta, Georgia, 1817–1967* (Columbia, SC: R. L. Bryan, 1967) 15-16; "Ware, Nicholas," *Biographical Dictionary of the United States Congress*, accessed 14 June 2015, http://bioguide.congress.gov/scripts/biodisplay.pl?index=W000148.

[91]Boykin, *History*, vol. 1, 104-105, 121. Washington L. Kilpatrick, *The Hephzibah Baptist Association Centennial, 1794-1894* (Augusta, GA: Richards & Shaver, 1894). Some churches, believing cooperative mission work unbiblical, opted not to join the organization.

[92]Minutes, 22 March 1822. The Rede's Creek Baptist Church was incorporated in 1806. See Jones and Dutcher, *Memorial History*, 378. In 1824 Rede's Creek returned to formal church status. See Charmain Z. Brackatt, "Church Has Rich History," *Augusta Chronicle*, 18 January 1998.

[93]Augusta's slaves, however, enjoyed more liberties than typical. See Cashin, *Old Springfield*, 16-38.

[94]Church records rarely refer to black persons, and early church records are void of slave members.

[95]"The Indian Performances," *Augusta Chronicle*, 28 November 1822.

[96]For more about the early Baptist missions movement, see Brian Stanley, *The History of the Baptist Missionary Society 1792-1992* (Edinburgh: T&T Clark, 1992).

[97]"Death of the Rev. Wm. Ward, of Serampore," *Augusta Chronicle*, 21 May 1823.

[98]*Augusta Chronicle*, 6 November 1823.

[99]"Just Published," *Augusta Chronicle*, 3 March 1824.

[100]Jordan, *Century of Service*, 15; Jones, *History of FBC*, 17.

[101]Minutes, 11 April 1824.

[102]Minutes, May-July 1824; Jordan, *Century of Service*, 16; Jones, *History of FBC*, 18; Jones and Dutcher, *Memorial History*, 338, 428-429, 482.

[103]Jones, *History of FBC*, 18.

[104]Minutes, 9 December 1824; "A Brief History of the First Baptist Church of Philadelphia," FBC Philadelphia, accessed 20 May 2015, http://www.firstbaptist-philadelphia.org/pages/history.html; Hutchinson, ed., *Baptist Memorial*, 312. The first Baptist denomination in America, formed at the First Baptist Church in Philadelphia in 1814, was the "General Missionary Convention of the Baptist Denomination of the United States for Foreign Missions," or the Triennial Convention, for short. The controversy Brantly observed in Philadelphia may have been over the subject of missions, an object of much contention in Baptist life of the 1820s, as many Christians condemned denominational missionary endeavors as foreign to scripture, and therefore theologically unsound. The congregation's current pastor, Henry Holcomb, an advocate of missions, had for some years as a writer and public speaker been a lightning road in the missions controversy. See Henry Holcomb, *The Whole Truth, Relative to the Controversy, Betwixt the American Baptists* (Philadelphia: J. H. Cunningham, 1820).

[105]Jordan, *Century of Service*, 16; Boykin, *History*, vol. 1, 115. "Hannah D'Antignac's American Revolution Pension Statement, 31 January 1839," accessed 20 May 2015, http://revwarapps.org/w4116.pdf; "History of the Medical College of Georgia, 1822-1828" (Augusta, GA: Georgia Regents University) accessed 20 May 2015, http://gru.edu/library/greenblatt/history/1822-1828.php. Antony's name was alternatively spelled "Anthony."

[106]Minutes, 12 March 1825; Jordan, *Century of Service*, 15; Jones, *History of FBC*, 18-19; Mustin operated a crockery store, selling kitchenware.

[107]Hutchinson, ed., *Baptist Memorial*, 312; Minutes, 2 April 1826; Jones, *History of FBC*, 19. Despite Brantly's resignation, Georgia Baptists retained him to represent them at the 1826 Triennial Convention. Boykin, *History*, vol. 1, 207.

[108]Jesse H. Campbell, *Georgia Baptists*, 21. The GBC in 1826 "Resolved, That as our beloved brother, the Rev. William T. Brantly, who has much endeared himself to us by his Christian deportment and faithful discharge of ministerial duties, is about to remove his residence from this State, we furnish him with a letter expressive of our affectionate regard and religious fellowship." The GBC also retained Brantly as a representative at the 1826 Triennial Convention. See Boykin, *History*, vol. 1, 121, 207.

[109]"A History of Sunbury Academy," accessed 17 May 2016, http://www.rootsweb.ancestry.com/~galiber3/history/academy.html; "Dr. James P.

Shannon, 1799-1859," accessed 17 May 2016, http://www.therestoration move-ment.com/_states/missouri/shannon.htm.

[110]"Signs of the Times—Missionaries (1800-1840)" (Liberty County Historical Society) accessed 17 May 2016, http://libertyhistory.org/timelines/timelines-1800-1849/131-signs-of-the-times-missionaries-; James Shannon Papers (Archives, University of Missouri) accessed 17 May 2016, http://www.rootsweb.ancestry.com/~galiber3/history/ academy.html; Minutes, May 1826; Jordan, *Century of Service*, 18; Boykin, *History*, vol. 1, 120.

[111]See Bruce T. Gourley, *Diverging Loyalties: Baptists in Middle Georgia During the Civil War* (Macon, GA: Mercer University Press, 2011) 158-198; also see Wills, *Discipline*.

[112]Jordan, *Century of Service*, 19; Minutes, August 1827.

[113]Minutes, 24 September 1826; 17 October 1826.

[114]Minutes, 12 July 1828.

[115]Minutes, 10 March 1826; Boykin, *History*, vol. 1, 177; Jones, *History of FBC*, 20; Jordan, *Century of Service*, 19.

[116]*Augusta Chronicle*, 1 April 1829. The Augusta Free School Society was "celebrated in the Baptist Church."

[117]"Dr. James P. Shannon, 1799-1859"; S. G. Hillyer, *Reminiscences of Georgia Baptists* (Atlanta: Foote & Davis, 1902) 15.

[118]*Augusta Chronicle*, 5, 8, 26 February 1828; Jordan, *Century of Service*, 19-20; Boykin, *History of the Baptist Denomination in Georgia*, vol. 2 (Atlanta: Jas. P. Harrison & Co., 1881) 547-548.

[119]*Augusta Chronicle*, 8 July 1829.

[120]"James Shannon" (Archives, University of Missouri), accessed 17 May 2016, http://muarchives.missouri.edu/c-rg1-s1.html.

[121]Cashin, "Paternalism," 13.

[122]Jones and Dutcher, *Memorial History*, 173, 292, 339-340; "History of the Medical Academy of Georgia: 1828-1836" (Augusta, GA: Georgia Regents University) accessed 26 May 2015, http://gru.edu/library/greenblatt/history/1828-1836.php; Jones and Dutcher, *Memorial History*, 254, 451, 480.

[123]Jordan, *Century of Service*, 20-21; Jones, *History of FBC*, 20.

[124]"Tryon, William Milton" (The Handbook of Texas, Texas State Historical Association) accessed 17 May 2016, https://www.tshaonline.org/handbook/online/articles/ftr19; "Celebration of Georgia Bicentennial: First Baptist Church, Augusta, Georgia, February 12, 1933," 8-9, Archives. Some references to Tryon in church records, including the centennial document, spell his middle name as "Melton."

[125]Jordan, *Century of Service*, 21. The Calvary Baptist Church did not survive, disbanding during World War I.

[126]Minutes, March 1832, April 1833, November 1834; Jones, *History of FBC*, 23. Sanders Walker may have been a colleague of Abraham Marshall who helped found the Kiokee Baptist Church. See Cashin, *Story of Augusta*, 18. Many Baptists throughout the 19th century remained opposed to circuses, theater, and sporting events. As late as the early 1900s baseball, for example, was often frowned upon.

[127]Minutes, August 1832, November 1834; Jordan, *Century of Service*, 21-22.

[128]Cashin, *Story of Augusta*, 87; Steve Storey, "Railroads" (*New Georgia Encyclopedia*) accessed 17 May 2016, http://www.georgiaencyclopedia.org/articles/business-economy/railroads.

[129]Cashin, *Story of Augusta*, 81, 82.

[130]Charles D. Mallory, *Memoirs of Elder Edmond Botsford* (Charleston, SC: Riley, 1832); Minutes, November 1834.

[131]Minutes, January 1835.

[132]Hutchinson, ed., *Baptist Memorial*, 312-313; *The Baptist Missionary Magazine*, 17 (1837) 69-70. Also see Jack U. Harwell, *An Old Friend With New Credentials: A History of the Christian Index* (Atlanta: GBC Executive Committee, 1972).

[133]Minutes, January-February 1835; Hutchinson, ed., *Baptist Memorial*, 313.

[134]Minutes, 30 March, 1 April 1835. "Embarrassments" typically referred to debts.

[135]Minutes, 3 May 1835.

[136]Ibid.

[137]Minutes, 9 May 1835.

[138]Minutes, 9 May, 13 June 1835. William T. Brantly remained as pastor of the FBC Philadelphia until 1837, thereupon resigning due to reasons of health. Moving to South Carolina, he pastored FBC of Charleston, edited a local newspaper, and then became president of the College of Charleston in 1838. He retained his pastoral and collegiate duties until a stroke in 1844 left him paralyzed. Moving back to Augusta to be with family, he died eight months later. See Boykin, *History*, vol. 2, 56-60, and John R. Shook, ed., *Dictionary of Early American Philosophers*, vol. 1 (Bristol, England: Thoemmes Contiuum, 2005) 138-139.

[139]Ira Mason Allen, *The Triennial Baptist Register*, no. 2 (Philadelphia: Baptist General Tract Society, 1936) 148.

[140]Minutes, July-September 1835.

[141]Jones and Dutcher, *Memorial History*, 321-322. See John B. Duff and Peter M. Mitchell, *The Nat Turner Rebellion: The Historical Event and the Modern Controversy* (New York: Joanna Cotler, 1971). In the decades following Nat Turner, some white Baptists of the South advocated for the right of slaves to read the Bible, if no other books. Such views were considered progressive and, in the eyes of many, quite dangerous.

[142]*Augusta Chronicle*, 14 February, 8 July, 22 July 1835. Regarding the history of abolitionism, see Richard S. Newman, *The Transformation of American Abolitionism: Fighting Slavery in the Early Republic* (Chapel Hill: University of North Carolina Press, 2002). Southern historical archaeologist Dr. J. W. Joseph considers the antebellum Springfield community "the capital of Southern African America." See http://african americanspringfield.org/, accessed 11 June 2015. Richmond County's Spirit Creek Baptist Church (founded 1800) and the First Ebenezer Baptist Church (founded 1812) are examples of local black Baptist churches supervised by white ministers prior to the Civil War.

[143]*Augusta Chronicle*, 29 July 1835.

[144]Jordan, *Century of Service*, 22. Cashin, "Paternalism, 25, states that the Green Street and Springfield congregations had no relationship prior to 1835. As noted previ-

ously, the minutes of FBCA indicate otherwise. Also, see chapter 5 regarding post-Civil War partnerships between FBCA and Springfield Baptist Church.

[145]Hutchinson, ed., *Baptist Memorial*, 378; Jones, *History of FBC*, 23; Minutes, November 1835, December 1835.

[146]Minutes, June, September 1835; Jones, *History of FBC*, 24-25. Many Baptist pastors of the era preached without the aid of notes.

[147]For an example of the early and mid-19th century debate over hell and eternal punishment, see Thomas B. Thayer, *The Origin and History of the Doctrine of Endless Punishment* (Boston: Universalist Publishing House, 1855). The eighth-century Anglo-Saxon word "hell," rooted in ancient pagan mythology, was popularized by such authors as Dante (14th century) and Milton (17th century). The usage of "hell" in English versions of scripture is used in place of two Hebrew words ("Sheol," or grave, and "Gehenna," the destination of the wicked) and two Greek words from mythology ("Hades," the underworld, and "Tartarus," the abyss). Early Baptist confessions (statements of faith) do not mention "hell." Only after the publication of Milton's *Paradise Lost* (1667) did Baptists introduce hell into some confessions of faith. The history of the word "hell" and the post-scriptural development of the concept of eternal punishment of the wicked, while understood by early Baptists, may have been largely forgotten in Baptist life by the 19th century.

[148]See typed copy of the church constitution inserted in the 1839 Minutes. The post-millennial view of the end of times was common at a time when many Westerners were convinced that expanding democracy and freedoms heralded the beginning of the thousand-year reign after which Christ would return to earth. The concept of Rapture, birthed in the 1830s, was considered to be heretical. Not until the early 20th century and the 1917 publication of the Schofield Bible would Rapture become a widely-accepted view among many evangelical Christians.

[149]Jordan, *Century of Service*, 22

[150]"Two Churches Severed Long Links," *Augusta Chronicle Herald*, Bicentennial Edition, 4 July 1976, 67; Jordan, *Century of Service*, 22. Finding no biblical support for abstinence, Baptist churches throughout the 19th century often served wine in communion services and sometimes paid preachers or evangelists partially in whiskey, in lieu of cash. Not until the post-Civil War era, having witnessed the excesses of drink in the armies of the North and South, did the abstinence movement in Baptist life gather momentum. As late as the second decade of the 20th century, however, the use of wine in Baptist communion services remained common.

[151]Minutes, June 1837, June 1838; Jones, *History of FBC*, 25. Sturgis ministered among the Cherokees immediately prior to the Cherokee nation's removal east of the Mississippi River in 1838 and 1839, a journey known as the "Trail of Tears."

[152]Jones, *History of FBC*, 24; Minutes, October 1838.

[153]Minutes, August 1837.

[154]Minutes, July 1838, July 1839; Jones, *History of FBC*, 25. William J. Northen and John Temple Graves, eds., *Men of Mark in Georgia*, vol. 2 (Atlanta: A. B. Caldwell, 1910).

[155]Jordan, *Century of Service*, 23; 51-52.

[156]Lucien Lamar Knight, *Georgia's Landmarks, Memorials and Legends*, vol. 1, pt. 2 (Gretna, LA: Pelican Publishing, 1913) 895.

¹⁵⁷Jones, *History of FBC*, 26.

¹⁵⁸See Frank Lawrence Owsley, "The Confederacy and King Cotton: A Study in Economic Coercion," *North Carolina Historical Review* 6/4 (1929): 371-397.

¹⁵⁹"Augusta Female Seminary, Augusta, Richmond County" file in "Baptist Educational Institutions of Georgia," Special Collections, Jack Tarver Library, Mercer University.

¹⁶⁰Minutes, May, June, 1840; Jordan, *Century of Service*, 24.

¹⁶¹Jordan, *Century of Service*, 24. Sherwood was Georgia's first gazetteer, or compiler of geographical indexes.

¹⁶²Jordan, *Century of Service*, 24-25. The theory of a textually perfect Bible, otherwise known as "inerrancy," was in its infancy in some ultra-conservative Christian circles of Brantly's time. Southern Baptists as a denomination did not embrace inerrancy until the 1990s. Regarding the Trinity, non-Trinitarians are welcome under the Baptist umbrella of freedom of conscience, but were, and are, relatively few. The theological concept of the Trinity was formulated in a politically-driven council of church leaders at Nicea in 325 A.D. The Nicene Creed thus produced was designed to separate true Christians from heretics, and for many centuries was used to persecute, and even kill, dissenters. Baptists were birthed in opposition to creeds, believing that creeds violated freedom of conscience. Today, some Baptists on the right hand of the theological spectrum do embrace creeds, including many Southern Baptist fundamentalists, as well as other conservative Baptists who wish to dissolve Baptists into the Roman Catholic Church (Bapto-Catholics). As to Arminianism (free will) and Calvinism (predestination), the strong Calvinistic influence in early Southern Baptist life largely dissipated by the 1890s, replaced with a widespread belief in free will. Currently, however, the SBC has once again theologically split between Calvinists and Arminians, with the Southern Baptist Theological Seminary in Louisville, Kentucky, serving as the flagship Calvinist center of SBC life. For more information, see: Doug Weaver, *In Search of the New Testament Church: The Baptist Story* (Macon, GA: Mercer University Press, 2008), and Bruce T. Gourley, *A Capsule History of Baptists* (Atlanta: Baptist History and Heritage Society, 2010).

¹⁶³Jordan, *Century of Service*, 25. By way of contrast, the Roman Catholic Church teaches that sacraments, of which Baptism and the Eucharist (Lord's Supper) are but two, convey salvific grace to the recipient.

¹⁶⁴Minutes, February, 18 April, 10 July, 7 November, 1841.

¹⁶⁵Minutes, 1841.

¹⁶⁶Michael J. Gagnon, "Antebellum Industrialization" (*New Georgia Encyclopedia*) accessed 27 June 2015, http://www.georgiaencyclopedia.org/articles/history-archaeology/antebellum-industrialization, 396-400. Early factories in Richmond County existed in a converted sawmill on Butler Creek (Bellville) and on Spirit Creek.

¹⁶⁷Cashin, "Paternalism," 20. In the larger picture, the slump in cotton prices began more than a decades-long migration of white males out of the South. Planters, utilizing free, slave labor, weathered the crisis. Poor white males in the rural South, competing against free labor, found it ever more difficult to earn even a hardscrabble living. In the 1850s more white males moved out of the Deep South than immigrated into the South, resulting in a decrease of white men in the region. The low numbers of white males re-

siding in the South, in turn, hampered the war effort in the 1860s. See Tommy W. Rogers, "The Great Population Exodus from South Carolina, 1850-1860," in *The South Carolina Historical Magazine* 68/1 (1967): 14-21.

[168]Cashin, "Paternalism," 20, 21; Leann Whites, "Paternalism and Protest in Augusta's Cotton Mills: What's Gender Got to Do With It?" in Cashin and Eskew, *Paternalism*, 74; Jones and Dutcher, *Memorial History*, 174.

[169]Minutes, 1 December 1844; Jordan, *Century of Service*, 26.

[170]Minutes, 7 September 1844.

[171]Glenn T. Eskew, "Paternalism Among Augusta's Methodists: Black, White, and Colored," in Cashin and Eskew, *Paternalism*, 89, 90.

[172]Robert Gardner, *A Decade of Debate and Division* (Macon, GA: Mercer University Press, 1995) 1-23.

[173]See Mary Burnham Putnam, *The Baptists and Slavery, 1840-1845* (Ann Arbor, MI: George Wahr, 1913) 34-72.

[174]*Christian Index*, 6 September 1844, 1-2; The byline of the *Index* letter is "Theopholis," the author's listed hometown, Augusta. Brantly Sr. was known as a Southern unionist who had long resisted the breakup of the Triennial Convention. See Robert Arthur Snyder, "William T. Brantly (1787-1845): A Southern Unionist and the Breakup of the Triennial Convention" (Ph.D. diss.): Southern Baptist Theological Seminary, 2005). At least one church member was of the planter status (owning twenty slaves or more): Ann Milledge, who according to the 1840 tax rolls, owned forty-six enslaved persons.

[175]John A. Chapman, *History of Edgefield County from the Earliest Settlement to 1897* (Newberry, SC: Elbert H. Aull, 1897) 366. Orville Vernon Burton, *In My Father's House Are Many Mansions: Family and Community in Edgefield, South Carolina* (Chapel Hill: University of North Carolina Press, 1987). Stephen Kantrowitz, *Ben Tillman and the Reconstruction of White Supremacy* (Chapel Hill: University of North Carolina Press, 2000). Some 20 percent of Edgefield District slaveowners were planters, a far higher percentage than across the river in Richmond County.

[176]Courtney L. Tollison, *Furman University* (Charleston, SC: Acadia Publishing, 2004). In 1822 Richard Furman, writing on behalf of white Baptist elites of South Carolina, assured the state's governor of their pro-slavery sentiments, declaring that "the right of holding slaves is clearly established in the Holy Scriptures, both by precept and example." See Richard Furman, *Exposition of the Views of the Baptists, Relative to the Coloured Population in the United States* (Charleston, SC: A. E. Miller, 1838). By 1851 Furman University was established in its current home of Greenville, South Carolina. From Furman the Southern Baptist Theological Seminary was created in 1858. For a discussion of slavery, profits, and capitalism in the antebellum South, see Edward E. Baptist, *The Half Has Never Been Told: Slavery and the Making of American Capitalism* (New York: Basic Books, 2014).

[177]Hortense Woodson, *Giant in the Land: A Biography of William Bullein Johnson, First President of the Southern Baptist Convention* (Nashville, TN: Broadman Press, 1950).

[178] Gardner, *Debate and Division*, 16-17.

[179]*Christian Index*, 14 March 1845.

¹⁸⁰"Board of the Triennial Convention," *Religious Herald*, 13 March 1845. Strangely, virtually all secondary accounts referring to this article fail to mention that Augusta was only one of two suggested locations where the 1845 South-wide gathering might be held. For many months previously, indecisive Virginia Baptist leaders had appeared on the defensive as Alabama and Georgia Baptists in vain looked to Virginians for direction on how to respond to Northern Baptists' refusal to appoint slaveholders as missionaries. "What position will Virginia take?" became an urgent question in the Deep South of the recognized leading role of Old Dominion. In January 1845 Virginian S. S. Sumner, responding to a recent editorial by GBC *Christian Index* editor Joseph Baker questioning whether Virginia Baptists were beholden to Northern influences, declared that "The position of the Mother of States, will be, to preserve and to defend, with moderation, but with firmness, the rights which divine, as well as human laws, have accorded to her." Yet, rather than taking the initiative in the matter, Sumner reiterated that Virginia Baptists would side with the South only if Northern Baptists were to dissolve "the co-operation of the religious communities." Sumner's piece was circulated in the Deep South. See Sumner's letter in *Religious Herald*, 16 January 1845, 3, and "Virginia and the Index," *Alabama Baptist*, 22 February 1845, 1.

¹⁸¹Gardner, *Debate and Division*, 17-18.

¹⁸²Regarding differences between Virginia and Charleston planters, see Cashin, *Story of Augusta*, 57-63. Also see Joseph Kelly, *America's Longest Siege: Charleston, Slavery and the Slow March Toward Civil War* (New York: Overlook Press, 2013). For the early history of the Charleston FBC, see Henry Allen Tupper, *Two Centuries of the First Baptist Church of South Carolina, 1683-1883* (Baltimore: R. H. Woodward, 1889).

¹⁸³William Eldridge Hatcher, *Life of J. B. Jeter* (Baltimore: H. M. Wharton, 1887). The only mention Jeter makes of Augusta pertains to the 1845 meeting. This account infers, incorrectly, that Jeter in the 13 March 1845 *Religious Herald* article put forth Augusta as his only suggestion for the meeting. Upon arriving in Augusta for the May meeting, Williams Sands wrote his impression of the town, his words indicating his prior unfamiliarity with the town and politely pointing out its deficiencies. "Augusta is a well built and very pleasant town—less flourishing since the formation of the railroad to Charleston, but preparations are [in the] making to obtain, by means of a canal, water power from the falls in the river, 9 miles distant, in order to engage vigorously in the manufacture of cotton. The streets are broad, not paved, and consequently very dusty. It contains a population from 7 to 8,000 souls, having rather decreased since the census was taken in 1840." See *Religious Herald*, 15 May 1845. For population statistics, see https://www.census.gov/population/www/documentation/twps0027/tab07.txt, accessed 18 May 2017; Cashin, *Story of Augusta*, 58, 113; Donnie B. Bellamy and Diane E. Walker, "Slaveholding in Antebellum Augusta and Richmond County, Georgia," *Phylon* 48 (1987): 165-177.

¹⁸⁴Isabella Jordan Whitney, "First Baptist Church, Augusta," *Christian Index*, 10 May 1945, 7.

¹⁸⁵From their beginnings in America in 1638 to 1845, Baptist congregations in America frequently evidenced a diversity of theology, even as no major denominational splits took place. Baptist denominational divisions that did take place tended to be more

disorganized than organized: the emergence of Free Will (anti-Calvinistic) Baptists in the 18th century and Primitive (anti-mission) Baptists in the early 19th century were perhaps the most notable schismatic developments. Until recent decades, denominational histories of the SBC presented the separation from the North as only tangentially related to slavery. This view reflected overarching Lost Cause mythology that denied slavery as the cause of the war. In this understanding of the formation of the SBC, missions commitment and ecclesial matters were often identified as the cause of separation, in particular to the structuring of the SBC as a denominational entity, compared to that of the Northern-based Triennial Convention. For an example, see William W. Barnes, *The Southern Baptist Convention: 1845-1953* (Nashville, TN: Broadman Press, 1954). Since the 1980s, however, most historians, Southern Baptist and otherwise, have freely acknowledged slavery as the overriding cause of the formation of the SBC.

[186]"Proceedings of the Southern Baptist Convention, Augusta, Georgia, 1845" (Richmond, VA: Ellyson, 1845); Minutes, FBCA, 23 and 30 April 1845. No one from Tennessee, Mississippi, or Florida attended the meeting; Kentucky and Louisiana each sent one delegate; and three from North Carolina traveled to Augusta.

[187] Jones, *History of FBC*, 28-30; *Augusta Chronicle*, 7 May 1845; Gardner, *Debate and Division*, 35.

[188]George Braxton Taylor, "Jeremiah Bell Jeter: Early Baptist Pastor and Writer" in *Virginia Baptist Ministers, Third Series* (Lynchburg, VA: J. P. Bell, 1912) 222.

[189]Gardner, *Debate and Division*, 35, 36.

[190]Ibid, 36.

[191]Proceedings, SBC, 1845; "The Southern Baptist Convention," *Christian Index*, 8 May 1845. William B. Johnson arrived at the convention with a draft constitution on hand, modeled on the organizational structure of the South Carolina Baptist Convention. Rather than establishing the foreign and home mission boards alongside the convention, they were established underneath the convention. During the remainder of the century, publishing enterprises and the Southern Baptist Theological Seminary were added to the roster of SBC entities.

[192]Proceedings, SBC, 1845, 1846; Gardner, *Debate and Division*, 36-39. SBC gatherings were subsequently changed to every second year in the 1850s, becoming annual occasions beginning in 1866.

[193]Gardner, *Debate and Division*, 50, 63-73. Barnes, now a Baptist, had been a founding trustee of the city's Episcopal church. See Cashin, *Story of Augusta*, 79.

[194]Gardner, *Debate and Division*, 29, 35-36, 65-73. At least one member of the Greene Street Baptist Church, Ann Milledge, owned enough slaves to qualify as a planter.

[195]Proceedings, SBC, 1853.

[196]Proceedings, SBC, 1845.

[197]Ibid.; William B. Johnson, "Address on the Origin of the Southern Baptist Convention," 12 May 1845.

[198]See C. C. Goen, *Broken Churches, Broken Nation* (Macon, GA: Mercer University Press, 1997).

[199]Minutes, 17 May 1845, August 1845; Gardner, *Debate and Division*, 33.

[200]Gardner, *Debate and Division*, 50-51. Turpin also maintained a "subscription," but did not attend future meetings of the SBC, the "subscription" perhaps as a representative of the American Baptist Publication Society, which retained, albeit in reduced form, a relationship with the SBC through the remainder of the 19th century. See Proceedings, SBC, 1846, 1853, 1855.

[201]Jones, *History of FBC*, 30-31; Minutes, 24 May 1846.

[202]Minutes, 10 January 1846; Bellamy and Walker, "Slaveholding," 172-174. Although not a plantation town, Augusta had a robust slave market supplied by South Carolina. White citizens tended to have strong feelings about slavery. One observer said of Augusta that "slavery is a topic upon which no man, and above all a foreigner, can open his lips without imminent personal danger unless it is to defend and uphold the system . . . all public discussion of the question is as effectually suppressed, as if these were a censorship of the press, or a holy inquisition." Even so, black citizens, free and enslaved alike, often found space within Augusta to flaunt the city's slave laws, and often with little negative consequence. See Cashin, "Paternalism," in Cashin and Eskew, *Paternalism in a Southern City*, 22-27. Regarding the Thankful Baptist Church, originally named Independent Baptist Church, see Leroy Davis, *A Clashing of the Soul: John Hope and the Dilemma of African American Leadership and Black Higher Education in the Early Twentieth Century* (Athens, GA: UGA Press, 1998) 27.

[203]Correspondence with Erick Montgomery, executive director, Historic Augusta Inc.; Cashin, *Story of Augusta*, 93-96; Whites, "Paternalism" in Cashin and Eskew, *Paternalism*, 75. Prior to the opening of the Augusta factory, James Coleman's sawmill opened in 1848 as the city's first operational mill. Child labor laws did not widely come into effect until the early 20th century.

[204]Cashin, *Story of Augusta*, 94-96, 102.

[205]*Augusta Chronicle*, 2 May 1849.

[206]Minutes, December 1847.

[207]Jones, *History of FBC*, 31. Minutes, 12 August 1848. Brantly pastored the Second Baptist Church of Atlanta during the Civil War. See *Sam Richard's Civil War Diary: A Chronicle of the Atlanta Home Front* (Athens, GA: UGA Press, 2009).

[208]Jones, *History of FBC*, 30-33; Jordan, *Century of Service*, 30; Minutes June 1849, October 1851.

[209]Jones, *History of FBC*, 31-32; Minutes, August 1849, 20 October 1852.

[210]Jordan, *History of FBC*, 30-31; Mrs. J. G. Binney, *Twenty-six years in Burmah: records of the life and work of Joseph G. Binney, D.D.* (Philadelphia: American Baptist Publication Society, 1880) 105ff.

[211]Binney, *Burmah*, 236-246.

[212]Jones, *History of FBC*, 34.

[213]Binney, *Burmah*, 246-256. During Binney's three-month absence in the summer of 1853, Albert Theodore Spalding served as interim pastor. See Minutes, summer 1853.

[214]Minutes, October 20, 1852; Jones, *History of FBC*, 34. Gas lighting became more available in Augusta in the 1850s.

[215]George H. Shriver, *Pilgrims Through the Years: A Bicentennial History of First Baptist Church, Savannah, Georgia* (Franklin, TN: Providence House Publishers, 1999) 34-35.

[216]Binney, *Burmah*, 256-257, 262.

[217]Ibid., 258; Jones, *History of FBC*, 34.

[218]Binney, *Burmah*, 257-260.

[219]Ibid, 262-272, 364ff; Jones, *History of FBC*, 34-35.

[220]Minutes, September 1855; Jordan, *Century of Service*, 32; Jones, *History of FBC*, 35.

[221]Minutes, November 1857, 12 February 1858, 21 February 1858, 12 February 1859, March 1859, 12 May 1860, August 1860, 13 October 1860; Jordan, *Century of Service*, 32; Jones, *History of FBC*, 35-36; Julia Walsh, "Rolling Religion Down the Hill: Millworkers and Churches in Augusta," in Cashin and Eskew, *Paternalism*, 182, 194, 195.

[222]Minutes, March 1859; Jordan, *Century of Service*, 32; Jones, *History of FBC*, 35-36.

[223]Minutes, 12 April 1856, 10 May 1856; "Ninth Annual Report of the Southern Baptist Publication Society, with the Proceedings of the Meeting held at Augusta, Geo., April 30th, 1856"; "Georgia Baptist Convention Minutes, 1857."

[224]Minutes, October 1857; Jones, *History of FBC*, 35-36.

[225]Minutes, November 1857.

[226]Minutes, 25 September 1859, October 1859, November 1859.

[227]Minutes, October 1859, November 1859, January 1860.

[228]Minutes, January 1860; Jordan, *Century of Service*, 33; Jones, *History of FBC*, 36-37; William Cathcart, *The Baptist Encyclopedia*, vol. 1 (Philadelphia: Louis H. Everts, 1881) 559-560. The cause of the schism is unclear, but may well have been politically related, with some members advocating secession sentiments and others Unionist sentiments.

[229]Jordan, *Century of Service*, 33. See C. Bill Mitchell, "The Life and Labors of Patrick Hues Mell," *Founders Journal* 76 (2009): 17-32.

[230]Cathcart, *Baptist Encyclopedia*, vol. 1, 559-560.

[231]Lincoln, often referred to in the Southern press from 1860 following as the "black president," was not included on presidential ballots in Augusta, whose citizens voted primarily for Democrat Stephen Douglas, an Illinoisan who campaigned on allowing Western citizens to decide whether or not to embrace slavery in their states and territories. Lincoln, on the other hand, campaigned on a platform of halting slavery's expansion westward. Southern elites were certain that Lincoln, who personally opposed slavery, would abolish the practice altogether. See Cashin, *Story of Augusta*, 115, and Eric Foner, *The Fiery Trial: Abraham Lincoln and American Slavery* (New York: W. W. Norton, 2011).

[232]*Augusta Daily Constitutionalist*, 1 January 1861.

[233]Some of Augusta's elites in the 1850s had actively pursued the dream of an expanding slave empire; Cashin, *Story of Augusta*, 114-116; *Augusta Daily Constitutionalist*, 22 January 1861; Bruce Gourley, "Baptists and the American Civil War: January 19,

1861," accessed 18 May 2016, http://civilwarbaptists.com/thisdayinhistory/1861-january-19/. While disdainful of blacks, many poor whites of Augusta and the larger South, sensing no benefit from secession, voted against it. An *Augusta Chronicle* article, reflecting the opposition voice, declared, "To say that we rejoice at such an act would be simple hypocrisy. We cannot and do not rejoice. We loved the union too much for that"; see Cashin, *Story*, 116. The popular vote was announced as for secession, but in 1972 new analysis of the historical data concluded that Georgians had voted against secession. See Michael P. Johnson, "A New Look at Popular Votes for Delegates to the Georgia Secession Convention," *Georgia Historical Quarterly*, LVI (1972): 259-275.

[234]For a Civil War era survey, see James M. McPherson, *Battle Cry of Freedom: The Civil War Era* (New York: Oxford University Press, 2003).

[235]Cashin, *Story of Augusta*, 118, 120, 121.

[236]See Gourley, *Diverging Loyalties*.

[237]Minutes, 9 November 1861; Jordan, *Century of Service*, 33.

[238]"Minutes of the General Assembly of the Presbyterian Church in the Confederate States of America, 1861" (Augusta: Steam Power Press Chronicle & Sentinel, 1861). Dr. Joseph R. Wilson, father of Woodrow Wilson, pastored the First Presbyterian congregation and served as clerk of the Assembly in which Presbyterians split North and South. See *Augusta Chronicle*, "Two churches severed long links," 4 July 1976.

[239]"Protestant Episcopal Church in the Confederate States of America Pastoral Letter from the Bishops of the Protestant Episcopal Church to the Clergy and Laity of the Church in the Confederate States of America, Delivered Before the General Council, in St. Paul's Church, Augusta, Saturday, Nov. 22d, 1862" (Augusta, GA: Steam Power Press Chronicle & Sentinel, 1862).

[240]While racism plagued the North as well as the South; most white Northern Christians by 1861 believed blacks deserved freedom. Among the various denominations, Baptists of the North were the most radical in their support for freedom for blacks, sentiments voiced in annual war-time gatherings among virtually all Baptist groups of the North. See Bruce T. Gourley, *Baptists and the American Civil War: Crucible of Faith and Freedom* (Macon, GA: Nurturing Faith, 2015).

[241]For nearly all white Southern Baptists, freedom applied to whites only. White Northern Baptists by and large believed that God willed freedom for all men. Black Baptists, free and enslaved, North and South, universally believed in freedom as God's will for all persons See Gourley, "Baptists and the American Civil War: In Their Own Words," www.civilwarbaptists.com; and Gourley, *Crucible*.

[242]"Proceedings of the Bible Convention of the Confederate States of America, Augusta, Ga., March 19th-21st, 1862"; Jordan, *Century of Service*, 33. Hard also served on the board of superintendents of the war-time Georgia Relief and Hospital Association. See "Report of the Executive Committee, Georgia Relief & Hospital Association to the Board of Superintendents," 29 October 1862, Archives.

[243]Jordan, *Century of Service*, 33.

[244]See civilwarbaptists.com.

[245]Minutes, April 1862, September 1862, November 1862; Cathcart, *Baptist Encyclopedia*, vol. 1, 304-305. The Augusta Baptist Missionary Society was formerly the Augusta Church Missionary Society.

[246]"Proceedings of the Ninth Biennial Session of the Southern Baptist Convention held in the Green Street Baptist Church, Augusta, Ga., May 8th, 9th, 10th, 11th and 12th, 1863." From 1863 through the remainder of the war, many Southern Baptist leaders routinely lamented the evil prevalent in the Confederate Army. Among the sins often attributed to soldiers were drunkenness, profanation of the Sabbath (Sunday), amusements (particularly card playing), reading of inappropriate literature, and sexual infidelity (prostitution being a problem in the camps). See civilwarbaptists.com.

[247]Minutes, 1863; Jones, *History of FBC*, 39; Cashin, *Story of Augusta*, 124; *Augusta Chronicle*, 4 July 1976.

[248]Whites, "Paternalism," in Cashin and Eskew, *Paternalism*, 75.

[249]Cashin, *Story of Augusta*, 125; Minutes, 1864; Sarah Conley Clayton and Robert Scott Davis, *Requiem for a Lost City: Memoir of Civil War Atlanta and the Old South* (Macon, GA: Mercer University Press, 1999) 119; Lansing Burrows, "'Nationality Insured!' Notes of a Sermon Delivered at the First Baptist Church of Augusta, Georgia, September 11th, 1864" (Augusta, GA: Jas. Nathan Ells, Baptist Banner Office, 1864).

[250]Burrows, "Nationality Insured!" The 1868 edition of the church's "Articles of Faith," for example, refers to the church as "First Baptist Church."

[251]Cashin, *Story of Augusta*, 125-127. See also Mark Weitz, *More Damning Than Slaughter: Desertion in the Confederate Army* (Lincoln, NE: University of Nebraska Press, 2008).

[252]Minutes, 5 April 1865, May 1865, 11 November 1865; Jones, *History of FBC*, 39.

[253]Minutes, 7 July 1865; "Huntington, Adoniram Judson, D.D.," in Cathcart, *Baptist Encyclopedia*, vol. 2 (Philadelphia: Louis H. Everts, 1880) 559-560.

[254]See William C. Davis, *The Cause Lost: Myths and Realities of the Confederacy* (Lawrence, KS: University of Kansas Press, 1996).

[255]See Cashin, *Story of Augusta*, 128-139. The federal forces, however, were not entirely welcome. Some Augustans during the years of Reconstruction resorted to violence against African-American soldiers stationed in the city.

[256]Minutes, 11 November 1865, 13 January 1866. The church reduced from fifteen to nine the number needed for a business meeting quorum.

[257]Jordan, *A Century of Service*, 33-34; Jones and Dutcher, *Memorial History of Augusta, Georgia*, 379.

[258]Cathcart, *The Baptist Encyclopedia*, vol. 1, 304-305.

[259]Minutes, 8 February 1866; July 1866; Jones, *History of FBC*, 40.

[260]Minutes, April 1867.

[261]Minutes, October 1868, November 1868. See also Minutes at large, 1865-1874.

[262]See Wills, *Democratic Religion*. Despite the overall lessening of disciplinary actions, shifting language related to disciplinary cases evidenced itself unevenly. For example, on October 13, 1883 the congregation "dropped from the roll of the church" Mrs. Ida Ashley, who had joined the Central Presbyterian Church of Atlanta, a lighter touch of language than the typical "excommunication." On the other hand, the language of

exclusion did not entirely fall by the wayside for some years. On 10 January 1885, for example, George S. Shackleford was "excluded" for failing to appear to defend himself against a disciplinary charge. Shackelford's absence likely signaled ambivalence concerning the nature of church membership, a significant factor in the waning of church discipline at this time. The same day, Edward Jackson was "excommunicated" for "having united with St. Luke's Methodist Church." For years by this point FBCA had cultivated good relations with other Protestant congregations in town, a fact seemingly at odds with the language of exclusion. More reflective of the direction of church discipline was language of September 16, 1885, at which time "the hand of fellowship was withdrawn from Mrs. Lizzy Derry Murphy by reason of her union with the St. Johns Methodist Church."

[263]Minutes, May 1867, January 1868; Jordan, *Century of Service*, 34; Jones, *History of FBC*, 40.

[264]Jordan, *Century of Service*, 34; Jones, *History of FBC*, 40, 42; Minutes, 13 January 1866, August 1866.

[265]Jordan, *Century of Service*, 34; Jones, *History of FBC*, 40, 42; Trustees Minutes, FBCA 1870s-1880s. See Gasper Loren Toole, *Ninety Years in Aiken County: Memoirs of Aiken County and Its People* (Aiken, SC: Walker, Evans & Cogswell, 1955) ch. 14. Among other positions, Hickman in the 1880s served as a director for the Georgia Railroad Bank (also known as the Georgia Railroad and Banking Company).

[266]*Augusta Chronicle*, 1 July 1866, 15 September 1871.

[267]Jordan, *Century of Service*, 34; Jones, *History of FBC*, 40, 42; Minutes, October 1867, January 1868, 1871; "Articles of Faith, Covenant, and Rules of Order, of the First Baptist Church, Greene Street, Augusta, Georgia," 1868, 19.

[268]Minutes, May 1867; see Shriver, *Pilgrims*.

[269]Minutes, May 1867, July 1867, June 1868.

[270]James Conquest Cross Black Papers, 1864-1899, The Southern Historical Collection, University of North Carolina; "Memorial Exercises of Augusta Bar Association, in Honor of J. C. C. Black," 9 November 1928, Archives. Black held many church leadership positions in the 1870s and 1880s: church trustee, Sunday School superintendent, church clerk (in the years 1870-71, replacing as clerk the venerable Eli Mustin who resigned the position after forty-six years), and moderator. He also helped expand the church's children's ministry. In public life Black arose to prominence in the 1870s as a great orator, in the two decades following serving on the city council, as city attorney, and as one of Georgia's leading politicians. He also founded the Augusta Orphan Asylum from 1879 to 1886. See Minutes, July 1870, 8 October 1870, 7 October 1871; Jones, *History of FBC*, 42; Cashin, *Story of Augusta*, 117, 146, 147, 159-164, 178, 180, 181, 199, 208, 221, 222, 229, 238. "Black, James Conquest Cross (1842-1928)," *Biographical Dictionary of the United States Congress*, accessed 8 June 2016, http://bioguide.congress.gov/scripts/biodisplay.pl?index=B000502.

[271]Minutes, July 1868, August 1868, May 1869; "Articles of Faith"; Jones, *History of FBC*, 40.

[272]Minutes, May 1869, June 1869; Jones, *History of FBC*, 40-41.

[273]Cashin, *Story of Augusta*, 145-159.

[274]Minutes, 17 October 1869; Jones, *History of FBC*, 41. The James Dixon who pastored FBCA was possibly the same James Dixon who pastored the Union Park Baptist Church in Chicago during the early 1860s. See Alfred T. Andreas, *History of Chicago*, vol. 1 (New York: Arno Press, 1975) 322; and Theodore James Elmore, *Family Memorials and Prose and Verse* (Savannah, GA: Morning News Steam Printing, 1880) xiv. Erick Montgomery's research indicates the Dixon's family Canadian background.

[275]Cashin, *Story of Augusta*, 145-146. Frank M. McKenney, *The Standing Army: The History of Georgia's County Monuments* (Alpharetta, GA: WH Wolfe, 1993) 99-103.

[276]Minutes, 12 November 1870.

[277]Bobby J. Donaldson, "Standing on a Volcano: The Leadership of William Jefferson White," in Cashin and Eskew, *Paternalism*, 138-140; Benjamin Brawley, *History of Morehouse College* (Atlanta: Morehouse College, 1917) 21-30.

[278]Jordan, *Century of Service*, 36; Minutes, 7 October 1876; Jones, *History of FBC*, 44-45.

[279]Jordan, *Century of Service*, 36-37; Jones, *History of FBC*, 42; Minutes, 7 January, 22 January, 10 June 1871. Curtis passed away in 1874, bequeathing to FBC $5,000 "to promote the cause of religion and education at Curtis Chapel." See Trustees Minutes, 2 January 1875, 5 June 1879.

[280]Minutes, 9 September, 7 October 1871.

[281]"History," Chinese Consolidated Benevolent Association, accessed 8 June 2016, http://ccbaaugusta.com/about-us/history/; Raymond T. Rufo, "The Augusta Chinese," 1995, unpublished. Brought to town against the will of city leaders by the construction firm hired to enlarge the canal, the Chinese workers arrived at a time of widespread national prejudice against Chinese immigrants. Willing to work for less than freedmen, they were initially tolerated in Augusta, eventually earning begrudging respect for their hard work.

[282]Jordan, *Century of Service*, 35-37; Jones, *History of FBC*, 42-43; Minutes, June 1873. The financial tension surfaced on 2 November 1870 when the church voted to place the financial affairs of the church in the hands of the deacons, rather than the pastor. Erick Montgomery's research indicates that Dixon moved to Indiana, where he may have become a Methodist, in addition to a newspaper editor.

[283]Jordan, *Century of Service*, 37; "Rev. Morton Bryan Wharton," accessed 8 June 2016, http://www.findagrave.com/cgi-bin/fg.cgi?page=gr&GRid=25829460.

[284]Jordan, *Century of Service*, 37-38. Trustees Minutes, 26 December 1875. The church annually selected delegates to attend the fall meeting of the Hepzibah Baptist Association, an annual gathering of area Southern Baptist churches featuring preaching and mission reports.

[285]Jordan, *Century of Service*, 39; see Shriver, *Pilgrims*.

[286]"Landrum, Rev. William Warren," Cathcart, *Encyclopedia*, vol. 1, 670; Jordan, *Century of Service*, 39.

[287]Cashin, *Story of Augusta*, 145-147. Mrs. Thomas J. Jackson, widow of Civil War hero Thomas "Stonewall" Jackson, attended the Confederate monument dedication ceremony.

[288]"Manual of the First Baptist Church, Greene Street, Augusta, Ga.," 1879, 17-23.

[289]Jones, *History of FBC*, 45-46.

[290]Minutes, September 1877; Jones, *History of FBC*, 45-46; Jordan, *Century of Service*, 39.

[291]Jones, *History of FBC*, 45-46; Minutes 1879, 13 September 1883, 13 October 1883. Julia Walsh, "Rolling Religion Down the Hill: Millworkers and Churches in Augusta," in Cashin and Eskew, "Paternalism," in Cashin and Eskew, *Paternalism*, 177-210.

[292]Eskew, "Paternalism," in Cashin and Eskew, *Paternalism*, 106. Of this era of Augusta's history, Channing Tobias, then in his young years and later one of the city's most notable black leaders, declared, "it was possible for a Negro in the Augusta of [that time] to aspire to the heights and to receive encouragement from white people in so doing." See Cashin, *Story of Augusta*, 164. For information on the Union Baptist Church, see Historic Augusta Inc., "Historic Downtown Augusta Church Tour," accessed 8 June 2016, http://www.historicaugusta. org/3820-2/.

[293]Jones, *History of FBC*, 45.

[294]Minutes 1878; Jordan, *Century of Service*, 40; see a transcript of the circa 1885 *Madisonian* article at http://files.usgwarchives.net/ga/morgan/newspapers/mustinma.txt, accessed 8 June 2016; Minutes, 16 April 1882. Brantly descendants remained in the church for many years afterward.

[295]Jordan, *Century of Service*, 41.

[296]Cashin, *Story of Augusta*, 152-155.

[297]Ibid., 153-154.

[298]Jones, *History of FBC*, 47; Jordan, *Century of Service*, 41.

[299]Minutes, 10 May 1883.

[300]"The Lansing Burrows Papers," Southern Baptist Historical Library and Archives, accessed 8 June 2016, http://www.sbhla.org/downloads/25.pdf.

[301]Ibid.

[302]Proceedings, SBC, 1880, 1, 12, 33; Proceedings, SBC, 1881, 2, 9, 10; Proceedings, SBC, 1882, 8; Proceedings, SBC, 1883, 36.

[303]Proceedings, SBC, 1845.

[304]Minutes, 22 July 1883, October-December 1883, 13 October 1885; Jones, *History of FBC*, 47.

[305]Minutes, 1884; Jones, *History of FBC*, 47-48. The minutes record, "The fire originated in the furnace and worked its way up to floor and after destroying the (?) attacked the pulpit." Following remodeling, the church expressed written thanks to the opera house and the fire department. The temporary services held in the opera house signified a departure from earlier decades, when opera was considered sinful.

[306]Minutes, January 1884, 4 May 1884; Jones, *History of FBC*, 47.

[307]Minutes, 8 December 1883, 12 January 1884. According to an insert in church minutes, membership in October 1884 stood at 428, with fifty-seven persons having joined and thirty-one leaving or dying within the past twelve months (the church year beginning each October). Contributions for the year included $471.20 for foreign missions, $180 for home missions, and $118.50 for state missions. The "Total Value of Church Property" stood at $40,000. "Sermon Preached at Unveiling of Memorial Pulpit to Thos. W. Coskery," undated, Archives.

[308]Minutes, October 1884. The announcement of the meeting is in church minutes, but no record exists of the meeting itself.

[309]Proceedings, SBC, 1875.

[310]Proceedings, SBC, 1884.

[311]"After It Is Over," *Religious Herald*, 22 May 1884, 2.

[312]See Lansing Burrows, "The Woman of Samaria," Sermon # 152 (1872), and "Priscilla," Sermon #160 (1872), in Lansing Burrows Papers, Southern Baptist Historical Library and Archives.

[313]FBCA Manuals of 1879 and 1889 list all members, providing a clear picture of how women far outnumbered men in the church. Isabella Jordan lists the following as involved in the Dorcas Ministry around the turn of the 20th century: Mrs. Burrows, Mrs. L. A. Dugan, Mrs. Thomas Phinizy, Mrs. John W. Walker, Miss Mary Rochester, Mrs. H. H. D'Antignac, Mrs. Holmes, Mrs. Latimer, Mrs. Law, Mrs. Eugenia Twiggs, Mrs. Albert Twiggs, Mrs. H. H. Hickman, Mrs. Fannie Walton, Miss Belle, Miss Mollie Coffin, Miss Mary Dobey, Mrs. W. S. Jones, Mrs. Bowen, Mrs. Ann Watson, Mrs. M. A. Rountree, Mrs. W. S. Jones, Mrs. Bowen, Mrs. Mary E. Robert, Miss Adele Verdery, Mrs. Z. McCord. See Jordan, *Century of Service*, 49-50.

[314]Minutes, October 1884; Jordan, *Century of Service*, 45.

[315]Minutes, January 1885.

[316]Minutes, 4 March 1885. During this era the discipline of history attained to a professional level, its ascendancy corresponding to the record-keeping concerns of FBC.

[317]Jones, *History of FBC*, 49.

[318]See Norma Basch, *In the Eyes of the Law: Women, Marriage, and Property in Nineteenth Century* (Ithaca, NY: Cornell University Press, 1982).

[319]The pre-war SBC depended upon the wealth of planters, money earned from the forced labor of slaves, to support missionary work. The war, however, abolished the slave economy of the South, wiping out the riches and denting the pride of planters. Coupled with a years-long economic recession, contributions to missions work, Southern Baptist and otherwise, plummeted. Whereas white elite males previously were dependent upon slave labor to fund missionary work, by the 1880s these same men found themselves reliant upon the free labor of white women. Pride, alongside patriarchy, most certainly played a role in their reticence to allow women a voice equal to their contributions.

[320]*Augusta Chronicle*, 18 August 1891, 5.

[321]Minutes, May 1885.

[322]"The Baptist Convention," *Augusta Chronicle*, 6 May 1885; *Augusta Chronicle*, 10 May 1885.

[323]*Augusta Chronicle*, 10 June 1885.

[324]Proceedings, SBC, 1885. The 1863 convention proceedings utilized an incorrect spelling, "Green" rather than "Greene."

[325]Proceedings, SBC, 1885.

[326]Fannie E. S. Heck, *In Royal Service: The Mission Work of Southern Baptist Women* (Richmond, VA: SBC FMB, 1913) 96-97. Proceedings, SBC 1885.

[327]Proceedings, SBC 1885, 119.

[328]Proceedings, SBC, 1898.

[329]*Augusta Chronicle*, "Baptist Convention," 9 May 1885; *Augusta Chronicle*, 22 May 1885.

[330]Proceedings, SBC, 1881, 30.

[331]"A Celestial Pilgrimage: A Pageant Written in Celebration of the Chinese Sunday School Centennial, 1885-1985," Archives.

[332]"History," Chinese Consolidated Benevolent Association, accessed 8 June 2016, http://ccbaaugusta.com/about-us/history/. Census records were likely incomplete, due to the discreet nature of many Chinese.

[333]Jones, *History of FBC*, 49. "Celestial Pilgrimage." "A Betrayal [Portrayal] of the Activity of the W.M.U. of the Fifty Years of Service," Archives.

[334]Rufo, "The Augusta Chinese," and *Augusta Chronicle*, 16 November 1894. In the 1880s and 1890s the minority Chinese community in Augusta stirred the prejudices of white citizens for several reasons: their foreign nationality and strange customs, frequent interracial marriages with blacks, and business successes. Some white merchants petitioned the city council to deny business licenses to Chinese citizens, but the council defended the rights of the immigrants to own their own businesses.

[335]Jones, *History of FBC*, 49, Jordan, *Century of Service*, 43. "Celestial Pilgrimage"; Rufo, "The Augusta Chinese."

[336]Jones *History of FBC*, 51.

[337]"Christmas Songs," *Augusta Chronicle*, 27 December 1885; Silas Xavier Floyd, *Life of Charles T. Walker* (Nashville: National Baptist Publishing Board, 1902) 42-43; "The Tabernacle Baptist Church," *Augusta Chronicle*, 13 December 1885.

[338]The 1888 WMU constitution is cited in Barnes, *The SBC*, 156.

[339]"Betrayal [Portrayal]"; "Events in FBC and BWMU History," undated, Archives.

[340]Jordan, *Century of Service*, 45.

[341]Ibid., 45-46; "Betrayal [Portrayal]."

[342]Ibid. Bothwell played a role in the early planning of the 1870s expansion of the Augusta Canal. In the course of his work with the canal, he may have become sympathetic to the plight of the city's Chinese population. See Jones and Dutcher, *Memorial History*, 413-414.

[343]Cashin, *Story of Augusta*, 152-153, 162-201; *Augusta Chronicle*, 17 May 1900.

[344]Digital copies of *Helping Hands* are available in the archives.

[345]Jordan, *Century of Service*, 46.

[346]Jones, *History of FBC*, 49-51; Minutes, 1888.

[347]Jordan, *Century of Service*, 46; Jones, *History of FBC*, 52; Minutes, 1893; Manual, 1889, 16-18.

[348]Jones, *History of FBC*, 51.

[349]"Historical Building Program, 1817-1939," booklet, Archives; Jordan, *Century of Service*, 50; Jones, *History of FBC*, 53; Minutes, 1893. Burrows advocated for a remodel, but realizing his voice was in the minority, led the way in seeking a unanimous vote for rebuilding.

[350]Jordan, *Century of Service*, 45; Jones, *History of FBC*, 52-53.

[351]Jones, *History of FBC*, 52.

[352]Jordan, *Century of Service*, 48-49; "D. R. Wright," *Helping Hands*, vol. 5, no. 1, 15 February 1891, 1; William M. Jordan obituary, accessed 8 June 2016, http://www.findagrave.com/cgi-bin/fg.cgi?page=dfl&GRid=19583370. Jordan also lists as notable men of this era who were faithfully active in the church but did not hold notable offices: John C. Lee, Z. W. Carwile, John Phinizy, and Judge E. H. Callaway.

[353]Minutes, 1 October 1893.

[354]"Guide to the American Baptist Education Society Records, 1887-1902," University of Chicago, accessed 8 June 2016, https://www.lib.uchicago.edu/e/scrc/finding aids/view.php?eadid=ICU.SPCL.BAPTISTEDU. Burrows is listed as recording secretary in *The Tribune Almanac and Political Register for 1894*, vol. 6, January 1894, 198.

[355]Taffey Hall, "Baptist Congress Proceedings Collection," Southern Baptist Historical Library and Archives, accessed 8 June 2016, http://www.sbhla.org/ downloads/40.pdf.

[356]*Eleventh Annual Session of the Baptist Congress, For the Discussion of Current Questions, Held in the First Baptist Church, Augusta, Ga., December 5th, 6th and 7th, 1893* (New York: Baptist Congress Publishing, 1894). Of 120 persons comprising the General Committee of the World Baptist Congress of 1893, only three were from the South, one being Burrows. For more about Walter Rauschenbusch, see Paul M. Minus, *Walter Rauschenbusch: American Reformer* (New York: MacMillian, 1988).

[357]Congress, 17, 18-113.

[358]Ibid, 114.

[359]Ibid, 114-115.

[360]Ibid, 115-116.

[361]See Gourley, *Diverging Loyalties* and Gourley, civilwarbaptists.com. Burrows was not alone in his post-war Christianizing of the Confederate army.

[362]Jordan, *Century of Service*, 54-55; "Rev. Lansing Burrow's Sermon at Thankful Baptist," *Augusta Chronicle*, 18 October 1897; *Augusta Chronicle*, 19 December 1897; "Funeral Yesterday. The Remains of Mr. George J. Howard Laid to Rest," *Augusta Chronicle*, 18 April 1898; *Augusta Chronicle*, 7 March 1898; *Augusta Chronicle*, 5 June 1898; "First Baptist Tonight," *Augusta Chronicle*, 30 July 1899.

[363]*Augusta Chronicle*, 22 May, 1 June, 5 June, 9 June 1898.

[364]James Adam Lester, *A History of the Georgia Baptist Convention, 1822-1972* (Atlanta: GBC Executive Committee, 1972) 266-267.

[365]"Dr. Burrows Leaves," *Augusta Chronicle*, 18 November 1899.

[366]Nell Irvin Painter, *Standing at Armageddon: A Grassroots History of the Progressive Era* (New York: W. W. Norton, 2008).

[367]For a summary of the Southern Progressive movement, see Jamil S. Zainaldin and John C. Inscoe, "Progressive Era," *New Georgia Encyclopedia*, accessed 23 November 2015, http://www.georgiaencyclopedia.org/articles/history-archaeology/progressive-era; Maria Annette Smith, "Race Relations in Augusta, Georgia 1900-1910 as Reflected in the *Augusta Chronicle* and Other Materials" (thesis, Atlanta University, 1975); Cashin, *Story of Augusta*, 183-199.

[368]See William Barton McCash and June Hall McCash, *The Jekyll Island Club: Southern Haven for America's Millionaires* (Athens, GA: UGA Press, 1989).

[369]*Augusta Chronicle*, 30 January 1898. Early 20th-century church bulletins extended an "Invitation to Hotel Guests."

[370]Cashin, *Story of Augusta*, 193-197. As John D. Rockefeller wintered in Augusta, brother William spent winters at his Jekyll Island home; Alice Louise Lytle, "The Sunny Side of Things," *Watson's Magazine* 5-4 (October 1910): 865.

[371]"Major Black Again Honored by Augusta Bar," *Augusta Chronicle*, 6 April 1928.

[372]George William Lasher, ed., *The Baptist Ministerial Directory in the United States of America* (Oxford, OH: Press of the Oxford News Company, 1899) 493; Annual, SBC, 1899; *Augusta Chronicle*, 23 April 1900; Jordan, *Century of Service*, 52-56.

[373]Jordan, *Century of Service*, 53; Cashin, *Story of Augusta*, 210-226.

[374]Jordan, *Century of Service*, 52; *Eighteenth Annual Session of the Baptist Congress, for the Discussion of Current Questions, Held in the First Baptist Church, Richmond, VA, November 20th, 21st and 22nd, 1900* (New York: Baptist Congress Publishing, 1900) 233-238. Melton spoke on similar Catholic themes in future Baptist Congress gatherings.

[375]*Augusta Chronicle*, 8 July 1901; *Augusta Chronicle*, 25 November 1900; Madison C. Peters, "Why I Became a Baptist," *Virginia Baptist Religious Herald*, 7 June 1900. In January 1901 another New Yorker filled the pulpit, Cecil L. Gates, an officer in the national Young Men's Christian Association (YMCA). See *Augusta Chronicle*, 20 January 1901; Mary C. Wadley, *Memorial of the Centennial Anniversary of the First Presbyterian Church, Augusta, Georgia: The Anniversary Exercises, May Fifteenth to Eighteenth, 1904* (Philadelphia: Allen, Lane & Scott, 1904) 131; "Christian Church," *Augusta Chronicle*, 29 December 1907; "Augusta, Ga. Preacher Becomes Red Cross Representative," *Christian Century*, 37-1 (1 July 1920): 19.

[376]*Augusta Chronicle*, 9 May 1901.

[377]*Augusta Chronicle*, 9 September 1901; 16 September 1901; 31 October 1901; 9-22 November 1901; 29 December 1901.

[378]*Augusta Chronicle*, 2 June 1901; 28 November 1901; 19 December 1901; 5, 8 July 1901; 19 August 1905. See John E. Wells and Robert E. Dalton, *The South Carolina Architects 1885-1930: A Biographical Dictionary* (Richmond, VA: New South Architectural Press, 1992) 44-49.

[379]"Contract Awarded," *Augusta Chronicle*, 5 June 1902; "Church Now Being Removed," *Augusta Chronicle*, 12 June 1902; Jordan, *Century of Service*, 53-56.

[380]Jordan, *Century of Service*, 54-55.

[381]*Augusta Chronicle*, 30 December 1902; 25 January 1903; 4 January 1903; 30 August 1903; 24 September 1903; 31 October 1903; 12 November 1903; 22 November 1903.

[382]*Augusta Chronicle*, 9, 16 August 1903. In September 1903 Bagby apparently enrolled in the Southern Baptist Theological Seminary in Louisville, Kentucky. In July 1904 he returned to the pulpit of FBCA while Melton was on vacation, this time with "Rev." in front of his name. See "Rev. A. Paul Bagby Preaches in Augusta," *Augusta Chronicle*, 2 July 1904. Bagby continued preaching periodically at FBCA.

[383]*Augusta Chronicle*, 1 February 1903; 15 October 1903; 1 November 1903.

[384]*Augusta Chronicle*, 3 December 1903; Jordan, *Century of Service*, 55-57; "175 Years of Heritage & Hope 1817-1992, FBCA," Archives. For more coverage, see *Augus-*

ta Chronicle, 6-8 December 1903. Church records of construction costs perished in the aforementioned fire.

[385]The architectural style of Beaux-Arts Classicism was common in America in the late nineteenth and early twentieth centuries. The description of Green Street is found in the 1911 edition of *Encyclopedia Britannica*, vol. 2, 904; "Highest Quality Clothes," *Augusta Chronicle*, 26 January 1909; *Augusta Chronicle*, 23 September 1917; "Historic Negro Society Finally Disbanded," *Augusta Chronicle*, 16 September 1907; *Augusta Chronicle*, 13 November 1907.

[386]*Augusta Chronicle*, 29 August 1903; "Unnecessary Force Used," *Augusta Chronicle*, 18 November 1904.

[387]*Augusta Chronicle*, 4, 30 January 1904. For information about the early hazards of electricity, see Earnest Freeberg, *The Age of Edison: Electric Light and the Invention of Modern America* (New York: Penguin Books, 2013); "Tribute to Memory of Mr. H. H. Hickman," *Augusta Chronicle*, 19 February 1904; "The Death Yesterday of Mrs. Mary A. Bouyer," *Augusta Chronicle*, 2 June 1904; Jones, *History of FBC*, 56.

[388]*Augusta Chronicle*, 31 January 1904; *Augusta Chronicle*, 13 March 1904; Minutes, Hephzibah Baptist Association, 1904; "First Baptist Church Informal Reception to Medical College Students a Great Success," *Augusta Chronicle*, 16 October 1907. The church hosted other entertainment events in the lecture room, at least one of which reflected the racial dynamics of the era. In February 1906 the black entertainer D. L. Leftwich performed at the church, where a "fine audience assembled and the evening with the old time Darkey was one of the utmost merriment and pleasure." See "Mr. D. L. Lefwich Gives Successful Entertainment," *Augusta Chronicle*, 6 February 1906. This type of self-mocking monologue by a black entertainer appealed to the many prejudices that white audiences held of blacks. Lefwich (or Leftwich in other accounts; see "Entertainment at Churchill," *Staunton Spectator and Vindicator*, 27 September 1901) apparently toured white churches of the South performing minstrel shows stereotypically depicting blacks as, in effect, clownish buffoons. While black entertainers thus made a mockery of their own race in order to please whites, it was the only public stage upon which to ply their wares. By the late 20th century this type of racist entertainment gave way to serious and significant contributions to uniquely black theater and music. See Randall Sandke, *Where the Dark and the Light Folks Meet: Race and the Mythology, Politics, and Business of Jazz* (Lanham, MD: Scarecrow Jazz, 2010) 76-77.

[389]"Church Notices," *Augusta Chronicle*, 14 February 1904; "Easter Egg Hunt on Court House Green," *Augusta Chronicle*, 4 April 1904. Easter, a day with pagan historical roots, remained little celebrated by Baptist churches of the South until around the 1930s. In 1906, for example, none of Augusta's Baptist churches presented an Easter program. See *Augusta Chronicle*, 15 April 1906; "Monster Picnic," *Augusta Chronicle*, 14 May 1904; *Augusta Chronicle*, 28 November 1904; "Rev. Roland D. Grant, D.D.," in *Granite Monthly: A New Hampshire Magazine*, vols. 43-44 (1912) 288; "Illustrated Lecture," *Cambridge Sentinel*, 29 October 1904, 3; "Davis Birthday," *Augusta Chronicle*, 3 June 1907. The church routinely hosted celebrations of Davis' birthday. See "Jefferson Davis Day," *Augusta Chronicle*, 1 June 1913. Following the war Williams emerged as a leading historian of the South and a prominent proponent of Lost Cause mythology, writing books about

Robert E. Lee, Stonewall Jackson, Jefferson Davis, and Fitzhugh Lee along with accounts of the war. For more information, see "J. William Jones Papers, 1861-1892," Library of Virginia, Richmond.

³⁹⁰"Anti-Saloon League," *Augusta Chronicle*, 16 March 1907; *Anti-Saloon League Yearbook, 1917* (Westerville, OH: Anti-Saloon League of America, 1917) 101-103; "Individual Duty Stop Dispensary," *Augusta Chronicle*, 16 December 1907. Illegal liquor sales continued in the months following state Prohibition, to which Melton called upon "every good citizen" to bring to a halt. See "Liquor Being Served and Many People Know," *Augusta Chronicle*, 8 June 1908. "First of Church Services Since Prohibition Law Became Effective Occur Today" and "Use Grape Juice for Communions," *Augusta Chronicle*, 5 January 1908. Southern Baptists' anti-liquor efforts continued throughout Prohibition and beyond.

³⁹¹"Melton Speaks," *Augusta Chronicle*, 17 May 1904; "Dr. Melton Goes East to Fill Engagements," *Augusta Chronicle*, 10 June 1904; "Dr. Melton Returns," *Augusta Chronicle*, 1 February 1906; *Augusta Chronicle*, 27 October 1907; Minutes, Hephzibah Baptist Association, 1907.

³⁹²Landrum frequently led revivals and other special services during Melton's pastorate. For example, see "Great Revival's Fitting Close," *Augusta Chronicle*, 30 April 1904; "Revival Very Successful," *Augusta Chronicle*, 22 April 1905; and "Large Attendance," *Augusta Chronicle*, 28 January 1907. Well thought of among the Baptists of Georgia, Landrum, pastor of FBC Atlanta, in May 1905 was selected by the trustees of Mercer University to succeed president P. D. Pollock, but declined. See *Augusta Chronicle*, 6 June 1905.

³⁹³"Men of First Baptist Free the Church of Debt," *Augusta Chronicle*, 6 November 1905. Although the women of the church played a significant role in paying off church debt, they were left out of the headlines. "A Stone Fence for the First Baptist Church," *Augusta Chronicle*, 12 December 1905; *Augusta Chronicle*, 30 August 1908.

³⁹⁴*Augusta Chronicle*, 28 January 1906; *Augusta Chronicle*, 21 September 1908; "Baptist Young People Form Organization," *Augusta Chronicle*, 23 September 1908. For a history of BYPU and Baptist Student Union, see: John Wesley Conley, *History of Baptist Young People's Union in America* (Philadelphia: Griffith and Rowland, 1913) and "Baptist Student Union Collection," Southern Baptist Historical Library and Archives, Nashville, Tennessee.

³⁹⁵Jordan, *Century of Service*, 57; Jones, *History of FBC*, 60; *Augusta Chronicle*, 9 and 29 November 1908; "Dr. Sparks W. Melton—The Triumph of a Life," Melton files, Archives.

³⁹⁶News reporters covered Rockefeller's travels. Many papers throughout the country carried news of Rockefeller's January 1908 visit to Tabernacle Baptist Church. The 31 January 1908 edition of the *Reidsville Review* (N.C.) noted: "John D. Rockefeller occupied his first Sunday morning in Augusta this winter listening to a sermon in the Tabernacle Baptist church (colored) by Rev. C. T. Walker, the 'Black Spurgeon' who got out of a sick bed to preach when informed that Mr. Rockefeller would be one of his congregation. After the sermon Mr. Rockefeller held a conference with Rev. Mr. Walker in the latter's study, when he 'made a very generous donation to the church.'" See also *Augusta*

Chronicle, 27 January 1908. For Taft's visit to Tabernacle Baptist, see S. B. Crawford, "Augusta's Black Heritage," *Augusta Chronicle Online*, 10 February 1997, accessed 14 November 2015, http://old.chronicle.augusta.com/stories/021097/fea_black2.html. An early advocate of civil rights, Walker attracted the attention of many prominent progressive politicians and businessmen. See Floyd, *Life of Charles T. Walker*. From the Hotel Bon Air on 18 January 1909 John D. Rockefeller wrote a letter to his son, John D. Jr. See "The Rockefellers: Father-Son Correspondence," *American Experience*, accessed 9 November 2015, http://www.pbs.org/wgbh/americanexperience/features/primary-resources/rockefellers-son/. The Georgia Archives contain a 24 January 1909 photo of William Howard Taft "at his winter home in the village of Summerville," accessed 14 November 2015, http://cdm.georgiaarchives.org:2011/cdm/singleitem/collection/vg2/id/13588/rec/35. For M. Ashby Jones, see "First Baptist Church Calls Pastor Sunday," *Augusta Chronicle*, 8 March 1909 and "Dr. Jones Accepts First Baptist Call," *Augusta Chronicle*, 29 March 1909. Buck Colbert Franklin, John Hope Franklin, and John Whittington Franklin, *My Life and an Era: Autobiography of Buck Colbert Franklin* (Baton Rouge: Louisiana State University Press, 1997) 114-115. M. Ashby Jones signed a public letter of endorsement of the Walker School on 11 January 1914. The letter referred to the school as important to "the white people" of Augusta. See *Augusta Chronicle*, 16 January 1914.

[397] References to Rockefeller attending FBCA are few, and are not included in church records nor reported in the *Augusta Chronicle* during the years Rockefeller wintered in Augusta. Years afterward at least three printed recollections place Rockefeller at FBCA on some occasions. These unverifiable accounts are likely apocryphal. See "Dinner Stories," *Augusta Chronicle*, 26 May 1925, and "By the Editor," 30 May 1937. In addition, one eyewitness placed Rockefeller at FBCA on a weekly basis, declaring that while in Augusta during the winters of 1915 and 1916, "Mr. Rockefeller was a regular visitor every Sunday at the First Baptist church in Greene Street, to which he would ride in his then modern auto." See "His 94th Birthday," *Augusta Chronicle*, 9 July 1933.

[398] *Augusta Chronicle*, 10 and 11 January 1909. See also Barton Myers, "Joseph M. Brown (1851-1932)," *New Georgia Encyclopedia*, accessed 14 November 2015, http://www.georgiaencyclopedia.org/articles/government-politics/joseph-m-brown-1851-1932.

[399] Jordan, *Century of Service*, 60; *Augusta Chronicle*, 13 May 1909; "First Baptist Minister to Speak Tomorrow Afternoon to Colored Y.M.C.A.," *Augusta Chronicle*, 23 October 1909; "Special Christmas Music at First Baptist Today," *Augusta Chronicle*, 19 December 1909; "Rev. M. Ashby Jones," *Augusta Chronicle*, 25 December 1909; 'Sermon to Masons by Rev. M. Ashby Jones," *Augusta Chronicle*, 25 December 1909. In the nineteenth and early twentieth centuries many urban Southern Baptist ministers were also Masons; "Rev. M. Ashby Jones the Lee Memorial Speaker," *Augusta Chronicle*, 31 December 1909; "Lee Memorial Service First Baptist Church," *Augusta Chronicle*, 19 January 1910. The Lee Memorial was an organization, initiated at the suggestion of former President Theodore Roosevelt, dedicated to honoring Confederate Gen. Robert E. Lee by raising funds to support Washington and Lee University, the institution that Lee presided over following the war. See *Washington and Lee University Bulletin* VI-3 (July

1907). FBC also hosted other Lee memorial services. See "Memorial Service to Robert E. Lee," *Augusta Chronicle*, 19 January 1913. Jones' annual Lee sermon in 1915 was titled "The Christian Soldier." See "Rev. M. Ashby Jones on 'The Christian Soldier,'" *Augusta Chronicle*, 17 January 1915. A Lee memorial service was also held at "Paine Negro College," likely not by the choice of black Augustans. See "Lee Memorial Service at Paine Negro College," *Augusta Chronicle*, 19 January 1913. For more information, see Michael Korda, *Clouds of Glory: The Life and Legend of Robert E. Lee* (New York: Harper, 2015).

[400]*Augusta Chronicle*, 16 August 1909; "Citizens to Confer on Negro Problem," *Augusta Chronicle*, 30 January 1912; "A Special Sermon," *Augusta Chronicle*, 3 February 1912. The "Negro Problem" broadly referred to the question of how Southern whites should treat the black race, a people until recent history the slaves of whites and whom many whites yet despised. Maintaining the separation of the races and the subjugation of African Americans required constant vigil. Whites, viewing blacks as inferior in every respect, often resorted to brutality, violence, and terrorism against blacks, even as leading African Americans struggled to better the lot of their race in the face of a brutal system of apartheid upheld by white political, social, cultural, and religious institutions. White fear and hatred of blacks found expression in numerous lynchings and killings at large in the early decades of the 20th century. Jones, from a perspective of paternalism, addressed the "Negro Problem" on more than one occasion. See "Rev. Dr. M. Ashby Jones to Speak to Negroes," *Augusta Chronicle*, 24 July 1913; "Principle Address by Dr. Ashby Jones," *Augusta Chronicle*, 10 March 1914; "Commencement Sermon," *Augusta Chronicle*, 3 May 1914.

[401]"Rev. E. Y. Mullins at First Baptist," *Augusta Chronicle*, 21 February 1910; *Augusta Chronicle*, 14 February 1910; "Juniors Banquet Tonight—Services at First Baptist Church by Dr. Melton Tomorrow," *Augusta Chronicle*, 11 June 1910. During his absences from the pulpit Jones sometimes invited two of his brothers who were also ministers, Howard Jones and Carter Helm Jones, to fill the Augusta pulpit. See Jordan, *Century of Service*, 60.

[402]"Woman's Missionary Union," *Augusta Chronicle*, 27 February 1910; "Commencement Sermon," *Augusta Chronicle*, 12 June 1910; "Dr. M. Ashby Jones Upholds Compulsory Education Bill," *Augusta Chronicle*, 25 July 1910

[403]"Entertainment at Baptist Sunday School," *Augusta Chronicle*, 23 December 1910.

[404]"Bothwell," *Augusta Chronicle*, 5 September 1909; "Memorial to the Late J. T. Bothwell at the First Baptist Church," *Augusta Chronicle*, 23 January 1910; "Funeral of Sam Kee," *Augusta Chronicle*, 20 September 1910. The murder made headlines throughout the South. See "Chinaman Murdered," *Charlotte News*, 17 September 1910.

[405]"Purchased, Through Alexander and Steiner, No. 1109 Greene Street for Home of Pastor—Consideration About $11,000," *Augusta Chronicle*, 10 August 1910; "New Deacons Elected," *Augusta Chronicle*, 6 December 1910.

[406]Alethia Edwards Nowell, *Trustees of the Town: Story of the Richmond Academy Trustees: 1780-1998* (Atlanta, GA: CI Publishing, 1998) 133; "T. Harry Garrett School History," Garrett Elementary School, accessed 14 November 2015 http://www.rcboe.org/domain/7095; "North Augusta Elementary, 100 Years of Educa-

tional Service," accessed 14 November 2015, http://naugel.acps.schoolfusion.us/modules/cms/pages.phtml?pageid=233127; Carwile is mentioned in Walter G. Cooper, *The Cotton States and International Exposition* (Atlanta: The Illustrator Company, 1896). Among other professional positions, Smith served on the board of the Georgia Chemical Works. See *The American Fertilizer* VIII-1 (July 1900) 25. For a sample of Kilpatrick's writing, see A. J. Kilpatrick, M. D., "The Value of Drinking-Water as Physiological and Therapeutic Agent," *Atlanta Medical and Surgical Journal*, XIV-1 (March 1897) 658-663. Regarding Wright, see *The American Contractor*, 15 February 1913, 79.

[407] *Twenty-Eighth Annual Session of the Baptist Congress, Held in the First Baptist Church, Augusta, Georgia, November 8, 9, and 10, 1910* (Chicago: University of Chicago Press, 1911). See Judge E. H. Callaway, "The Agricultural Needs of the South," *The Christian Educator* 19-1 (February 1919) 8. Callaway argued for retaining Negroes as the primary tenant farmers of the South rather than turning to immigrants. He displayed the prevailing paternalistic attitude of the day among middle to upper class white citizens of the South, assuming that farming was the best to which most African Americans could or wanted to achieve.

[408] *Twenty-Eighth Annual Session*, 5-10, 82.

[409] Ibid., 200-201. The annual Baptist Congress meetings continued for only two more years, the last one taking place, appropriately, in New York State.

[410] *Augusta Chronicle*, 8 February 1911; "Summerville Historic District," National Park Service, accessed 16 November 2015, http://www.nps.gov/nr/travel/augusta/summervillehd.html; *Augusta Chronicle*, 29 May 1912. The integration of the Bible and business arrived in earnest within America's business community by the 1920s. See Bruce Barton, *The Man Nobody Knows: A Discovery of the Real Jesus* (Indianapolis: Bobbs Merrill, 1925).

[411] Cashin, *Story of Augusta*, 208-209. Booker T. Washington advocated working with the narrow, subservient space allowed by whites for the betterment of the blacks, a position of which Black and Augusta's other white leaders approved. See Booker T. Washington, *The Negro Problem* (New York: J. Pott & Company, 1903).

[412] For example, see *Augusta Chronicle*, 3-18 August 1912. Among many outstanding church musicians during this era was J. Atlee Young of the Peabody Conservatory of Music, Baltimore, Maryland. Young served as organist and choir director during the second decade of the 20th century. See "Announcement," *Augusta Chronicle*, 2 September 1914; and a J. Atlee Young brochure at http://sdrc.lib.uiowa.edu/traveling-culture/chau1/pdf/youngj/1/brochure.pdf, accessed 18 November 2015. For Easter 1916 the church choir and a group of "the best musicians in Augusta" performed John Stainer's *Crucifixion*. "At First Baptist," *Augusta Chronicle*, 21 April 1916.

[413] "Men Attend Church Without Hats, Coats," *Augusta Chronicle*, 30 June 1911; *Augusta Chronicle*, 19 October 1911; *Augusta Chronicle*, 11-12 December 1911; *Augusta Chronicle*, 26 January 1913; *Augusta Chronicle*, 20 and 22 April 1912; "Deed to First Baptist Lot Recorded After 96 Years," *Augusta Chronicle*, 17 May 1916.

[414] "Memorial Service to Unveil Window," *Augusta Chronicle*, 8 December 1912; "Delightful Banquet at Bon Air Last Night," *Augusta Chronicle*, 8 January 1913; "In Spirited Sermon at First Baptist Church Order of Commercial Travelers is Lauded," *Augusta*

Chronicle, 28 April 1913; "Thanksgiving Dinner Given by Commercial Travelers," *Spartanburg Herald*, 29 November 1913; "Series of Sermons by Rev. M. A. Jones," *Augusta Chronicle*, 23 February 1913; "Windows Unveiled," *Augusta Chronicle*, 9 December 1912; "Faddoul Moghabghab to Address Augustans," *Augusta Chronicle*, 18 March 1913.

[415]"Sunday School Sends Missionaries to China," *Augusta Chronicle*, 29 April 1913; "Baptists to Observe All Over the United States: Congregation of First Baptist Church to Observe 100th Anniversary of First Foreign Missionary Work," *Augusta Chronicle*, 10 December 1913. The modern missions movement was birthed at the turn of the 19th century. Previously, Baptists were essentially not engaged in missions work apart from revivals and establishing churches. The lack of missions reflected the influence of Calvinism, a theology that discouraged missionary activity. For a brief survey, see Gourley, *Capsule History of Baptists*; "Items of Interest About S.S.___ Found in Pageant," n.d., Archives; Cheryl Wong, "Between Light and Shadows: The Chinese Community in Augusta," 1931, Archives.

[416]"J. B. Cousins to Preach at First Baptist Church," *Augusta Chronicle*, 31 May 1913.

[417]*Augusta Chronicle*, 15 September 1913.

[418]"Good Friday: Dr. Ashby Jones Will, in His Sermon This Evening, Discuss the Question of Holidays in Public Schools," *Augusta Chronicle*, 3 May 1914; "Good Friday is Not a School Holiday," *Augusta Chronicle*, 4 May 1914. The practice of public schools, in some instances, observing Good Friday as a holiday evolved in later decades. Some states allowing such observances did so on religious grounds, others on practical grounds of allowing teachers and students to have a three-day weekend.

[419]*Augusta Chronicle*, 6 August 1916, and "A Powerful Appeal for Religious Freedom," *Augusta Chronicle*, 7 August 1916. The bill to which Jones referenced was Act 548 of the Georgia General Assembly of 1916, otherwise known as the Veasey Bill. If passed it would have allowed the state to intrude into the operations of Catholic institutions. The bill was proposed at a time when many Protestant politicians, and many Baptist leaders, were virulently anti-Catholic.

[420]"Debate Tonight," *Augusta Chronicle*, 30 November 1913; "Woman's Suffrage," *Augusta Chronicle*, 21 November 1913. For more information, see Eleanor Flexner, *Century of Struggle: The Woman's Rights Movement in the United States* (Boston: Belknap Press, 1959, 1975).

[421]"A Sermon on Peace at First Baptist Church," *Augusta Chronicle*, 13 February 1915; "Rev. M. Ashby Jones on International Issues," *Augusta Chronicle*, 13 June 1915; "Not For 'Peace at Any Price' But 'Character at Any Cost,'" *Augusta Chronicle*, 14 June 1915. Jones preached his peace sermon at the suggestion of the Church Peace Union, a multi-denominational organization seeking an end to military armament and warfare. See "Resolutions Passed by the Church Peace Union, at Its First Meeting, 10 February 1914," accessed 18 November 2015, http://www.carnegiecouncil.org/about/ history/ church_peace_union.html. Presciently, the Union formed four months prior to World War I. American Protestants since the early 19th century embraced a post-millennial theology, a biblical interpretation of the end times espousing a millennium of peace, prosperity, and progress prior to the return of Christ. Northern Christians viewed victory

over the South in the American Civil War as progress for humanity. National prosperity, westward expansion, and technological advances in the latter part of the century further fueled post-millennialism. Global death and destruction wrought by WWI, however, shelved popular post-millennial theology in favor of pre-millennial theology, a belief that world conditions would degenerate prior to the return of Christ, who would thereafter reign over earth during a peaceful millennium. The war that would transform popular end times theology escalated in February 1915 as Germany began unrestricted submarine warfare in British waters. A German submarine torpedoed the British Ocean liner *Lusitania* on May 7, 1915 off the coast of Ireland.

[422]Jones, *History of FBC*, 54-55; correspondence with Erick Montgomery, Historic Augusta, Inc.

[423]*Augusta Chronicle*, 26 June 1916, 4 December 1916.

[424]Minutes, 27 May 1917.

[425]"Not the Land of America; It is Her Soul That is in Jeopardy," *Augusta Chronicle*, 2 April 1917; "American Soldiers Called to Defend the American Home, and the Religious Aspect of the Situation," *Manufacturer's Record*, 26 April 1917, 53; "Red Cross Meeting at First Baptist Church," *Augusta Chronicle*, 6 April 1917; "Mr. Taft to Speak on Red Cross Today," *Augusta Chronicle*, 11 April 1917. For a survey of World War I, see Ian F. W. Beckett, *The Great War: 1914-1918* (New York: Routledge, 2007).

[426]"Red Cross Rally at Baptist Church," *Augusta Chronicle*, 17 June 1917; "Open Air Service," *Augusta Chronicle*, 9 July 1917; "Veterans Will Attend Service at First Baptist," *Augusta Chronicle*, 3 June 1917; *Augusta Chronicle*, 22 July 1917.

[427]"Resignation of Dr. Ashby Jones," *Augusta Chronicle*, 13 August 1917; "Dr. Jones' Resignation Accepted With Regret," *Augusta Chronicle*, 20 August 1917; "First Baptist Church," *Augusta Chronicle*, 30 September 1917.

[428]For a history of Georgia's military contributions to World War I, including Camp Hancock, see Gerald E. Shenk, "Race, Manhood, and Power: Mobilizing Rural Georgia for World War I," *Georgia Historical Quarterly* 81 (Fall 1997): 622-62.

[429]"Rest Room for Soldiers at First Baptist Church," *Augusta Chronicle*, 8 September 1917; Jordan, *Century of Service*, 61. Baptists South and North worked together ministering to soldiers stationed in Augusta. See Deacons Minutes, 3 November 1918.

[430]Based on the absence of coverage in the *Augusta Chronicle* during June 1930.

[431]Minutes, 30 September 1917. Vines' salary was set at $4,000 plus a pastoral residence. "Vines, William Madison (1867-1952)," (Alabama Authors, University of Alabama University Libraries), accessed 20 November 2015, http://www.lib.ua.edu/ Alabama_Authors/?p=2074.

[432]Jordan, *Century of Service*, 62-64.

[433]Ibid., 63-64; "Girls of First Baptist Church to Meet Today," *Augusta Chronicle*, 15 March 1918. *The Patriotic League: An Interpretation for Leaders* (New York: Patriotic League, 1917) accessed 21 November 2015, https://archive.org/details/patrioticleaguei00patr; "Present Service Flag at First Baptist," *Augusta Chronicle*, 2 February 1918; Jones, *History of FBC*, 63; "First Baptist Women to Hold a Day of Prayer Tuesday," *Augusta Chronicle*, 7 April 1918; "Services for Soldiers at the First Baptist Church," *Augusta*

Chronicle, 13 July 1918. The church's volleyball court was popular with young people. See Minutes, 27 May 1917.

[434]"Miss Annie Shumate With Soldiers Welfare Committee," *Augusta Chronicle*, 2 December 1917; Jordan, *Century of Service*, 64.

[435]Jordan, *Century of Service*, 64; "Miss Dorothy Lehman Reaches Augusta Today," *Augusta Chronicle*, 29 June 1918; Jones, *History of FBC*, 63.

[436]Jordan, *Century of Service*, 65; Jones, *History of FBC*, 64; Minutes, December 1918; "Resigned Last Night as Pastor of First Baptist," *Augusta Chronicle*, 3 December 1918.

[437]Jones, *History of FBC*, 64; Minutes, 27 April 1919; 13 July 1919; "Dr. Edward L. Grace at First Baptist Sunday," *Augusta Chronicle*, 2 August 1919. Throughout 1918, new members added at a robust pace. Reflecting a post-war recession, Grace's initial salary was $3500—$500 less than that of Vines. Regarding Augusta's celebration of the end of the war, see Cashin, *Story of Augusta*, 224.

[438]"Woman's Club Holds Splendid Meeting at Albion Hotel," *Augusta Chronicle*, 5 October 1919; *Augusta Chronicle*, 10 November 1919.

[439]Minutes, 22 October 1919, 3 December 1919; Jordan, *Century of Service*, 66-67.

[440]*Augusta Chronicle*, 28 September-1 October 1919; Jordan, *Century of Service*, 67; Minutes, 5 May 1920; George W. Truett, "Baptists and Religious Liberty," 16 May 1920, accessed 22 November 2015, http://www.mainstreambaptists.org/mob/truett_sermon.htm.

[441]Jordan, *Century of Service*, 68-72; Jones, *History of FBC*, 66; "Eric W. Hardy Director of Educational Work at First Baptist Church," *Augusta Chronicle*, 20 June 1920.

[442]Minutes, 17 December 1919.

[443]Jones, *History of FBC*, 67; "First Baptist History by Mrs. Isabella Jordan," *Augusta Chronicle*, 29 August 1920; "Centennial Celebration of First Baptist Church Exercises Begin Today in Honor of Birthday," *Augusta Chronicle*, 8 May 1821; "Centennial of FBC" program, 8-11 May 1921, Archives.

[444]*Augusta Chronicle*, 20 February 1921.

[445]"The Remarkable Tribute Paid to Charles T. Walker, Col., By the People of Augusta," *Augusta Chronicle*, 7 August 1921; Cashin, *Story of Augusta*, 228-229.

[446] Cashin, *Story of Augusta*, 229-246.

[447]These observations are a composite portrait derived from church minutes; Jones, *History of FBC*; and *Augusta Chronicle* articles of the 1920s. The church motto often appeared in the *Augusta Chronicle* during the 1920s. Sunday School classes included two Roger Williams classes, named after the first Baptist in America. Revivals often resulted in many converts, including fourteen on 1 April 1923. The talented playwright, Dorothy Lehman Sumerau, often wrote scripts for holiday pageants. The FBCA Sunday School basketball team played in the Savannah Sunday School League. For his 1924 one-month summer vacation, Edward L. Grace and his wife drove to Canada and back.

[448]Minutes, May 1922.

[449]Minutes, May 1922, 14 and 16 July 1922; *Augusta Chronicle*, 19 April 1923. Church archives contain "Letters of Lucy Wright" in Chinese Sunday School files, and

Emily Oliver Wright and Anna Wright Jordan, compilers, "Her Destination—Back to China, 1943-45: Letters of Lucy Wright," 1979, honoring the 100th anniversary of Wright's birth.

[450]Minutes, Hephzibah Baptist Association, 1923, 7, 22.

[451]Ibid., 9. The claim of the Southern Baptist Convention achieving greater success on world mission fields than any other denomination foreshadowed a century-long narrative of self-congratulatory and self-serving rhetoric on the part of Southern Baptist leaders.

[452]Minutes, Hephzibah Baptist Association, 1923, 18-19. Prohibition remained a concern of Baptists of the association throughout the decade and into the thirties.

[453]"A. M. Nichols, In Address to Augusta Preachers, Favors Local Prohibition Survey," *Augusta Chronicle*, 5 January 1925; "Pussyfoot Johnson Noted Lecturer Here Tonight," *Augusta Chronicle*, 9 March 1927; *Augusta Chronicle*, 6 and 8 March 1928.

[454]"James Clay, Known to Augusta As 'Patient Blind Man', is Dead," *Augusta Chronicle*, 22 November 1924; "Twenty Years Ago Today in Augusta," *Augusta Chronicle*, 22 November 1944.

[455]"Dr. Grace Announces Subject for Sunday," *Augusta Chronicle*, 1 December 1923; "First Baptist Women to Give Reception Today for Social Workers," *Augusta Chronicle*, 14 April 1924; for example, see "First Baptist W. M. U.," *Augusta Chronicle*, 20 February 1927.

[456]*Augusta Chronicle*, 28 January 1923; 16 March 1923; "The Church v. War at First Baptist," *Augusta Chronicle*, 7 September 1924.

[457]See Edward L. Larson, *Summer for the Gods: The Scopes Trial and America's Continuing Debate Over Science and Religion* (New York: Basic Books, 2006).

[458]See William E. Ellis, *A Man of Books and a Man of the People: E. Y. Mullins and the Crisis of Moderate Southern Baptist Leadership* (Macon, GA: Mercer University Press, 1985).

[459]Annual, Southern Baptist Convention, 1924; *Augusta Chronicle*, 16 and 19 May 1924.

[460]"Makes Reference to Dr. John Fox," *Augusta Chronicle*, 1 December 1924. The writer apparently mistakenly printed "John" Fox. Fox's firing made national news. See "Dixie Baptist College Fired 'Evolution Prof,'" *Chicago Tribune*, 12 October 1924. See also Ronald L. Numbers, *The Creationists: The Evolution of Scientific Creationism* (Berkeley: University of California Press, 1993) 48.

[461]The full text of the Butler Act is available online at http://law2.umkc.edu/faculty/projects/ftrials/scopes/tennstat.htm, accessed 9 June 2016.

[462]Annual, Southern Baptist Convention, 1925. The text of the 1925 Baptist Faith and Message is available at http://www.utm.edu/staff/caldwell/bfm/1925/, accessed 27 November 2015. For an insider history of Baptist fundamentalism, see David O. Beale, *In Pursuit of Purity: American Fundamentalism Since 1850* (Greenville, SC: Bob Jones University Press, 1986).

[463]See Larson, *Summer for the Gods*.

[464]"Judge Callaway," *Augusta Chronicle*, 27 July 1925.

[465]*Augusta Chronicle*, 19 August 1925.

466"Noted Lecturer to Preach Here Sunday," *Augusta Chronicle*, 4 July 1925; "Protestant Churches Celebrate Tonight," Augusta Chronicle, 28 October 1925.

467"Beautiful Tribute to Dr. W. W. Landrum by Major James C. C. Black," *Augusta Chronicle*, 1 February 1926; Minutes, January 1926; *Augusta Chronicle*, 17 February 1929. For more on the problems of early electricity, see Freeberg, *Age of Edison*.

468*Augusta Chronicle*, 4 July 1926 and 9 January 1927.

469Minutes, 25 September 1927; "1st Baptist Church," *Augusta Chronicle*, 26 September 1927; "Dr. Edward L. Grace," *Augusta Chronicle*, 30 October 1927; Jones, *History of FBC*, 69.

470"A Landing Place in Time," *Augusta Chronicle*, 5 October 1997. Unimpressed by the airfield, derided by many as a mere "cornfield," the citizens of Augusta voted Daniels out of office in 1928.

471"First Baptist to Hear Judge Callaway," *Augusta Chronicle*, 25 December 1927. Notable Baptists including Frank Shelby Groner, president of the Baptist General Convention of Texas, and J. L. Rosser, scholar and historian, also filled the pulpit following Grace's departure. See "Rev. Frank S. Groner Speaks Here Sunday," *Augusta Chronicle*, 19 May 1928; "Dr. J. L. Rosser Will Preach First Baptist Sermons Here Sunday," *Augusta Chronicle*, 9 June 1928; "Beautiful Cantata to be Given at First Baptist Church Sunday Evening," *Augusta Chronicle*, 15 December 1927.

472"Major Black Again Honored by Augusta Bar," *Augusta Chronicle*, 6 April 1928; "Major James C. C. Black," *Augusta Chronicle*, 2 October 1928; "Beautiful Resolutions Adopted to Memory of Late Major J. C. C. Black," *Augusta Chronicle*, 13 November 1928; Minutes, 3 February 1929; "Memorial Service to Late Maj. Black," *Augusta Chronicle*, 4 February 1929. Black was perhaps the last remaining Confederate veteran church member.

473Minutes, 2 September 1928; "Call to be Pastor of First Baptist," *Augusta Chronicle*, 25 September 1928.

474*Augusta Chronicle*, 22 June 1929; "Men's Bible Class to Announce the Winners Next Week," *Augusta Chronicle*, 16 March 1929. The class at least some of the time was large enough that it met in the church's "main auditorium." See "John I. Phinizy Bible Class Meets Today," *Augusta Chronicle*, 25 June 1933; "Wiener Roast Today at First Baptist," *Augusta Chronicle*, 16 February 1929; "First Baptist Royal Ambassadors to Meet," *Augusta Chronicle*, 9 May 1929; "Family Day at 1st Baptist Church," *Augusta Chronicle*, 14 April 1929.

475"First Baptist W. M. S.," *Augusta Chronicle*, 23 March 1929; see Henry Louis Gates Jr. and Gene Andrew Jarrett, eds., *The New Negro: Readings on Race, Representation, and African American Culture, 1892-1938* (Princeton, NJ: Princeton University Press, 2007); *Augusta Chronicle*, 25 April 1929.

476"Television Progresses," *Augusta Chronicle*, 15 December 1929.

477"Sermon on 'Failure,'" *Augusta Chronicle*, 29 June 1929; Minutes, 9 September 1929.

478"First Baptist W. M. S.," *Augusta Chronicle*, 27 October 1929.

479"Tomorrow Morning Yale Professor Will Fill Pulpit of First Baptist Church," *Augusta Chronicle*, 1 February 1930; "Yale Professor Addresses Huge Crowd at First Baptist Church; Says Jesus was 10,000 Years in Advance of His Times and a 'Charming Person'," *Augusta Chronicle*, 3 February 1930; also see *Augusta Chronicle*, 19 and 29 January 1931, 23 January 1934.

[480]"Dr. Charles Barker," *Augusta Chronicle*, 4 January 1931.

[481]"Augusta on the Air," *Augusta Chronicle*, 6 July 1930.

[482]*Augusta Chronicle*, 8 February 1931.

[483]"Forty-Three Drunks, 21 Drunk and Disorderly Persons Jailed," *Augusta Chronicle*, 15 February 1931; "Memorial from the GBC," Annual, Southern Baptist Convention, 1931.

[484]"Bobby Jones to Build His Ideal Golf Course on Berckman's Place," *Augusta Chronicle*, 15 July 1931.

[485]*Augusta Chronicle*, 1 May 1931; "Princess Rahme Haider," *Ellensburg Daily Record*, 17 August 1918. Palestine was the pre-World War II name of the lands controlled by Britain that now comprise the nation of Israel. Following the Holocaust and World War II, Britain allowed Jewish leaders to remove Palestinians from the land.

[486]*Augusta Chronicle*, 27 July 1931; unnamed and undated document, "History of Chinese S.S." folder, Archives, FBCA; "A Celestial Pilgrimage" pageant program, 1985, Chinese Sunday School Scrapbook, Archives; *Augusta Chronicle*, 26 November 1933.

[487]"'Deadly Virtues' is Subject for Morning Sermon," *Augusta Chronicle*, 25 October 1931; "'Ghosts' is Theme for Sunday Sermon," *Augusta Chronicle*, 31 October 1931; "Rev. Frederick E. Smith Addresses Club; Singers Render Anthem," *Augusta Chronicle*, 25 November 1931; "Judge Enoch H. Callaway," *Augusta Chronicle*, 11 June 1932.

[488]"Educator to Fill Pulpit of First Baptist Church Tomorrow," *Augusta Chronicle*, 14 May 1932.

[489]Annual, Southern Baptist Convention, 1932.

[490]"Baptist Minister Announces Sermon," *Augusta Chronicle*, 15 January 1933; "At First Baptist," *Augusta Chronicle*, 22 January 1933; *Augusta Chronicle*, 13 February 1933; "Baptist Minister Speaks Today on Licensed Whiskey," *Augusta Chronicle*, 10 December 1933; "Striking Scene Enacted in Courtroom of Recorder," *Augusta Chronicle*, 10 September 1935.

[491]"Augusta Churches, Education Board Looted by Thieves," *Augusta Chronicle*, 10 March 1933. A 15 July 1933 *Augusta Chronicle* headline read, "Loan Banks Urged to Spur Building." For more about the Great Depression, see Amity Shlaes, *The Forgotten Man: A New History of the Great Depression* (New York: Harper Perennial, 2008).

[492]"Honorary Official of Baptist Convention Will Speak at Local Churches," *Augusta Chronicle*, 12 July 1934; "Huey Long Wouldn't be Bad as President of U.S." *Augusta Chronicle*, 24 November 1934. For more about the New Deal, see Eric Rauchway, *The Great Depression and the New Deal: A Very Short Introduction* (New York: Oxford University Press, 2008). Regarding conservative Christian opposition to Roosevelt and the New Deal, see Allan Lichtman, *White Protestant Nation: The Rise of the American Conservative Movement* (New York: Grove Press, 2009).

[493]"Celebration of Georgia Bicentennial," 1933, Archives; Jones, *History of FBC*, 71.

494"Mercer University Century Birthday Will Also be Observed," *Augusta Chronicle*, 7 February 1933.

495 Lester, *A History of the Georgia Baptist Convention*, 493-511; "Honorary Degree at Mercer Won by Augusta Minister," *Augusta Chronicle*, 12 May 1933.

496 Some Woman's Missionary Society events lasted all day. See "First Baptist W.M.S. to Have All-Day Meeting," *Augusta Chronicle*, 20 March 1935. The church's WMS celebrated its 50th anniversary in 1935; "Wins Speaker's Contest," *Augusta Chronicle*, 3 April 1933. *Chronicle* articles about FBCA activities speak of various events during the Great Depression in the same glowing, often extravagant terms as in the 1920s, giving the impression that the church's social and financial status allowed for continuity despite citywide and national adversity; "'Matter of Morale' Sermon Topic at the First Baptist," *Augusta Chronicle*, 11 June 1933; "Church Announcement," *Augusta Chronicle*, 23 July 1933; "Smith Speaks on Money and Work at First Baptist," *Augusta Chronicle*, 9 September 1933.

497"Marion S. Symms," *Augusta Chronicle*, 22 December 1933; "First Baptist," *Augusta Chronicle*, 6 May 1934; "Christ is a Living Force Within Lives, Rev. Smith States in Easter Sermon," *Augusta Chronicle*, 22 April 1935; "Hephzibah W.M.U. Holds Sessions at First Baptist Church," *Augusta Chronicle*, 12 July 1936; "Mrs. Mary Verdery Dies at Residence," *Augusta Chronicle*, 1 March 1936.

498"Kathleen Mallory Comes Here as Guest of First Baptist Circle," *Augusta Chronicle*, 5 April 1934. National Woman's Missionary Union headquarters were in Birmingham, Alabama; *Augusta Chronicle*, 25 May 1935; "Lecturer Will Tell Story of Passion Play at First Baptist," *Augusta Chronicle*, 20 May 1934.

499"First Baptist," *Augusta Chronicle*, 8 September 1934; Minutes, 1 October 1936. Deacons after "prayerful consideration" granted Smith's request, and agreed to pay him at half-salary during his sojourn. The phrase "prayerful consideration" in church records at large is often a polite euphemism indicating differences of opinion on a matter; "The Fred Smiths Sail into a Land of Romance," *Augusta Chronicle*, 28 October 1935.

500Minutes, 1 November 1935; "Pastor Returns: Sparks W. Melton Will Conduct Services at First Baptist Church," *Augusta Chronicle*, 18 October 1935; "Dr. M. Ashby Jones at First Baptist," *Augusta Chronicle*, 16 November 1935; "Dr. Jones Will Deliver Address on General Lee," *Augusta Chronicle*, 17 January 1936.

501"Lights and Shadows," *Augusta Chronicle*, 29 November 1935; "Mr. B. P. Jordan," *Augusta Chronicle*, 14 December 1935.

502"Dr. Phelps Will Give Talk at First Baptist Church," *Augusta Chronicle*, 22 February 1936; "Interesting Trip," *Augusta Chronicle*, 15 March 1936; "Perkins-Cullum House, 501 Greene Street," Historic Augusta, accessed 9 June 2016, http://www.historicaugusta.org/properties/2015-perkins-cullum-house-510-greene-street/. Cullum was likely a close friend of Mrs. Smith; "Augusta Pastor on Program of Scotch Church," *Augusta Chronicle*, 12 May 1936.

503"Wonders of 'Queen Mary' Described by Augustan," *Augusta Chronicle*, 28 August 1936; Minutes, 27 September 1936. The record stresses that Smith was terminated with "no charges" against him "but because it was felt the Church needed a change in Pastors." Left unsaid are motives for dismissal. The six deacons who offered their resignations that subsequently were not accepted were John Phinizy, Marion Symms, H. J. Miller, Paul Mustin, L. S. Moody, and C. A. Scruggs; Minutes, October 1936. The date is smudged, making the exact day of the letter uncertain; Minutes, 1 November 1936; "Augustan Offered Pulpit of Greenville (Miss.) First Church," *Augusta Chronicle*, 6 November 1936.

[504]*Augusta Chronicle*, 12 September 1936. The focus on location may indicate that Augusta even at that time was significantly expanding westward, prompting church leaders to inform newcomers of the church's place in the city; Minutes, 6 October 1936; *Augusta Chronicle*, 4 November 1936; Minutes, 15 November 1936; "Hephzibah W.M.U. Executive Board Holds Rally at First Baptist Church," *Augusta Chronicle*, 18 October 1936. Greene served as the Young People's director; "First Baptist," *Augusta Chronicle*, 31 October 1936, 26 December 1936; "Movement Started by First Baptist to Buy New Organ," *Augusta Chronicle*, 7 December 1936; Minutes, 7 and 20 December 1936, 7 January 1937; "Organ Recital to be Given at First Baptist Thursday," *Augusta Chronicle*, 28 March 1937. Other organ concerts followed. For example, see "Music Lovers Will Attend Concert at First Baptist," *Augusta Chronicle*, 14 July 1937.

[505]Minutes, 3 April 1937. "New Pastor Named at First Baptist," *Augusta Chronicle*, 23 April 1937. Caudill's preaching query reflected his social gospel convictions at a time when social concerns were of limited concern among Southern Baptists at large. See George W. Cornell, "Southern Baptists Point Out Substantial Growth Progress," (St. Petersburg, Florida) *Evening Independent*, 20 May 1959.

[506]Bulletin, FBCA, 16 January 1938; "Virgil Fox," *Augusta Chronicle*, 9 January 1938; Bulletin, 13 March 1938; "W.M.U. Will Hold Golden Jubilee," *Augusta Chronicle*, 16 March 1938; Bulletin, 12 September 1937, 3 September 1939; "First Baptist Plans Temperance Picture," *Augusta Chronicle*, 5 June 1938. See also "Prayer Service," *Augusta Chronicle*, 15 April 1938.

[507]Adolph Hitler speech in Passau 27 October 1928 Bundesarchiv Berlin-Zehlendorf, from Richard Steigmann-Gall, *Holy Reich: Nazi conceptions of Christianity, 1919-1945* (Cambridge: Cambridge University Press. 2003) 60-61. For a bibliography of religion and Nazi Germany, see https://en.wikipedia.org/wiki/Religion_in_Nazi_Germany#cite_note-33, accessed 2 April 2016. *Fifth Baptist World Congress, Berlin, August 4-10. 1934*" (London: Baptist World Alliance, 1934). Archie Grinalds, "Baptists Face Clash With Nazi Principles at World Baptist Alliance Session in Berlin," *Augusta Chronicle*, 26 April 1934. Even German Baptists were seduced by Hitler's religious rhetoric. See David Roach, "Baptists 'Humbled' by Failure to Oppose Nazis," *Baptist Press*, 18 December 2014, accessed 2 April 2016, http://www.bpnews.net/43382/baptists-humbled-by-failure-to-oppose-nazis. The American Protestant press often downplayed the evils of Nazism; see Robert W. Ross, *So It Was True: The American Protestant Press and the Nazi Persecution of the Jews* (Eugene, OR.: Wipf & Stock, 1980). For a survey of American reaction to Hitler and Nazism, see Lichtman, *White Protestant Nation;* "St. Cecilians to Present Cantata Sunday at First Baptist Church," *Augusta Chronicle*, 8 April 1938.

[508]*Augusta Chronicle*, 8 April 1938; "Futility of War," *Augusta Chronicle*, 2 February 1938. Caudill's words echoed post-World War I Southern Baptist calls for disarmament,

including at the 1932 SBC annual meeting; "Dillard Speaks," *Augusta Chronicle*, 16 November 1938.

[509]"First Baptist," *Augusta Chronicle*, 23 December 1939. The year's Christmas musical was titled "Holy City." See "Outstanding Music at First Baptist," *Augusta Chronicle*, 10 December 1939; "Baptists Break Ground for New Building," *Augusta Chronicle*, 22 November 1939; "Dedication Program, New Education Building," 8 September 1940, Archives; Jones, *History of FBC*, 77, 83; "First Baptist BTU to Install Leaders," *Augusta Chronicle*, 5 November 1939.

[510]"At Church Site," *Augusta Chronicle*, 5 January 1940; "Claire Coci, Organist, at First Bapist Church," *Augusta Chronicle*, 9 January 1940; "First Baptist," *Augusta Chronicle*, 20 April 1940; Bulletins, 1938-1942.

[511]"Rotary Progress Seen by Leader," *Augusta Chronicle*, 25 September 1940.

[512]"First Baptist," *Augusta Chronicle*, 16 August 1941. For more information on the use of radio by the church, see "Baptists Plan New Broadcast Programs," *Augusta Chronicle*, 19 February 1940. Prayer for peace began in May 1940. See "First Baptist Announces Daily Prayer Periods to Plead for Peace," *Augusta Chronicle*, 29 May 1940.

[513]*Augusta Chronicle*, 17 January 1940; 12 and 22 February 1941; "Outdoor Service," *Augusta Chronicle*, 31 May 1941; *Augusta Chronicle*, 25 April 1941; *Augusta Chronicle*, 4 April 1941; "Commencement Speaker," *Augusta Chronicle*, 21 May 1941.

[514]"Sermon on Vice Kept off Radio," *Augusta Chronicle*, 22 September 1941.

[515]"First Baptist Church," *Augusta Chronicle*, 24 October 1941; Bulletin, 7 December 1941.

[516]"Prayers at Noon: First Baptist Begins Services During Crisis," *Augusta Chronicle*, 9 December 1941.

[517]Bulletin, 4 January 1942; *Augusta Chronicle*, 3 January 1942. The sermon title was "The Christian's Position on the Present Crisis."; "Foreign Missions Week of Prayer at First Baptist," *Augusta Chronicle*, 30 November 1942.

[518]"Service Honor Roll Unveiled at First Baptist," *Augusta Chronicle*, 10 August 1942; Jones, *History of FBC*, 80-83; Minutes, 9 August 1943.

[519]John Boyette, "Masters Took Break During World War II," *Augusta Chronicle*, 19 February 2015, accessed 4 January 2016, http://www.augusta.com/masters/story/ history/masters-took-break-during-world-war-ii.

[520]"21 Persons, Firms Fined for Failure to Douse Lights," *Augusta Chronicle*, 7 October 1942. Other than Pearl Harbor, enemy aircraft never actually threatened the United States.

[521]"Victory Garden Contest to be Sponsored by Church," *Augusta Chronicle*, 1 March 1943; "Problems of World Discussed at First Baptist Revival," *Augusta Chronicle*, 15 July 1943. The revival was apparently the first summer revival the church conducted.

[522]"Receives Degree," *Augusta Chronicle*, 11 May 1942; Minutes, May 1943; Jones, *History of FBC*, 81-82.

[523]"Mayor Proclaims China Week Here," *Augusta Chronicle*, 12 April 1942; Jones, *History of FBC*, 81-82.

[524]Alethia Edwards Nowell, *Trustees of the Town: Story of the Richmond Academy Trustees: 1780-1998* (Atlanta, GA: CI Publishing, 1998) 133; "Mr. Paul Mustin," *Augus-*

ta Chronicle, 26 May 1943; "Rev. Paul Caudill to Leave Augusta," *Augusta Chronicle,* 31 January 1944; Jones, *History of FBC,* 83; Minutes, 20 February 1944. Caudill's wife, Netta Sue, later wrote a biography of her husband's life in which she devoted a chapter to "The Church Where the SBC Was Founded." She reminisced of the "majestic" sanctuary and recalled that many church members "were of Augusta's gentry." Dr. Caudill was as comfortable eating with mill workers as with wealthy families. Netta Sue spoke of their time in Augusta as "a pastoral family's dream," despite the couple having lost to death a baby girl, Mary Jane, at only eight days of age. See Netta Sue Caudill McKnight, *They Call Him Pastor: The Life and Ministry of R. Paul Caudill* (Self-published, 2000) 114-127.

[525]"Dr. Sparks Melton at First Baptist," *Augusta Chronicle,* 15 July 1944; Jones, *History of FBC,* 85; *Augusta Chronicle,* 12 May 1944; Annual, Southern Baptist Convention, 1944.

[526]Jones, *History of FBC,* 84-86; Huyck letter to FBC, 30 August 1983, Archives; Bulletin, 6 August 1944.

[527]Jones, *History of FBC,* 85-87.

[528]Bulletin, 24 December 1944; Jones, *History of FBC,* 88.

[529]The plaque, presented by Mrs. Minnie Halford in memory of her son, Richard, was dedicated 30 May 1948.

[530]"World Traveler to Speak at First Baptist Church," *Augusta Chronicle,* 27 September 1945; "Russian War Relief," *Augusta Chronicle,* 24 November 1945; "Overflow Crowds Attend First Baptist Church," *Augusta Chronicle,* 22 October 1945; Isabella Jordan Whitney, "First Baptist Church, Augusta," *Christian Index,* 10 May 1945, 5-7, 12; Jones, *History of FBC,* 91.

[531]Jones, *History of FBC,* 89-90; Annual, Southern Baptist Convention, 1945; "Southern Baptist Convention Centennial," *Augusta Chronicle,* 19 April 1945; "Centennial Scenes," *Augusta Chronicle,* 10 May 1945.

[532]Jones, *History of FBC,* 88-93; "Addition Planned at First Baptist," *Augusta Chronicle,* 18 November 1945; "Program, Georgia Baptist Sunday School Convention, FBC Augusta, April 23, 24, 25, 1946," Archives.

[533]Jones, *History of FBC,* 91-95. Of Garrett a January 1946 church resolution stated: "As a man he was temperate, generous, valiant, chaste, faithful and honest. Through the virtues of homely philosophy, wit and humor, he kept as few men the most intimate human touch. Possessed of these noble virtues, transfused with the spirit of Christ, he stood out as a great, generous, God-fearing and God-honoring personality."

[534]James M. Gregory, "Internal Migration: Twentieth Century and Beyond," in *Oxford Encyclopedia of American Social History* (New York: Oxford University Press, 2012) 540-545; 2010 Census of Population and Housing, Population and Housing Unit Counts, CPH-2-5, U.S. Government Printing Office, Washington, DC: U.S. Census Bureau 2012, 20-26.

[535]Jones, *History of FBC,* 96-98. Church growth, rather than doctrinal and moral purity concerns of an earlier era, characterized Southern Baptist literature. Billy Graham was not yet a national figure.

[536]David Aikman, *Billy Graham: His Life and Influence* (Nashville: Thomas Nelson, 2007) 68. Media magnate William Randolph Hearst, impressed with Graham's anti-

communist message, provided the national newspaper exposure during the crusade that made Billy Graham a household name.

[537]Marshall Frady, *Billy Graham: A Parable of American Righteousness* (New York: Simon & Schuster, 1979) 238-239. Graham was a member of Augusta's Curtis Baptist Church, a former mission church of FBCA, in the early 1950s. He never attended nor preached in the church. "A Rich History," *Augusta Chronicle*, 6 January 2001.

[538]Jones, *History of FBC*, 98-105; Minutes, 1951-1952.

[539]Minutes, 1953.

[540] For more information about Augusta of the 1950s into the 1980s, see Cashin, *Story of Augusta*.

[541] "Proclamation 2978—National Day of Prayer, 1952," 17 June 1952; Jeffery Owen Jones, "The Man Who Wrote the Pledge of Allegiance," *Smithsonian*, November 2003; "History of 'In God We Trust,'" United States Department of the Treasury, accessed 3 April 2016, https://www.treasury.gov/about/education/Pages/in-god-we-trust.aspx. Christian Amendment resolutions, S. J. Resolution 29 and H. J. Resolution 156.

[542]Bulletin, FBCA, 5 April 1953, 12 July 1953, 29 March 1953.

[543]Bulletin, 19 April 1953.

[544]Bulletin, 15 March 1953, 6 December 1953, 22 November 1953.

[545]Bulletin, 15 March 1953, 14 June 1954; Rich Thompson, "The Road We Travel," accessed 3 March 2016, http://www.theroadwetravel.net/2007/11/ed-stetzer-quotes-from-this-weekend.html. Other prominent Southern Baptist leaders filling the Augusta pulpit included Sydnor L. Sealey, the newly-elected president of Southeastern Baptist Theological Seminary in North Carolina. Sealey had preached at FBCA years earlier. The SBC's "Million More in '54" campaign did not reach its goal.

[546]Minutes, FBCA, 19 April 1953; Bulletin, 3 May 1953, 19 April 1953.

[547]Minutes, 15 July 1953; H. R. Creamer, chairman, board of deacons, letter to FBCA, 6 June 1953, Archives, FBCA; "A Biographical Sketch of Dr. R. J. (Jack) Robinson," n.d., Archives; "New President is First and Foremost a Preacher," *Christian Index*, 19 November 1970, 6; Jones, *History of FBC*, 109; "Texas Minister is Named Pastor of First Baptist," *Augusta Chronicle*, 19 July 1953; L. Katherine Cook, "Robinson Interview No. 1," Oral History Memoir, Baylor University Institute for Oral History, 20 May 1982, 22.

[548]Bulletin, 16 August 1953.

[549]Bulletin, 2 August 1953, 3 May 1953.

[550]Cashin, *Story of Augusta*, 287.

[551]Bulletin, 21 June 1953, 28 June 1953, 20 September 1953, 18 October 1953.

[552]Bulletin, 11 October 1953, 28 March 1954, 11 April 1954, 4 April 1954.

[553]Bulletin, 18 April 1954, 25 April 1954.

[554]Bulletin, 2 May 1954, 6 June 1954, 25 July 1954.

[555]Bulletin, 6 September 1953, May-December 1954; Jones, *History of FBC*, 111-112, 120.

[556]Jones, *History of FBC*, 115-118, 121.

[557]Ibid., 113-115; Bulletin, 10 May 1953.

[558]Jones, *History of FBC*, 116, 120, 123-124. A plaque placed on the third floor of the Telfair building read, "Protect his memory and preserve his story, Remain his lasting monument to God's Glory. THIS FLOOR FOR THE TEACHING OF GOD'S WORD IS LOVINGLY DEDICATED TO THE MEMORY OF J. C. C. BLACK 1841-1928 SOLDIER OF THE CONFEDERACY—LAWYER—CONGRESSMAN—CHRISTIAN—STATESMAN Major Black joined FBC in October 1867. He was a faithful and devoted servant of the Lord throughout his long and illustrious career. He served as Chairman of the Board of Deacons, church clerk, Chairman of the Board of Trustees, and for many years as a teacher in the Sunday School. He was one of the motivating factors in the Missionary work of the church. His efforts directly contributed to the organization of numerous Baptist Churches in this area and the Chinese Sunday School of FBC. By His Daughters Merial Black Carey and Katherine Black 1957 'Men who see the invisible, hear the inaudible, believe the incredible, think the unthinkable, are the men who do the impossible.'"

[559]Bulletin, 22 August 1954. Far more expensive was the cost—$225,000—to air condition the church's remaining buildings in 1960. See Jones, *History of FBC*, 129.

[560]Bulletin, 6 September 1953; Jones, Jones, *History of FBC*, 112. For example, missionary efforts other than foreign missions included Sunday School offerings for the GBC Children's Home. See Bulletin, 3 May 1953.

[561]Jones, *History of FBC*, 111, 115, 123.

[562]Ibid., 155; Bulletin, 20 December 1953.

[563]Bulletins, December 1955; Jones 119-122, 138.

[564]Jones, *History of FBC*, 123, 126, 127; "A Biographical Sketch of Dr. R. J. (Jack) Robinson," n.d., Archives. Robinson was also voted by Texas sports writers as the greatest high school basketball player in Texas history.

[565]Jones, *History of FBC*, 116, 124, 127.

[566]Ibid., 126, 127.

[567]Ibid., 128-130; Bulletin, 21 August 1960.

[568]James Lester, "Jack Robinson: Augusta's Olympic Pastor," *People*, 3-3 (December 1972) 18. Bulletin, 14 August, 4 September 1960. During Robinson's pastorate church members annually voted on their favorite sermon through a "Preach-It-Again" contest.

[569]Bulletin, 28 August 1960, 4 September 1960, 18 September 1960. Opposition to church-state separation escalated in the 1980s through the Religious Right movement. See Rob Boston, *Why the Religious Right is Wrong About Separation of Church and State* (Buffalo, NY: Prometheus Books, 2002).

[570]Minutes, 14 November 1962; Jones, *History of FBC*, 135. The U.S. Supreme Court in *Engel v. Vitale* (1962) ruled as unconstitutional official prayers in public schools. The right of individual students to pray of their own initiative was not restricted, and is not to the present day.

[571]Bulletin, 18 September 1960, 2 October 1960; Jones, *History of FBC*, 131.

[572]"New President is First and Foremost a Preacher," 6; "Robinson Appreciation Day, Sunday, September 8th," promotional material, Archives; "Augustan Winner of Encyclopedias," Robinson files, Archives.

[573] Kamille Bostick, "Civil Rights in Georgia: Augusta," UGA: Freedom on Film, accessed 26 March, http://civilrights.uga.edu/cities/augusta/; Cook, "Robinson Interview No. 1," 21, 49. Robinson's statement is largely true. Few Southern Baptist leaders dared advocate for integration.

[574] Jones, *History of FBC*, 130-133, 139.

[575] "Mr. Roscoe McGahee," Obituary, *Augusta Chronicle*, 10 August 2001; correspondence with Robert Anderson, March 2016. By 1964, thirteen ushers manned the sanctuary. See Jones, *History of FBC*, 137.

[576] Jones, *History of FBC*, 131-135, 141, 142.

[577] Four Great Sundays notebooks, Archives.

[578] Bulletin, 19 August 1962; "Sesquicentennial Minutes, 1965-1968," Archives; "Four Great Sundays" files, Archives; Jones, *History of FBC*, 135-144; "Music Ministry Synopsis," May 1989, Music Ministry Programs and Photographs File, Archives. The entirety of the staff of fourteen included: Mrs. B. K. Barnes, Miss Myra E. Haig, Miss Carol Harley, Mr. Sidney E. Hatfield, Mr. and Mrs. Jacques M. Kearns, Mrs. Mertie Martin, Mr. Sidney A. Richardson, Dr. R. Jackson Robinson, Mr. and Mrs. Wendall D. Sloan, and Rev. and Mrs. Allen N. Stickney.

[579] Church sesquicentennial materials, Archives, including events program; Jones, *History of FBC*, 145-147. Graham preached at the invitation of Robinson, the two men by then long acquainted.

[580] Jones, *History of FBC*, 147.

[581] According to a 1990 typed letter signed by J. Newton Thompson and in the FBC Scrapbook, the 1964 group of forward-looking men consisted of: John C. Bell, T. Richard Daniel, Sherman Drawdy, A. Roy Krouse, Daniel B. Matheny, E. Frank Napier, Robert C. Norman, R. J. Robinson (pastor), Wendall Sloan (education director), J. Dan Smith, William P. Stevens, J. Newton Thompson, and William A. Trotter; "Redreaming Our Dream, FBC," Archives. Author's interview with Martha and Dick Daniel, 2014. Martha related that the inability of FBCA to acquire the two adjacent lots was viewed by many members as a sign from God that the time had come to relocate the church.

[582] Bulletin, 5 May 1968; "Redreaming Our Dream"; author's interview with Dick and Martha Daniel, 2014.

[583] Walton Way lawsuit files, Archives; Interviews with Jack Robinson and Dick Daniel, 2014. The three legal decisions were: *Goodwin v. First Baptist*, 225 Ga. 448 (1969), 226 Ga. 254 (1970), and 227 Ga. 603 (1971).

[584] "20th Anniversary Celebration Service," 9 September 1973, Archives; Great Sunday files, Archives. Charlotte Robinson also served on the women's board of University Hospital.

[585] *Christian Index*, 15 August 1968, 18; Bulletin, 6 December 1970; Bulletin, 3 January 1971.

[586] Bulletin, 3 January 1971.

[587] Ibid. The Supreme Court dismissed the case with a unanimous vote. Daniel interview, 2014.

[588]"New President is First and Foremost a Preacher," *Christian Index*, 19 November 1970, 6; "A Biographical Sketch of Dr. R. J. (Jack) Robinson," Archives; Bulletin, 3 January 1971. The large gatherings of the GBC were held in the Bell Auditorium adjacent to the church.

[589]Adam Folk, "Residents Recall 1970 Riot That Rocked Augusta," *Augusta Chronicle*, 10 May 2010; Cathy Geyso, "Reunion Stirs Area Memories," *Augusta Chronicle*, 8 July 1990; "458 F. 2d 486 - *Acree v. County Board of Education of Richmond County Georgia*," 31 March 1972.

[590]Jack R. Robinson, "Presidential Address, GBC, Savannah, Ga., 13 November 1972," 6, 11, Archives. "Dr. Robinson Resigns as Minister of FBC," Bulletin, 25 August 1974.

[591]For more information on how Southern Baptists responded to Civil Rights and racial integration, see: Mark Newman, *Getting Right With God: Southern Baptists and Desegregation, 1945-1995* (Tuscaloosa: University of Alabama Press, 2001) and Andrew M. Manis, *Southern Civil Religions in Conflict: Civil Rights and the Culture Wars* (Macon, GA: Mercer University Press, 2002). Several long-time members of FBCA related to the author that during the Civil Rights years the church refused to allow blacks into the sanctuary.

[592]"Redreaming Our Dream, FBC," Archives; "A Portrait of FBC of Augusta," Mrs. T. C. Bannister, 1980, Archives; interview with Dick and Martha Daniels, 2014. Kidd served from 1971 to 1974.

[593]Bulletin, 3 February 1973; Bulletin, 1 April 1973; "Redreaming."

[594]Robinson 20th Anniversary Program, 9 September 1973, Archives.

[595]"FBC History," undated document, Archives.

[596]"A Biographical Sketch of Dr. R. J. (Jack) Robinson," Archives; "Dr. R. J. Robinson Resigns at Insistence of Physicians," *Augusta Chronicle*, 19 August 1974; R. J. Robinson letter to Dr. George A. Christenberry, church moderator, 18 August 1974; R. J. Robinson letter to FBC, 19 August 1974; "A personal note from Charlotte Robinson" to church, 19 August 1974. Both letters are in archives. In December 1974 Robinson declined an offer by the church's pulpit search Committee to return. He remained in Augusta in a business position before returning to ministry apart from the church. See Bulletin, 22 December 1974.

[597]See Bulletins, 11 August 11-29, December 1974.

[598]Bulletin, FBCA, "Final Services Held," 24 August 1975; Bulletin, 31 August 1975; Bulletin, 19 October 1975; "The Dedication Service of the New Walton Way Facilities of the First Baptist Church, Augusta, GA," 19 October 1975; Interview with Daniel and Martha Daniel, 2014.

[599]For more information, see http://www.augustaga.gov/292/Riverwalk, accessed 19 June 2016.

[600]Bulletin, 25 April 1976.

[601]Balentine file, Archives, FBCA; Bulletin, 6 July 1975; "A Portrait of FBC of Augusta," Mrs. T. C. Bannister, 1980, Archives.

[602]Bulletin, 18 January 1976

[603]"Women's Religious Roles Discussed," *Augusta Chronicle*, 5 December 1975

[604]Minutes, FBCA, 21 June 1978; "First Baptist Amends Constitution on Deacon Eligibility and Election," *Interpreter*, July 1978; "Deacon Election Results Announced," *Interpreter*, 19 October 1978

[605]Bulletins, 1976.

[606]"1977-1978 Schedule of Activities and Directory of Buildings," Archives.

[607]*Interpreter*, 12 January 1978. For more about the fundamentalist takeover (or conservative resurgence) of the SBC from the perspective of the victors, see Paige Patterson, *Anatomy of a Reformation: The Southern Baptist Convention, 1978-2004* (Fort Worth, TX: Southwestern Baptist Theological Seminary, 2005).

[608]Bulletins, 1976-1977; *Interpreter*, 31 March 1977.

[609]"Neighborhood Prayer Parties," *Interpreter*, 24 August 1978; "20th Anniversary Television Recognition," *Interpreter*, 21 September 1978; "First Baptist Approves New Budget," *Interpreter*, 5 October 1978; campaign brochures and literature, Archives.

[610]See Bill J. Leonard, *God's Last and Only Hope: The Fragmentation of the Southern Baptist Convention* (Grand Rapids, MI: Eerdmans, 1990); Nancy Ammerman, *Baptist Battles: Social Change and Religious Conflict in the Southern Baptist Convention* (New Brunswick, NJ: Rutgers University Press, 1990); and Ruth Murray Brown, *For a "Christian America": A History of the Religious Right* (Amherst, NY: Prometheus Books, 2002).

[611]"FBC History" document, n.d., Archives; Interview with Anna Bannister, 2014; Bulletin, 28 October 1979; "Historical Perspectives: First Baptist: A Church Growing Through Challenging Times," 27 October 1979. Balentine addressed the GBC as the organization's featured speaker in 1979, his sermon titled "With Christ in Concern for the Lost." See Minutes, GBC, 1979.

[612]"The FBC Sanctuary Building, Augusta, GA," n.d., Archives.

[613]Staff files, Archives; Ibid.; Balentine Files, Archives.

[614]President of Shorter College from 1982-1986, afterward Balentine pastored churches in North Carolina and Georgia and was and assisted in the founding of the Baptist House of Studies at Duke University Divinity School. He passed away in 2006. George L. Balentine obituary, *Augusta Chronicle*, 30 April 2006.

[615]Charles Bugg files, Archives.

[616]Bulletin, 20 March 1983; Chris Peacock, "First Baptist to Inaugurate Sanctuary," *Augusta Chronicle*, 20 March 1983; "The FBC Sanctuary Building, Augusta, GA," n.d., Archives.

[617]Sanctuary Dedication program, 4 September 1983, Archives; Chris Peacock, "Pastor's Homecoming Celebrates New, Old," *Augusta Chronicle*, 5 September 1983; "A Panel Discussion: FBC Sanctuary History," 23 March 2006, DVD, Archives.

[618]Bulletins, September 1983; "Sermons from the Sanctuary Dedication," CD, Archives.

[619]"Redeeming Our Dream, FBC," n.d., Archives

[620]Interview with Charles Bugg, 2014; Educational Building file, Archives; "Pastor Warns of Possible Dangers Connected with 'Electronic Church,'" *Augusta Chronicle*, 3 May 1985. Jerry Falwell's television ministry remained among the most popular in America, with Falwell increasingly advocating for abolishment of church-state separation, a position that increasingly tarnished the image of Baptists in the public eye. The late

1980s was marked by the fall of two prominent televangelists, Jim Bakker and Jimmy Swaggart, due to sex scandals.

[621]Interview, Bugg, 2014. "Augusta Pastor is Chairman," *Christian Index*, 4 April 1985. In a pivotal moment in 1988 the Denominational Study Committee met with Adrian Rogers, popular Southern Baptist pastor and one of the architects of the progressing fundamentalist takeover of the SBC, while Rogers was in town for an M-Night (Church Training) event. Committee members, according to Bugg, were stunned to learn that Rogers' church contributed a mere 2 percent to the Cooperative Program (CP), Southern Baptists' unified giving program—far less than FBCA contributed. This revelation led some members to begin reevaluating their commitment to the CP at a time when the SBC increasingly failed to reflect the theology and values of the congregation.

[622]Interview, Bugg, 2014; Charles B. Bugg, *Getting on Top When Life Gets Us Down: 15 Sermons on Christian Living* (Nashville: Broadman, 1990); Paul Nowell (Associated Press), "Baptist Pastor's Personal Tragedy Leads to Renewed Faith," *Nashua Telegraph*, 26 February 1994.

[623]Interview, Bugg, 2014.

[624]Youth files and church staff files, Archives.

[625]Robert Norman and Thomas Blanchard both passed away in 2000. Guy Jennings passed away in 2006. Patricia Mangum died in 2016, and Debbie Williams in 2010. Also, interview with Martha Daniel, 2014. Following twenty years as secretary, Martin resigned in 1991.

[626]1987-1988 Woman's Missionary Union Yearbook, Archives

[627]"Music Ministry Synopsis," May 1989, Music Ministry Programs and Photographs File, Archives.

[628]Interview with Rodger Murchison, 2015; Richard Rogers, "Augusta Minister Releases Guide for Grief," WRDW12, 23 September 2011, accessed 15 June 2016, http://www.wrdw.com/home/headlines/Augusta_minister_releases_a_Guide_for_Grief_130435268.html. See Rodger Murchison, *Guide for Grief* (Canton, MI: David Crumm Media, 2001).

[629]James Dotson, "Dr. Bugg to Accept Professorship," *Augusta Chronicle*, 15 April 1989. Charles Bugg read his resignation letter of 12 April 1989. Charles Bugg file, Archives; Interview, Bugg, 2014.

[630]"Denominational Study Committee Report," 24 January 1990, Archives. The Alliance of Baptists was formed in 1987 as a liberal alternative organization for Southern Baptists. Of the many volumes penned about the fundamentalist Southern Baptist controversy, among the more helpful are: Leonard, *God's Last and Only Hope*; Ammerman, *Baptist Battles*; Walter B. Shurden, ed., *Struggle for the Soul of the SBC: Moderate Responses to the Fundamentalist Movement* (Macon, GA: Mercer University Press, 1994); Grady C. Cothen, *The New SBC: Fundamentalism's Impact on the Southern Baptist Convention* (Macon, GA: Smyth & Helwys, 1995); Walter B. Shurden and Randy Sheply, eds., *Going for the Jugular: A Documentary History of the SBC Holy War* (Macon, GA: Mercer University Press, 1996); Fisher Humphreys, *The Way We Were: How Southern Baptist Theology Has Changed and What It Means to Us All* (Macon, GA: Smyth & Helwys, 2002); Carl L.

Kell, ed., *Exiled: Voices of the Southern Baptist Holy War* (Knoxville: University of Tennessee Press, 2006).

[631]Timothy Owings file, Archives; Interview with Timothy Owings, 2014.

[632]James Dotson, "New Pastor Says Church is Healthy," *Augusta Chronicle*, 12 May 1990; Pamele R. Durso, *A Short History of the Cooperative Baptist Fellowship* (Brentwood, TN: Baptist History and Heritage Society, 2006); Aaron D. Weaver, ed., *Stories of the Cooperative Baptist Fellowship* (Macon, GA: Nurturing Faith, 2016); Interview, Murchison, 2014; Denominational files, Archives.

[633]Interview with Timothy and Kathie Owings, 2014; Missions files, Archives.

[634]Interview, Owings, 2014; Cathy Geyso, "Reunion Stirs Area Memories," *Augusta Chronicle*, 8 July 1990; Chinese Sunday School files and scrapbook, Archives.

[635]*Interpreter*, 1991.

[636]Allison Kennedy, "Ministers Bringing Augustans Together With City Programs," *Augusta Chronicle*, 27 February 1994; Interview, Owings, 2014; Virginia Norton, "Pastors to Share Wealth in Pulpit Exchange, Joint Service," *Augusta Chronicle*, 24 April 1999.

[637]Bill Sanders, "'Midday' Anchor's Departing," *Augusta Chronicle*, 13 October 1994; Virginia Norton, "Broadcasting Faith: Augusta Pastor Reaching a Growing Audience on Radio," *Augusta Chronicle*, 8 March 1997; Timothy L. Owings, *Hearing God in a Noisy World* (Macon, GA: Smyth & Helwys, 1998).

[638]Interview, Timothy and Kathie Owings, 2014.

[639]Herb Hollinger, "Augusta SBC 150th Celebration Yields 'A Time to Remember'," *Baptist Press*, 12 May 1995. One month later the SBC, annually assembled in Atlanta passed a "Resolution on Racial Reconciliation" that echoed the apology for racism voiced at FBCA May 8-10, 1995.

[640]Music files, Archives; Interview, Owings, 2014.

[641]Archives; Larry Mize, "More than a Masters title required for infinite worth," *Baptist Courier*, 31 March 1994; Interview, Owings, 2014.

[642]"Dedication of Sanctuary Addition and Covered Walkways" program, 1 October 2000.

[643]Interview, Owings, 2014.

[644]"2000 Church Vision Statement," Archives. In the formal statement, each sentence is its own paragraph.

[645]*Visions*, Cooperative Baptist Fellowship of Georgia, January/February 2001; "Jimmy Carter Renounces Southern Baptist Convention," United Press International, 20 October 2000; Edlyn Elliott letter, accessed 16 June 2016, http://www.adherents.com/largecom/baptist_SBC_Carter.html. Thereafter the SBC, GBC, and many local Baptist associations increasingly excluded from membership churches pastored by women.

[646]Jacob Malone obituary, *Augusta Chronicle*, 1 September 2013; Joni B. Hannigan, "Global Outreach 2002 at Olympics: 1,000 Volunteers from 21 States," *Baptist Press*, 22 February 2002.

[647]Deacons Minutes, 10 February 2003.

[648]"Church Creates a Joyful Festival," *Augusta Chronicle*, 8 March 2003; "Lewis Festival Has Developed Over the Years," *Augusta Chronicle*, 9 March 2006.

[649]Trustees records, February-May 2003, Archives; "Members Demand Answers," *Augusta Chronicle*, 9 June 2003; Kelly Jasper, "Ex-First Baptist Pastor Puts Resignation Behind Him," *Augusta Chronicle*, 28 August 2011; Interview, Owings, 2014. Following his resignation, Owings and his family remained in Augusta and he began a new career as a financial professional.

[650]Anna Olive Jones Bannister, "Church History" (14 July 2014), accessed 16 June 2016, http://www.n-georgia.com/nps-augusta-canal-first-bapt-church.html.

[651]Gregory DeLoach files, Archives.

[652]DeLoach files; Interview with Gregory DeLocach, 2014. In a conversation, DeLoach related to the author that all he ever wanted to do was pastor a church.

[653]See *Interpreter*, Summer 2007; "The Baptist Story: A Series of Sermons," Archives.

[654]DeLoach was reflecting on his reading of religious historian Dianna Butler Bass.

[655]Conversations with Rodger Murchison and Gregory Deloach; http://fbcaugusta.org/contemporary-worship/, accessed 17 June 2016.

[656]Deacons Minutes, 8 February 2010, 11 July 2011

[657]Storey Chapel files, including Storey Chapel Dedication Program, Archives; Malone obituary; Kelly Jasper, "First Baptist Plans to Wear Out New Facility," *Augusta Chronicle*, 10 June 2011; Kelly Jasper, "First Baptist Church Celebrates Campus Growth," *Augusta Chronicle*, 12 June 2011.

[658]Jonathan Overstreet and Kelly Jasper, "Local Mission Team Member Dies in Chile," *Augusta Chronicle*, 21 March 2010; Kelly Jasper, "First Baptist Doctors on a Mission of Love, Healing," *Augusta Chronicle*, 18 February 2011.

[659]Interview, DeLoach, 2014. For a brief snapshot in time of the ascendant, "missional" concept during DeLoach's early years in Augusta, see Alan Hirsch, "Defining Missional," *Christianity Today Leadership Journal* (Fall 2008), accessed 16 June 2016, http://www.christianitytoday.com/le/2008/fall/17.20.html.

[660]Deacons Minutes, 14 May 2012, 13 August 2012. The capital campaign was divided between debt relief (90 percent) and missional work (10 percent).

[661]Ordination Council report, 28 July 2009; Ordination Council report, 19 August 2011 (both in Archives); Newsletter, Baptist Women in Ministry, September 2014; Deacons Minutes, 9 January 2012

[662]Deacons Minutes, 9 January 2012, 14 May 2012, 13 February 2012; Minutes, 24 October 2012; Deacons Minutes, 12 November 2012, 13 August 2012, 13 February 2012. Interview, Murchison, 2014.

[663]"New Role for First Baptist Pastor Greg DeLoach," *Augusta Chronicle*, 12 November 2015.

[664]http://fbcaugusta.org/ministry-team/, accessed 24 June 2016.

Index

Duncan, Harvey M., 266, 268
Duncan, Lynn H., 268
Dye, Martin M., 55, 64, 65, 67, 71, 78, 79, 266
Eakes, J.H., 119, 120
Earnest, Chubby T., 268
Earnest, Larry, 273
Echols, Jeremy, 276
Edenfield, Deborah, 233
Edenfield, Jimmy, 233
Edwards, M.B., 266
Eisenhower, Dwight D., 173, 174, 176, 179
Elkin, Alex, 230
Elkin, Andrew, 230
Elkin, Paul, 230, 234, 268
Elkin, Rebecca, 230, 234, 268
Eller, S. Gary, 268
Elliott, Edlyn, 216
Elliott, Ralph, 201
Ellis, Gladys, 234
Ellis, James, 234
Eng, Bert, 256
Engels, Nettie B., 268
Engler, Harold S., 268
Engler, Josephine R., 268
Ensley Jr., Howard, 268
Eubank, Jackie, 188
Evans, Alfred, 234
Evans, L. Bridges, 266, 268, 272
Evans, George W., 266
Evans, Kay, 234
Evans, Lawton Bridges, 154, 181
Evans, Nick, 215
Everett, Alice, 230
Everett, Ann, 230
Everett, Jean W., 230, 234
Everett, Jeannie, 230
Everett, Ted, 230
Everett, Theodore, 234
Fair, Jane Eve, 256
Falwell, Jerry, 202
Faulk Jr., F.M., 268
Faulk, Ann, 268
Fellers, E.E. ("Bo"), 266, 268, 272
Fennell, J.F., 266
Ferrell, Lee, 232
Ferrell, Tim, 232
Fickhesen, Gary, 275
Fields, M. Ann, 268
Fiske Jr., Julian, 183, 234
Fiske, Carolyn Cox, 234
Fiske, Chiles, 234

Fiske, Chip, 234
Fiske, Jewelle DeLaughter, 273
Fiske, Joy, 234
Fiske, Julian Chiles, 268
Fiske, Julian F., 266, 268
Fiske, Ray, 234
Fleming, William M., 194
Fletcher Jr., William Lawrence, 231
Fletcher, Anna Kim Polatty, 231, 232, 277, 278
Fletcher, W. Lawrence, 231, 232, 268, 272, 277
Fletcher, Will, 232
Flowers, Jeff W., 268
Fortson Jr., Lombard, 235
Fortson, Barbara, 235
Fortune, Jack C., 168
Fosdick, Harry Emerson, 127
Foster, Mary, 41
Foster, Nathaniel Greene, 68, 262
Fowler Jr., William T., 268
Fowler, Patti, 205, 218, 225, 231, 245, 248, 273, 274, 275
Fox, Henry L., 146
Fox, Joseph C., 268
Fox, Virgil, 160
Freeman, T.M., 266
Frits, Beth C., 269
Frits, Michael J., 269
Frye, Jay, 269
Fuller, Andrew, 19, 36
Fuller, Richard, 48, 53, 82
Furman, Richard, 58
Galey, Leah, 225, 274
Galloway, Ronald F., 269
Galphin, John Milledge, 33
Gardner, Sabrina, 41
Garner, John, 23
Garner, Sara, 23
Garnto, Kelly, 225
Garrett, Hilton C., 197, 273
Garrett, Mary Ellen, 256
Garrett, T. Harry, 126, 127, 137, 158, 166, 168, 169, 266
Garrison, Mrs. Glen, 239, 240
Garrison, Searcy S., 196
Gary, T. Reed, 269
Geer, Anita, 231, 234
Geer, David, 231
Geer, H. Calvin, 231, 234, 266, 269, 270
Geer, James, 231
Geer, Mrs. W.F., 234